Das vorliegende Lehrwerk **Logistics Milestones** richtet sich hauptsächlich an Auszubildende im Beruf Speditionskaufmann / -frau, aber auch an alle, die im Logistik-Dienstleistungsgewerbe tätig sind und zeichnet sich insbesondere durch folgende Elemente aus:

- Berücksichtigung der Incoterms® 2010 (gültig ab 01.01.2011)
- Einbeziehung neuester Entwicklungen in der Arbeitswelt, z. B. durch realitätsnahe Arbeitsaufträge wie Recherchen im Internet
- Konsequente Berücksichtigung neuester Lehrpläne (Lernfelder) sowie durchgängiges Sprachkompetenztraining nach dem Gemeinsamen Europäischen Referenzrahmen (Sprachstufen B1 / B2)
- Möglichkeit zur Binnendifferenzierung durch gekennzeichnete Aufgaben mit höherem Schwierigkeitsgrad
- Umfangreiches Seh- / Hörverstehenstraining durch u. a. Originalvideos von der BBC sowie zahlreiche Audios
- Vokabelarbeit mit der „Word Bank" sowie mit den Vokabellernlisten, dem unitbegleitenden Vokabular und dem Glossar über Online-Link
- Vertieftes Vokabel-, Grammatik- und Hörverstehenstraining in den Workbooks 1 und 2, inklusive Audio-CD-ROM mit allen Schülerbuch- und Workbook-Audios
- Gezielte Prüfungsvorbereitung auf das KMK-Fremdsprachenzertifikat im Lehrwerk und im Workbook 2

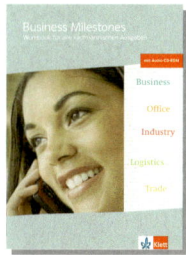

Workbook 1:
Business Milestones Workbook mit Audio-CD-ROM,
978-3-12-808265-3

Workbook 2:
Business Milestones Workbook mit Prüfungsvorbereitung
KMK-Fremdsprachenzertifikat und mit Audio-CD-ROM,
978-3-12-808266-0

Lernhilfen	**Symbole**	
WORDBANK Schlüsselvokabular	◎ A1.27	Audioverweis
Info-Box Faktenwissen	◎ V4	Videoverweis
Communicating across cultures Interkulturelle Kompetenz	Phrases	Verweis auf Phrases
	P, M, I, R	Produktion, Mediation, Interaktion oder Rezeption
Language and grammar Grammatik	Example:	z. B. Beispieldialoge
Video lounge authentische Videos	Online-Link	Vokabellernlisten, unitbegleitendes Vokabular und Glossar über Online-Link
	KMK	Aufgaben zur Vorbereitung auf die Prüfung zum KMK-Fremdsprachenzertifikat Englisch
	🌐	Internet-Recherchen
	✳	„Advanced"-Aufgaben

Unit 1
Introducing yourself

WORD BANK

I'm / my name is • I'm from • I was born in / on • to work as a … • to be a … • to work at / with / for … • to be interested in • to be into • trainee • apprentice • traineeship / apprenticeship • vocational school • to attend school • to be on a programme • to take part in • to train / to be training as a … • to train to be a … • to be training to become a … • to do a traineeship as a … • to qualify as a … • clerk • management assistant • consultant • specialist

In business it is often necessary to introduce yourself. It is therefore important to know what to say and what information to include. You may, for instance need to explain your professional role or duties in the firm. In a business situation introductions and greetings are often more formal than those among friends in a casual situation. It is important to choose the right style.

Decide which of the following phrases would be used in a formal and which in a casual situation. Match the phrases with the photos above.

1
Good afternoon, Mr Perigault. Nice to see you again.

2
Hello Janina. How's things?

3
How do you do, Mr Yamato? Pleased to meet you.

4
Hi, Ian. How are you doing?

Online-Link
808264-0001

A Talking about yourself

Students at a vocational school in Germany are asked to introduce themselves to a new English assistant who is to spend half a year at their school.

1 **Take the roles of the assistant and the students and read the introductions.**

Rona: Good morning. I'm Rona Mansfield. I come from Dulwich in South London and I'll be working here as an assistant teacher for the next six months. It would be good if a few of you could introduce yourselves so I can begin to learn your names. Perhaps you could tell me briefly what job you're training for and what your interests are. Hello, what's your name?

Stefanie: Hello. I'm Stefanie Krieger. I'm from Cologne but I was born in Hamburg. I'll be 17 next Monday. I'm doing a traineeship at Kabel AG in Leverkusen to become an office administration clerk. I'm very interested in computers and enjoy designing websites. I do quite a lot of sport, including aerobics and badminton.

Rona: Thank you, Stefanie, I'll remember the birthday! And what's your name?

Haris: Hi. My name's Haris Akbar. I'm from Cologne. I am 19 years old. I'm training at Schulz und Schmalenbach as an export clerk. I am very interested in football and support Werder Bremen. I work out regularly at a local gym. I love music. "The Devils" are my favourite group.

Rona: Thank you, Haris. My taste in music is a touch more traditional. Can you tell me something about yourself?

Antonella: My name is Antonella Piccolino but my friends call me Nella. Like Stefanie, I also work at Kabel AG but I'm training to be an Industrie-kauffrau, that's an industrial clerk or industrial business management assistant. I was born in Bergheim in 1992. Originally my family comes from Sicily. I'm very interested in the Italian language and Italian cooking. I also go to a fitness centre three times a week because I'm into body-building.

Rona: Gosh, I can see we'd better watch what we say. Right, we can continue with the introductions later. Could you make a plan of the classroom where everybody's sitting with names – first names and family names.

2 Say whether the following statements from page 7 are TRUE or FALSE.

R

1. Stefanie Krieger was born in Cologne.
2. She is training to be an office administration clerk.
3. She doesn't like working with a computer.

4. Haris Akbar is doing a traineeship to become an industrial clerk.
5. He is between 20 and 30 years old.
6. He supports a football club from Bavaria.

7. Antonella Piccolino is at the same firm as Haris Akbar.
8. Her hobby is cooking Italian dishes.
9. She tries to keep fit.

3 Complete the following introduction using the words from the box.

at • from • in (3x) • near • to • on

I was born **2** Garforth **3** 23 March 1964. Garforth is a small town **5** Leeds **6** the UK. My family comes **7** the West Indies. I work **8** an advertising agency and I'm taking part **9** a training programme for advertising assistants. I regularly go **10** a gym for a work-out.

4 Listen to the following introductions and answer the questions.

R

A1.1

Thorsten

1. Where does Thorsten come from?
2. What is he training as?
3. What is his hobby?

Ludmilla

1. How long has Ludmilla been living in Germany?
2. How old is she?

Ayshe

1. When was Ayshe born?
2. What is she training to become?
3. What does she do in her free time?

5 Work in groups and make up similar introductions with the help of the
P following hints.

Phrases >

Training or working as:	industrial clerk/industrial business management assistant, office administration clerk/office management assistant, wholesale and export clerk/management assistant in wholesale and foreign trade, bank clerk/bank business management assistant, management assistant in advertising, freight forwarding and logistics services clerk/management assistant in freight forwarding, IT specialist, management assistant in retail business, publisher's assistant/management assistant in publishing, insurance clerk/insurance business management assistant
Firms:	ENKA AG, Schuster & Schneider, Taufrisch OHG, Kohlhaas & Söhne, Globistik-Transport KG, Sportsmarketing GmbH, Online-Consulting
Hobbies:	Swimming, reading fantasy novels, cycling, volleyball, Sci-Fi films, buying clothes, computer games, horses, snowboarding, clubbing

Language and grammar
Work in groups of four. Introduce yourself briefly in writing.
You may use imaginary details if you wish. Read the introduction
out to your group.

Phrases >

Language and grammar: Introducing yourself

Antonella sagt: I **was** born in Bergheim in 1992.	Auf Deutsch hätte sie gesagt: Ich **bin** 1992 in Bergheim geboren.
Im Englischen werden Geburtszeitpunkt und Geburtsort mit simple past angegeben:	
My father **was** born in Italy. Haris **was** born on 7 July 1992.	Mein Vater ist in Italien geboren. Haris ist am 7. Juli 1992 geboren.
Außerdem wird im Englischen erst der Ort genannt und danach der Zeitpunkt: I was born **in Bergheim in 1992**.	Im Deutschen ist die Reihenfolge umgekehrt: Ich bin **1992 in Bergheim** geboren.
Haris sagt: I'm training as **an** export clerk. She's **a** travel consultant. He works as **a** programmer.	Auf Deutsch hätte er gesagt: Ich mache eine Ausbildung als Exportkaufmann. Sie ist Reiseverkehrskauffrau. Er arbeitet als Programmierer.
Im Englischen steht zur Angabe des Berufes der unbestimmte Artikel: **a travel consultant.** Im Deutschen steht kein Artikel: **Reiseverkehrskauffrau.**	
I am **a** publisher's assistant. I am training as **a** bank clerk or bank business management assistant.	Ich bin Verlagskaufmann. Ich mache eine Ausbildung als Bank-kaufmann.

Communicating across cultures: Introducing and greeting people

In English-speaking countries people often give only their first name when introducing themselves - "Hi, I'm Jonathan". In more formal contexts they give their first name and surname but never just their surname as is usual in Germany - "I'm Jennifer Ashton". Often people add; "Please call me Jennifer".
"How do you do" is a formal greeting which is nowadays rarely used. The other person also says "How do you do" and will probably add "Pleased to meet you".
A usual greeting is "Hello, how are you?" The other person says something like "Fine, thanks / not so bad / so-so" and immediately adds "How are you?" Friends usually say something like "Hi, Justin. How are you doing?" or "Hello, Sarah, how's things?"
Sarah might reply: "Fine, how's things with you?"

B Young people talk about their (future) professions

Rona Mansfield meets more students at the vocational college and asks them to introduce themselves and tell her what training programme they're on:

Oliver:	Hello, I'm Oliver: I'm training to become an office management assistant.
Jeannine:	My name's Jeannine: I'm on the trainee programme of a high street bank.
David:	I'm David: I'm an insurance business management assistant.
Jennifer:	Hi, I'm Jennifer: I want to train as an advertising assistant.
Antje:	I'm Antje: I hope to be a restaurant manager.
Rosa:	Hi, I'm Rosa: I am interested in qualifying as a foreign language correspondent.
Dennis:	I'm Dennis: I want to get on to a training programme for retail management assistants.
Niko:	I'm Niko: I want to train as an event management assistant.
Simone:	Hi, I'm Simone: I'm applying to train as an IT specialist.
Janina:	Hello, my name's Janina: I work for a wholesaler in the electrical goods industry.
Mike:	I'm Mike: I'm a trainee export clerk.
Dragan:	I'm Dragan: I'm training to be a management assistant in publishing.
Hasan:	Good morning. I'm Hasan: I am planning to train as an industrial clerk or industrial business management assistant.

My name's Samira. I am taking part in an ITC programme.

Hello, I'm Sabrina. I'm training to be a travel consultant.

1 Read the introductions on page 10 and match the German occupations with their English paraphrases.

1. Kauffrau für Tourismus und Freizeit
2. Kaufmann im Einzelhandel
3. Fremdsprachenkorrespondentin
4. Kaufmann für Spedition und Logistikdienstleistung
5. Veranstaltungskauffrau
6. Industriekauffrau
7. Automobilkaufmann
8. Kaufmann für Bürokommunikation
9. Kauffrau für Marketing-kommunikation
10. Kaufmann im Groß- und Außenhandel
11. Kauffrau für Versicherung und Finanzen
12. Informatikkaufmann
13. Bankkaufmann

a. advertising assistant/management assistant in advertising
b. bank clerk/bank business management assistant
c. automobile sales management assistant
d. management assistant in event organisation
e. management assistant for freight forwarding and logistics
f. industrial clerk/industrial business management assistant
g. insurance clerk/insurance business management assistant
h. IT consultant/management assistant in informatics
i. management assistant in office communication
j. retail business management assistant
k. secretary with foreign languages/foreign language correspondent
l. management assistant for tourism and leisure
m. wholesale and export clerk/management assistant in wholesale and foreign trade

2 Übertragen Sie die folgenden Aussagen ins Englische.

M

1. Ich habe eine Ausbildung als Industriekaufmann gemacht.
2. Ich möchte eine Ausbildung als Automobilkaufmann machen.
3. Ich möchte als Fremdsprachen-korrespondentin ausgebildet werden.
4. Ich will Versicherungskaufmann werden.
5. Ich nehme an einem IT-Weiter-bildungsprogramm teil.
6. Ich bewerbe mich um einen Ausbildungsplatz als Bürokauffrau.
7. Ich mache eine Ausbildung als Kauffrau im Einzelhandel.
8. Ich arbeite bei einem Großhändler.
9. Ich möchte gerne eine Ausbildung als Werbekaufmann machen.

3 Work in groups of three. Act out the following conversation, inserting your own
I / P names and training courses.

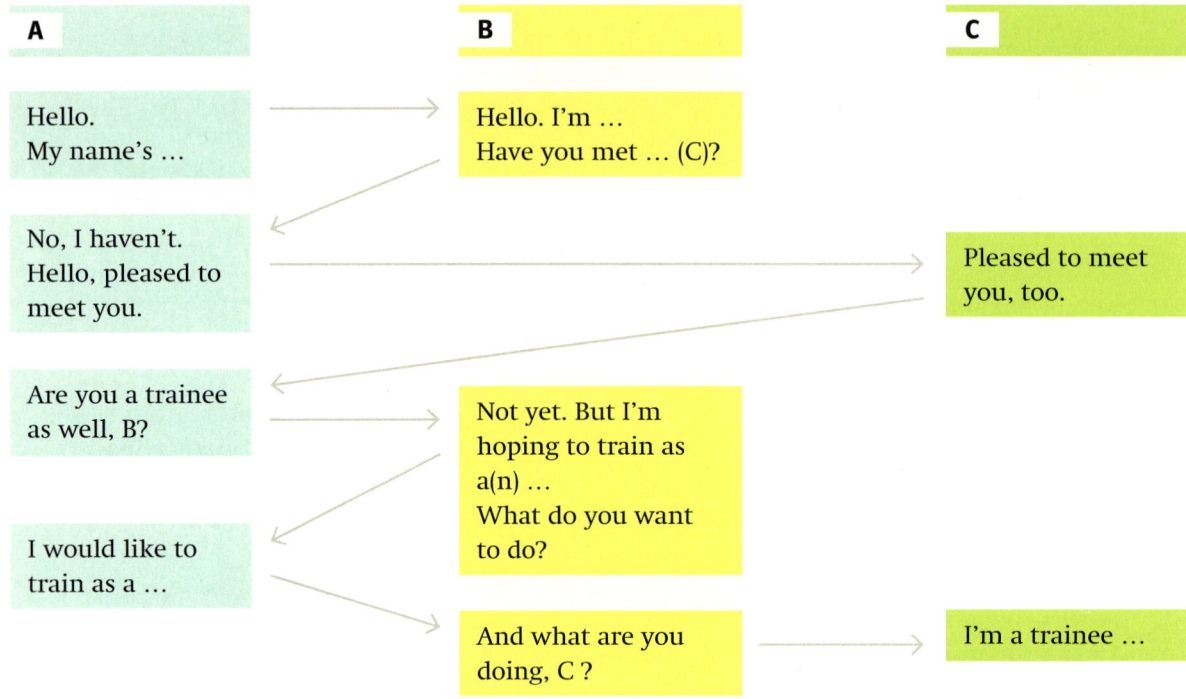

| **A** | **B** | **C** |

Hello.
My name's …

Hello. I'm …
Have you met … (C)?

No, I haven't.
Hello, pleased to
meet you.

Pleased to meet
you, too.

Are you a trainee
as well, B?

Not yet. But I'm
hoping to train as
a(n) …
What do you want
to do?

I would like to
train as a …

And what are you
doing, C ?

I'm a trainee …

4 Work in groups of three. Use the phrases from the conversation above and make
I / P similar dialogues.

Phrases ▸

5 Listen to the following dialogue and say which of the following
R statements are true for Patrick and Janina.
◎ A1.2

1. I'm training to become an industrial clerk.
2. I want to train as an export clerk.
3. I'm in the electrical goods industry.
4. There are good prospects of promotion.
5. I'm allowed to advise customers.
6. I get on well with the people I work with.
7. I can use my English.
8. I can work on my own.

6 Work in groups of two. Introduce yourselves and say what you do.
I Ask each other what you like or dislike in your job.

Phrases ▸

7 Search the Internet for two of the following international job titles. Note down
the details of one job ad. Compare and discuss your findings with the group.

freight forwarding clerk • trainee advertising assistant • insurance clerk •
IT assistant • trainee assistant events • bilingual secretary / secretary or PA with
foreign languages • trainee tourism assistant / tourism clerk

Communicating across cultures: The German "dual training" system

The German "dual training" system combining on the job apprenticeships / traineeships with vocational school has no direct systematic equivalent in Britain and the USA. This is also true of the large number of protected job titles with a prescribed course of training in Germany. However, in Britain, for example, there are many training programmes, traineeships and apprenticeships in more traditional skilled occupations (plumber, electrician, etc.), also vocational courses leading to an NVQ (National Vocational Qualification). Most trainee programmes (except traditional apprentices) are shorter than in Germany and people often do additional courses later (e.g. in CLAIT = computer literacy and information technology) leading to a national or international qualification.

As a result of these differences German job titles can often not be translated literally. It is necessary to paraphrase them in such a way that a foreign employer can get a realistic idea of the range of activity covered.

The statement "Ich mache eine Ausbildung zum Industriekaufmann bei der ENCOR AG" could be paraphrased as follows: "I am on a 3-year training programme with ENCOR AG to qualify as an industrial clerk / industrial business management assistant specialising in the commercial side of an industrial business. During the training programme I have to attend courses at vocational school either two days a week or in blocks of several weeks at a time. At the end of the training period I sit for an examination before the local chamber of commerce."

Basic structure of the German education system

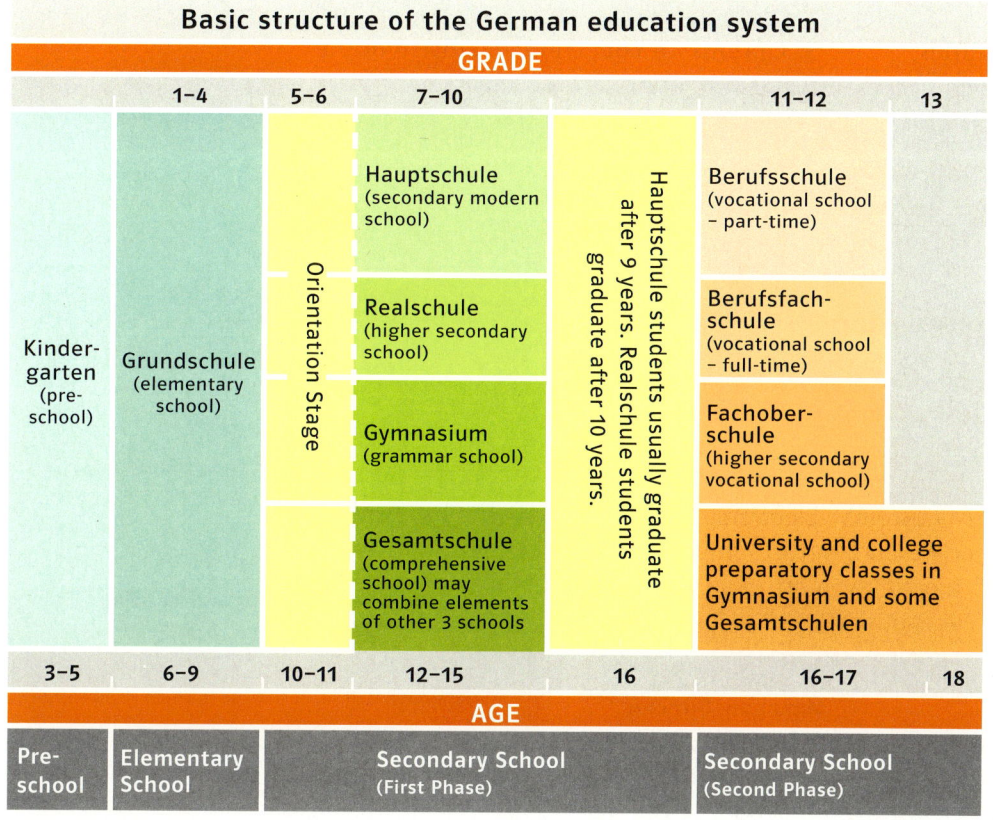

GRADE						
1–4	5–6	7–10		11–12	13	

Kinder-garten (pre-school)

Grundschule (elementary school)

Orientation Stage

Hauptschule (secondary modern school)

Realschule (higher secondary school)

Gymnasium (grammar school)

Gesamtschule (comprehensive school) may combine elements of other 3 schools

Hauptschule students usually graduate after 9 years. Realschule students graduate after 10 years.

Berufsschule (vocational school – part-time)

Berufsfach-schule (vocational school – full-time)

Fachober-schule (higher secondary vocational school)

University and college preparatory classes in Gymnasium and some Gesamtschulen

AGE						
3–5	6–9	10–11	12–15	16	16–17	18

Pre-school	Elementary School	Secondary School (First Phase)	Secondary School (Second Phase)

Logistics expert

1 A forwarding agent's job

1
M In groups of three, look at the word cloud and find as many German equivalents as possible. Then compare your results in class.

2
R
◎ A 2.5 Neil Carter works for the international forwarding company Routiers Mâcon Logistics at Heathrow airport. He works at the Perishables Handling Centre. Listen to the first part of an interview (for the second part, see UNIT 2) and take notes on the following aspects.

1. Number of facilities
2. Transport modes
3. Options for collection and distribution
4. Tasks of a forwarding agent

3
R / P
◎ A 2.5 Listen again and write down the questions asked by the interviewer. Then work with a partner and answer the questions for the company you work for.

`Phrases ▶`

2 Company organisation

1
R Use the organisation chart and list the departments in the box under the three headings: General Administration, Sales and Logistics.

> Accounts and Finance • Advertising and Public Relations • Air Freight • Customer Service • Customs • Electronic Data Processing (EDP) • Export • Groupage • Human Resources (HR) • Import • Inland Waterways Freight • Insurance • Multi-modal Transport • Rail Freight • Road Freight • Sea and Ocean Freight • Warehousing

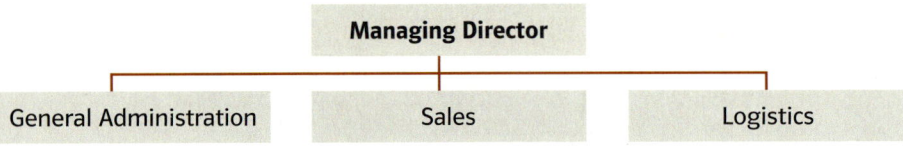

2 Use the prompts in the speech bubbles and make sentences about the work
P   done in the different departments of a company.

Phrases ▶

Example: 1. In the HR department job interviews are conducted.

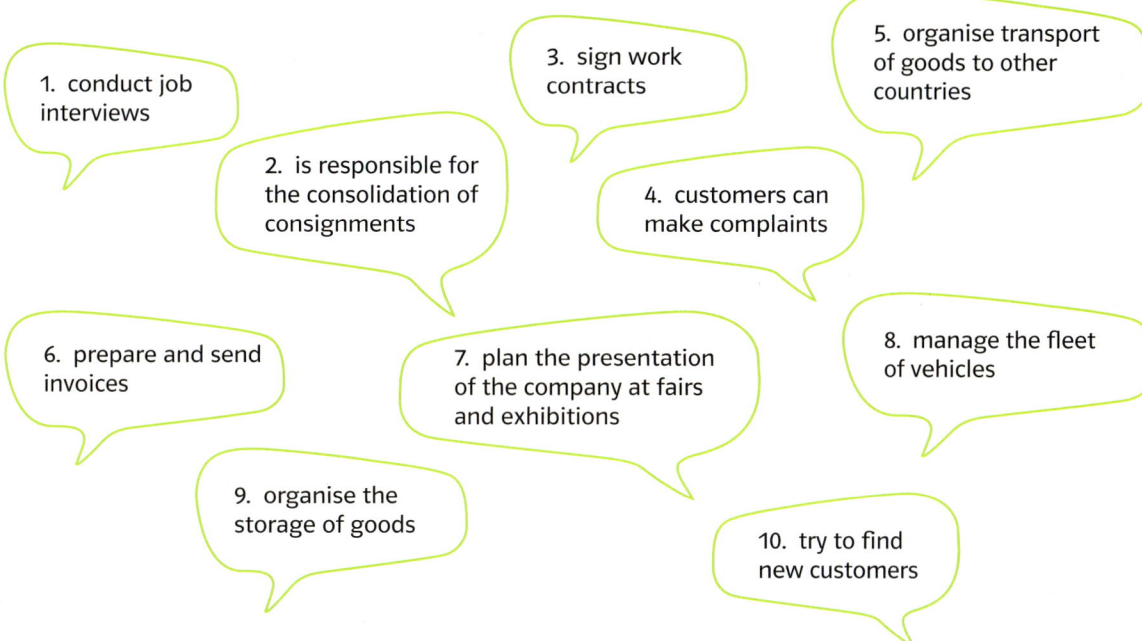

1. conduct job interviews

2. is responsible for the consolidation of consignments

3. sign work contracts

4. customers can make complaints

5. organise transport of goods to other countries

6. prepare and send invoices

7. plan the presentation of the company at fairs and exhibitions

8. manage the fleet of vehicles

9. organise the storage of goods

10. try to find new customers

3 Job titles

Job titles are complicated and can cause confusion. For example, the English
equivalent of the German term *"Manager"* can be "… director" as in "managing
director", but also "head of … department" as in "head of the purchasing
department" (who might also be called the "chief buyer" at other companies).

1 Use the table to invent a job title for yourself by choosing one word from
I   each column. Think about what a person with such a title would do in a
     real company. Your partner will then try to find out which job title you have
     invented by asking up to ten questions about your job tasks. Then take turns.

Job title fabricator		
air freight	development	analyst
customs	excellence	assistant
export	goods	coordinator
finance	management	director
groupage	optimisation	manager
import	planning	officer
transport	quality	specialist

2 Describe the job of a "property maintenance officer" in no more than three
P   sentences. (There's one working at your vocational college!)

Phrases: Introducing yourself and others

To introduce yourself

I'm Peter./My name is Henry Myers.	Ich heiße Peter./Ich heiße Henry Myers.
Please call me Henry.	Nennen Sie mich doch Henry.
My surname is Hillary, my first name is Tom.	Mein Familienname ist Hillary, mein Vorname Tom.
How are you? (How are you doing?)	Wie geht es Ihnen/Dir? (informelle Begrüßung)
I'm from Berlin, and I am 20 years old.	Ich stamme aus Berlin und bin 20 Jahre alt.
I'm British/Irish.	Ich bin Brite/Ire.
I **was** born in Cyprus on 7 August 1982.	Ich bin am 7. August 1982 in Zypern geboren.
Have you met Mr Martens?	Kennen Sie Herrn Martens?
May I introduce Dr. Bolt to you?	Darf ich Ihnen Herrn Dr. Bolt vorstellen?
Pleased/Nice to meet you.	Ich freue mich, Sie kennen zu lernen.
And how are you?	Und (wie geht es) Ihnen?
Didn't we meet at the Boat Fair?	Haben wir uns nicht schon auf der Boot-Messe kennen gelernt?
I've heard a lot **about** you **from** Mr Winter.	Herr Winter hat mir schon viel von Ihnen erzählt.

To talk about your hobbies and interests

I am interested in computers.	Ich interessiere mich für Computer.
I love travelling more than anything else.	Ich reise schrecklich gern.
I like to go clubbing.	Ich gehe gern in die Disco.
I'm **into** body-building.	Ich interessiere mich für Bodybuilding.
I do a lot of diving.	Ich gehe oft tauchen.

To talk about your training or your work

I'm a trainee export clerk.	Ich mache eine Ausbildung zum Exportkaufmann.
I'm training to become	Ich mache eine Lehre als
an industrial clerk/industrial business management assistant	Industriekaufmann/-frau
a wholesale and export clerk/management assistant in wholesale and foreign trade	Kaufmann/-frau im Groß- und Außenhandel

an office administration clerk/office management assistant	Kaufmann/-frau für Bürokommunikation
a freight forwarding and logistics services clerk/management assistant in freight forwarding and logistics	Kaufmann/-frau für Spedition und Logistikdienstleistung
a bank clerk/bank business management assistant	Bankkaufmann/-frau
a retail clerk/management assistant in retail business	Kaufmann/-frau im Einzelhandel
a management assistant for tourism and leisure	Kaufmann/-frau für Tourismus und Freizeit
a publisher's assistant	Verlags-/Medienkaufmann/-frau
an insurance clerk/insurance business management assistant	Kaufmann/-frau für Versicherungen und Finanzen
a management assistant in advertising	Kaufmann/-frau für Marketing-kommunikation
a management assistant in event organisation	Veranstaltungskaufmann/-frau
an automobile sales management assistant	Automobilkaufmann/-frau
I'm taking part in an ITC programme.	Ich nehme an einem ITC-Ausbildungsprogramm teil.
I'm in the catering **industry**.	Ich bin in der Cateringbranche.
I work **at** SITCOM Ltd.	Ich arbeite bei SITCOM Ltd.
I **attend** vocational school.	Ich besuche die Berufsschule.
What are you doing job-wise, Nina?	Nina, was machst du beruflich?
What are you training to be, Timo?	Was machst du für eine Ausbildung, Timo?
What do you like **about** your job?	Was gefällt dir an deiner Arbeit?
What industry are you in?	In welcher Branche arbeitest du?

To say what you like or dislike about your training or your work

I like my job because I get on well with the people I work with.	Ich mag meine Arbeit, weil ich mich mit meinen Kollegen gut verstehe.
I can work **on** my own.	Ich kann selbstständig arbeiten.
There are good prospects **of** promotion.	Die Aufstiegschancen sind gut.
I have to key in data all day long.	Den ganzen Tag muss ich Daten eingeben.
I have to work a lot of overtime.	Ich muss viele Überstunden machen.

Unit 2
Taking care of visitors

WORD BANK

visitor • visit • refreshments • to greet • to receive • to welcome • to meet • flight • hotel • weather • hobbies • sports • to entertain • to chat • directions • floor plan • map • layout • premises • to go • to turn • to follow • restaurant • menu • meal • dish • to invite • to choose

Greeting visitors to your company and making them feel welcome may be an important part of your job. You should always be friendly and helpful as first impressions are often very important. You may have to entertain them until the person they want to see appears. The language in which both you and they can communicate will often be English, even when the visitors do not come from an English-speaking country. English is rapidly becoming a lingua franca in Europe.

1 Match the phrases with the photos above.

1
Welcome to Schneider GmbH. Did you have any trouble finding us?

2
Have you met Ms Reuter? She is our marketing manager.

3
Go along the corridor. The conference room is the second door on the right.

4
Did you have a pleasant flight?

Online-Link
808264-0002

2 Translate the following statements from the introductory text into German.

M

1. Greeting visitors may be an important part of your job.
2. First impressions are often very important.
3. You may have to entertain visitors until the person they want to see appears.
4. The language in which both you and they can communicate will often be English.

A Greeting visitors

Marcel Krenz, an export clerk at International Snacks GmbH, a German food processing company, has been asked by his boss, Markus Diepholz, to receive Kirsty Burnham and Kevin Sears who represent a major British catering chain. They are interested in the wide range of snacks and lunch boxes the company produces.

1 Read the above text, listen to the dialogue and answer the following questions.

R

A1.3

1. Who is Marcel Krenz?
2. What are his visitors from Britain interested in?
3. What refreshments do Kirsty Burnham and Kevin Sears prefer?
4. What is Kevin's position?
5. What is Frau Wieland in charge of?
6. Where have Kirsty Burnham and Frau Wieland met before?
7. Why has Marcel Krenz been asked to receive the visitors?

2 Match the expressions on the left with those on the right.

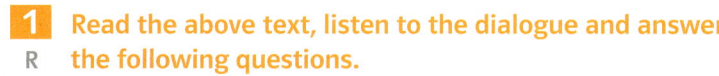

1. a food processing company	a. a large assortment of snacks
2. a major chain	b. she is responsible for sales to the EU
3. a wide range of snacks	c. a few minutes
4. I'll let him know you're here	d. we already know each other
5. a couple of minutes	e. water with gas bubbles
6. a sparkling mineral water	f. a company using raw materials to make food products
7. she's on the export staff	g. an important company with many branches
8. she's in charge of sales to the EU	h. I would like to introduce you to Frau Wieland
9. I'd like you to meet Frau Wieland	i. she is a member of the export sales personnel
10. we've already met	j. I will inform him that you have arrived

19

B Making conversation

Marcel and the visitors from Britain chat while waiting for Herr Diepholz.

1 Listen to the CD and complete the following dialogue on a separate sheet of paper.

R
A 1.4

Marcel: Did you have a pleasant flight?

Kirsty: Oh yes, the flight was very straightforward – **1**. There was a bit of turbulence, though. I'm afraid I don't like that.

Marcel: **2** does the flight from Manchester take?

Kevin: It only takes about one and a half hours. But we **3** as a result of the time difference.

Marcel: Of course. What was **4** in Manchester? Was it as good as it is here?

Kirsty: Surprisingly, yes. We have been having **5** lately. It's almost like summer. But generally Manchester gets a lot of rain. From the Atlantic – it's on the west side, you know.

Marcel: Yes, I've heard it gets a lot of rain. **6** is Manchester United doing?

Kitsty: No idea, I'm afraid. I'm **7** a football person. Kevin is, aren't you? Ask him.

Kevin: They're still among the top teams and **8** in the Champions' League quarter finals.

Marcel: I know, they may be playing Bayern Munich next … ! I've heard that Manchester is a very vibrant place.

Kirsty: It certainly is. It's become a **9** city. Lots of gigs and clubs. All the old industry has gone and the old buildings have been renovated. You'd like it. You ought to come some time.

Marcel: I'd like to. Are there any **10**?

Kevin: Definitely. It's amazing how cheap they are if you book **11**. If you search the internet you can save a lot of money.

Marcel: Well, that's really … Ah, here comes Herr Diepholz …

2 Complete the following conversations with the words from the boxes.

Dialogue 1

> afraid • doing • flight • like • proud • time

You: How was your **1**?

Visitor: Rather bumpy, I'm **2**.

You: I'm sorry to hear that. What was the weather **3** in Glasgow?

Visitor: Oh, it was the same as here, overcast and windy. But that's nothing unusual for this **4** of the year.

You: How are Glasgow Rangers **5**?

Visitor: They play in the UEFA Europa League, we're rather **6** of them. I support Celtic, though.

Dialogue 2

apart • by • for • from • how • there

You: Where do you come **1**, Miss Spears?
Visitor: I'm from South Africa. Just now I've come from Berlin **2** train.
You: **3** was the train ride? Was the train punctual?
Visitor: Actually, the train was 10 minutes late, **4** from that the ride was quite
          pleasant, though.
You: South Africa must be a wonderful country. At least that's what
          everybody here says who's been **5**.
Visitor: You should come and see **6** yourself. There's a lot to see and do for
          tourists.

3 Match the questions with the answers.

1. Can I offer you a cold drink?   a. No, thank you. I'll keep it on. I'm cold.
2. Is this your first visit to Germany?   b. No, thanks. I'm on a diet.
3. Did you have a good flight?   c. Yes, please. Perhaps your company brochure?
4. Would you like something to read?   d. Very sunny. We could do with some rain.
5. What was the weather like in Portugal?   e. No, it's not my thing. I prefer cycling.
6. May I take your coat?   f. Yes, it is.
7. Do you take milk and sugar?   g. Oh no. There was a lot of turbulence.
8. Are you interested in tennis?   h. Thank you. An apple juice would be fine.

4 Restore the correct order of this jumbled dialogue.

1. Barmaid (in pub): Yes, it's freezing, isn't it? And this awful drizzle.
2. Customer: It's not like June at all.
3. Barmaid: They say its going to improve for the weekend, though.
4. Customer: Isn't the weather dreadful!

Communicating across cultures: Small Talk

In Britain the weather is very changeable, which makes it a constant topic of conversation:

The weather is wonderful, superb, lovely,
very good. The weather is awful, ghastly,
dreadful, terrible.

Example:
Newsagent: Good morning. How are you today?
Customer: Fine. Isn't it a beautiful day?
Newsagent: Wonderful. Let's hope it stays like this.
Customer: I'm afraid the weather forecast says rain.

5 Role play: Work in pairs. Make up dialogues using the following prompts and the phrases at the end of the Unit.

Phrases

> Student A:
> How was your trip?

> Student B:
> Rather tedious, there was a tailback on the motorway from Frankfurt.

Student A asks about:	Student B replies using these expressions:
flight / trip / journey	pleasant, rather tedious, lots of turbulence, tailback on the motorway, long delay at the airport, etc.
weather	sunny, overcast, slight drizzle, fog, gale-force winds, snow, is going to improve, cold for the time of the year, quite warm, pouring rain, windy, etc.
first visit to …	oh yes, many times, once before, but not much time to see anything, no never, long been wanting to visit …, etc.
hotel	nice and quiet, service first-class, a bit far from the exhibition centre, rather noisy, excellent restaurant, etc.
visitor's home town	small place in Wisconsin, has changed a lot in recent years, many tourists visit it, has vibrant business centre, scenic village in the mountains, busy port in India, etc.
sports events	not very interested in golf, watch as many tournaments as possible, would like to see the match, support XYZ club, etc.

C Giving directions

Kirsty Burnham has lost her way in the office building. She is standing at the reception desk. The receptionist directs her to Herr Diepholz' – the managing director's – office.

1 Take the role of the receptionist. Use the floor plan, the phrases below and the phrases at the end of the unit.

Phrases >

Herr Diepholz' office is on the right / left hand side.

The ladies' room / restroom is on your left / right.

Go down the stairs.

Go up the stairs.

Take the lift to the first / second floor.

Go down to the ground floor.

Go along the corridor.

Second floor, Advertising Department

| Assistant | Managing Director | Stairs | Confe-rence Room |
Secretary
Advertising Assistants
Lift
Storage
Gents
Ladies
Open Plan Office
Storage | Kitchen
Advertising Manager
Assistant
Secretary

First floor, Marketing and Sales Department

Secretary
Secretary
Assistant
Marketing Manager
Lift
Kitchen
Gents
Ladies
Open Plan Office
Assistant | Sales Manager | Stairs | Data Processing
Storage | Secretary | Research Manager
Secretary
Marketing Assistants
Sales Assistants

Ground floor, Finance and Personnel Department

Company Training Manager
Secretary
Kitchen
Lift
Medical Room
Gents
Ladies
Lounge Area
Chief Accountant | Secretary | Stairs
Canteen
Stationery Room | Post Room
Main entrance
Receptionist

If you turn left / right you will see Mr / Ms … office on your right / left.

Take the first entrance to the right / left.

Go across the hall.

2 Work in pairs. Explain to each other the way to certain rooms.

I

1. Your partner is at the main entrance. He asks you: "Could you tell me the way to the Sales Manager's office?"
2. You are in the canteen. You ask your partner:" Where is the conference room, please?"
3. Your partner is leaving the Advertising Manager's office. He asks you: "Would you mind telling me where the medical room is?"
4. You are in the Marketing Assistants' room. You ask your partner: "I need to freshen up a bit. Could you tell me the way to the ladies'/the men's toilets/restroom (Am)?"

3 The visitors from England want to see some of the famous sights in Munich.

P Use the map on page 25 and direct them from the station (Hauptbahnhof) to the following destinations:
Hofbräuhaus [1], Frauenkirche [2], Englischer Garten [3].

Phrases

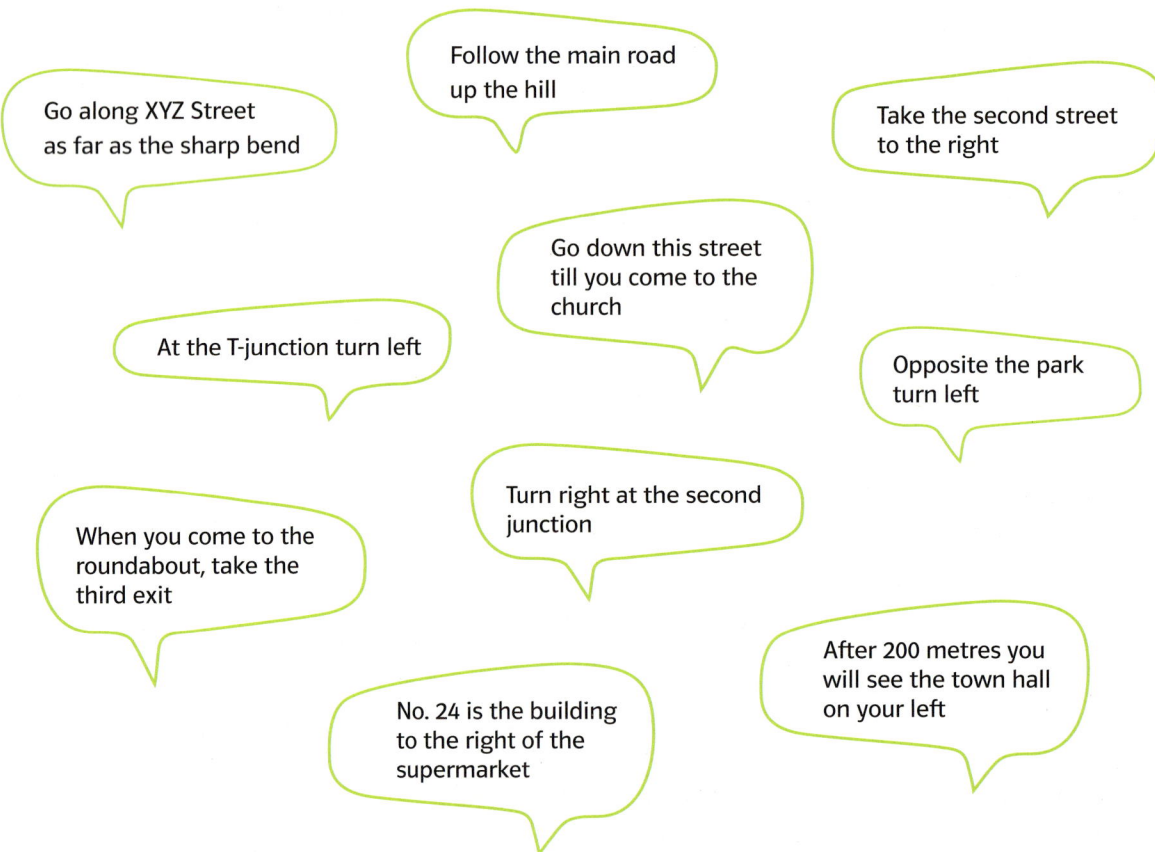

Go along XYZ Street as far as the sharp bend

Follow the main road up the hill

Take the second street to the right

Go down this street till you come to the church

At the T-junction turn left

Opposite the park turn left

Turn right at the second junction

When you come to the roundabout, take the third exit

After 200 metres you will see the town hall on your left

No. 24 is the building to the right of the supermarket

4
R
◎ A1.5

Listen to the explanations given by the Tourist Information assistant and find out which famous sights the visitors will be seeing during their stroll through the town centre of Munich.

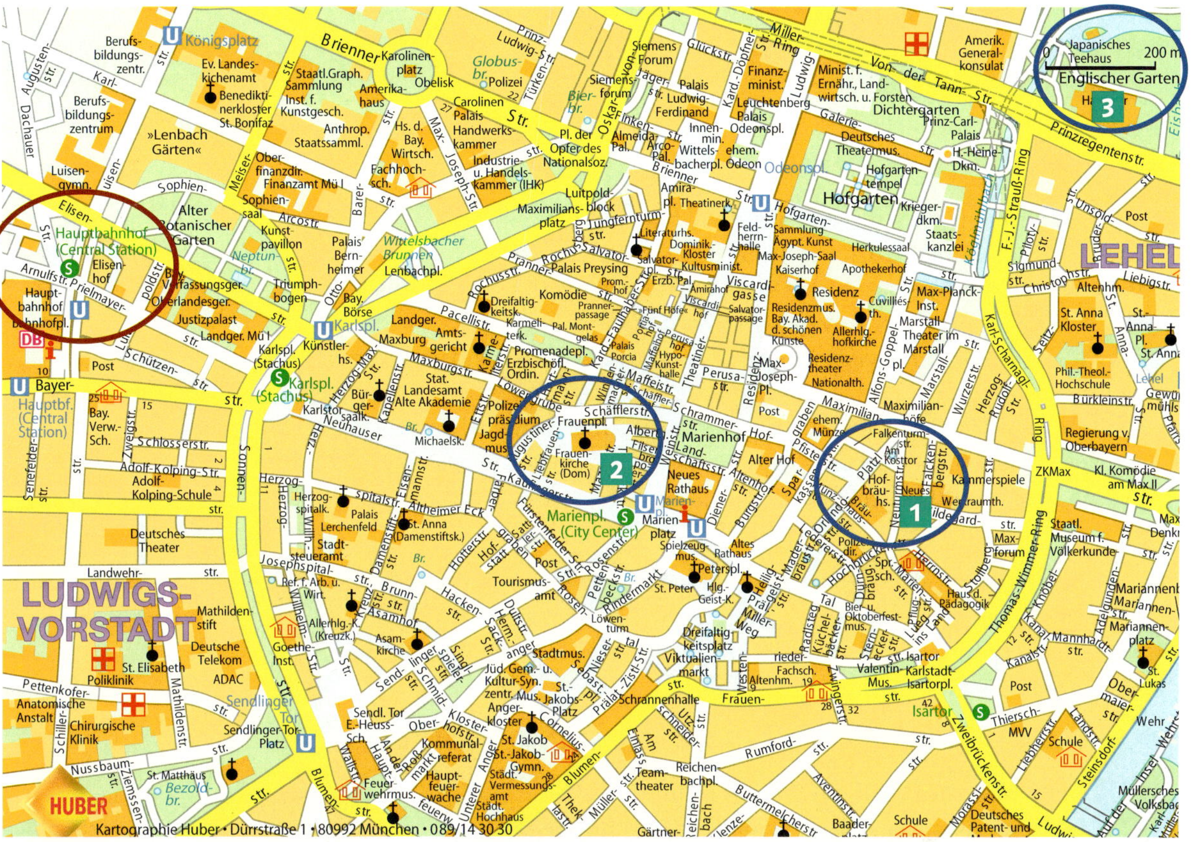

5 David Stedman has been visiting your headquarters in Berlin. He now has an appointment at your offices in Inselstraße, Düsseldorf. He has been told that the office is within walking distance of the main station. As he has some time on his hands before his appointment he would like to have instructions how to get there on foot.

Click on to a map of Düsseldorf on the internet and e-mail the instructions to him (davidstedman@aol.com).

D Describing the layout of the premises and carrying out a tour of the firm for visitors

Markus Diepholz and Marcel Krenz take Kirsty Burnham and Kevin Sears on a tour of the company's premises.

1 **Listen to the dialogue and decide whether the following statements are TRUE or FALSE.**
R
◎ A1.6
1. All the administrative work is dealt with at the offices.
2. The senior staff also work in the open-plan offices.
3. Marcel Krenz' office has a nice view of the surrounding countryside.
4. The canteen also provides vegetarian snacks.
5. Herr Diepholz and his visitors cross the car park to reach the kitchen facilities.
6. Freshness and hygiene are the most important considerations.
7. International Snacks are planning to do some market research on what people feel about their packaging.

2 **You are Kevin Sears. Write a memo in English on the tour of the premises of**
P **International Snacks.**
   Remember: A memo has to be brief, clear and to the point.

> **+ + MEMO + + MEMO + + MEMO + + MEMO + + MEMO + +**
>
> **To:** Michael Kent, General Manager
> **From:** Kevin Sears, Assistant to Kirsty Burnham
> **Date:** Wednesday, 23 March 201_
> **Subject:** Our tour of the Premises of International Snacks, Düsseldorf

3 **Sie sind Marcel Krenz. Verfassen Sie eine kurze Aktennotiz in Deutsch über die**
KMK **Betriebsbesichtigung und die Reaktionen der britischen Besucher.**

> ## MEMO
>
> **Für:** Geschäftsleitung
> **Von:** Marcel Krenz, Exportsachbearbeiter
> **Datum:** 20.03.201_
> **Betreff:** Betriebsbesichtigung mit Kirsty Burnham und Kevin Sears von Global Catering, Manchester, UK

E Taking foreign visitors to a restaurant

Herr Diepholz invites Kirsty and Kevin to lunch
and asks Marcel to join them and interpret.

1 **Listen to the dialogue and write down what**
R **Kirsty and Kevin order (starter, main course,**
A1.7 **dessert, drinks).**

Speisekarte

Vorspeisen

Pikante Brokkoli-Pastetchen

Gefüllte Steinpilze

Kraftbrühe mit Ei

Lauchcremesuppe

Avocado-Kaltschale

Hauptgerichte

Schweinebraten mit Rotkohl und Salzkartoffeln

Rinderrouladen mit Blumenkohl und Kartoffelpüree

Rheinischer Sauerbraten mit Rotkohl und Kartoffelklößen

Wiener Schnitzel mit Pommes frites und Salat

Wildgulasch mit Speckknödeln und Preiselbeeren

Forelle Müllerin-Art

Lauch-Soufflé

Gemüsebratlinge

Nachspeisen

Gemischtes Eis

Rote Grütze mit Sahne

Bayerische Creme

Käseplatte

2 **Find the correct equivalents.**

1. Bockwurst
2. Bratkartoffeln
3. Bratwurst
4. Erbsensuppe
5. Frikadellen
6. Gurkensalat
7. Kartoffelbrei
8. Kartoffelsuppe
9. Pommes frites
10. Rinderbraten
11. Rindfleischbrühe
12. Schokoladenpudding
13. Schweinebraten

a. beef broth
b. chocolate pudding
c. cucumber salad
d. French fries
e. fried potatoes
f. grilled sausage
g. mashed potatoes
h. meatballs
i. pea soup
j. potato soup
k. roast beef
l. roast pork
m. large frankfurter

Communicating across cultures: Describing dishes

For a number of typical German dishes there are no direct translations. You will have to describe them to your visitors from abroad. These expressions may help you:

Which part of the meal is it?
It's a starter.
It's the main course.
It's a dessert.
What kind of food is it?
It's meat (pork, beef, veal, lamb).
It's poultry (chicken, turkey).
It's fish (salmon, trout, plaice, haddock).
It's game (venison, rabbit).
It's a sort of pasta (spaghetti, noodles).
It's a vegetable (peas, beans, carrots, green peppers, cauliflower, cabbage, Brussels sprouts, asparagus).

How is it made?
It's made of mashed potatoes, ground / minced meat, chopped onions.
It's filled / stuffed with (rice, minced meat, vegetables).
It's boiled (baked, stewed, grilled, fried, smoked).
What does it taste like?
It's hot / spicy.
It's sweet / sour.
It's tart.
It's savoury.
It tastes a bit like (yoghurt, veal, mousse au chocolat).

3 Study the explanations and find out which of the German dishes
R   they refer to.

> Jägerschnitzel · Kopfsalat · Rote Grütze · Semmelknödel ·
> Spätzle

1. It's a dessert. It's a jelly made of red berries thickened with
   corn starch. It's not too sweet. Quite tart, in fact.
2. They go with a main course. They're dumplings made of
   white bread with eggs and parsley. They're rather filling,
   though.
3. It's a schnitzel, a sort of pork escalope with sauce and
   mushrooms.
4. It's a kind of home-made pasta, typical of the South West of
   Germany.
5. It's lettuce with oil and vinegar dressing.

✳ **4** Ask the amateur chefs among you to explain two of the   Phrases ▶
M   following dishes in English to your group. Use the expressions at
     the end of the unit.

> Zigeunerschnitzel · Sauerkraut · gemischter Salat · gefüllte
> Paprikaschoten · Milchreis · Hackbraten · Linseneintopf

✳ **5** Choose a starter, a main course and a dessert from the menu on   Phrases ▶
M   page 27 and explain it to a foreign visitor. Use the phrases at the
     end of the unit.

✳ **6** Work in groups. Explain your favourite dishes to the group.
P

> **Communicating across cultures:**
> **Going to restaurants in Britain**
>
> You may have to wait to be seated. A waiter will ask how many you are and indicate a table.
> Of course, you can say something like: "Couldn't we sit over there in the window?"
>
> The waiter / waitress may ask you whether you want to order drinks straight away. After you have
> had time to study the menu, the waiter or waitress will say: "Are you ready to order, madam?"
> If you are not, you could say: "We're not quite ready. We need a moment or two."
>
> When the food comes, he / she will probably say: "Enjoy your meal" or sometimes just "Enjoy!"
> However, there is nothing like "Guten Appetit" that you can say to your companions / guests.
>
> Complaining is very difficult. You should at all costs avoid being aggressive or loud – this will not
> get you anywhere. Be nice, understanding, humorous if possible.
>
> Finally, when you want to pay, you say: "Could I have the bill, please."

Language and grammar 1
Choose the correct form of the verbs.

1. I `give` you a ring towards the end of the week.
2. We `let` you `know` as soon as possible.
3. If you `wash` the dishes, I `dry` .
4. I `ask` Joanna if she `want` to come.
5. You `chop` the mushrooms and I `cook` the pasta.
6. I `pass` on the message when I `see` her on Friday.
7. I `pick` him up at the station if you `want` .
8. He `help` you with your move if you `give` him a ring on Wednesday.
9. I `give` you a lift if you like.
10. David `stand` in for you if necessary.

Language and grammar 2
Translate the following text.

Wir übergeben die Sendung morgen früh der Spedition Fuhrmann Logistik
und hoffen, dass die Ware übermorgen wohlbehalten bei Ihnen ankommt. Wir
helfen Ihnen gerne, wenn Sie noch weitere Fragen haben. Wir sind sicher, dass
unsere exquisiten Schuhe Ihren Kunden gefallen und dass sich diese Artikel in
Großbritannien gut verkaufen lassen.

Language and grammar: Will-future	
Die "will"-Zukunftsform (meistens in der abgeschwächten Form I'll, we'll) wird im Englischen bei spontanen Entscheidungen benutzt und entspricht dem Präsens im Deutschen.	
Marcel Krenz says:	I'll give Herr Diepholz a ring and let him know you're here.
Kevin Sears says:	I'll have black coffee.
Marcel Krenz says:	I'll just ring through and order them.
Sit down and I'll make some coffee.	= Setz dich hin. Ich koche Kaffee.
You keep an eye on the spaghetti and I'll make the salad.	= Pass du auf die Spaghetti auf. Ich mache den Salat.
Allerdings wird "will" nicht in Nebensätzen der Bedingung und der Zeit verwendet.	
I'll fetch the newspapers if you make the tea.	= Ich hole die Zeitungen, wenn du Tee machst.
I'll tell him as soon as he arrives.	= Ich sage es ihm, sobald er ankommt.

Logistics expert

1 Warehouses

1 Look up the words in the box in a dictionary. Then describe the photos.

P

canopy • cardboard box • fork-lift truck • loading dock • pallet • pallet jack •
roller door • semi-trailer • shelf • storage • warehouse

2 Read the text and complete the summary with the words in the box on
R page 32. There are more words than you will need.

Commercial buildings used for the **storage of goods** are called
"warehouses". In Hamburg or Amsterdam, for example, old storage
buildings have become an important part of the local cultural heritage.
Modern warehouses today are usually plain buildings in industrial areas on
the outskirts of towns.

Goods usually arrive on trucks in containers, placed on ISO standard pallets,
and are unloaded at the loading docks by fork-lift trucks. In the storage area
the pallets are stored in racks or shelves. Special software organises the
optimal placement of the goods for easy retrieval.

After the goods are received and put away, the next step in the workflow
is to prepare the **shipping of the orders** to the customers. In some
warehouses, the goods may be picked by an automated storage and retrieval
system (ASRS) and moved on conveyor belts to the picking station. In a
"person-to-goods" warehouse, the order picker walks up and down the
aisles, using a pick list and a picking cart, until the order is complete and
ready to be shipped.

The warehousing process is coordinated by a **warehouse management
system** (WMS). This is a software programme which keeps an accurate
inventory of incoming and outgoing goods. In fully automated warehouses,
pallets and products are moved on conveyor belts and by cranes. This type
of warehouse is often used for refrigerated goods.

conveyor belts • fork-lift trucks • industrial area • inventory • ISO pallets •
loading docks • picked • picking list • picking station • refrigerated goods •
warehouses

Nowadays, old **1** are often used as luxury apartments. At modern
warehouses the goods usually arrive packed on **2**. Inside the warehouse,
the goods are moved by **3** or on **4**. The goods are unloaded at the **5**. In the
preparation of orders, the goods must be **6** from the shelves. The **7** tells
the order picker which goods to pick. The list of incoming and outgoing
goods is called: **8**. Automated warehouses are often used for **9**.

2   At the Perishables Handling Centre

1 Use the illustration to describe the way the goods move through the PHC
P   until they are loaded onto the lorries for on-carriage.

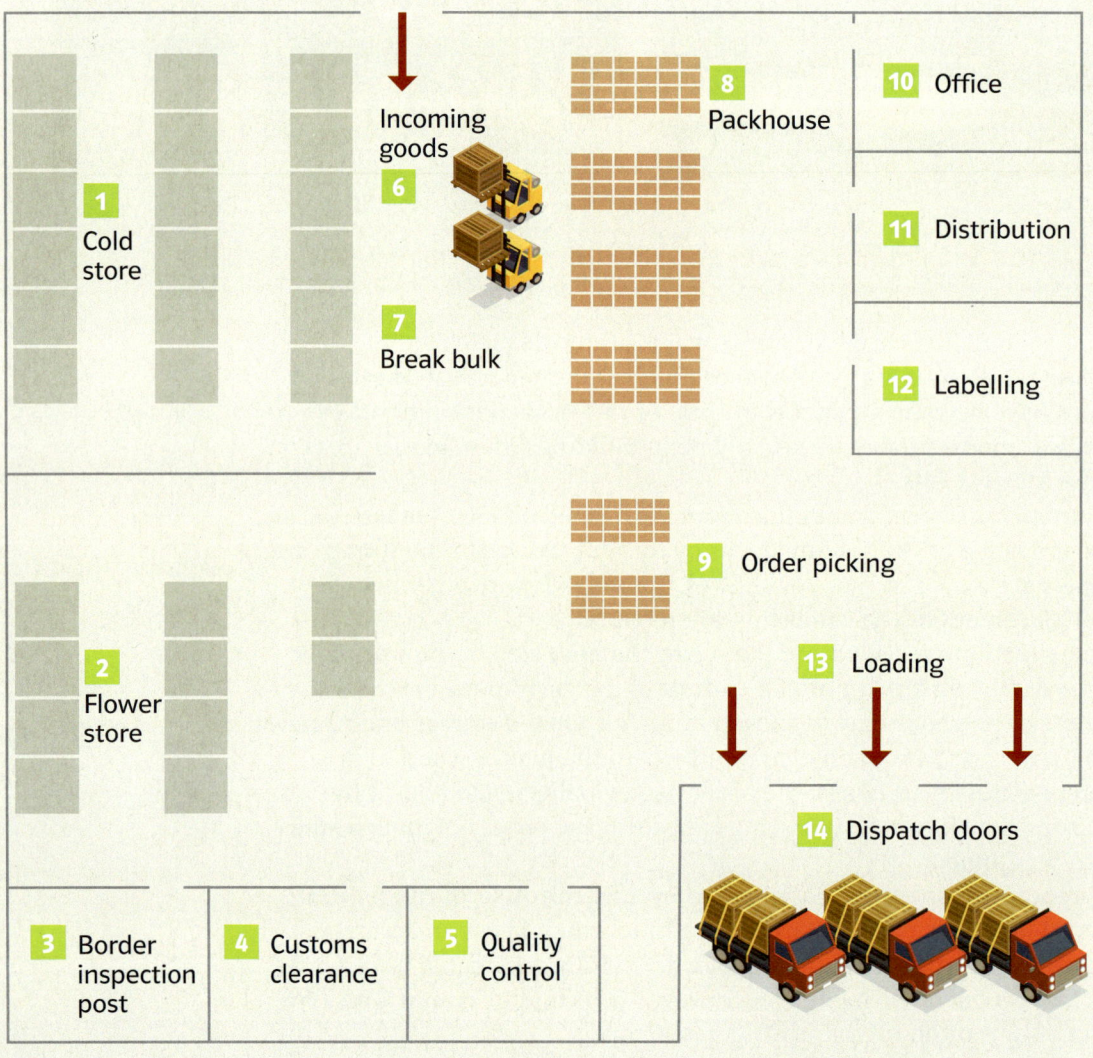

2
R
A 2.6

Neil Carter continues talking about his work at the PHC in Heathrow airport. Listen to the second part of the interview (for the first part, see UNIT 1). Then answer the following questions.

1. Give three examples of perishable goods mentioned in the interview. Then think of three more examples not mentioned in the interview.
2. At what temperature are goods stored at the PHC?
3. Describe the process of "breaking bulk".
4. Which extra services does the PHC offer to its clients?
5. How does the PHC keep control of incoming and outgoing goods?
6. Describe the most basic service which is offered to customers.
7. What is the highest level of service?

3 **Work in groups and find out what happens in a quality control check for the following products. Use the internet and report your findings in class.**
P

1. fruit and vegetables
2. livestock
3. frozen meat
4. chemicals

3 Dealing with measurements and calculations

Info: Calculations, sizes and dimensions

Special signs

.	full stop / dot	'	foot	33	double three
:	colon	"	inch	333	triple three / three, double three
–	hyphen / dash	/	slash		
"..."	quotation marks	\	backslash	( )	brackets
'...'	inverted commas	A	capital A	[ ]	square brackets
;	semicolon	*A*	capital A in italics	@	at
!	exclamation mark	a	small a		

Volumes
m² square metre   m³ cubic metre

Shapes
round like a circle   square like a cube   rectangular   cylindrical

Decimal numbers
0.1   UK: oh point one / nought point one / US: zero point one
0.015   UK: oh point oh one five / US: zero point zero one five
0.170   UK: oh point one seven oh / US: zero point one seven zero

Mathematical symbols

$1 + 3$	one plus three / add one and three
$4 - 1$	four minus one / subtract one from four
7×2	seven times two / multiply seven by two
$9 : 3$	nine divided by three
$7 + 8 = 15$	seven plus eight is fifteen / equals fifteen / makes fifteen
$10 > 5$	ten is more / greater than five
$111 < 113$	one hundred and eleven is less / smaller than one hundred and thirteen

Fractions

½ a half ⅓ a third / one third ¼ a quarter ⅜ three eighths % per cent / percent

Sizes and dimensions

Length The twenty foot container is nearly six metres long. / Its length is nearly six metres.

Width The vessel is 33 metres wide. / Its width is 33 metres.

Height The cargo unit is 3.65 metres high. / Its height is 3.65 metres.

Size The wooden crate is 2 by 2 by 1 metres, which makes 4 cubic metres in all. / The wooden box measures 2 by 2 by 1 metres. / Its measurements are 2 by 2 by 1 metres.

Weight The gross weight of the crate is 356 kg. The net weight of the scooter is 305 kg. So the tare weight of the crate and the seaworthy packing material must be 51 kg. The total gross weight of a lorry is 40 tons. The maximum payload is 26 tons – so the dead weight of the lorry must be 14 tons.

Conversion

Metric	Imperial
1 millimetre (mm)	0.03937 in
1 centimetre (cm) 10 mm	0.3937 in
1 metre (m) 100 cm	1.0936 yd
1 kilometre (km) 1000 m	0.6214 mile

Imperial	Metric
1 foot (1')	0.3048 m
1 inch (in)	2.54 cm
1 foot (ft) 12 in	0.3048 m
1 yard (yd) 3 ft	0.9144 m
1 mile (1760 yd)	1.6093 km
1 int nautical mile (2025.4 yd)	1.853 km
3 foot 3 inches (3'3")	1.0 metre (exactly 39.37 inches or 3.281 feet)

Say the following aloud. Use the info box above for help.

P

1. 0.165×255
2. $3' \times 4' \times 1'3"$
3. $20.4 \, m^2$
4. ⅝
5. $23 + 17 = 40$
6. $2.5 \, m \times 2 \, m \times 3 \, m$
7. 12.5%
8. $16.05 \, mm$
9. $35.28 \, m^3$
10. $48 : 8 = 6$

Phrases: Taking care of visitors

To welcome visitors

Good afternoon. Can I help you?/What can I do for you?	Guten Tag. Was kann ich für Sie tun?
Please take **a seat**.	Bitte nehmen Sie Platz.
Can I offer you some refreshments?	Darf ich Ihnen etwas anbieten?
Coffee with milk and sugar, tea, herbal tea, fruit juice, sparkling/still mineral water, coke?	Kaffee mit Milch und Zucker, schwarzer Tee, Kräutertee, Fruchtsaft, Mineralwasser mit/ohne Kohlensäure, Cola?
Frau Sievers **is expecting** you.	Frau Sievers erwartet Sie.
I'm afraid, Frau Sievers is still in a meeting.	Frau Sievers ist leider noch in einer Besprechung.
She will be **with** you in a few minutes.	Sie wird in ein paar Minuten da sein.

To make conversation

Did you have a pleasant flight?	Hatten Sie einen angenehmen Flug?
How was the **journey**?	Wie war die Fahrt?
Have you ever been to Oldenburg before?	Waren Sie schon einmal in Oldenburg?
Where do you come **from**?	Wo kommen Sie her?
What was the weather **like** in Belfast?	Wie war das Wetter in Belfast?
Would you like to see something **of** Bonn?	Möchten Sie in Bonn etwas besichtigen?
Are you satisfied with your hotel?	Sind Sie mit dem Hotel zufrieden?
I'll have an orange juice.	Ich nehme einen Orangensaft.
No thanks, I don't take milk or sugar.	Nein danke, ich nehme weder Milch noch Zucker.
The flight was rather bumpy.	Der Flug war ziemlich unruhig.
The trip was very pleasant. Thank you.	Danke. Die Fahrt war sehr angenehm.
Actually, I have been to Oldenburg twice, in 1999 and in 2002.	Ich war tatsächlich schon zweimal in Oldenburg, 1990 und 2002.
The weather was fine. Not a cloud **in** the sky.	Das Wetter war schön. Kein Wölkchen am Himmel.
We've had a lot of rain lately.	In der letzten Zeit hat es bei uns viel geregnet.
I'd like to visit Beethoven's house.	Ich möchte mir gerne das Beethoven-Haus ansehen.

The hotel will do. It's **on** a rather noisy street, though.	Das Hotel geht einigermaßen. Es liegt allerdings an einer ziemlich lauten Straße.
The hotel is excellent. Very quiet.	Das Hotel ist ausgezeichnet. Sehr ruhig.

To give directions

GB	USA	Germany
second floor	third floor	2. Etage
first floor	second floor	1. Etage
ground floor	first floor	Erdgeschoss
basement	basement	Untergeschoss/Keller

Take the lift to the third floor.	Fahren Sie mit dem Aufzug in den dritten Stock.
Go up/down (the stairs) to the 2nd floor.	Gehen Sie (die Treppe) hinauf/hinunter zum 2. Stock.
Herr Diepholz' office is on the **right hand** side.	Das Büro von Herrn Diepholz ist auf der rechten Seite.
At the junction **turn** right/left.	Gehen/Fahren Sie an der Kreuzung nach rechts/links.
Go **straight ahead** to …	Gehen/Fahren Sie gerade aus bis …
Go down this street till you come to the …	Gehen/Fahren Sie auf dieser Straße weiter bis Sie zu … kommen.
When you come to the roundabout, take the 3rd exit.	Am Kreisverkehr nehmen Sie die dritte Ausfahrt.
Follow the main road up the hill.	Fahren Sie die Hauptstraße weiter bergauf.
After 200 yards you will see the church **to** your left.	Nach (ca.) 200 m sehen Sie die Kirche auf der linken Seite.

To take visitors on a tour of your firm's premises

We would like to show you **round** the company's premises.	Wir möchten Ihnen unsere Firma auf einem Rundgang zeigen.
We have two open-plan offices.	Wir haben zwei Großraumbüros.
These are our production facilities.	Hier sehen Sie unsere Fertigungsanlagen.
We'll go through this door which leads to the canteen.	Wir gehen durch diese Türe, die zur Kantine führt.

The canteen looks very modern and airy.	Die Kantine wirkt sehr modern und luftig.
We leave this building and **cross** the car park.	Wir verlassen jetzt dieses Gebäude und gehen über den Parkplatz.
I think we had better be getting back to our office now.	Ich glaube wir sollten jetzt lieber ins Büro zurückgehen.
Our visit has certainly been very interesting.	Unser Besuch war wirklich sehr interessant.

To take visitors to a restaurant

This is a typical German restaurant.	Das ist ein typisch deutsches Restaurant.
Let's have a look **at** the menu?	Wollen wir uns die Speisekarte ansehen?
What **about** you? What are you having?	Wie ist es mit Ihnen/Dir? Was nehmen Sie/ was nimmst Du?
Are you having a starter?	Nimmst Du/Nehmen Sie eine Vorspeise?
I think I'll just have a main course.	Ich nehme nur ein Hauptgericht.
Could I have a starter as a main course?	Kann ich eine Vorspeise als Hauptgericht nehmen?
It's a sort of pasta.	Es sind Teigwaren.
It's cabbage stuffed with minced meat.	Es ist Kohl mit einer Hackfleischfüllung.
It tastes a bit like mushrooms.	Es schmeckt ein bisschen wie Pilze.
I'm not hungry enough for a 3-course meal.	Ein Menü mit 3 Gängen ist mir zuviel.
I'd like a German beer.	Ich möchte ein deutsches Bier.
Would you like a salad as a starter?	Möchten Sie einen Salat als Vorspeise?
I'll have the lamb cutlets with beans.	Ich nehme die Lammkoteletts mit Bohnen.
I prefer chicken **to** fish.	Ich esse lieber Geflügel als Fisch.
I'm **a** vegetarian.	Ich bin Vegetarier/in.
My wife would like the trout with almonds.	Meine Frau möchte die Forelle mit Mandeln.
What about some ice cream as a dessert?	Wie wär's mit Eis als Nachtisch?
I'd **rather** have some cheese.	Ich hätte lieber etwas Käse.
It was delicious but I'm afraid I can't eat any more.	Es hat sehr gut geschmeckt, aber ich bin leider schon satt.
I'm going to do without a dessert.	Ich verzichte auf eine Nachspeise.

A

B

Unit 3
The company and its products and services

WORD BANK

image • history • range of products • company brochure • global player • start-up business • family-owned firm • workforce • manufacturing • provision of services • business idea • stock corporation • public limited company • private limited company • to found • to establish • to manufacture • to provide • old-established • modern • traditional • leading • small • medium-sized • state-of-the-art

When companies describe themselves in their sales literature they generally attempt to create a particular image. They may refer to the firm's history to emphasise qualities such as experience and reliability. If they do not have a long history behind them, they may prefer to emphasise that they are a young, dynamic, forward-looking company, providing new products and services.

1 List the adjectives and expressions from the box under the categories given below:

old-established • flexible • dynamic • reliable • with many years' experience • young • forward-looking • taking advantage of the new media • solid • state-of-the-art

Example:

traditional	modern
old-established	state-of-the-art

Online-Link
808264-0003

2 Find examples of traditional and young companies in Germany and other countries.

3 Choose the adjectives from the box on page 38 which best describe the company you are training at. Is it a traditional or a young company? Give details.

A Introducing a firm and giving a brief history

While waiting for an interview at Herkules AG, Sandra Kohl studies the company brochure in English. It begins with an article on the history of the firm.

Herkules
the global sports brand

Back in 1922 the shoemaker Heinrich Schuster made the first sports shoes for the local sports club, the TSV Neustadt. Very soon sportsmen from neighbouring clubs ordered sports shoes from Mr. Schuster and two years later he employed a staff of 25. In 1927 he rented a factory building and bought the machinery required for industrial manufacturing. The company continued to prosper until World War II. In 1948 Heinrich Schuster's son Helmut took over and changed the company's name to Herkules. At the Olympic Games in Melbourne in 1956 several of the athletes competing wore Herkules shoes.

A few years later Helmut Schuster added footballs and other types of ball to Herkules's range of products and in the early 70s took up the production of sports bags. Meanwhile Herkules employed 3400 people and its products featured in all the Olympic Games and World Championships.

Olympic Games

By 2010 the workforce had risen to 12,500 and Herkules had become the market leader in the EU and a global player with production sites in Germany, Portugal, Morocco, Malaysia and Taiwan.

1 Read the text on page 39 and ask the questions which would produce the
R following answers.

Example:
Question:
1. Who founded the company?

Answers:
1. The company was founded by **Heinrich Schuster**.
2. Mass production began **in 1927**.
3. **Olympic Games and World Championships** are of particular importance
   for the company.
4. Apart from shoes the company produces **bags and balls**.
5. Herkules has got production sites in **Germany, Portugal, Morocco, Malaysia
   and Taiwan**.

2 Find the missing prepositions from the box with the help of the text on page 39.
R

by • from • in (2x) • of • over • until • up • to (2x) • with

Back **1** 1922 Heinrich Schuster made the first sports shoes.
Sportsmen **2** neighbouring clubs ordered sports shoes.
Two years later he was employing a staff **3** 25.
The company prospered **4** World War II.
In 1948 Schuster's son Helmut took **5** and changed the name **6** Herkules.
In the early 70s Herkules took **7** the production of bags.
Herkules' products featured **8** all the Olympic Games.
9 1990 the number of staff had risen **10** 9,500.
Herkules is a global player **11** production sites in several countries.

3 Read the text on Herkules again and find words or phrases that mean the same as
R the following expressions.

1. people employed by a firm
2. production on a large scale
3. an assortment of articles
4. the company that has a dominant position in a given market
5. a company that is active worldwide

✳ **4** Sandra Kohl informiert eine Freundin über die Firma Herkules.
KMK Verfassen Sie hierfür eine schriftliche Zusammenfassung der wichtigsten Fakten in
Deutsch, die ca. 80 Wörter umfasst. Gehen Sie dabei kurz auf folgende Punkte ein:

• Entwicklung des Unternehmens
• Produkte
• gegenwärtige Stellung des Unternehmens

5 Read the introduction below, then listen to
R   Martha Dinsdale describing her firm and
A 1.8 complete the following text.

Christian Kleine, an IT specialist, is interested
in doing a short practical abroad. At a job
fair he meets Martha Dinsdale, managing
director of Smartmart Ltd, who describes the
development of her firm.

"Our company, Smartmart Ltd., was **1** in 1999. Our business **2** was to provide
an online market for private individuals or **3** companies with something to **4**
who do not want to spend a lot of **5** online selling it themselves. This, as we
all **6**, can be very time-consuming! It's not everybody's idea of an **7** way to
spend an evening! Some people do not feel sufficiently secure with the **8** to do
their own buying and selling. But, it is amazing how many **9** have things to
sell and how many potential **10** there are. After we had completed a feasibility
study, we **11** through the local chamber of commerce for financial and other **12**
in establishing a start-up business. Our **13** expenditure was for designing and
setting up an attractive and efficient **14** which would be capable of dealing
with a large **15** of hits. There's no point in opening up **16** on the internet with
an inadequate or badly designed website. We were quite overwhelmed by the
amount of **17**. Our business has grown in line with the other big **18** marts. We
charge a commission of 10% on sales completed, i.e. the **19** pays. We are now
making a healthy **20** and in two or three years' time we will be thinking in
terms of going public."

6 Match the English expressions with their German equivalents.

1. private individuals	a. 10 % Provision verlangen
2. time-consuming	b. Auslagen, Ausgaben
3. sufficient	c. ausreichend, genügend
4. amazing	d. bei der örtlichen IHK beantragen
5. feasibility study	e. erstaunlich
6. apply through the local chamber of commerce	f. finanzielle Unterstützung
	g. Machbarkeitsstudie
7. financial support	h. neugegründetes Unternehmen
8. start-up business	i. Online-Markt
9. expenditure	j. Privatpersonen
10. inadequate	k. sich in eine Aktiengesellschaft umwandeln
11. overwhelmed	
12. online mart	l. überwältigt
13. charge a commission of 10%	m. unzureichend, unzulänglich
14. go public	n. zeitraubend

7 Answer the following questions on Martha's talk.

R

1. When was the company founded?
2. What was their business idea?
3. Why did they think people would use their services?
4. What was their most expensive investment?
5. How does the company earn its living?

8 Christian Kleine fasst die Informationen, die ihm Martha Dinsdale über ihre Firma gegeben hat, auf Deutsch in einer Gesprächsnotiz für seine Personalabteilung zusammen. Bitte übernehmen Sie seine Rolle.

KMK

Gesprächsnotiz

Empfänger: _Personalabteilung_

Verfasser: _Christian Kleine, IT-Support_   Datum: _____

Gesprächspartner: _Martha Dinsdale von Smartmart Ltd._

Betreff: _Vorstellung von Smartmart Ltd._

✳ **9** Describe your own company in writing. Model your description on the descriptions of other companies in this unit.

P

Communicating across cultures:
Joint stock companies *(Kapitalgesellschaften)* **in the USA and Britain**

The British **Public Limited Company** (abbreviated to **PLC** or **plc** after the company name) and the American **Stock Corporation** (abbreviated to **Inc.** or **Corp.**) are roughly comparable to the German Aktiengesellschaft. The British **Private Limited Company** (abbreviated to **Ltd**) and the American **Closed Corporation** are approximately equivalent to the German GmbH. British and American joint stock companies are managed by a **Board of Directors** under the leadership of a Chief Executive Officer (CEO) (chairman of the board or managing director), who may also hold the title of Chairman or President. The head of a **Private Limited Company** is generally called the Managing Director.

10 Search the Internet for some of the following global players. Make notes on their products or services in English. Compare your notes with the group.

Tata Group • GlaxoSmithKline • Arcelormittal • Antofagasta • RWE Group • Berkshire Hathaway • Verizon • De Beers • China Mobile • Rio Tinto Zinc • HSBC • Selesio AG • Sir Robert McAlpine

B Describing products and services

At home Sandra Kohl looks at Herkules' homepage on the internet. Sandra clicks on the button "about us" to learn more about the company. The following website appears.

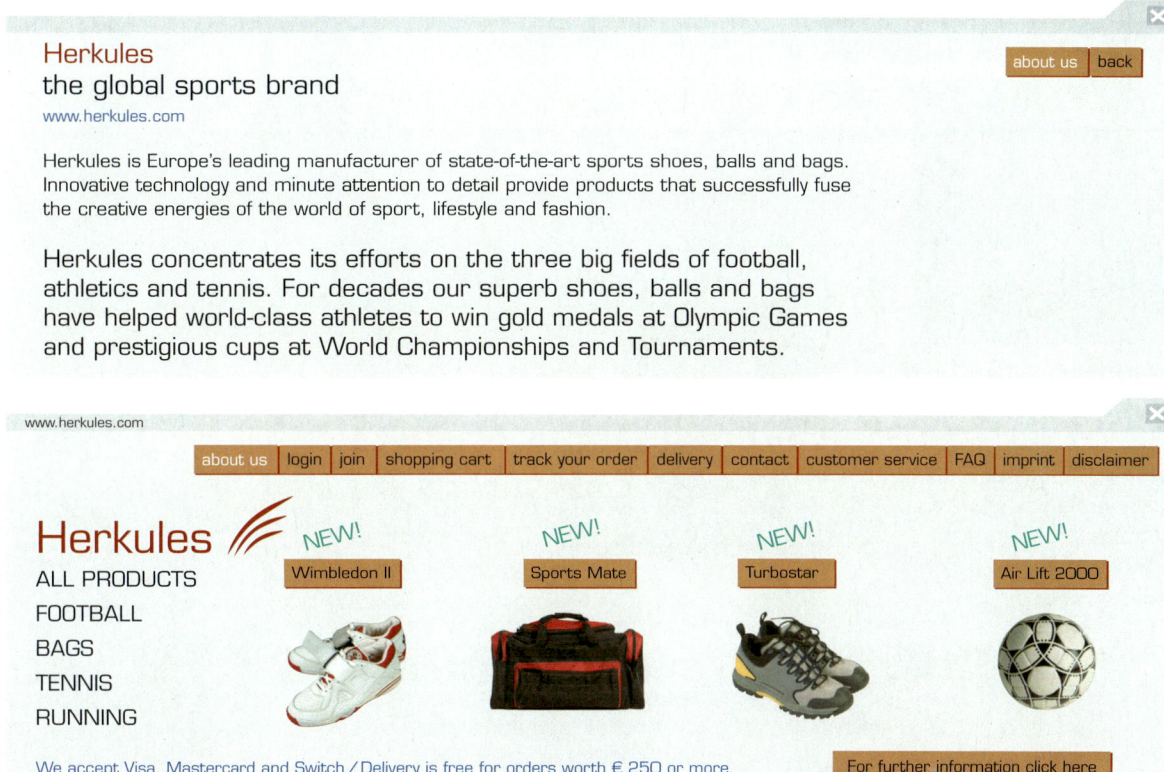

Herkules
the global sports brand
www.herkules.com

about us | back

Herkules is Europe's leading manufacturer of state-of-the-art sports shoes, balls and bags. Innovative technology and minute attention to detail provide products that successfully fuse the creative energies of the world of sport, lifestyle and fashion.

Herkules concentrates its efforts on the three big fields of football, athletics and tennis. For decades our superb shoes, balls and bags have helped world-class athletes to win gold medals at Olympic Games and prestigious cups at World Championships and Tournaments.

www.herkules.com

about us | login | join | shopping cart | track your order | delivery | contact | customer service | FAQ | imprint | disclaimer

Herkules

ALL PRODUCTS
FOOTBALL
BAGS
TENNIS
RUNNING

NEW! Wimbledon II

NEW! Sports Mate

NEW! Turbostar

NEW! Air Lift 2000

We accept Visa, Mastercard and Switch / Delivery is free for orders worth € 250 or more.

For further information click here

1 **Which buttons do you click on if you want to find out more about the following?**

1. the firm
2. all their products
3. particular product groups
4. individual products
5. details about delivery
6. frequently asked questions
7. how to place an order
8. repairs

2 **Replace the adjectives in brackets with appropriate expressions from the box.**

> excellent • the most modern • very careful • highly regarded

1. Herkules is Europe's leading manufacturer of (state-of-the-art) **1** sports shoes.
2. Innovative technology and (minute) **2** attention to detail provide products that fuse the creative energies of the world of sport, lifestyle and fashion.
3. For decades our (superb) **3** shoes and bags have helped world-class athletes to win gold medals at Olympic Games and (prestigious) **4** Cups at World Championships and Tournaments.

43

3

R/M Match the German statements on the next page with the following English statements.

Tatjana: The company I work for is a leading manufacturer of precision instruments.

Janine: I work for a small upmarket advertising agency. We specialise in media companies.

Patrizia: I work for a medium-sized company manufacturing organic cosmetic preparations.

Sinan: I work for a small family firm making a wide range of high quality furniture.

Markus: My company are IT consultants providing customised solutions for corporate clients.

Holger: I work for a small catering company specialising in providing lunches for local companies. We offer a lot of vegetarian dishes. We're basically a small start-up.

Jörg: My company is a whole-saler stocking a wide range of electrical products.

Claudia: The company I work for is a major retailer of food and some non-food products. I work in the admin section.

V1   Video lounge   Sport and leisure

BBC Motion Gallery

You are about to see a video on the sport and leisure industry. While watching the video, keep the following questions in mind:

1. How are the three presenters dressed? Which do you find most natural and convincing? Why?
2. Which different fitness club products does the video mention?
3. What does the first presenter mean when she says fitness has become a lifestyle business?
4. According to the video what is the overall economic situation of the fitness and leisure club industry?

Discuss your answers with the class.

1. Ich arbeite für ein mittelständisches Unternehmen, das Biokosmetik herstellt.
2. Meine Firma ist eine IT-Beratungsgesellschaft und bietet Firmenkunden maßgeschneiderte Lösungen an.
3. Die Firma, bei der ich arbeite, ist ein bedeutender Einzelhändler für Lebensmittel und Non-Food-Produkte.
4. Ich arbeite bei einem kleinen Partyservice, der sich auf Mittagessen für die Firmen in der Umgebung spezialisiert hat.
5. Meine Firma ist ein führender Hersteller von Präzisionsinstrumenten.
6. Ich arbeite bei einem Familienunternehmen, das hochwertige Möbel herstellt.
7. Ich arbeite bei einer kleinen exklusiven Werbeagentur.
8. Bei meiner Firma handelt es sich um eine Großhandlung mit einem breiten Sortiment von Elektroartikeln.

4 **Write similar descriptions of two firms' products or services with the help of the following hints.**
P

Types of firms	medium-sized enterprise, import/export company, large manufacturer, start-up company, wholesaler, retail chain, family-owned firm, IT consultancy, publishing house, advertising agency, catering firm, Public Limited Company, Private Limited Company, Stock Corporation
Products/services	household appliances, IT services, exotic fruit, steel tubes, creation of advertising material, groceries, silk fabrics, audio books, clocks and watches, cleaning services, office software
Descriptions	modern, upmarket, high-quality, fresh, in demand, excellent, unique, interesting, attractive, reliable, thorough, long-lasting, state-of-the-art, customised, inexpensive

We specialise in …

Our products/services are …

We are …

We offer …

I work for …

Example:
I work for a family-owned firm specializing in the manufacture of state-of-the-art steel tubes.

5 **Work in groups. Describe the firm you are training at and its products and/or services to your group. Use the phrases at the end of the unit.**
P

Phrases ▶

6 Dolmetschen Sie folgende Aussagen:

M

1. „Ich arbeite bei einer mittelgroßen Werbeagentur. Wir stellen attraktives Werbematerial für eine Lebensmittel-Einzelhandelskette her."

2. „Meine Firma ist auf die Herstellung einzigartiger Seidenstoffe höchster Qualität spezialisiert."

3. „Wir bieten maßgeschneiderte Lösungen für Bürosoftware an."

4. „Wir sind ein junger Musikverlag mit einem anspruchsvollen Sortiment von Titeln."

✳ 7 Project work: Work together with two other students to set up your own company. See Exercise 5 for useful expressions.

I/P

Phrases

Step 1: Discuss the following questions:
– What is your business idea?
– How can you find out whether your idea is any good?
– Where can you get help, financial or otherwise?
– What are the most essential investments to enable you to begin trading?

Step 2: Think up a good name for your company.

Step 3: Divide the work among yourselves:
– Student A creates an eye-catching logo.
– Student B designs a business card incorporating the logo.
– Student C designs a company letterhead also incorporating the logo.

Step 4: Present the result to the class.

6 Language and grammar 1

Find out whether the periods of time mentioned in the following sentences are entirely in the past or whether they continue to the present. Then choose the correct tense for the verbs in brackets.

1. It all (begin) in 1975.
2. Two years later he (launch) the new product.
3. The company (be successful) for many years now.
4. Since 2002 we (offer) these unique marketing services.
5. By now Herkules (become) a global player.
6. Last September Robert Hanks (start) a new business in the USA.
7. In the past there (be) a big demand for such systems.
8. But in the meantime they (be replaced) by faster systems.
9. So far we (have) no complaints.
10. I (speak) to him only yesterday.

Language and grammar: Simple Past and Present Perfect

Wird ein Zeitraum genannt, der vollständig in der Vergangenheit liegt, steht "simple past".

Back **in 1922** Heinrich Schuster **made** the first sports shoes.
At the Olympic Games several athletes **competed** wearing Herkules shoes.
A few years later he **added** footballs to the range of products.
Our company **was founded in 1999**.

Wenn ein Zeitraum genannt wird, der bis in die Gegenwart reicht, steht "present perfect".

For decades our superb shoes **have helped** athletes to win gold medals.
In the meantime ACE **has become** the market leader in Germany.
Since the beginning of the 90s **we have specialised** in real-time solutions.
I **have been** in my present department **for three months**.

Language and grammar 2
Decide which of the alternatives in brackets are correct.

1. I (am/have been) a trainee (for/since) 4 months.
2. We (see/have seen) a number of employees leave (for/since) 1998.
3. We (have specialised/specialise) in providing networking systems (for/since) more than a year.
4. She (wants/has wanted) to live in Berlin (since/for) she was 17 years old.
5. We (have known/know) the company (since/for) it was founded in 1983.
6. I (am thinking/have been thinking) of changing my job (since/for) a long time.
7. We (place/have placed) orders with this company (since/for) its foundation.

Language and grammar: "since" and "for"

"since" bezieht sich auf den Anfang des Zeitraums
since Christmas
since 24 June
since my last report

"for" bezieht sich auf den Zeitraum selbst
for 3 weeks
for several days
for a couple of years

Merke: Im Deutschen wird „seit" mit der Gegenwart verwendet, "since" und "for" stehen im Englischen mit "present perfect".

Ich **bin seit** drei Jahren bei Topline-Computers beschäftigt.
Seit Januar **bin** ich der Abteilungsleiter.

I **have been** employed with Topline-Computers **for three years** now.
Since January I have been head of the department.

Logistics expert

1 Different modes of transport

1 Match the modes of transport (a.–d.) listed in the table below to the photos above.
R/P Then complete the table with numbers from 1 (low / short) to 5 (high / long). Use the table to write a text comparing the different forms of transport.

	Cost	Speed	Distance	Ideal cargo (give examples)
a. Road freight				
b. Rail freight				
c. Sea freight				
d. Air freight				

2 Which logistics service(s) would be most suitable in the following cases?
P Give reasons for your choice and compare your results with a partner.

1. An English boat builder wants to transport a boat to the Berlin Boat Show.
2. A Danish food manufacturer plans to launch a product on the German market. He has neither a German subsidiary nor the necessary logistics.
3. A Swedish steel company has to ship a steelworks to Saudi Arabia.
4. Fritz Schneider Backwaren OHG has a contract to send five boxes of pumpernickel to New York every week. The boxes are $1\,m^3$.
5. A German coffee importer has bought one shipload of Puerto Rican coffee. He needs door-to-door transport from the plantation via Puerto Limon to his warehouse in the free port of Hamburg.

2 Transport and packaging

✳ 1 **Work with a partner and read the following text. Find a headline for each**
R / M **paragraph and find visualisations for the main aspects presented in the text.**
Then write a summary of the text in German.

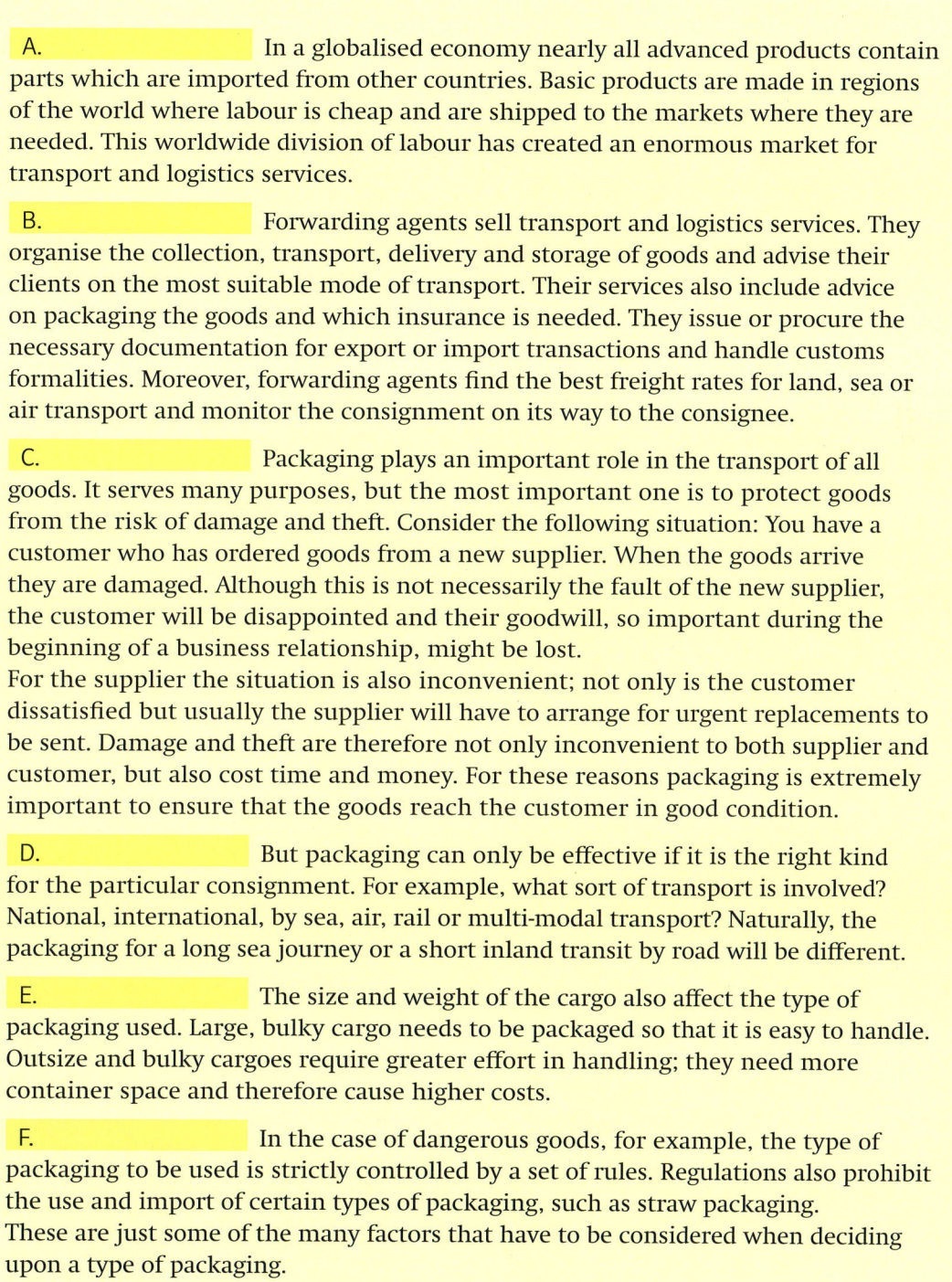

A. 　　　　　　　　　In a globalised economy nearly all advanced products contain parts which are imported from other countries. Basic products are made in regions of the world where labour is cheap and are shipped to the markets where they are needed. This worldwide division of labour has created an enormous market for transport and logistics services.

B. 　　　　　　　　　Forwarding agents sell transport and logistics services. They organise the collection, transport, delivery and storage of goods and advise their clients on the most suitable mode of transport. Their services also include advice on packaging the goods and which insurance is needed. They issue or procure the necessary documentation for export or import transactions and handle customs formalities. Moreover, forwarding agents find the best freight rates for land, sea or air transport and monitor the consignment on its way to the consignee.

C. 　　　　　　　　　Packaging plays an important role in the transport of all goods. It serves many purposes, but the most important one is to protect goods from the risk of damage and theft. Consider the following situation: You have a customer who has ordered goods from a new supplier. When the goods arrive they are damaged. Although this is not necessarily the fault of the new supplier, the customer will be disappointed and their goodwill, so important during the beginning of a business relationship, might be lost.
For the supplier the situation is also inconvenient; not only is the customer dissatisfied but usually the supplier will have to arrange for urgent replacements to be sent. Damage and theft are therefore not only inconvenient to both supplier and customer, but also cost time and money. For these reasons packaging is extremely important to ensure that the goods reach the customer in good condition.

D. 　　　　　　　　　But packaging can only be effective if it is the right kind for the particular consignment. For example, what sort of transport is involved? National, international, by sea, air, rail or multi-modal transport? Naturally, the packaging for a long sea journey or a short inland transit by road will be different.

E. 　　　　　　　　　The size and weight of the cargo also affect the type of packaging used. Large, bulky cargo needs to be packaged so that it is easy to handle. Outsize and bulky cargoes require greater effort in handling; they need more container space and therefore cause higher costs.

F. 　　　　　　　　　In the case of dangerous goods, for example, the type of packaging to be used is strictly controlled by a set of rules. Regulations also prohibit the use and import of certain types of packaging, such as straw packaging.
These are just some of the many factors that have to be considered when deciding upon a type of packaging.

2 Complete the following packaging rules by matching the numbers (1.–9.)
R   with the letters (a.–i.).

1. The nature of the item/article, the route
   and destination, and the different means of
   transport involved
2. The more fragile the goods are
3. The product must be fixed within the package
4. A consignment of many smaller packages
   should be put into one
5. Bulky goods must be packed in crates, boxes
   or containers
6. A waterproof lining should be used to protect
   the inner sales packaging. Add a polystyrene
   foil
7. Make sure that the packages are adequately
   sealed. Make use of
8. For bales, bundles, crates, etc. make use of
   modern banding and strapping. Use
9. Check if there are any restrictions for
   packaging materials. Some countries

a. protective pieces to shield corners
   and edges when using straps.
b. prohibit the use of e.g. high-grade
   wood, straw or wood wool.
c. the greater the degree of packaging
   needed.
d. in order to facilitate handling and
   stowage.
e. to the interior of the outer package.
f. carton or container in order to
   facilitate handling and stowage
   and to reduce the danger of theft.
g. are important factors that influence
   the kind of packaging used.
h. either waterproof sealing tape,
   nails, screws, ropes or customs-
   approved seals.
i. by cushioning materials.

3 Mr Green gibt bei Clarkson Transports einen Warentransport in Auftrag.
KMK Hören Sie aufmerksam zu und notieren Sie die Angaben zu den folgenden
A 2.7 Punkten auf Deutsch. Sie hören das Telefongespräch zweimal.

1. Maße der Ware

2. Gewicht der Ware

3. Transportart

4. Ankunftsdatum

5. Empfängeradresse

6. Warenkennzeichnung

7. Versicherungswert

8. Faxnummer von
   Clarkson Transports

3 Cargo marking

International marking symbols facilitate the correct handling of cargoes. These symbols are instructions or information for stevedores and dockers telling them how to handle a consignment, for example "keep dry", "fragile", "handle with care". Such symbols are essential as they reduce the risk of faulty handling and unnecessary damage. Below are some of the most commonly used symbols.

1 Match the caution marks (1.–7.) with the instructions (a.–g.).
R

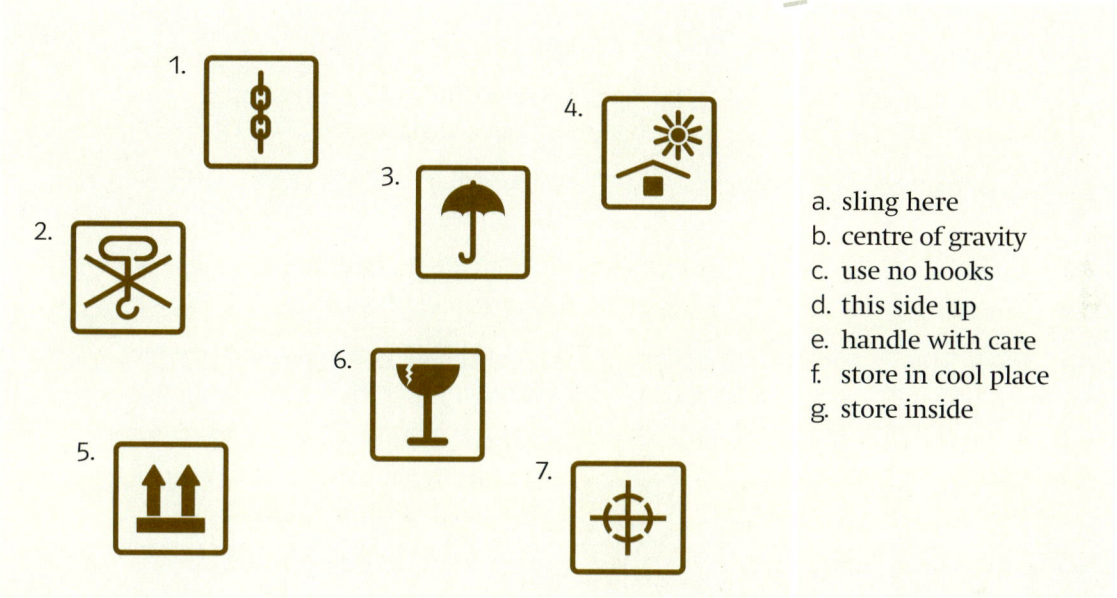

a. sling here
b. centre of gravity
c. use no hooks
d. this side up
e. handle with care
f. store in cool place
g. store inside

2 Work in pairs. Make a list of eight different types of goods and find
P suitable caution marks for them.

Phrases: The company and its products and services

To introduce your firm

Our company was founded in 1972.	Unsere Firma wurde 1972 gegründet.
Our business idea was …	Unsere Geschäftsidee bestand darin …
In 1998 we were taken over by …	1998 wurden wir von … übernommen.
We are a leading manufacturer **of** …	Wir sind ein führender Hersteller von …
I work for an upmarket advertising agency.	Ich arbeite bei einer exklusiven Werbeagentur.
We are a **medium-sized** family firm.	Wir sind ein mittelständisches Familien-unternehmen.
We are a wholesaler **specializing in** …	Wir sind ein Großhandelsunternehmen und sind spezialisiert auf …
My company is a major food retailer.	Meine Firma ist ein bedeutender Lebensmittel-einzelhändler.
We are a start-up company offering customized solutions.	Wir sind ein junges Unternehmen, das maßgeschneiderte Lösungen anbietet.
We are a chain of organic cosmetics suppliers.	Wir sind eine Kette von Anbietern biologischer Kosmetikprodukte.
The legal form of our company is a public limited company.	Juristisch gesehen ist unsere Firma eine (britische) Kapitalgesellschaft, vergleichbar einer deutschen Aktiengesellschaft.
FastTrack Inc. is a stock corporation.	FastTrack Inc. ist eine (US-)Kapitalgesellschaft.

To describe your firm's products / services

We manufacture state-of-the-art solutions.	Wir bieten Lösungen nach dem neuesten Stand der Technik an.
Our high-quality products are well-known **all over** the world. They are unique.	Unsere erstklassigen Produkte sind weltbekannt. Sie sind einzigartig.
Our instruments are both reliable and long-lasting.	Unsere Instrumente sind zuverlässig und haben eine lange Lebensdauer.
The software we offer is carefully adapted to suit your requirements.	Unsere Software wird Ihren Bedürfnissen sorgfältig angepasst.
We make a wide range of high-quality furniture.	Wir stellen ein breites Sortiment hochwertiger Möbel her.
We import exotic fruit **from** South America.	Wir importieren tropische Früchte aus Südamerika.
The travel agency I work for **specialises in** upmarket package tours.	Das Reisebüro, bei dem ich arbeite, ist auf exklusive Pauschalreisen spezialisiert.

Unit 4
The office

front office · back office · open-plan office · office supplies · furniture · electronic equipment · internet access · catering equipment · organization chart · department · business unit · head · assistant · superior · colleague · to be in charge of · to be responsible for · to report to

Offices may be spacious open-plan, purpose-built areas in a major company, individual small rooms to accommodate two to three people, or elegant premises at a prestigious address in a converted building. They may be back offices where employees have no contact with the public, or front offices to which the public have access.

1 **Match the following types of office with the pictures above.**

1. front office
2. back office
3. manager's office
4. open plan

2 **Tell your group in which type of office you would prefer to work and give reasons for your preferences.**

I'd like to work in a(n) … office because …

I'd prefer to work in a(n) … office because …

Online-Link
808264-0004

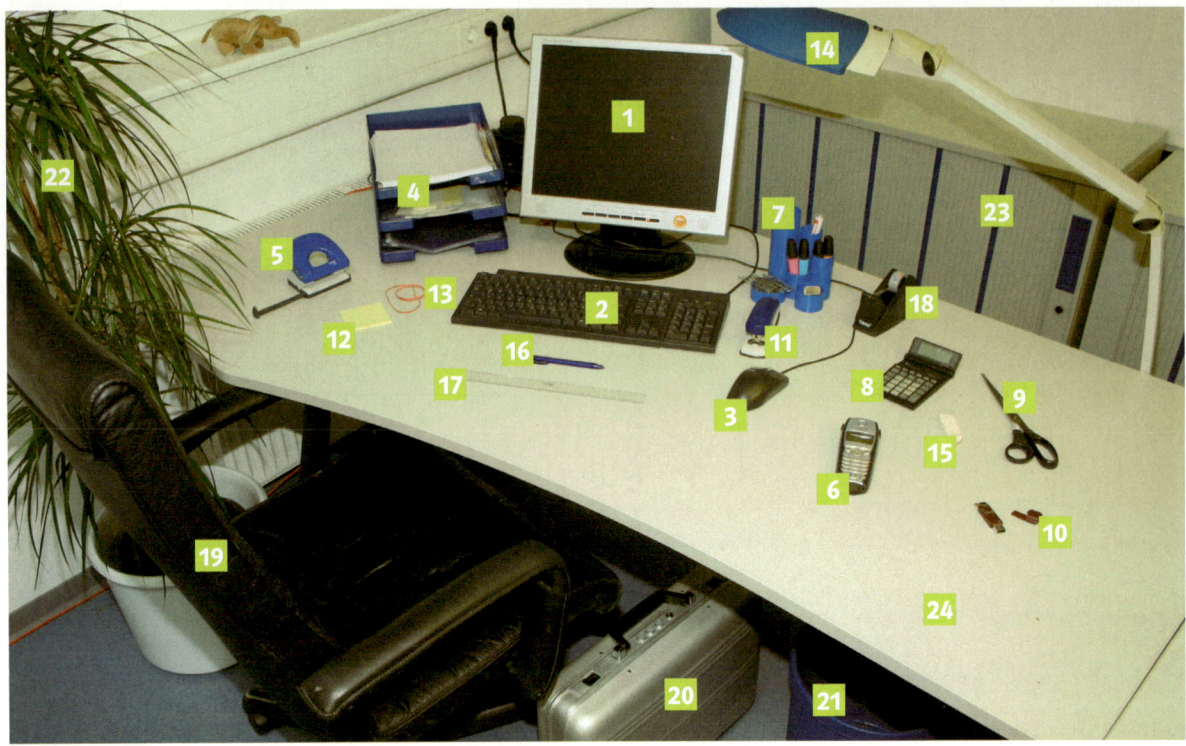

A The office environment

1 Match the following pieces of office equipment with the numbered items above.

a. calculator
b. scotch tape/sellotape
c. biro
d. desk
e. note pad
f. trays
g. filing cabinet
h. aluminium briefcase
i. keyboard

j. memory stick
k. monitor
l. desk tidy
m. pair of scissors
n. wastepaper bin
o. ruler
p. punch
q. rubber/eraser

r. pot plant
s. desk lamp
t. mobile phone
u. stapling machine/stapler
v. swivel chair
w. mouse
x. elastic band

2 Use the following prepositions and describe the position of the equipment you see in the picture.

The keyboard is The …	on • under • behind • between • in front of • next to • on the right of • opposite • near • on top of	the desk. the …

3 List the items shown on page 54 under the following categories:

Office supplies / Stationery	Furniture	Electrical equipment / Hardware
rubber	desk	computer

4 How many computer terms and abbreviations can you find in the puzzle below? Make a list. Compare your lists in class.

Computer terms puzzle

	A	B	C	D	E	F	G	H	I	J
1	I	B	M	O	D	E	M	Q	R	H
2	T	O	E	S	L	A	N	P	X	A
3	D	O	M	T	C	D	R	O	M	R
4	E	T	O	O	L	B	A	R	O	D
5	S	B	R	O	W	S	E	T	N	D
6	K	E	Y	B	O	A	R	D	I	I
7	T	E	R	M	I	N	A	L	T	S
8	O	S	C	A	N	N	E	R	O	K
9	P	C	C	C	U	R	S	O	R	M
10	D	O	W	N	L	O	A	D	X	B

5 Work in groups. Make up similar puzzles with other computer terms and
P / I abbreviations. Ask the other groups to find the terms and abbreviations.

6 Listen to Anita, Ali and Nadine describing the office environment in which they work and take notes. Work in pairs and compare your notes.

R
◎ A1.9

7 Draw a grid like the following. Use your notes and fill in the grid. Then listen to the dialogue again, complete the grid and answer the questions below.

R
◎ A1.9

	Office (front office – open plan or back office?)	Office equipment (PC? Photocopier? Scanner? …?)
Anita	…	…
Ali	…	…
Nadine	…	…

1. What does Anita like about her office?
2. What does Ali like about his office?
3. What does Nadine like about her office?

8 Translate the following statements from the dialogue into German.

M

1. I work in a large open-plan office with about 20 other people. It is spacious and airy with large windows. Fortunately, there is air-conditioning.
2. Our offices are situated in an old villa in the centre of Hanover. The office I work in is a front office.
3. The view from the windows is not very exciting – the office looks out on to the car park.
4. Our office has a wide range of equipment. We all have PCs with internet access.
5. I like the privacy of a small office – you don't get the feeling there's somebody looking over your shoulder the whole time. We all get on very well together.

9 Describe your own office.

P

10 Check out the latest products of three manufacturers of photocopiers and scanners, including any innovative features. Make notes and compare your findings with the group.

B Catering in the office

1 Übertragen Sie die Aussagen von Anita, Nadine und Ali ins Deutsche.

KMK

Anita We have a small kitchen attached to the office with a fridge and tea and coffee making facilities. Our official coffee break is a quarter of an hour at 10.30 am and 3 pm.
At lunchtime we go to the canteen. There is quite a good range of hot and cold snacks, some of them vegetarian. My friend Alexandra is a vegetarian so we usually have a fresh vegetable soup and a salad with fruit as a dessert. We both watch our figures and the canteen is very good about giving calorie counts.

Nadine We have a tea and coffee machine in the office and a kitchen at the end of the corridor with a microwave. We don't have a set coffee break but lunch is from 12.30 to 1.15 pm. Our company is too small to have a canteen so we either bring sandwiches or convenience food that we can warm up in the microwave. There is an upmarket supermarket nearby with an interesting range of good quality convenience food with things like fresh soups and Chinese and Thai dishes. We sometimes go out to a pub but the lunch break is really too short for that.

Ali We have a small kitchen with a coffee machine and fridge. Only Amelie is allowed to touch it. We have an hour lunch break.
We don't have a canteen either. So we usually bring sandwiches or go out. There's a snack bar nearby that has quite an interesting range of snacks and a pub with not very appetising meatballs and filled rolls. Quite often, when we're working to a deadline, we just eat a sandwich at our desks and an apple.

2 Match the words on the left with the explanations on the right.

1. calorie count	a. equipment for making coffee
2. coffee making facilities	b. pre-prepared food
3. convenience food	c. small restaurant/shop producing light/quick food
4. snack bar	d. high-quality supermarket
5. upmarket supermarket	e. energy content

3 What are the catering arrangements like at your firm? Work in pairs to produce a brief description in writing that you can read out to the other students.

Phrases ▶

C   The company's organization chart

1 Study the organization chart below and complete the following text.

R

Nadine works for a car sales company. The **1** is Jochen Küppers who is one of the two owners of the firm. His personal assistant is his elderly **2** Eva Cebulla. Nadine's superior, Jessica Rathsmann, a trained accountant, is the head of the **3** Department, and a motor-car mechanic, Markus Nehring, is in charge of **4**. The **5** manager is Natalie Hoffmann, the managing director's sister-in-law. Eddy Gerstenberg, an engineer, is the head of the **6** Department. André Fontaine, who is training to become a car sales management assistant, reports to him.

The car sales company is organized like this:

Managing Director
Jochen Küppers

Secretary
Eva Cebulla

Administration and Finance	**Purchasing**	**Sales**	**Customer Service**
Jessica Rathsmann	Natalie Hoffmann	Eddy Gerstenberg	Markus Nehring
Nadine Boedeker		André Fontaine	

Info: Large companies

The larger a company is the more complex its organisation tends to be. Large companies are headed by a chief executive officer (CEO) or a chairman of the board. They have many different business units and departments, such as a personnel, legal or marketing department. The scope of an individual employee's responsibilities will also be smaller and his or her duties more specialised in a large company than in a small one.

2 Study the above texts and find the equivalents of the German titles.

R

Geschäftsführer • Einkaufsleiter • Vorstandsvorsitzender •
Automobilkaufmann • Leiter des Kundendienstes • Personalchef •
Leiter des Rechnungswesens • Persönliche Assistentin

3
I Work in pairs. Partner A asks Partner B about his / her current department.
Then change roles.

Phrases

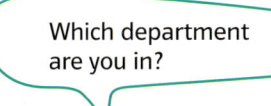

Which department are you in?

I work in the … department.

Partner A	Partner B
Who is your boss?	The head of our department is …
What is he/she responsible for?	She is in charge of …
Who does she report to?	Her superior is …
What's your general manager's name?	Our general manager is called …
Who are your colleagues?	My colleagues are …
What are you responsible for?	I process/I'm in charge of …

4
R Listen to five trainees describing to their friends what they or their colleagues do
in the departments they are in. Find out which departments they are working in.

A 1.10

	Christine	Harun	Annette	Simon	Christos
Department?	…	…	…	…	…

Language and grammar 1
Translate the following sentences.

1. Unsere Firma ist zu klein für einen eigenen Parkplatz.
2. Diese Frage zu beantworten ist für mich zu kompliziert.
3. Nun ist es zu spät für eine Bewerbung.
4. Es ist noch zu früh, darüber zu entscheiden.
5. Sie kam als Letzte zu der Besprechung.
6. Unser Unternehmen ist das einzige, das diese Lösung anbietet.

Language and grammar 2
Choose the correct form of the verbs in brackets.

1. We are having problems (find) qualified programmers.
2. We look forward to (get) your comments on this matter.
3. It is no use (buy) a new one, if it is still the same model.
4. They are having difficulties (meet) the deadline.
5. I am not used to (drive) big cars like this.
6. I object to (have) my work criticised when it's not justified.

Language and grammar: Infinitive and gerund

Nach "too ...", "the first", "the last", "the only one" steht im Englischen der Infinitiv:

Our company is	too small	**to have** a canteen.
This problem is	too difficult for us	**to solve** without help.
It is	too late for you	**to apply** for the job.
She was	the first	**to come.**
He was	the last	**to arrive.**
He was	the only one	**to take part.**

In folgenden Fällen sind deutsche Sprecher auch versucht, einen Infinitiv zu benutzen.

Es steht aber das Gerund:

I am looking forward **to receiving** your reply.

I am looking forward **to being shown** their new flat.

I am not used **to speaking** in public.

I object **to being forced** to work overtime.

I am having problems **understanding** him.

We had no difficulty **persuading** him.

It is no use **waiting** for the new regulations.

Communicating across cultures: Addressing people

In English-speaking countries hierarchical differences may be less pronounced than in German companies. Certainly, they are not so obvious from the way people address each other as first names are generally used. Immediate superiors are also usually addressed by their first name. Where there is a considerable difference in status the titles Mr / Mrs / Miss and surname may be used when addressing a superior.

In Britain or the USA business contacts will very quickly address you by your first name and try to establish an informal atmosphere. When introducing yourself to English-speaking people, always give both your first name and your surname. If they firstname you, you should, of course, do the same.

In schools students usually address teachers with the title (Mr / Mrs / Miss) and surname and in shops and restaurants customers may be addressed as sir / madam, e.g.: Are you ready to order, sir? Can I help you, madam? It is important simply to recognise this – you will not have to use it yourself.

Note:

As we have already seen there is often no one-to-one equivalent to German job titles. Similarly there is no direct equivalent to the much used German word "Sachbearbeiter". It may correspond to "the person dealing with the case / our order" or "the person in charge of ..." .

Phrases: The office

To describe the office

I work in an open-plan office.	Ich arbeite in einem Großraumbüro.
I work in a small office for two people.	Ich arbeite in einem kleinen Büro für zwei Personen.
She works in the back office.	Sie arbeitet in einem Büro ohne Publikumsverkehr.
I prefer working in a front office.	Ich arbeite lieber in einem Büro mit Publikumsverkehr.
My office is spacious and airy.	Mein Büro ist geräumig und luftig.
The office looks **out on to** the car park.	Vom Büro sieht man auf den Parkplatz.
We all have PCs with internet access.	Wir haben alle einen PC mit Zugang zum Internet.
There is a photocopier, a fax machine and file shredders.	Wir haben einen Kopierer, ein Faxgerät und Aktenvernichter.
The senior staff use the computer projectors for presentations.	Die leitenden Angestellten verwenden die Beamer für ihre Präsentationen.

To introduce the people in the office

He is the overall **boss**, the managing director.	Er ist der oberste Chef, der Geschäftsführer.
Mr Kent is the chief executive.	Herr Kent ist der Vorstandsvorsitzende.
She is **head** of department.	Sie ist die Abteilungsleiterin.
He **reports to** Frau Niemeyer.	Er untersteht Frau Niemeyer.
Frau Niemeyer is our superior.	Frau Niemeyer ist unsere Vorgesetzte.
She is assistant / secretary **to** Mr Kent.	Sie ist Herrn Kents Assistentin / Sekretärin.
I am **in charge of** exports.	Ich bin Exportsachbearbeiterin.
I am responsible for sales to the EU.	Ich bearbeite / bin zuständig für den Verkauf in die EU-Länder.
He deals with / processes / handles complaints.	Er bearbeitet Mängelrügen.
He makes sure that instalments are paid **on** time.	Er kümmert sich um den pünktlichen Eingang der Ratenzahlungen.
Robert is one of the partners of our firm.	Robert ist einer der Partner in unserer Firma.
I hope to be **taken on** after I've finished my course.	Ich hoffe nach der Ausbildung übernommen zu werden.

To talk about catering in the office

Our official coffee break is a quarter of an hour.	Offiziell haben wir eine Viertelstunde Kaffeepause.
We have a small kitchen with a fridge, a coffee machine and a microwave.	Wir haben eine kleine Küche mit Kühlschrank, Kaffeemaschine und Mikrowelle.
At lunchtime we go to the canteen.	Zum Mittagessen gehen wir in die Kantine.
We either bring sandwiches or convenience food.	Wir bringen entweder belegte Brote oder ein Fertiggericht mit.
The canteen caters for vegetarians, too.	Die Kantine bietet auch Gerichte für Vegetarier.

To describe your company's organization chart

He is our **chief executive officer**.	Er ist der Chef unserer Firma.
The department Administration and Finance is subdivided into five units.	Die Abteilung Verwaltung und Finanzen besteht aus fünf Bereichen.
The Marketing Department is part of Sales.	Die Marketing-Abteilung gehört zum Verkauf.
IT Support is responsible for all our IT equipment.	IT-Support ist zuständig für alle IT-Anlagen.
We are an international company and our **personnel** department is called "human resources".	Wir sind ein internationales Unternehmen und unsere Personalabteilung heißt „Human Resources".
The head of our legal department is a lawyer specializing in company law.	Der Leiter unserer Rechtsabteilung ist ein Fachanwalt für Gesellschaftsrecht.
Our company is divided **into** five business units.	Unsere Firma ist in fünf Geschäftsfelder unterteilt.

Unit 5
Telephoning

WORD BANK

telephone • number • extension • handset • landline • answering machine • mobile / cell phone • mailbox • text message • telephone alphabet • symbols • codes • to put through • to hold • to catch • to spell • to repeat • to take down • to read back • slowly • clearly • precisely

The telephone has long been an essential tool of business communication but in the past few years it has been revolutionised by the privatisation of state telecom companies and the advent of mobile telephony. People can call and be called wherever they happen to be. Even if a person is not available to take calls a text message can be sent or a message can be left on their voice-mail.

1 Read the text and match the expressions on the left with the explanations on
R   the right.

1. essential tool	a. telephoning without fixed lines
2. privatisation	b. arrival
3. advent	c. selling state-owned enterprises to the public
4. mobile telephony	d. mailbox
5. voice-mail	e. important instrument

2 Describe the telephone situations above.
P

63

Online-Link
808264-0005

A Appliances and components

1 Read the following sentences and translate them into German. Use the words
M below.

Handy

Telefonbuch

Festnetztelefonanlage

Hörer

Besetztzeichen

Onlineverzeichnis

Telefonauskunft

Anrufbeantworter

Freizeichen

Festnetzleitung

1. My fixed line handset includes an answering machine.
2. It is important to replace the receiver carefully otherwise anyone ringing will get the engaged signal.
3. When you pick up the receiver you hear the dialling tone.
4. The latest innovation is to combine landline and mobile phones – when you leave your home the landline becomes a mobile.
5. My telephone handset can also be used to send and receive fax messages.
6. Most people have a copy of the old-fashioned local telephone directory with a business section. Sometimes the Yellow Pages are in a separate book.
7. However, post offices no longer keep a complete nationwide set of telephone directories.
8. Many people have online directories.
9. The traditional Directory Enquiries has been replaced by a number of competing companies.
10. The applications of mobile phones / cell(ular) phones are increasing all the time.

2 Work in groups. Describe to your group the telephoning equipment you have at
P the office, at home and for mobile communication.

B Receiving and redirecting calls

1 Restore the correct order of the two jumbled dialogues and write them out.

R

Dialogue 1

1. Receptionist: Delphi Materials. Good afternoon. How can I help you?
2. Caller: No, thanks. I'll call back later.
3. Receptionist: Just a moment, Mr Martin. I'll put you through to Louisa Bates …
Oh, I'm sorry, her extension is engaged at the moment. Would you like to hold?
4. Caller: Hello. This is Robert Martin from Komplettbau in Erfurt, Germany. I'd like to speak to someone in accounts, please.

Dialogue 2

1. Receptionist: May I ask what it's about?
2. Caller: It's about the dreadful beds we had to sleep in. My back is still aching.
3. Receptionist: Could you give me your name please?
4. Caller: My name is Jakob Grailing and I need to speak to your general manager.
5. Receptionist: Just a second. I'll connect you to Customer Relations.
6. Caller: Hi. The reason I'm calling is …
7. Receptionist: Florida Leisure Park. Good morning. What can I do for you?

2 Listen to the following telephone conversation between Marcel Krenz of International Snacks GmbH and Jennifer Glover, a receptionist at Global Catering in Manchester and say whether the following statements are TRUE or FALSE.

R

 A 1.11

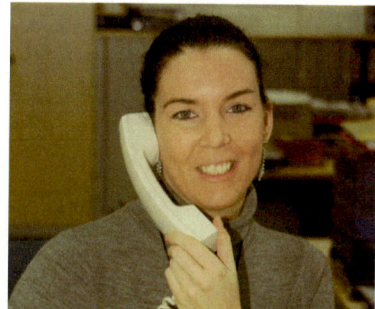

1. Jonathan Ashley works for Omnipolis Research Consultants Ltd.
2. Marcel Krenz wishes to speak to Jennifer Glover.
3. Jennifer Glover knows for certain that Kirsty Burnham is not in.
4. Marcel Krenz prefers to be put on hold.
5. Marcel Krenz has got Kirsty Burnham's mobile phone number.
6. Marcel Krenz does not want to be put through to Kevin Sears.

3 Hören Sie sich die Dialoge noch einmal an und finden Sie heraus, wie
KMK Folgendes auf Englisch formuliert wird.

A 1.11

1. Was sagt Jonathan Ashley, als das Telefon klingelt?
2. Was sagt Marcel Krenz, als er sich verwählt hat?
3. Wie stellt sich Marcel Krenz bei Ms Glover vor?
4. Was sagt Jennifer Glover, während Sie Marcel Krenz durchzustellen versucht?
5. Was antwortet Marcel Krenz auf die Frage, ob er jemand anderen sprechen möchte?
6. Was sagt Jennifer Glover, als sie wissen will, ob Marcel warten möchte oder ob sie zurückrufen soll?
7. Mit welchen Worten schlägt Jennifer Glover vor, Kirsty auf ihrem Handy anzurufen?
8. Wie formuliert Marcel die Bitte, zu Kevin Sears durchgestellt zu werden?

4 Beantworten Sie die Fragen zu nachstehendem Text schriftlich auf Deutsch.
KMK

1. Warum schicken viele Menschen einem Geschäftspartner lieber eine E-Mail als ihn anzurufen?
2. Wovor haben wir Angst, wenn wir ein Auslandsgespräch führen sollen?
3. Welche Aspekte der Kommunikation fehlen bei einem Telefongespräch?
4. Was soll man tun, wenn man nicht versteht, was der Gesprächspartner sagt?

Info:
Telephoning in a foreign language

Telephoning in a foreign language can be rather frightening. No wonder people often prefer to send an e-mail where they can plan what they want to say and need not fear immediate comeback. However, a telephone call is sometimes unavoidable and one wonders: Will I understand what they are saying? What do I say if I can't? Can I just hang up in embarrassment? Will I be able to express what I want to say? Will they laugh if I make some awful mistake? We all know these kinds of fears when we have to ring someone abroad. And, to some extent, the fears are justified. The non-verbal side of communication is missing. We can't see the person's face, their lips and gestures. They can't see our gestures and the look of despair on our faces! It's best to remain calm and ask them to speak slowly and repeat anything that is not clear.

5
R
A1.12

In her first week at Herkules Sandra Kohl finds herself alone in the office and it is precisely then that the telephone rings.

Work with a partner. Listen to the telephone conversation twice. Partner A makes a note of the phrases Sandra uses to ensure that she understands what Jim Farquhar is saying. Partner B makes a note of the strategies and phrases Jim Farquhar uses to make Sandra understand him and feel good about her English. Then compare your findings.

6
R / M

Complete the telephone phrases below using words from the box. Then translate the phrases into German.

cut • get • line • repeat • slowly • speak • quite • what

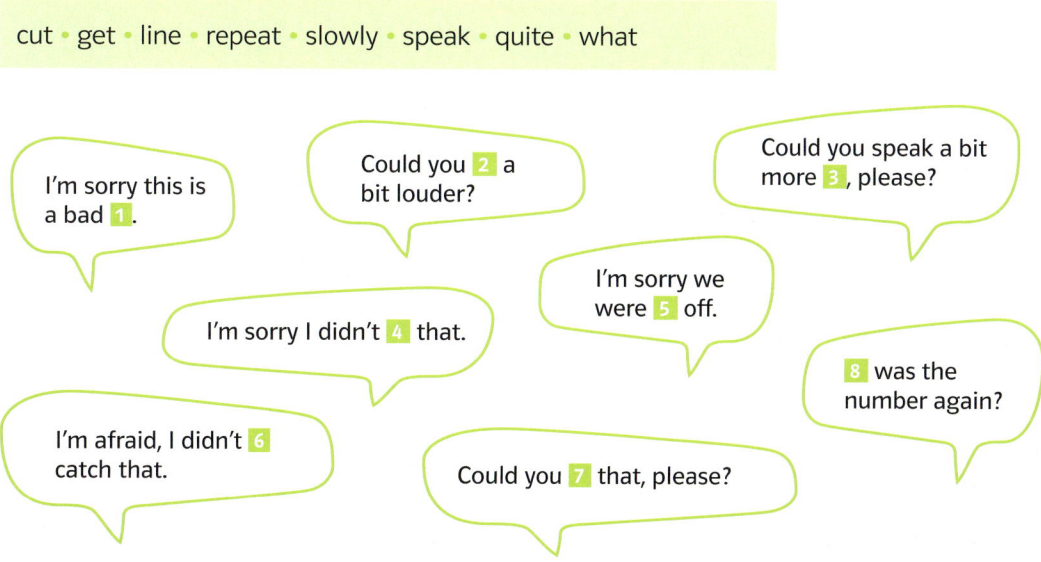

I'm sorry this is a bad **1** .

Could you **2** a bit louder?

Could you speak a bit more **3** , please?

I'm sorry I didn't **4** that.

I'm sorry we were **5** off.

8 was the number again?

I'm afraid, I didn't **6** catch that.

Could you **7** that, please?

7 Roleplay this telephone conversation with a partner. Use the phrases at the end of the unit.

Phrases

Firma: Heinz GmbH, Dresden	Company: Baltic Car Supplies, Tallinn, Estonia
Nehmen Sie den Anruf entgegen.	Nennen Sie Ihren Namen und den Namen der Firma. Sie möchten Frau Lange sprechen.
Sagen Sie, dass Sie den Anrufer schlecht verstehen und bitten Sie ihn, etwas lauter zu sprechen.	Sprechen Sie etwas lauter und fragen Sie, ob Sie jetzt besser zu verstehen sind.
Es ist jetzt besser. Fragen Sie, worum es geht.	Es geht um eine Rechnung.
Bitten Sie den Anrufer einen Moment zu warten und verbinden Sie ihn mit Frau Lange.	Bedanken Sie sich.
Sagen Sie, dass die Leitung leider im Moment besetzt ist und fragen Sie, ob der Anrufer warten möchte.	Sagen Sie, dass Sie lieber später zurückrufen möchten und fragen Sie nach der Durchwahl.
Die Durchwahl ist 23. Frau Lange wird bis 16 Uhr im Büro sein.	Sie haben das nicht richtig verstanden und bitten um Wiederholung.
Wiederholen Sie die vorherige Information.	Bedanken Sie sich und verabschieden Sie sich.
Antworten Sie und verabschieden Sie sich.	

8 Work in pairs. Sit back to back. Use your notes from Exercise 5 and the phrases at the end of the unit. Then act out a similar dialogue.

Phrases

C Taking messages

✱ **1** **Übertragen Sie den folgenden Text ins Deutsche.**
KMK

> **Info: How to take a message**
>
> When taking messages it is important to make sure that you take down all the relevant details. You should first make sure that you take down the name of the caller. It is usually necessary to ask him / her to spell names and addresses. Be sure to get the postcode.
>
> It is essential to note down telephone numbers accurately. Failure to do so will lead to a lot of problems. Read back telephone numbers to check that you have got them right. Telephone numbers are often read differently in different countries. In Britain numbers are simply given in the order they occur, eg: 0044 020 363 2991 = oh oh four four – oh two oh - three six three – two nine nine one. Instead of **oh** Americans usually say **zero**. People often say: double oh or: two double nine one. If necessary, ask the caller to repeat the number more slowly.
>
> Get callers to spell e-mail addresses precisely. Even the slightest mistake results in e-mails being sent back. @ is pronounced at, (.) is read as dot, (cf "dotcoms" = internet companies), (/) is pronounced slash and (–) is read as hyphen or dash or minus.
>
> Your company may have a special form for recording telephone messages.

2 **There are different international telephone alphabets but people very often make**
R **up their own as they go along. Spell the following names and addresses using the**
A 1.13 **international telephone alphabet on page 70. Then listen and check.**

> Brian Urquart • Jonathan McEwan • Trevelyan Networking Ltd • Peterborough • Heidi Schlösser • Detlev Jaegermeyer • Jörg Eyrich • Silberstein • Chemnitz • Ditzhuizen • Mbamali • Werchojansk • Ian McWhirter • Appletreewick in Wharfedale • Georg Süsterhenn • Bad Oeynhausen

3 **Spell the following names and addresses using your own telephone alphabet.**

> Mississippi • Philadelphia • Rhondda • Le Havre • Eyjafiallajökull • Energize Ltd. • Joachim • Fort Myers • Wolfgang Somborn • Kiel • Mississauga Enterprises Inc. • Maldives Travel Lounge

International telephone alphabet

S for Sierra
C for Charlie
H for …
U … …
L … …
Z … …

H for Hotel
E for Echo
N for …
S … …
H … …
U … …
I … …

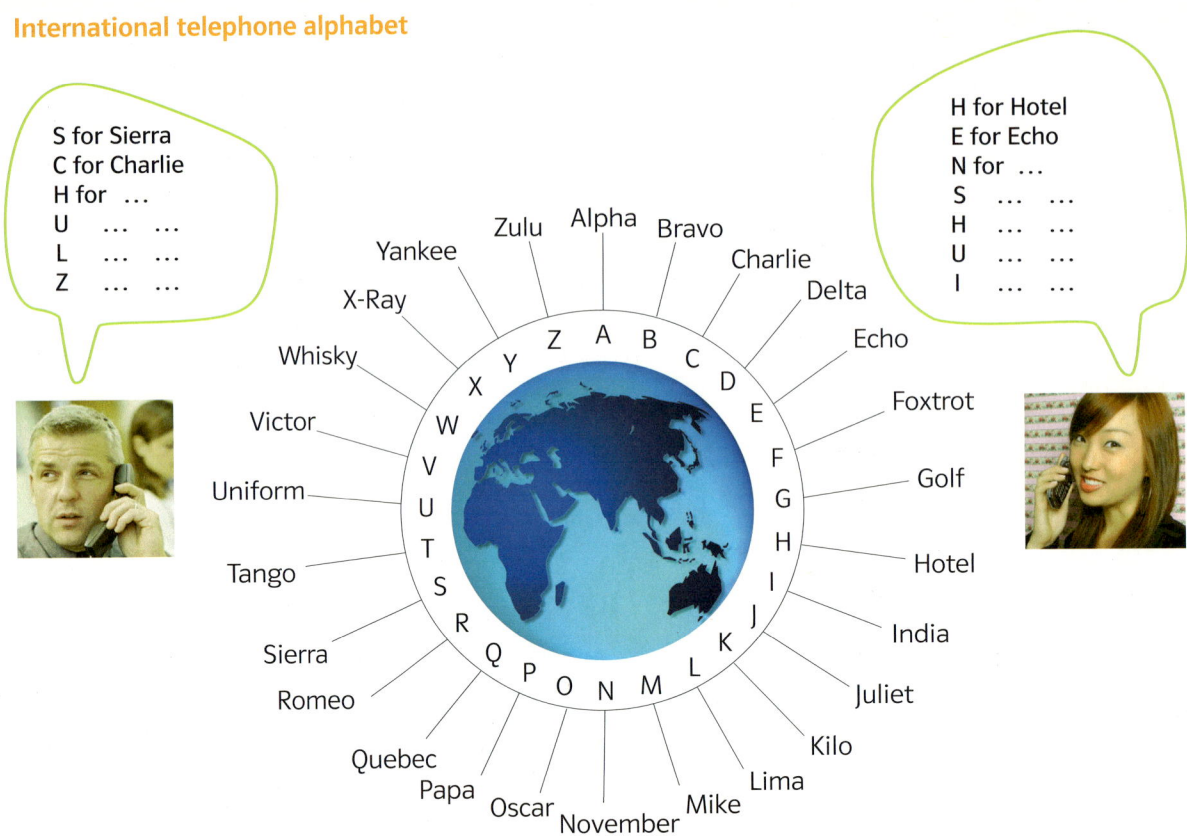

Zulu Alpha Bravo
Yankee Charlie
X-Ray Delta
Whisky Echo
Victor Foxtrot
Uniform Golf
Tango Hotel
Sierra India
Romeo Juliet
Quebec Kilo
Papa Lima
Oscar Mike
November

Y Z A B
X C
W D
V E
U F
T G
S H
R I
Q J
P O N M L K

4 Work in pairs: Sit back to back and spell your name and the name and address of your company using the international telephone alphabet. Then change roles and check the results.

Phrases ▸

Symbol:	Name:	Example:
'	apostrophe	O'Connor
@	at	info@
A/a	capital letters/small letters	USA/asap
-	hyphen/dash/minus	t-online
Ö	o-umlaut/oe/o with 2 dots	Möller
:	colon	http:
/	slash/stroke	org/gla/
\	backslash	\docs.nt\
.	dot	.de
_	understroke	tourist_org.

Codes / numbers:

+49	(0)711	664376-0	34
country code	area code	office number	extension
04275	Leipzig		
post / zip code	city		

5 Work in groups. Group A uses the role card below and dictates the following
KMK telephone numbers, e-mail addresses and websites. Group B uses the role card
on page 254 and dictates the information given there. Then check your results.

> **Role card: Partner A**   **Role card partner B ⇨ page 254**
>
> 1. +44 (1234) 687791
> 2. (0203) 4670976
> 3. (051) 27 81 13 - 12
> 4. (0171) 25333980
> 5. info@terstegen.com
> 6. dieter.wilhelmsen@abconsulting.de
> 7. www.mittelpunkt.de/abo
> 8. info@sykescottages.com

6 First copy the form below. Then listen to the conversation and take the message.
R / P
A 1.14

```
TELEPHONE MESSAGE
Message for:
Message taken by:                    Date:
Caller:
Subject:
```

7 You are David Verhoeven. You receive a telephone call from the UK. See on
R / P page 72 for what you yourself say in the conversation with Mr Jones.
A 1.15

First copy the form below. Then listen to the conversation and make a note of the
message in German.

```
TELEFONNOTIZ
Nachricht für:
aufgenommen von:                    am:
Anrufer:
Betreff:
```

David Verhoeven:	Anton Hein GmbH, Erkelenz, guten Tag.
David Verhoeven:	Good morning, Mr Jones. I'm afraid Mrs van Steuben is away on a business trip. She is not due back before the beginning of next week. Is there anyone else you'd like to speak to?
David Verhoeven:	Certainly. No problem.
David Verhoeven:	Right. Could you give me your name and your boss's name again, please?
David Verhoeven:	It's David Verhoeven. I'd better spell my second name: V for Victoria, E for egg, R for Richard, H for happy, O for ox, E for Egg, V for Victoria, E for egg and N for nice. I hope you got that alright.
David Verhoeven:	I'll make sure she gets your message. The name of your company was CyberWorld, wasn't it? I didn't catch the name of the town, though.
David Verhoeven:	Thank you and thank you very much for ringing. Goodbye.

8 Work in pairs. Copy the English and the German forms for telephone messages. Sit back to back. Partner A "rings" partner B and leaves a short message. Partner B takes down the message, either in German or in English – depending on the recipient. Then change roles. Use the role card on page 254.

`Phrases`

Example:

Partner A: "This is Pavel Banka speaking. I've got a message for Herr Meister, your purchasing manager. Please tell him that the MP3 Player C27 is again in stock and that I could ship them tomorrow morning. Ask Herr Meister to ring me as soon as possible."

Partner B takes down the message on a form.

```
TELEFONNOTIZ

Nachricht für:      Herrn Meister, Einkauf

aufgenommen von:  (Ihr Name)                    am:

Anrufer:            Pavel Banka

Betreff:            MP3 Player C27 wieder vorrätig

Herr Banka könnte die C27-Player morgen früh absenden.

Bittet möglichst bald um Rückruf.
```

9 Work in pairs. Sit back to back and practise taking messages. Use the phrases at the end of the unit.

`Phrases`

D   Making telephone calls

1   **Listen to the conversation and note down the missing expressions on a separate sheet of paper.**

R
A 1.16

Voice:	Good morning. Cardboard Box Company, John Hough speaking.
Nadine Pfeiffer:	Good morning. `1` your packaging materials. My boss `2` your sales literature.
John Hough:	Certainly, `3` you our literature. `4` the name and address of your company.
Nadine Pfeiffer:	The name of the company is Hülshoff GmbH.
John Hough:	`5`, please.
Nadine Pfeiffer:	H for Harry, `6`, L for lemon, S for sugar, H for Harry, O for Otto, double F for Frederick, and then G m b H. The street is Zülpicher Str 131, 50001 Köln, that's Cologne and it's spelt K for knock, O for Otto with two dots, L for lovely and N for nice.
John Hough:	Oh dear, `7` the street as well.
Nadine Pfeiffer:	Z for Zoe; U for ugly with two dots; L for lovely; P for princess; `8`; C for carrot; H for Henrietta; E for egg and R for Ritz.
John Hough:	Brilliant. I will send you the sales literature immediately and `9` you again. By the way, `10` name?
Nadine Pfeiffer:	Yes, Huff. `11`?

John Hough:	I'm afraid not. It's spelt H O U G H, that is H for Henry, O for orange, U for united, G for Green and H for Henry again. My first name's John **12** !
Nadine Pfeiffer:	Thank you very much. Goodbye.
John Hough:	Thank you. **13** the literature in a couple of days. Goodbye.

2

R

⊚ A 1.17

First copy the form below. Then listen to the telephone conversation between Lucy Batt and Chloe Stott and fill in the form Chloe has prepared for her boss's information.

Contact person:

Days of arrival and departure:

Size and location of the cottage:

Charge per week:

Additional charges:

Half the total rent plus booking charges to be paid by:

Balance to be paid by:

Modes of payment:

Mode of booking:

3 Roleplay this telephone conversation with a partner.

KMK

Phrases ▶

**Employee at Form und Raum GmbH
(eigener Name)**

**British customer
John Willoughby,
Exclusive Interiors, London**

Melden Sie sich am Telefon.

Stellen Sie sich vor. Sie haben die neuen Lampen der deutschen Firma auf einer Ausstellung gesehen und möchten eventuell einige bestellen.

Sie sind gerade allein im Büro. Fragen Sie, ob der Anrufer eine Nachricht hinterlassen möchte.

Sie möchten, dass jemand so bald wie möglich zurückruft. Sie geben Ihre Telefonnummer in London an:
(020 897 3884).

Sie bitten den Anrufer, die Telefon-nummer langsam zu wiederholen. Den Namen haben Sie auch nicht verstanden. Er soll ihn bitte buchstabieren.

Buchstabieren Sie den Namen und wiederholen Sie die Telefonnummer langsam und deutlich. Sie sind heute bis 18.00 Uhr britischer Zeit im Büro.

Es wird auf jeden Fall jemand im Laufe des Nachmittags anrufen.

Sie bedanken sich und verabschieden sich.

Sie verabschieden sich ebenfalls.

E Leaving a message on an answering machine

Info: A message on an answering machine

1. Begin by saying "Good morning" etc. Do not say your name first as the first few words may get "lost".
2. Pronounce your name very clearly, give your company's name as well and mention the place / country you are calling from, if necessary.
3. Be as concise and polite as possible when leaving the message.
4. Repeat figures and spell names, if necessary.
5. At the end repeat your name and dictate your telephone number slowly.

**Kopieren Sie den Vordruck, hören Sie die Nachricht ab und fassen Sie sie
auf Deutsch in einer Telefonnotiz zusammen.**

KMK

A 1.18

```
TELEFONNOTIZ

Nachricht für:

aufgenommen von:                    am:

Anrufer:

Betreff:
```

Language and grammar
Choose the correct prepositions.

1. The meeting will be held from 2 pm (until/to) 4 pm.
2. Thank you for your letter (from/of) 9 December.
3. We are prepared to wait (until/by) next Friday.
4. We enclose a description of our facilities (by/of) an independent expert.
5. We have received numerous enquiries (of/from) start-up companies.
6. The tickets will have to be confirmed (by/until) the middle of next week.
7. We haven't heard (of/from) him recently.
8. The book (of/by) a well-known writer is available in paperback.
9. We expect to receive the consignment (by/until) Friday at the latest.
10. I've never heard (of/from) the firm. Are you sure you've got the name right?
11. It's a study (of/by) the CBI (Confederation of British Industry).
12. He has to get to the airport (until/by) 4 pm.

Language and grammar: Tricky prepositions –
getting the wrong one may change the meaning

by / until   bis
I need the report **by** Monday means that you must get it on Monday (or sooner) because from then on you will need it for your work. Example: The goods must reach us **by** the end of next week.

I need the report **until** Monday means that you need it only until Monday and will then be finished with it.
Example: The import licence is valid **until** 31 August. (You say: until **the thirty-first of** August.)

from ... to   von ... bis
This year's shoe fair will take place **from** 30 June **to** 4 August. (You say: ... from **the thirtieth of** June to **the fourth of** August.)
Wrong: from 30 June ~~until~~ 4 August

from, of, by   von / vom
The date of a communication is preceded by "of" or "dated":
Example: We refer to your offer **of** 2 November. (You say: ... of **the second of** November.)
Wrong: We refer to your offer ~~from~~ 2 November.

Where the communication came from is expressed by "from":
Example: We received a complaint **from** one of our customers.
Wrong: We received a complaint ~~of~~ one of our customers.

The author is introduced by means of the preposition "by":
Example: This is shown in a report **by** an independent study group.
Wrong: This is shown in a report ~~of~~ an independent study group.

Logistics expert

1 Arranging transport

Logistics has become a key competitive quality factor for industry and trade. In order to offer reliable service and individual solutions even for extremely sensitive, hazardous or bulky consignments, careful planning is necessary.

1 **Make a list of all the information a forwarding agent must**
P **get before organising the shipment of goods.**

Phrases

2 **Sarah Dean, logistics manager at Wind Power Inc., phones Orca Shipping GmbH,**
R **a company specialising in heavy-lift shipping, to discuss details of a consignment**
of wind turbines destined for Norway. Read the dialogue and complete it with the
questions (a.–f.) below.

Hannes: Good morning. Orca Shipping Bremen, Hannes Buchwald speaking.

Sarah: Hi, Hannes, this is Sarah from Wind Power Inc. We need wind turbines to be shipped from Atlanta to an offshore wind park in Norway.

Hannes: Sure, we can arrange that for you. But I need the details first. **1**?

Sarah: Of course, it's 124/346 WP.

Hannes: Thanks, Sarah. Now let's get down to business. **2**

Sarah: I don't know exactly. But the rotor blades are seven tons each at least.

Hannes: **3**?

Sarah: The tower comes in segments of 30 foot 4 in length and about 25 feet in diameter. The blades measure roughly 90 feet by 12 by 4.

Hannes: **4**?

Sarah: The turbine is dismantled into three blades and six tower segments.

Hannes: I'd advise stowage in layers to reduce the number of shipments.

Sarah: **5**? They're rather valuable, you know.

Hannes: Don't worry. A sufficient number of lashings will ensure cargo security.

Sarah: That sounds great. **6**?

Hannes: If you send me all the details now, I'll have it ready by Monday.

Sarah: That's great. Thank you very much. Bye for now.

Hannes: You're welcome. Goodbye.

e. What does the shipment weigh?

a. And what are the measurements?

c. Could you first give me your reference number?

b. But how do you prevent them from moving during transport?

d. How many pieces does the consignment consist of?

f. When can you send me a firm offer?

3 Hannes needs some more details from Sarah to make a firm offer. Roleplay their telephone conversation with a partner using the information below.

I

Phrases ▶

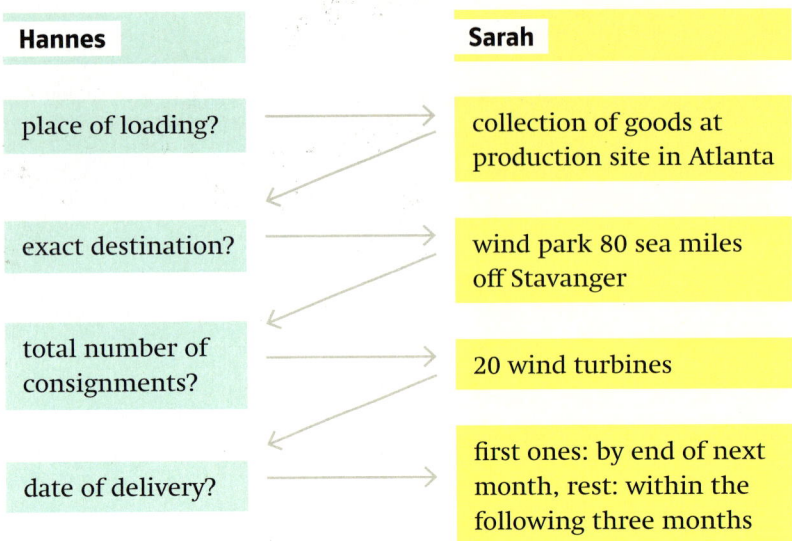

Hannes	Sarah
place of loading?	collection of goods at production site in Atlanta
exact destination?	wind park 80 sea miles off Stavanger
total number of consignments?	20 wind turbines
date of delivery?	first ones: by end of next month, rest: within the following three months

2 Loading and unloading goods

✳ **1** Orca Shipping has published a manual on how to load heavy or bulky consignments. Read the extract and find the English equivalents of the German terms.

M

> **Loading instructions for trailers**
> - Make sure you know your permitted axle and gross weights and the vehicle's tare weight.
> - Lift sensitive goods with slings rather than hooks.
> - Distribute your load evenly to avoid axle overload.
> - Place heavy items at the bottom and lighter or fragile ones on top.
> - To prevent moving, do not leave room between parts of the load.
> - Make sufficient use of strapping and chocks.

1. Achse
2. Bruttogewicht
3. Bremsklotz
4. erlaubt
5. Haken
6. Leergewicht
7. Riemen
8. Schlinge
9. verteilen
10. zerbrechlich

2 Hannes telefoniert mit dem verantwortlichen Frachtaufseher im Hafen von Savannah, Georgia, um die wichtigsten Aspekte der Ver- und Entladung der Windkraftanlagen zu klären. Notieren Sie die besprochenen Punkte in einer Telefonnotiz auf Deutsch.

KMK

◎ A 2.8

```
TELEFONNOTIZ

Ansprechpartner:

Betreff:

Details:
```

Phrases: Telephoning

To make friendly remarks at the beginning of a telephone conversation

Oh, hello Nadine. Nice to hear **from** you. How are things **over there**?	Hallo Nadine. Schön von Dir zu hören. Wie geht's denn so?
Good morning Mrs Glover. I hope you had a pleasant holiday.	Guten Morgen Mrs. Glover. Ich hoffe, Sie hatten einen angenehmen Urlaub.
Good afternoon Mr McEwan. **What's** the weather in Scotland **like**?	Guten Tag Mr. McEwan. Wie ist das Wetter in Schottland?

Reactions

Fine, thank you. And how are you?	Gut, vielen Dank. Und wie geht es Ihnen?
Thank you, it was really very relaxing.	Danke, es war wirklich sehr erholsam.
We've had an awful lot of rain recently, I'm afraid. What's it like in Germany?	Es hat in der letzten Zeit leider schrecklich viel geregnet. Wie ist das Wetter in Deutschland?

To ask the caller to speak more slowly, to spell sth., to repeat sth.

Oh sorry. I didn't quite catch that. Could you repeat it more slowly, please?	Es tut mir Leid, das habe ich nicht verstanden. Könnten Sie es etwas langsamer wiederholen?
Could you possibly spell that? Is that the name of the town?	Könnten Sie das vielleicht buchstabieren? Ist das der Name der Stadt?
I'm afraid I didn't get the telephone number. Could you give me it again, please?	Leider habe ich die Telefonnummer nicht mitbekommen. Würden Sie sie bitte wiederholen?

To ask for somebody

Could I speak **to** Ms Burnham, please?	Könnte ich bitte Ms. Burnham sprechen?
Could you put me **through** to Mr Hough?	Könnten Sie mich mit Mr. Hough verbinden?
Could you give me his/her extension, please?	Könnten Sie mir bitte seine/ihre Durchwahl geben?
I'd like to speak to someone from the sales department.	Ich möchte gern jemanden im Verkauf sprechen.

To say that someone is not available

I'm afraid Kirsty Burnham is not in the office at the moment.	Kirsty Burnham ist z. Zt. leider nicht in ihrem Büro.
… is in a meeting.	… ist in einer Besprechung.
… has someone **with** her.	… hat Besuch.

… is **on** a business trip.	… ist auf Geschäftsreise.
… is out **at** lunch.	… ist zu Tisch.
… is no longer **with** the company.	… ist nicht mehr bei unserer Firma.

To offer to ring back or take a message

I'm afraid Mr Hough is speaking **on** the other line. Would you prefer to hold or shall I ask him to ring back?	Mr. Hough spricht leider gerade auf der anderen Leitung. Möchten Sie warten, oder soll er Sie zurückrufen?
Can he call you back this afternoon?	Kann er Sie heute Nachmittag zurückrufen?
Can I give him a message?	Kann ich ihm etwas ausrichten?
Would you like to leave a message?	Möchten Sie eine Nachricht hinterlassen?

Reactions

Thank you. I'll ring back later.	Danke sehr. Ich rufe später zurück.
I'm afraid I won't be in the office this afternoon. I'll give you my mobile number.	Ich bedaure, ich bin heute Nachmittag außer Haus. Ich gebe Ihnen meine Handy-Nummer.
Yes, please. Could you tell him that …?	Ja bitte. Könnten Sie ihm ausrichten, dass …?

To refer someone to someone else

I'm afraid … I don't know the details. … I am not familiar **with** this order. … I am not in charge of this transaction. I'll put you through to Mr Sears.	Leider … kenne ich mich damit nicht aus. … weiß ich über diesen Auftrag nicht Bescheid. … bearbeite ich diesen Vorgang nicht. Ich stelle Sie zu Mr. Sears durch.
Shall I put you through **to** his secretary?	Soll ich Sie mit seiner Sekretärin verbinden?
Would you like to speak **to** somebody in the accounts department?	Möchten Sie mit jemandem aus der Abteilung Rechnungswesen sprechen?

Reactions

Yes, please. She may be able to help.	Ja bitte. Sie kann mir vielleicht helfen.
No thanks, I really need to speak **to** the export manager.	Nein danke. Ich muss unbedingt mit dem Exportleiter sprechen.

To ask for / about something

Would you please let me know if …?	Ich möchte gern wissen, ob …?
I'd like to ask **whether** it would be possible to …	Wäre es möglich, dass …

Could you possibly …?	Könnten Sie/Könntest Du …?
Do you think you could …?	Könnten Sie/Könntest Du vielleicht …?
You'd be doing us a great favour if you could …	Sie täten uns einen großen Gefallen, wenn Sie …
Please **make sure** that …	Bitte sorgen Sie dafür, dass …
I would really appreciate **it** if you could …	Ich wäre Ihnen sehr dankbar, wenn Sie …

Reactions

Certainly.	Ja, natürlich.
I see no reason why not.	Natürlich. Warum nicht.
Certainly. No problem.	Klar. Kein Problem.
I will certainly do my very best.	Ich werde bestimmt mein Bestes tun.
Definitely. I'll see to it myself.	Ganz bestimmt. Ich werde mich selbst darum kümmern.

To refuse something

I'm afraid we can't agree **to** your proposal.	Leider können wir uns mit Ihrem Vorschlag nicht einverstanden erklären.
We find this level of service quite unacceptable.	Für uns ist diese Art von Kundendienst absolut inakzeptabel.
This is unfortunately not what we had in mind.	Leider hatten wir uns das nicht so vorgestellt.

Reactions

That is a pity.	Das ist wirklich schade.
That is most regrettable.	Das ist überaus bedauerlich.
I can quite understand. We are trying hard to improve things.	Das kann ich verstehen. Wir bemühen uns nach Kräften um eine Verbesserung.
There must have been a misunderstanding.	Hier muss ein Missverständnis vorliegen.

To apologise

I'm terribly sorry but …	Es tut mir schrecklich Leid, aber …
I really must apologise for the inconvenience we've caused you.	Ich möchte mich für die Ihnen entstandenen Unannehmlichkeiten vielmals entschuldigen.
I'm very sorry. Thank you for being so understanding.	Es tut mir sehr Leid. Vielen Dank für Ihr Verständnis.
I can only repeat that I'm very sorry **for** the delay.	Ich kann mich nur nochmals für die Verzögerung entschuldigen.

Reactions

It could happen to anyone.	Das hätte jedem passieren können.
It's a mistake that is very easily made.	So ein Fehler kommt oft vor.
Don't worry. The main thing is that the mistake has been rectified.	Machen Sie sich keine Gedanken. Hauptsache, der Fehler ist behoben.
Well, let's just hope it doesn't happen again.	Hoffen wir nur, dass es nicht noch einmal geschieht.
It has caused us a lot of embarrassment.	Es war für uns sehr peinlich.

To play for time

Can I ring you back? I need to look **at** the file.	Kann ich Sie zurückrufen? Ich muss erst die Unterlagen einsehen.
I'll have to have a word with the line manager.	Ich muss die Sache erst mit dem Bereichsleiter besprechen.
I'm afraid I can't access the file **on** my monitor at the moment. Can I ring you back?	Leider habe ich im Moment auf meinem Computer keinen Zugriff auf die Datei. Kann ich Sie zurückrufen?
I'm afraid I can't give you a definitive answer **at** the moment. I'll get back to you this afternoon if that's OK.	Leider kann ich Ihnen z. Zt. keinen endgültigen Bescheid geben. Wenn es Ihnen recht ist, rufe ich Sie deswegen heute Nachmittag zurück.

Reactions

I'm afraid you said that the last time I rang. I'm not prepared to be put **off** again.	Das haben Sie schon beim letzten Mal gesagt. Ich lasse mich nicht noch einmal so abspeisen.
Certainly, but please give me your extension so that I can ring you direct if necessary.	Natürlich, geben Sie mir aber doch bitte Ihre Durchwahl, damit ich Sie nötigenfalls direkt anrufen kann.
I wish to settle the matter now. I should be grateful if you would put me through to the person responsible.	Ich möchte die Angelegenheit jetzt klären. Bitte stellen Sie mich zu dem entsprechenden Sachbearbeiter durch.
Fine. I look forward to hearing from you. I leave the office **at** 4pm your time.	Schön. Ich erwarte Ihren Anruf. Ich bin bis 4 Uhr Ihrer Zeit im Büro.

To insist that something is done by a certain date

We need the goods **by** Wednesday **at** the very latest.	Wir benötigen die Ware bis spätestens Mittwoch.
We definitely need the documents **by** 3 May.	Wir müssen die Unterlagen unbedingt bis zum 3. Mai erhalten.
Can we rely **on** that?	Können wir uns darauf verlassen?
Please make sure it arrives **no** later **than** the end of April.	Bitte sorgen Sie dafür, dass es spätestens Ende April eintrifft.
Monday 31 July is the final deadline.	Montag, der 31. Juli ist der letzte Termin.

To promise something

We promise you that …	Wir versprechen Ihnen, dass …
You have my word. The documents will reach you **by** Monday.	Ich gebe Ihnen mein Wort. Die Dokumente treffen spätestens Montag bei Ihnen ein.
We will certainly **ensure** that …	Wir werden bestimmt dafür sorgen, dass …
The goods will be definitely dispatched tomorrow.	Die Ware wird mit Sicherheit morgen abgeschickt.

To end the conversation

Goodbye Miss Pfeiffer. Thank you for calling.	Auf Wiederhören, Frau Pfeiffer. Vielen Dank für Ihren Anruf.
Thank you. Goodbye. Have a nice weekend.	Danke schön. Auf Wiederhören. Schönes Wochenende!
Sorry, I must have got a wrong number.	Entschuldigung, ich habe mich verwählt.

Reactions

Goodbye Mr Hough. You'll be hearing from us again soon.	Auf Wiederhören Mr. Hough. Sie werden bald wieder von uns hören.
Goodbye. You too.	Auf Wiederhören. Gleichfalls.

Unit 6
Making arrangements

WORD BANK

arrangements • booking •
reservation • flight • destination •
departure • arrival • hotel •
accommodation • ensuite
bathroom • diary • appointment •
conference • meeting • topic •
agenda • minutes • fair •
exhibition • application • stand •
to organise • to book • to hire •
to attend • to record

An important part of the job of secretarial or clerical staff is to make
arrangements on behalf of management. This may include managing
the boss's diary and making or rescheduling appointments, booking
flights or train tickets, making hotel reservations and hiring cars.
A secretary may be required to organise meetings and conferences and to take
part in order to keep a record of what is said and decided. It is her job to generally
facilitate proceedings, making sure that the participants have everything they need.
Many companies take part in trade fairs and exhibitions and it may be the task of
the secretary to book stand space and help organise the company's participation.
Finally, the secretary will be responsible for welcoming visitors, often from abroad.
Obviously, a good command of foreign languages is an absolute must.

Study the text and answer the following questions.

R / P
1. Why may a secretary be asked to be present at a meeting?
2. What are the various duties of a secretary as given in the text? Make a list and
   translate it into German.

Online-Link
808264-0006

A Flights and accommodation

1

R

A1.19

Global Catering in Manchester has meanwhile taken over a German company and renamed it Global Catering München GmbH. Executives from the German, British and American companies are to meet for a conference in Munich before flying on to Madrid to attend an international food fair.

Melanie Schmiedel, personal assistant (PA) to Udo Moersen, manager of Global Catering München GmbH, has been asked to organise the conference from 5th to 7th September at the company's premises in Munich. She decides to start by ringing her opposite number at the company's headquarters in Manchester.

Listen to the dialogue and complete the following sentences:

1. The conference is to take place in **1** on **2**
2. The sales manager is going **3**
3. Melanie Schmiedel will book rooms for **4** at **5**
4. Jackie Rowland asks whether the Munich hotel caters for **6**
5. Lunch will be provided by **7**
6. Jackie Rowland will book the flights from **8** to **9**
7. Melanie Schmiedel sends Jackie Rowland a copy of **10**

2

P

Taking the role of Melanie Schmiedel send two e-mails confirming the hotel reservation at Zum Goldenen Ochsen, Wittelsbacher Allee 57, 81220 München to Naomi Rodgers at the American company on Rodgers.GlobalCateringusa@aol.com and to Jackie Rowland on Rowland.GlobalCateringuk@aol.com answering Jackie Rowland's query and asking whether the Americans have any special wishes as far as catering is concerned. Executives will be picked up at the airport. You require flight times and the names of the American executives.

To:	Rowland.GlobalCateringuk@aol.com	Cc:
From:	schmiedel.GlobalCateringmunich@aol.com	Date:
Subject:		

3

R

A 1.20

Melanie Schmiedel then rings the Hotel Granada in Madrid to make arrangements for the six executives attending the International Food Fair from 7 to 9 September.

Listen to the conversation twice and answer the following questions:

1. What rooms does Melanie want to book?
2. What are the special features of the rooms she is offered?
3. What are the nationalities of the executives?
4. What meal will the executives receive automatically?
5. What arrangements are there for the evening meals?
6. What special catering arrangements are necessary for Kirsty Burnham?
7. How will the executives get to the exhibition grounds?
8. Why are they advised against hiring a car?

Flight	Departure Time	Arrival Time	Destination
ZY 207	8.45 am	11.30 am	Madrid
ZY 213	6.30 pm	9.15 pm	Munich

Melanie has meanwhile booked the flights from Munich to Madrid. The flight ZY 207 leaves Munich at 8.45 am on 7 September and arrives in Madrid at 11.30 am. Return flight ZY 213 is at 6.30 pm on 9 September.

4

P

Taking the role of Melanie Schmiedel send an e-mail to the Granada Hotel informing them of the flight number and times and giving the names of the six executives. Ask them to confirm that the executives will be picked up at the airport.

Phrases

5

P

In your role as Melanie Schmiedel send an e-mail to Naomi Rodgers cc Jackie Rowland giving information about the flight from Munich to Madrid and the hotel booking in Madrid.

Phrases

6 Work with a partner. Act out the following dialogue with the help of the prompts.

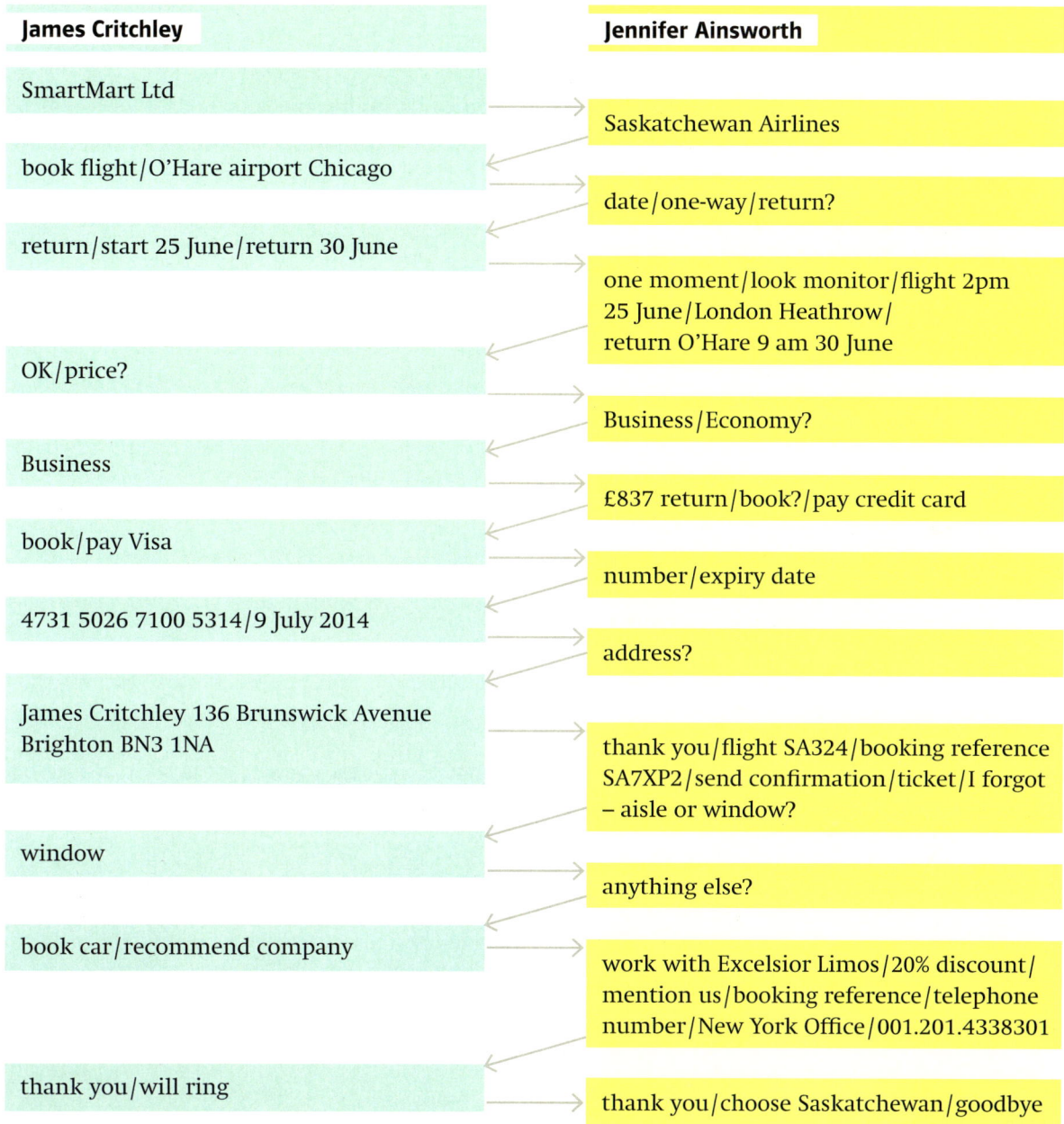

James Critchley	Jennifer Ainsworth
SmartMart Ltd	
	Saskatchewan Airlines
book flight/O'Hare airport Chicago	
	date/one-way/return?
return/start 25 June/return 30 June	
	one moment/look monitor/flight 2pm 25 June/London Heathrow/ return O'Hare 9 am 30 June
OK/price?	
	Business/Economy?
Business	
	£837 return/book?/pay credit card
book/pay Visa	
	number/expiry date
4731 5026 7100 5314/9 July 2014	
	address?
James Critchley 136 Brunswick Avenue Brighton BN3 1NA	
	thank you/flight SA324/booking reference SA7XP2/send confirmation/ticket/I forgot – aisle or window?
window	
	anything else?
book car/recommend company	
	work with Excelsior Limos/20% discount/ mention us/booking reference/telephone number/New York Office/001.201.4338301
thank you/will ring	
	thank you/choose Saskatchewan/goodbye

7 Your boss asks you to check out times and prices of business class flights to Mumbai, India (direct flights from your nearest airport). Make notes on the options.

* **8** Work with a partner. Act out the following dialogue with the help of the role cards.

Phrases ▸

Role card: Partner A   **Role card partner B** ⇨ **page 255**

Sie sind Ivor Friedmann von der Mietwagenfirma Excelsior Limos Inc. in Chicago und erhalten einen Anruf von James Critchley von der britischen Firma SmartMart Ltd. **Nehmen Sie den Anruf entgegen.**

- Mietwagen verschiedener Kategorien (Kompakt- bis Luxusklasse) zur Abholung am Flughafen bereit
- Preis für Kompaktklasse $200 pro Woche, Preis pro Tag $50
- keine Beschränkung der Anzahl der gefahrenen Meilen
- Versicherung im Preis enthalten, bei Unfall muss der Kunde allerdings 10% der Kosten selbst tragen
- Zusatzversicherung zur Deckung der 10% Selbstbeteiligung (excess coverage): $60 pro Woche
- 20% Rabatt für Kunden der Saskatchewan Airlines
- Gesamtpreis: $200 plus $60 Zusatzversicherung minus $40 Rabatt = $220
- Zahlung per Kreditkarte erwünscht unter Angabe der Kreditkartennummer und des Verfallsdatums sowie der Adresse des Kunden

---

B   Meetings, conferences and fairs

1   Making an appointment

Melanie Schmiedel's boss Udo Moersen is to go to Manchester for one day to discuss the integration of the German company into the group and the new product range with Kirsty Burnham. He asks his PA to arrange a day to fit in with Ms Burnham's agenda. He would arrive about 9.30 and stay till 2.45. He would prefer Wednesday.

Melanie Schmiedel has Herr Moersen's diary in front of her and rings Jackie Rowland, who likewise refers to Ms Burnham's diary. They try to decide which day it would be possible to meet. Kirsty Burnham would like to invite Udo Moersen out to a pub for a working lunch, if he would like that.

1 Sit back to back with your partner (Role card B) and act out the dialogue between them in which they arrange an appointment in Manchester and cover the other points mentioned.

Phrases ▶

Role card: Partner A	Role card partner B ⇨ page 255

Terminkalender von Udo Moersen

Montag	**13. Juni**
9 Uhr: Treffen mit Lieferanten Pauli & Co; 11.30 Ad.Slot Internetwerbung Frau Franzen	

Dienstag	**14. Juni**
Einzelhändler im Großraum München ab 9 Uhr bis ca 15.30 Uhr	

Mittwoch	**15. Juni**

Donnerstag 16. Juni
Geburtstag meiner Frau, 20.00 Uhr Tisch bei Da Pino reserviert

Freitag 17. Juni
11 Uhr: Besprechung der Produktplanung mit Xaver;
13–14 Uhr Mitarbeiterbesprechung

Communicating across cultures: Tips for visitors to the UK

Trains:
There are no supplementary charges for faster trains in Britain (the Eurostar to Brussels and Paris is more expensive!). Trains that stop at many stations are obviously slower than those that rarely stop. How often and where they stop is given on the indicator and timetables. It is very important to make sure that the train stops where you want to get off! Do not assume that all trains will stop at the same station on your return journey. Each train may stop at a different selection of stations.

Pubs:
Pubs are an important institution in Britain and are a popular venue at lunchtime for an informal meal. Many provide food at lunchtime, less often in the evening. As a rule there is no waiter service. You go to the bar to buy drinks where turn-taking is observed although there is no visible queue. If the pub is crowded it may be a good idea to discreetly wave a 10 pound note to let the barman / barmaid know you are waiting. Often English people buy rounds, saying things like "What's yours?" or "What are you having?".

Everybody is in principle expected to buy a round. If you don't, there may be an embarrassed silence. Food is also ordered and paid for at the bar and is brought to the table where you are sitting. All drinks and food are paid for straight away.

Tipping (taxis and restaurants):
In Germany you frequently tip by rounding up the amount of the bill. If the taxi fare is Euro 8.10 you might say Euro 8.50 or Euro 9.00. In Britain a taxi driver would not know what you meant. If the fare is £5.30 you could give the driver a £10 pound note and say "please give me change for £6". In restaurants the bill is generally brought on a little tray. You put enough money on the tray to pay the bill. The waiter returns, takes the tray away and comes back again with your change on the tray. You then decide what to put on the tray as a tip. It does not have to be a percentage of the bill.

2
KMK **Ihr Chef muss geschäftlich zum ersten Mal nach England. Geben Sie ihm einige Tipps. Fassen Sie dazu die Informationen in der Box (Communicating across cultures) zusammen.**

2 Preparing the agenda

1
KMK **Übertragen Sie die Agenda ins Deutsche.**

Melanie Schmiedel has now received the draft agenda of the conference in Munich on 6 and 7 September as drawn up by her boss.

Agenda

1. Welcoming guests
2. Minutes of the last conference in Boston, USA
3. Report on the Munich company and its integration in the group by Xaver Ertl
4. Presentation by Kirsty Burnham on the development of Global Catering's sales
5. Report by Kevin Sears on the development of Global Catering's European business
6. Consumer health concerns – from obesity to organic food – recent market research presented by Jeanne-Anne Taylor
7. Presentation on the role of international trade fairs in Global Catering's marketing strategy by Udo Moersen
8. Other business

2
P **In your role as Melanie Schmiedel send an e-mail to Jackie Rowland at Global Catering UK and Naomi Rodgers at Global Catering USA enclosing the above draft agenda as an attachment, requesting notification of any additions or modifications in the course of the following week.**

Phrases ▶

3 Preparing a meeting

Read the following text and make a list of the most important points.

R

As PA to Udo Moersen Melanie Schmiedel has been asked to assist at the conference in Munich.

This involves supervising the preparation of the room, making sure that there is an adequate supply of tea, coffee, soft drinks and mineral water (sparkling and still) available.

Any equipment required such as a computer projector, whiteboard or flip chart with a supply of board markers must be available and in working order.

Her boss may require files, additional information, or he may need to make telephone calls etc.

She must be on hand to provide any assistance necessary. Some of the German executives' English leaves much to be desired and so she may be asked to interpret or translate.

◉V2 Video lounge Hospitality   **BBC** Motion Gallery

This video deals with the hotel and catering trade.
Keep the following questions in mind while watching the video:

1. Does Judith like her job? What are the disadvantages?
2. What problem does the sector face that is highlighted several times in the course of the video?
3. What – mentioned towards the end of the video – is the sector doing to solve this problem?
4. What is Wayne Spencer's job title? Describe his appearance.
5. What particular skills do people working in this industry require?

Discuss your answers with the class.

4 Taking the minutes

 Translate fhe first three paragraphs of the following text.

The minutes

It is important for an accurate written record of the transactions of a meeting or conference to be kept. It is essential for those involved to be able to refer back to the minutes and see what was said and, in particular, what was agreed. The minutes are evidence in law of the proceedings of the meeting.

The names of those present and any apologies for non-attendance must be recorded. In this case there are the six executives with Udo Moersen acting as chairman or chair and a number of other employees of the Munich company and finally, Melanie Schmiedel.

Especially in a discussion it is difficult to keep a word for word account of what is being said. The person taking the minutes may be able to note down only the most important points. It is particularly important that any figures or dates should be recorded accurately.

The minutes have to be presented to those present at a later date for approval or corrections.

Melanie Schmiedel has also been asked to take the minutes. As most of the topics on the agenda are presentations which will be available in written form her minute-taking will be largely restricted to the questions and answers following the presentations.

5 Booking an exhibition stand

Melanie now has to ring the exhibition authorities in Madrid to check that their order for a stand is OK. After checking her records she sees that she returned the application about two months ago.

Melanie Schmiedel:	Good morning. Melanie Schmiedel from Global Catering in Munich speaking. I'm afraid I don't speak Spanish. Do you speak English or German?
Exhibition authorities:	I do speak English. What can I do for you? By the way my name's Rosa de la Fuente.
Melanie Schmiedel:	I'd like to check our stand reservation for the International Food Fair. I sent off the application form two months ago but I have not received confirmation yet.
Rosa de la Fuente:	Just a second. Let me check my monitor. Yes, here it is. Global Catering. A corner stand, 25m^2, with kitchenette and conference area. Is that OK?
Melanie Schmiedel:	Excellent. When will you be sending out the confirmations?
Rosa de la Fuente:	In a couple of weeks at the latest, I should think. But you can assume that everything's OK.
Melanie Schmiedel:	We shall need an interpreter with English and German. Can you recommend anyone?
Rosa de la Fuente:	I would get in touch with the Multilingua Agencia by e-mail under multilinguaservices@aol.com or send them a fax. The telephone number is 0034 91 4022468 and the fax number is the same with a 9 at the end instead of the 8. I'm sure they'll be able to recommend someone suitable.
Melanie Schmiedel:	Brilliant. I'll get in touch with them right away. Thank you very much. Goodbye.
Rosa de la Fuente:	Thank you for ringing. Bye.

1 **R** **Lesen Sie den Dialog, decken Sie den Text dann ab und drücken Sie Folgendes auf Englisch aus.**

1. Sie sprechen kein Spanisch.
2. Sie möchten die Standreservierung überprüfen.
3. Sie haben einen Eckstand von 25 m^2 mit Teeküche und Besprechungsraum gebucht.
4. Sie wollen wissen, wann die Bestätigungen herausgeschickt werden.
5. Sie brauchen eine Dolmetscherin für Englisch und Deutsch.

2
P Write a fax as Melanie Schmiedel to the Multilingua Agencia (see page 93) giving details of your requirements. Set out your fax as in the form below.

TELEFAX TRANSMISSION
Global Catering München GmbH

Nymphenburger Allee 93
80335 München
Tel.: (0049) (0)89277183
Fax: (0049) (0)89277190

To: Attention:
From: Fax: (0034) (91)4022469
Date: Pages (incl. this one):
Subject:

Language and grammar
Translate the following sentences.

1. Als Anhang senden wir Ihnen unsere neueste Preisliste.
2. Gestern habe ich von 13:00 Uhr bis 16:30 Uhr auf Ihren Anruf gewartet.
3. Pro Woche versenden wir zwischen 20 und 30 Angebote.
4. Wir investieren regelmäßig 5% unseres Gewinns in neue Technologien.
5. Leider warten wir noch immer auf Ihre Überweisung.
6. Zur Zeit versuchen unsere Mitbewerber eine Firma in USA zu übernehmen.
7. Wegen des Booms in China steigen die Stahlpreise weltweit.
8. Er organisiert die Konferenz, die nächste Woche stattfindet, und wir buchen die Hotelzimmer.

Language and grammar: Continuous form (Verlaufsform)

Die Verlaufsform (he is writing an e-mail) dient zur Beschreibung einer gerade vor sich gehenden Handlung sowie einer allmählichen Entwicklung, häufig markiert durch **now, just, still, when, while, since, for** etc.	Our competitors **are trying** to undercut our prices. They **are** still **waiting** for a reply. Prices **have been rising** in the last few months. We **are thinking** of buying a house.
Da die einfache Verbform (he writes 50 e-mails a day) ausdrückt, dass etwas immer so ist oder immer wieder geschieht, ist die Verwendung der Verlaufsform in bestimmten Fällen unerlässlich, um klar zu machen, dass etwas nur von vorübergehender Natur ist.	They **are having** problems with their suppliers (= at the present time). They **have** problems with their suppliers (= often / always). I **am living** with my parents at the moment (= but I'm looking for a flat of my own). I **live** in Dresden (= permanently).
Die Verlaufsform kann für feste Planungen und Abmachungen auch für die Zukunft benutzt werden.	He is giving a presentation at the conference. I am picking him up at the airport next Friday (= this has been arranged).

Logistics expert

Scheduling transport

Most companies rely on the fast delivery of their goods but must also keep their costs down. So a forwarder must advise customers on the most appropriate mode of transport depending on the nature of the consignment.

1 Read the following text and complete it with the words in the box.
R/M Then summarize the text in German.

> destinations • domestic • door-to-door • drop-off • facilitating •
> globalisation • pick-up • size • transport chains • urgency

The logistics industry has faced important changes in recent years. Not only have a lot of borders come down and political systems changed, **1** a massive increase in the world-wide shipping of goods, but the **2** of markets has led to an increase in combined transport to distant **3** around the globe.

Although **4** transport by lorry still makes up the core of **5** business, competitive forwarders must provide for all needs. They have to offer complete **6**, combining different means of transport (e. g. road and air or road, sea and rail). Distance and accessibility of the **7** and **8** points are crucial factors for the choice of transport but **9** and type of goods as well as cost and **10** must also be taken into consideration.

2 Work with a partner and ask each other about the missing information in
P your chart. Partner A uses the role card below, Partner B uses the role card on page 256.

Role card: Partner A		Role card partner B ⇨ page 256	
Departure time FRA	Destination	Duration of flight	Arrival time
06.30 am	San Francisco	?	?
09.15 am	Cape Town	?	?
?	Singapore	12:00 h	05.45 am
?	Rio de Janeiro	12:00 h	10.00 pm

3 Wind Power Inc. needs to send some spare parts to Norway. So Sarah Dean calls
R Hannes Buchwald at Orca Shipping GmbH. Read the dialogue and complete it
with the expressions given below.

Hannes: Orca Shipping Bremen GmbH, Hannes Buchwald speaking. How can I
help you?

Sarah: Hello, Hannes, this is Sarah Dean of Wind Power Inc. We're having
problems with some of our wind turbines in Norway and we have to send
spare parts there.

Hannes: Is it very **1** ?

Sarah: Actually, it is. The parts must be there **2** .

Hannes: Well, transport by vessel isn't an option then, as it takes about four
weeks. So it's got to be **3** by road and air. There isn't any regular
air service from Atlanta to Oslo but we have scheduled flights to
Frankfurt **4** . **5** is 07.30 am and the flight only takes nine hours.

Sarah: And how do we ship the consignment from Frankfurt to Stavanger?

Hannes: I'd advise **6** . Sending general cargo by charterplanes is extremely
expensive and you would only gain about **7** compared to road transport.

Sarah: So, what's **8** our spare parts could be in Stavanger?

Hannes: If nothing goes wrong they could be there **9** .

Sarah: That is good news! Thanks a lot, Hannes.

Hannes: You're **10** .

e. multi-modal transport

h. urgent

a. by the end of the week

c. half a day

i. welcome

f. road haulage

b. daily

d. Local departure time

j. within 48 hours

g. the earliest date

✱ 4 Führen Sie in Partnerarbeit einen Dialog mithilfe der Vorgaben auf den
KMK Rollenkarten.

Phrases ▷

| Role card: Partner A | Role card partner B ⇨ page 256 |

Sie arbeiten für die Spedition Nah & Fern. Sie werden von der Firma Weigand
wegen eines Warentransports von Frankfurt nach Kapstadt angerufen.

- Erfragen Sie die Art der Ware.
- Fragen Sie nach dem Umfang der Lieferung.
- Empfehlen Sie See- oder Flugtransport und begründen Sie dies.
- Informieren Sie über Transportzeiten (Seeweg: ca. vier Wochen, Flugweg:
  mit Verladen und Entladen ca. 30 Stunden).
- Geben Sie Auskunft über Abflug- und Ankunftszeiten bei Flugtransport
  (Abflug FRA: 9.15 Uhr, Ankunft CPT: 21.35 Uhr).

Phrases: Making arrangements

To book flights or trains

Please reserve a window/aisle seat **on** the 8.30 am flight to Munich.	Bitte reservieren Sie einen Platz am Fenster/Gang für den Flug um 8:30 Uhr nach München.
Are you travelling economy or business class?	Fliegen Sie Economy- oder Business-Class?
I would like to reserve a window seat on the 9.15 ICE train to Hamburg.	Ich möchte einen Fensterplatz des ICE um 9:15 Uhr nach Hamburg reservieren lassen.
Is that first or second class, one way or return?	Erster oder zweiter Klasse? Einfach oder hin und zurück?
Is there a supplementary charge for the InterCity to Edinburgh?	Muss für den Intercity nach Edinburgh ein Zuschlag bezahlt werden?
There is no supplementary charge.	Es wird kein Zuschlag erhoben.
You are booked **on** flight no ZY 652 **on** 23 March, departing London Gatwick **at** 7.30 am, arriving Munich 10.15 am.	Sie sind am 23. März für Flug Nr. ZY 652 gebucht, Abflug London Gatwick um 7:30 Uhr, Ankunft München 10:15 Uhr.
You should check in two hours before departure to allow **for** security.	Sie sollten wegen der Sicherheitsüberprüfung zwei Stunden vor Abflug einchecken.

To book hotel or conference rooms

We require a single/double room with **ensuite** bathroom.	Wir benötigen ein Einzel-/Doppelzimmer mit Bad.
I should like to book an executive suite for three nights **from** 3 **to** 6 March with Internet access.	Ich möchte eine Präsidentensuite mit Internetzugang für drei Nächte vom 3. bis 6. März buchen.
We require a conference room **to seat** 25–30 people.	Wir brauchen ein Besprechungszimmer für 25–30 Personen.
For our annual general meeting we need an assembly hall **of** at least 500 square metres equipped with a stage and a big screen.	Für unsere Jahreshauptversammlung brauchen wir einen Versammlungssaal von mindestens 500 Quadratmetern mit Bühne und Großbildschirm.
I should be grateful if you could confirm the booking **in** writing/**by** e-mail/**by** fax.	Wir wären für eine Bestätigung der Buchung per Brief/E-Mail/Fax dankbar.
Is it possible to order a buffet lunch?	Besteht die Möglichkeit ein Mittagsbuffet zu bestellen?
We regret that we have to cancel the reservation. We realise that it is very short notice.	Wir bedauern, diese Reservierung stornieren zu müssen. Wir sind uns dessen bewusst, dass dies sehr kurzfristig geschieht.

To make appointments

I'm afraid I'm engaged all day on Wednesday.	Leider bin ich am Mittwoch den ganzen Tag besetzt.
Friday would suit me fine.	Freitag würde mir gut passen.
I'd prefer Thursday morning.	Donnerstag Morgen wäre mir lieber.
It's Monday **at** 11, then.	Also bleibt es bei Montag um 11 Uhr.
Could we meet **on** Monday 17 at 10 am?	Könnten wir uns am Montag, den 17. um 10 Uhr vormittags treffen?
– Certainly. Monday at 10 am is fine.	– Ja, sicher. Montag 10 Uhr ist o.k.
Would Tuesday suit you?	Würde Ihnen Dienstag passen?
– Not so good. My diary's full, I'm afraid. Wednesday would be better.	– Eigentlich nicht. Mein Terminkalender ist leider voll. Mittwoch wäre besser.
I'm free all day Wednesday.	Am Mittwoch geht es den ganzen Tag.

To prepare the agenda

A draft agenda has already been drawn up.	Ein Entwurf für die Tagesordnung ist bereits erstellt worden.
Notification of any additions or changes is requested within a week.	Es wird gebeten, eventuelle Zusätze oder Änderungen innerhalb einer Woche anzugeben.

To prepare and assist at a meeting

He/She is chairing the meeting.	Er/Sie leitet die Sitzung.
He is the chairman, he/She is the chairperson.	Er/Sie ist der/die Vorsitzende.
Perhaps you could each introduce **yourself** briefly indicating your role in the company.	Vielleicht könnten Sie sich kurz vorstellen und dabei auf Ihre Stellung in der Firma eingehen.
Has everyone got a copy of the agenda?	Haben alle eine Kopie der Tagesordnung bekommen?
We shall adjourn **for** lunch **at** …	Um … unterbrechen wir für das Mittagessen.
Lunch will be provided by our own caterers.	Unser eigener Versorgungsbetrieb wird das Mittagessen liefern.
Are there any further comments?	Gibt es noch Wortmeldungen?
Shall we take a vote?	Sollen wir nun abstimmen?
The proposal is accepted.	Damit ist der Vorschlag angenommen.

To book an exhibition stand

We are interested in displaying our products **at** the Madrid Motor Show.	Wir sind daran interessiert, unsere Produkte auf der Automobilmesse in Madrid auszustellen.
Our company wishes to reserve floor space for a stand **covering** 8 x 15 metres.	Unsere Firma möchte die für einen Stand von 8 x 15 Metern benötigte Ausstellungsfläche reservieren lassen.
We are interested in introducing our software solutions at this years's Computer Fair and would like to ask you to send us your information package with application forms.	Wir sind daran interessiert, unsere Software-Lösungen bei der diesjährigen Computermesse vorzustellen und möchten Sie bitten, uns Ihre Messe-Information mit Anmeldeformularen zu schicken.
We wish to book a stand in the main exhibition hall.	Wir möchten einen Stand in der Hauptausstellungshalle buchen.

To organise the necessary equipment

Our stand must have internet access and it must be equipped with telephone lines.	Unser Stand muss Internetzugang haben und er muss mit Telefonleitungen ausgestattet sein.
First-class catering services will also be required.	Wir benötigen ebenfalls erstklassigen Catering-Service.

To write invitations

The chairman will be pleased to welcome you **at** our annual dinner **at** the Park Hotel.	Der Vorsitzende gibt sich die Ehre, Sie zu unserem alljährlichen festlichen Abendessen im Park Hotel begrüßen.
The reception will be held in our main hall **between** 10 am **and** 3 pm.	Der Empfang findet zwischen 10 und 15 Uhr in unserer Haupthalle statt.

To have a stand built and dismantled

Are you in a position to design an eye-catching stand for us and erect it before 15 March?	Sind Sie in der Lage, für uns einen ins Auge fallenden Stand zu entwerfen und vor dem 15. März aufzubauen?
Can you help us remove the heavy exhibits and dismantle the stand?	Können Sie uns dabei helfen, die schweren Ausstellungsstücke zu entfernen und den Stand abzubauen?

Unit 7
Making presentations

WORD BANK

presentation • audience • delivery • content • prompt cards • key words • points • introduction • main body • conclusion • visual aids • eye-contact • body language • handout • to prepare • to rehearse • to deliver • statistics • developments • degree • percentage • comparisons • rankings • graphs • diagrams • bar chart • line graph • pie chart • to visualise • to describe • to rise • to fall • to remain unchanged • to fluctuate • to account for • slight • steady • dramatic

You may be required to present your company and its products – either informally or on a more formal level. This may range from the introduction of a specific product or products to presenting the company as a whole. Although many may feel a bit scared of standing up before an audience, the ability to make good oral presentations is a key skill. However, it is a skill that can be acquired and improved by practice. It is important, above all, to remember that the style and manner of delivery is as important as the content.

Translate the following sentences into German.

M

1. You may feel scared of standing up before an audience.
2. Making a good oral presentation is a key skill.
3. This skill can be acquired and improved.
4. Style of delivery is as important as content.
5. You may be required to make a presentation on your company and its products.

Online-Link
808264-0007

A Preparing a presentation

You have been asked to give a presentation of your company and its products. The presentation will be brief. You have a maximum of 5 minutes at your disposal. The following hints should help you to prepare.

Start by deciding what you want to include and what your objectives are. Remember that there are limits to the number of facts your audience can absorb. The following are intended as helpful hints:

How to make a presentation

- Do not write out your presentation in full. Use numbered prompt cards with key words. They are the best way to avoid forgetting important points.
- Your presentation should have an introduction, main body and conclusion.
- First give a brief overview of points to be covered.
- Divide up the main body according to the number of important points.
- Finish with a conclusion.

Use expressions like:

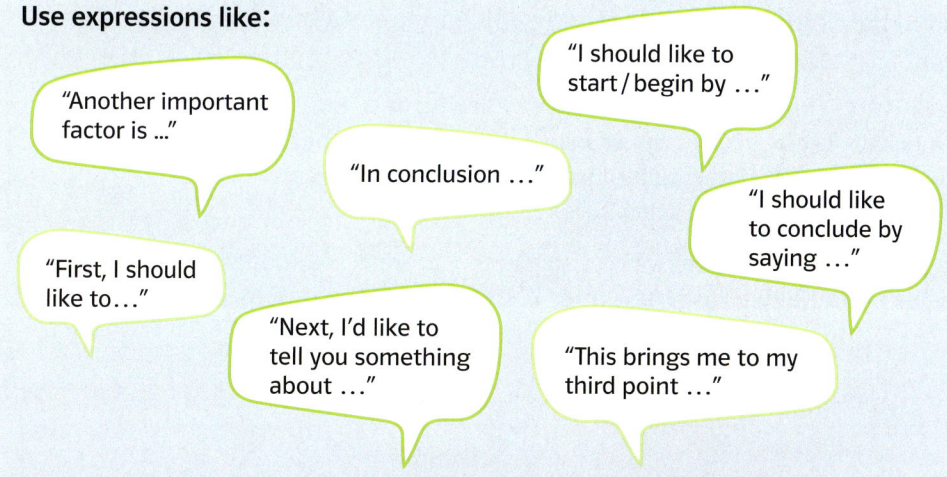

"Another important factor is …"

"I should like to start / begin by …"

"In conclusion …"

"I should like to conclude by saying …"

"First, I should like to…"

"Next, I'd like to tell you something about …"

"This brings me to my third point …"

in order to signal the different sections of your presentation.

Reinforce what you say by **visual aids**, such as powerpoint slides. Visual aids help you to explain complicated ideas more easily and arouse and hold the interest of your audience and make your presentation look more professional. If you print them out they may double as a handout.

Visual aids may take the form of overhead transparencies or computer files showing graphs, pictures, flowcharts, brief statements/cues (e.g. the key words from your prompt cards). Here are a few helpful hints:

- Limit the text to six lines.
- Use no more than six words per line.
- Print the text in large letters, using upper and lower case letters.
- Use dark colours, such as black, red, blue or green.

1

KMK Fassen Sie den Text über die Vorbereitung einer Präsentation unter Beantwortung folgender Fragen auf Deutsch zusammen.

1. Warum soll eine Präsentation nicht schriftlich ausformuliert werden?
2. Wie soll eine Präsentation gegliedert sein?
3. Welche Vorteile bietet Anschauungsmaterial?
4. Wie müssen Folien aussehen, damit sie wirken?

2

R
A1.21 Now listen to a presentation by Udo Moersen from the German subsidiary of Global Catering and complete the following text.

Good morning, ladies and gentlemen. **1** a few words about our company. Since last January we have been a part of Global Catering Manchester but we are an old-established Munich company producing a range of Bavarian specialities.

We have now entered the rapidly growing market for convenience foods, **2** a range of freshly prepared dishes to quality supermarkets and delicatessens and **3** the catering for company board meetings, conferences etc.

In Munich and internationally **4** of young business people (male and female) who do not have the leisure to cook but who still demand high-quality, imaginative, prepared meals which they can quickly pop into their briefcases on their way home.

Our sales figures show that this is a growth market (I don't want to bore you **5** which I hope you have all received). We are also exporting Bavarian specialities to Britain and the USA via Global Catering and its subsidiaries. At the same time we are importing British and American specialities to Germany.

6 that we look forward to rapid growth in these markets. Catering is a modern industry with massive potential whose importance is still underestimated in Germany **7**.

3

R
A1.21 Udo Moersen used the following prompt cards for his presentation.
Listen again and restore the correct order of his jumbled prompt cards.

① conclusion: growth industry

② part of Global Catering but old Munich company. Bavarian specialities!

③ target group: busy young professionals

④ supermarkets / delicatessens / corporate catering

⑤ sales figures (see handout!) exports to USA / UK; imports

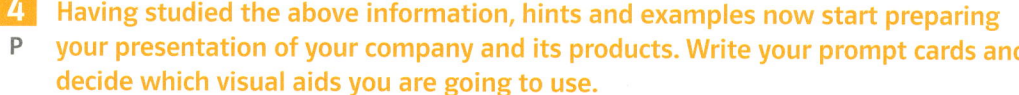

✳ 4
P
Having studied the above information, hints and examples now start preparing your presentation of your company and its products. Write your prompt cards and decide which visual aids you are going to use.

Content of your presentation:
- size, type, location, activities of company
- products in general, selection of products, services
- main markets, domestic/export
- sales figures
- special features of products e.g. state-of-the-art, environmentally friendly

5
As your British boss frequently has to give presentations at changing venues, she has asked you to find information on the latest computer projectors. She is especially interested in lightweight compact models that are easy to carry and cost under $ 500. Use the internet to find this information and make notes for her in English.

B Delivering a presentation

> ### Useful tips
>
> It is a good idea NOT to read out a prepared text. It is easy to bore your audience. You make a much more lively impression if you speak freely using prompt cards and visual aids to remind you of the various points. This also helps to ensure that your body language is natural. If you are planning to use equipment such as an overhead projector or a computer projector, make sure a) they are working and b) you know how to operate them. Practise and rehearse your presentation, preferably with real people as an audience.
>
> - Do not speak too quickly (in order to get the whole thing over as quickly as possible!)
> - Speak clearly – make sure everybody can hear you.
> - Do not speak monotonously – you will sound as if you are boring yourself and will bore your audience!
> - Do not wave your arms around mechanically – your gestures should be appropriate.
> - Look at your audience, establish eye contact.
> - Look happy and confident. Smile.
>
> It is very helpful for the person making the presentation to be given constructive, concrete and detailed feedback. Only in this way can they become aware of how they come across and how this can be changed. This is a prerequisite for developing skills in oral presentation.

1
KMK
Ein Kollege muss eine Präsentation halten und hat Sie um Rat gebeten. Schreiben Sie ihm eine E-Mail auf Deutsch und geben Sie ihm Hinweise für eine Präsentation unter Verwendung der Informationen in „Useful tips".

✳ 2 **Now give your presentation on your company and its products to your fellow**
P/I **students. The other students listen to the presentation and assess it according**
to the following evaluation scheme. The audience should award points out of ten
under each heading (on a separate sheet of paper).

Evaluation of presentation/checklist:

		Points
Preparation	evidence of careful preparation	▪
Structure	introduction, main body – clear emphasis on small number of important points – conclusion	▪
Content	relevance, well-substantiated with facts and figures	▪
Visual aids	appropriate use of simple, easy-to-understand visual aids	▪
Delivery	not too fast, eye contact, appropriate body language, confident, relaxed	▪
Language	no jargon, straightforward, use of signalling expressions like: "I should like to begin/conclude by …"	▪
Overall impression	lively, humorous, easy to follow, right length	▪

✳ 3 **The following is an example of a more ambitious presentation using visual**
R **aids. At an investment seminar Daniela Webb gives a brief presentation on the**
Limpopo Mining Company and its products, using a computer projector. Make a
list of expressions that would be useful in any presentation.

"Good morning, ladies and gentlemen. I should like to give a brief presentation on our company and its products in the context of this investment seminar.

I'll begin by showing you a graph illustrating the rising demand for zinc and copper worldwide and the development of production at our sites in Asia and Africa. As a result of the strength of the world economy and particularly rapid growth in China and India demand for our products has soared dramatically over the last two years.

At the same time we are investing strongly in the development of our sites. This is a photograph of construction work on our new site in Kazakhstan. As you can see from this graph, production there jumped by 20% last year. We are also spending a large slice of our profits on exploration.
The pie chart shows what proportion of our expenditure goes on the construction and development of sites and the exploration of new sites.

In conclusion, I should like to emphasise that demand for our products is expected to be strong in the foreseeable future. I am sure that this brief presentation will have shown you that Limpopo Mining shares will add some excitement to your investment portfolio.

Thank you very much indeed for your time. I shall be very pleased to answer any questions you may have."

Language and grammar: Describing graphs

Statistics are easier to read if they are presented in the form of bar charts, line graphs or pie charts. When making a presentation, you may have to describe graphs. The expressions given on the following page will be helpful.

Developments over time can be visualised by **line graphs**.

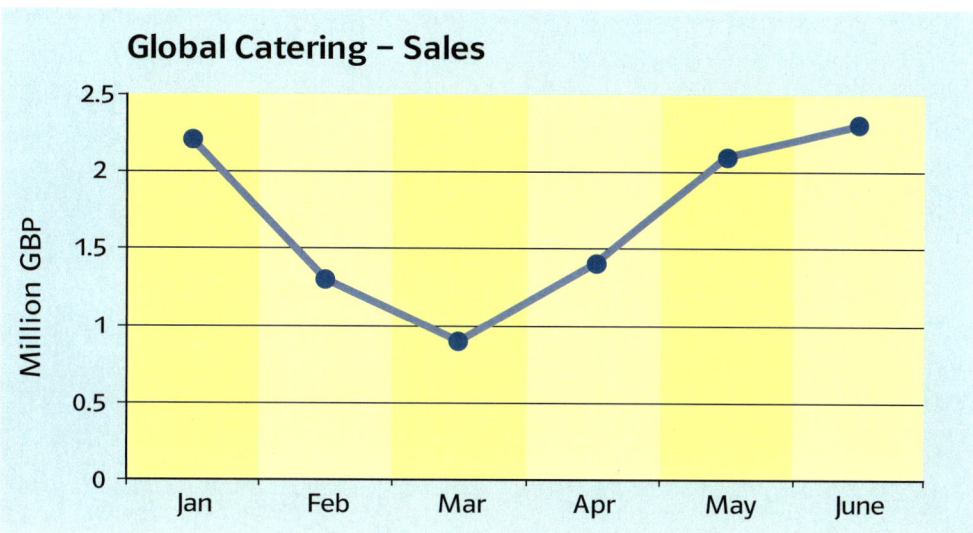

V3 Video lounge Presentations

lingua tv

This video shows a presentation given by a senior Purple Fashion executive. After watching it answer the following questions:

1. Does the presenter make a natural impression?
2. Do you find her gestures and smile convincing?
3. Why is it not necessary to take notes?
4. When does she plan to answer questions?
5. When and where was Purple Fashion founded?
6. Is this her actual presentation?
7. What in her view is Purple Fashion's "obsession"?

To describe developments

1. upwards		
to rise / increase / go up / jump **by ... from ... to ...** to reach a peak / maximum of ...	Between May and July exports rose by 5% from 10,000 units to 10,050 units. In June prices reached a peak of €75.	
2. unchanged		
to remain / stay unchanged / stable / flat **at ...** to fluctuate **between ... and ...**	Sales remained unchanged at 750m units. In the second quarter oil prices fluctuated between 42 and 61 dollars per barrel.	
3. downwards		
to fall / decline / go down / drop / slump **by ... from ... to ...** to reach a low / minimum **of ...** / the lowest point **at ...**	Last year the average price dropped by 2% from € 100 to €98. In March the lowest point was reached at 28 dollars.	

At a meeting Kirsty Burnham from Global Catering in Manchester presents her company to a gathering of potential customers. She refers to the last half year's sales and to the line graph on the preceding page.

4   **Read her description and find the correct prepositions from the box.**

at • by • from • of • of • to • to • to

In January sales stood **1** 2.2 million pounds. Then there was a dramatic decline **2** GBP 1.3m in February. Sales continued to fall steadily and reached the minimum **3** 0.9m in March. Between March and May, however, sales jumped **4** 0.9m **5** 2.1m. In June sales had risen **7** around 9% **6** the peak **8** 2.3 million pounds.

5   **Choose the correct adjective or adverb. See *Language and grammar* in Unit 9.**

1. In January imports fell (sharp/sharply).
2. Sales remained (constant/constantly) for three months.
3. A (slight/slightly) increase in prices had been expected.
4. There was a (gradual/gradually) fall in turnover.
5. Oil prices have been rising (dramatic/dramatically).

To describe the speed or degree of change

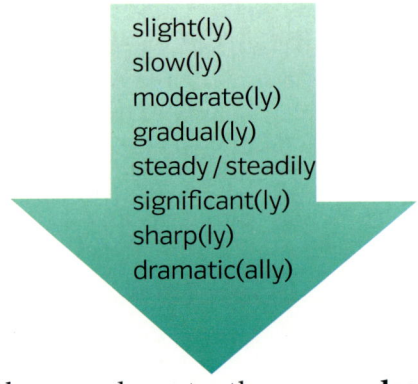

slight(ly)
slow(ly)
moderate(ly)
gradual(ly)
steady / steadily
significant(ly)
sharp(ly)
dramatic(ally)

In the second quarter there was a **dramatic** increase in sales. In June imports rose **sharply**.

Phrases: Making presentations

To make a presentation

I should like to start **by** telling you something about my company/organisation.	Zunächst möchte ich Ihnen etwas über meine Firma/mein Unternehmen sagen.
First, I should like to introduce my company briefly.	Als Erstes möchte ich Ihnen mein Unternehmen kurz vorstellen.
My presentation will deal **with** …	Meine Präsentation behandelt …
I intend to keep my presentation as brief as possible.	Ich möchte meine Präsentation so kurz wie möglich halten.
I would like to focus **on** the following points/areas/products/services:	Ich möchte mich auf folgende Punkte/Gebiete/Produkte/Dienstleistungen konzentrieren:
I would welcome any questions **at** the end of my presentation.	Ich wäre gern bereit, etwaige Fragen am Ende meiner Präsentation zu beantworten.
Has everyone received a copy of the handout?	Haben alle den Handzettel bekommen?
The handout summarises the main points and gives an overview of the relevant figures and statistics.	Der Handzettel enthält die Hauptpunkte und gibt einen Überblick über die entsprechenden Zahlen und Statistiken.

To structure the main part of your presentation

Now my second point is …	Ich komme nun zu Punkt 2 …
Thirdly, let me give you some basic statistics.	Drittens darf ich Ihnen ein paar grundlegende Statistiken zeigen.
The gist of the matter/central issue is …	Der Kernpunkt/die zentrale Frage ist …
I should now like to move **on** to the next topic.	Ich möchte nun gern zum nächsten Thema kommen.
An excellent example **of** this is …	Ein hervorragendes Beispiel dafür ist …
I should like to give you an example to illustrate this point.	Ich möchte diesen Punkt mit einem Beispiel erläutern.
A distinct trend emerges **from** the figures.	Aus den Zahlen geht ein deutlicher Trend hervor.
In this connection it is worth mentioning …	In diesem Zusammenhang sollte man erwähnen, …

To conclude your presentation

To sum **up** we can say that …	Zusammenfassend kann man sagen, dass …
I should like to finish **by** saying/thanking the organisers/pointing out …	Ich möchte schließen mit der Bemerkung/dem Dank an die Organisatoren/dem Hinweis …

Unit 8
Form of written communication

WORD BANK

e-mail • facsimile message • letter • sender • letterhead • addressee • recipient • attention line • reference line • date • attachment • subject • salutation • initials • complimentary close • signature • covering page • enclosure • structure • paragraph • style • linking words • to attach • to delete • to forward

Written communication plays an essential role in business in cases where documentation in writing is required. It may, for instance, also be used to ensure that misunderstandings cannot arise. However, in recent years the traditional letter has increasingly been replaced by new, quicker and frequently less formal media. In business correspondence the letter has now largely been replaced by e-mails and to a lesser degree by faxes.

1 Work with a partner. Make a grid for yourself like the one below. Then read the text that follows
R and fill in your grid. Compare the result with your partner's information in the grid.

	Advantages	Disadvantages
E-Mail		
Letter		
Fax		

Online-Link
808264-0008

The advantages of **e-mails** are too well-known to require explanation here. However, there are a number of disadvantages. Spam is a major time waster. According to one source 95% of e-mails sent worldwide are spam. Hence the need to install spam filters. Security is also a major issue. E-mails and attachments may be used to transfer spyware and other viruses. Privacy is also a problem – you cannot be sure that your e-mails are not being read by an unauthorised third party. Finally, authenticity – who is the e-mail really from? – is a further issue undermining the reliability and safety of e-mails which can be addressed by installing digital signatures. Sometimes one might feel it's safer to entrust one's important message to the old-fashioned snail-mail!

In international business transactions **faxes** are used to communicate with partners in countries where the e-mail system is still unsatisfactory or unreliable. Faxes are also preferred to e-mails whenever business people want their partners to have some written (and possibly signed) evidence of a transaction. Faxes, like e-mails, may also be used where speed is essential, e.g. for offers. Signatures on faxes are nowadays recognised as evidence even by the courts.

The business **letter** is still widely used in legal contexts, in connection with formal contracts and complaints. Such letters are often "faxed and posted", i.e. sent by fax and by post. Only a letter ensures that the communication is not read by an unauthorised person. Letters also serve as covering letters when a catalogue or similar enclosure is to be sent.

✷ **2** **Translate the following English sentences into German.**

M

1. Letters have largely been replaced by e-mails.
2. E-mails can be addressed to several people at the same time.
3. Worms and viruses may make it necessary to instal protective software.
4. It is a disadvantage that e-mails cannot easily be signed.
5. In some countries the e-mail system is unsatisfactory or unreliable.
6. It may sometimes be necessary to have written evidence of a transaction.
7. Business letters are still widely used in connection with formal contracts.
8. A letter is less likely to be read by unauthorised persons.

A   Layout and components of business correspondence

1   E-Mails*

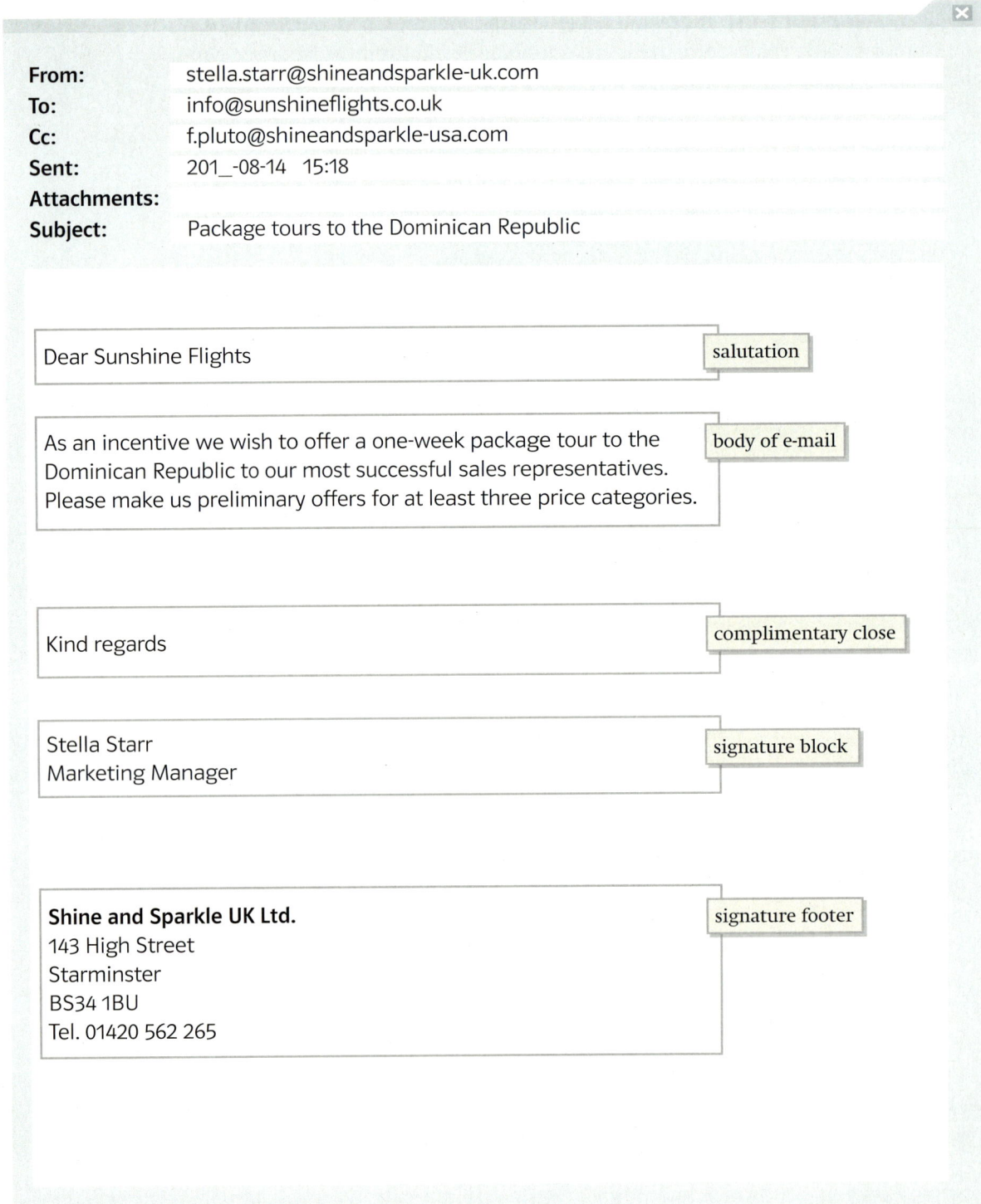

From:	stella.starr@shineandsparkle-uk.com
To:	info@sunshineflights.co.uk
Cc:	f.pluto@shineandsparkle-usa.com
Sent:	201_-08-14 15:18
Attachments:	
Subject:	Package tours to the Dominican Republic

Dear Sunshine Flights   salutation

As an incentive we wish to offer a one-week package tour to the   body of e-mail
Dominican Republic to our most successful sales representatives.
Please make us preliminary offers for at least three price categories.

Kind regards   complimentary close

Stella Starr   signature block
Marketing Manager

Shine and Sparkle UK Ltd.   signature footer
143 High Street
Starminster
BS34 1BU
Tel. 01420 562 265

* Both ways of spelling are acceptable, **e-mail** and **email**.

Info: E-mails

From:	Your e-mail address will appear automatically.
To:	Be careful not to make the slightest mistake when entering the recipient's address, or else the e-mail will be returned.
Cc:	The abbreviation stands for "carbon copy". With old-style typewriters copies used to be made by inserting carbon paper between the blank sheets of paper. This is where you enter the addresses of the persons to whom you wish the message to be forwarded.
Bcc:	Addresses listed under "Blind Carbon Copy" do not appear in the message header of the other recipients.
Sent:	Instead of "Sent" you may find the word "Date". The correct date and time will be entered automatically.
Attachments:	Any kind of file, such as word documents (.doc), excel sheets (.xls), pictures (e.g. .jpg), etc. can be attached to an e-mail.
Subject:	You should always mention the precise subject matter of your correspondence. Firstly it will help your business partner to deal with your mail and secondly it will prevent him / her from deleting it for fear of viruses.
Salutation:	Very formal salutations like "Dear Sirs" or "Gentlemen:" are not used in e-mails. Use "Dear …" instead. In the English-speaking world correspondence is personalised whenever possible: Dear Fiona Dear Ms Starr or even (to avoid "Dear Sirs"): Dear Sunshine Flights
Body of the e-mail:	Note that the first word starts with a capital letter.
Complimentary close:	There is a range of expressions to choose from, like: With best / kind regards Kind / Best regards Regards Best wishes or (very formal in e-mails) Yours sincerely
Signature block:	Write your title or department below your name. In Britain women often add (Miss) or (Mrs) in brackets after their name, e.g. Janine Smith (Miss), if they wish to be addressed in this way.
Signature footer:	Add your company's full name, address and telephone number to all e-mails you send to persons or companies who may not know you or your firm.

Do not use special characters like ß, ä, ö or ü. They may come out very strangely at the other end! Use ss, ae, oe and ue instead.

1 Choose the appropriate alternative from the brackets.

1. You may (enclose/attach) files to an e-mail.
2. You should always watch out for (viruses/germs).
3. Make sure that you (wipe out/delete) suspicious e-mails.
4. E-mails can be (passed on/forwarded) to third parties.
5. Do not forget to mention the (theme/subject) of your e-mail.
6. E-mails always start with the (complimentary close/salutation).
7. The recipient or (addressee/sender) is the person the e-mail is sent to.

2 Study the example e-mail on page 110. Then restore the correct order of the jumbled elements below and rewrite the e-mail.

(1)	**Sent:**	201_-11-09
(2)	**Cc:**	walter-elliot@kellynchhall.ie
(3)		Thank you. Kind regards Nancy
(4)	**From:**	nancy.steele@jenningsfood.com
(5)		Jennings Food Ltd. Delaford Industrial Estate Barton GU7 3AB Tel. 01430 37968
(6)		Sorry to inform you that the 150 picnic hampers as per yesterday's order have not yet arrived. Please make sure that we get them by tomorrow 11 a.m. at the very latest.
(7)		Dear Kitty
(8)	**To:**	k.bennet@longbourne.co.uk
(9)	**Subject:**	Late delivery

3 Search the Internet and find out about "netiquette" and "texting abbreviations". Make notes and compare your findings with the group. Send a text message in English using appropriate abbreviations to one of your classmates.

Info: How to write e-mails

- Keep messages short and to the point.
- Focus on one subject per message and include a relevant subject title for the message.
- Include your signature footer when communicating with persons who may not know you personally.
- Capitalize words only to highlight an important point. Capitalizing is generally felt to be like SHOUTING!
- Be sparing in your use of exclamation marks.
- Never send chain letters through the Internet.
- Be professional and be careful what you say. E-mails are easily forwarded.
- Be careful when using sarcasm and humour.
- Never assume that your e-mails will be read only by you and the recipient.
- Emoticons like :-) for "happy" or ;-) for "only joking" should be reserved for communication with business partners with whom you are on a familiar footing.
- Use abbreviations sparingly as you cannot be sure that your partner in a foreign country is familiar with them.

 4 Your colleague does not speak English. Explain the above information to him
M   in German.

You might begin like this:
„Ich habe im Internet interessante Hinweise über das, was man bei E-Mails beachten soll, gefunden. Der Text beginnt mit der Ermahnung E-Mails kurz und präzise zu formulieren. Man soll sich auf ein Thema pro Mail beschränken und einen passenden Betreff wählen …"

2 Faxes

There is no established layout for faxes (facsimile messages). Firms are free to design their own covering page. A typical one could look like this:

Herkules
the global sports brand

Ziegelberg 8–12
89331 Neustadt
Tel. +49 8358 888-0
Fax +49 8358 88820
www.Herkules.com

Telefax Message

To: India Sports
112 Delhi Road, Meerut-250 001
Uttar Pradesh, India

Attention: Mr. Kunal Mahajan

Fax: +91 121 2512275

From: Laura Bayerle, Purchasing Department

Date: 1 Feb 201_

Pages: (incl. this page) 1

Subject: Our order No. ABF / 16 of 20 January

Dear Mr. Mahajan

If it is possible, we should like to increase our order for item 345 (plain navy T-shirts) from 1750 to 2000 units for the sizes L and XL.

Please let me know by return whether you are in a position to dispatch the extra articles together with the rest of our order.

Thank you very much.

Regards

Laura Bayerle

Laura Bayerle

If you do not receive all the pages, please advise us as soon as possible.

Info: Fax

The **names, addresses, telephone** and **fax numbers** of both the sender and the addressee should be recorded on the fax. The **date** is also essential as well as an appropriate **subject line**. As fax transmissions are sometimes interrupted, the **number of pages** is mentioned to show the recipient whether any pages are missing. If you send a business letter by fax, write the recipient's fax number below the inside address and refer to the total number of pages on the first page.

1 Use the fax on page 114 as an example and rewrite the following fax using the
P correct spacing and punctuation.

> Getränke König Am Sprudelbach 17 06122 Halle Tel. 0345 785634 Fax 0345 785635 Telefax To BIG Beverages Ltd 38 Cromwell Road Chipping OX7 5SR UK Fax +44 1608 647919 Attention Ms Maggy Lane From Nicole Sachse Import Department Date 31 Jan 201_ Pages incl. this one 1 Subject Our order for 500 bottles of Tropicana Fruit Juice of 28 Jan Dear Ms Lane I am sorry to cause you trouble but our client has just informed us that he needs the fruit juice as early as Friday next week I trust you will be able to bring forward delivery by three days Thank you for your co-operation Best wishes *Nicole Sachse* Nicole Sachse

2 Study the fax on page 114. Then restore the correct order of the jumbled elements
R / P below and rewrite the fax.

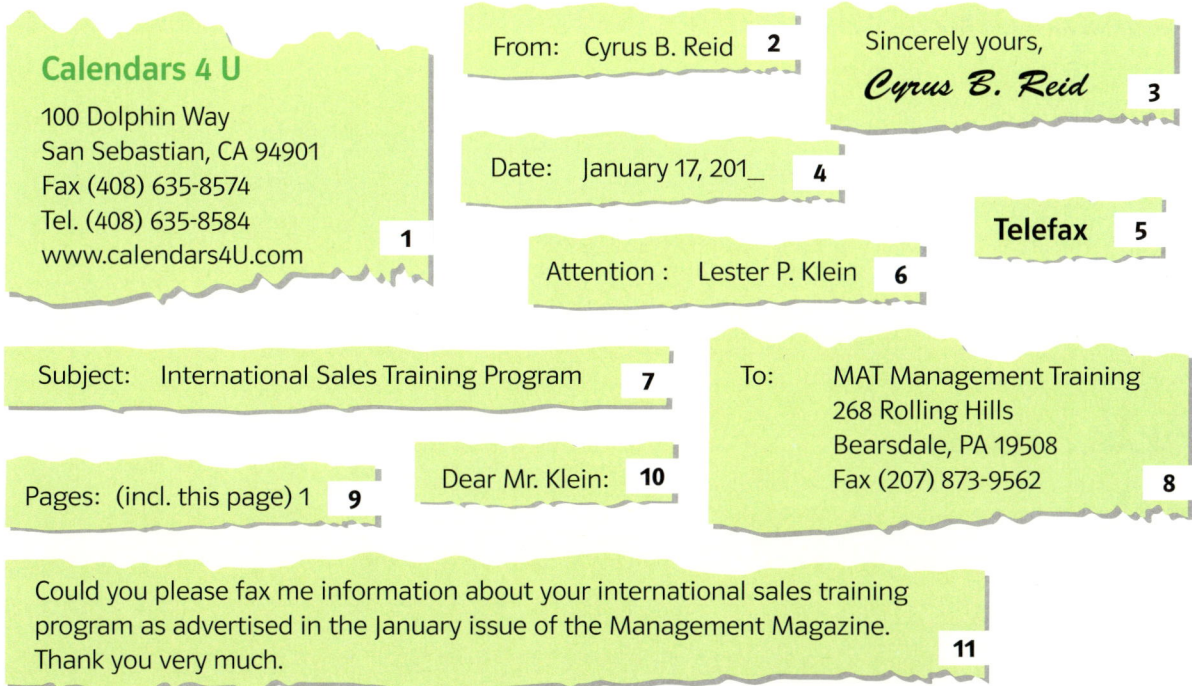

Calendars 4 U
100 Dolphin Way
San Sebastian, CA 94901
Fax (408) 635-8574
Tel. (408) 635-8584
www.calendars4U.com   **1**

From: Cyrus B. Reid   **2**

Sincerely yours,
Cyrus B. Reid   **3**

Date: January 17, 201_   **4**

Telefax   **5**

Attention :   Lester P. Klein   **6**

Subject: International Sales Training Program   **7**

To: MAT Management Training
268 Rolling Hills
Bearsdale, PA 19508
Fax (207) 873-9562   **8**

Pages: (incl. this page) 1   **9**

Dear Mr. Klein: **10**

Could you please fax me information about your international sales training program as advertised in the January issue of the Management Magazine. Thank you very much.   **11**

3 Business letters

1 Match the numbers (1–11) in the following business letter with the letters (A–K)
R in the definitions given on the following pages.

International Snacks GmbH (1)

Fürstenstr. 19
40547 Düsseldorf
Tel. 0211 577563
Fax 0211 577566
E-Mail info@internationalsnacks.de
www.internationalsnacks.de

RH / rf (2)

14 August 201_ (3)

Global Catering (4)
17 Nelson Square
Manchester
MA17 3DF
UK

Attention: Ms Kirsty Burnham (5)

Dear Ms Burnham (6)

Brochure on rules and regulations (7)

As promised on the occasion of your recent visit to our company I am sending you
enclosed the translation of the brochure on the German rules and regulations for
food processing in the catering industry.

May I take this opportunity of thanking you and Mr. Sears for your visit.
My colleagues and I greatly enjoyed meeting you in person. (8)

Yours sincerely (9)
International Snacks GmbH (10)

Markus Diepholz

Markus Diepholz
Export Manager

Enc. (11)

A Letterhead shows a company's logo, name and address, its telephone, fax and e-mail numbers and its Internet address.

B Reference line may show the initials of the signatory and the secretary or references to files or departments.

C Date

As 07/08/12 would mean 7 August 2012 for an Englishman and 8 July 2012 for an American, it is advisable to write out the month. The following ways of writing the date are recommended:

7 August 2012   or   7 Aug 2012   or   August 7, 2012

Note that the year is written out in full.

Giving the year first, then the month and then the day is rapidly becoming accepted worldwide: 2012-08-07.

D Inside address

British usage	North American usage
Messrs J. McDream & Co. 91 Malvern Road Ashford Kent CA3 6AH UK	Samantha Duvet The Mattress Corporation 1386 Munras Avenue Monterey, CA 93940 USA

Note that in British business letters Messrs, Mr, Mrs, Ms and Miss are written on the same line as the name. In the USA they are often omitted altogether. Messrs is only used for smaller firms, such as partnerships. Do not write Messrs if the company's name is followed by "Ltd", Plc", "Inc." or "Corp.". Ms should be used whenever the marital status of the female addressee is not known.

Note that in Great Britain the postal code is written on its own line below the place name, whereas in USA and Canada it is placed after the place name on the same line.

When letters are written to foreign countries, the name of the country should be shown on the final line of the inside address.

E Attention line ensures that the letter is dealt with by a specific person. You may write **Attention:**, **For the attention of …:**, or (less formal) **FAO:**
As an alternative the person's name may be included in the inside address. This is a must if the recipient is addressed by name in the salutation.

Global Catering 17 Nelson Square Manchester MA17 3DF UK Attention: Ms Kirsty Burnham	Ms Kirsty Burnham Global Catering 17 Nelson Square Manchester MA17 3DF UK

F Salutation (UK)

Dear Sirs, Dear Sir/Madam

Dear Ms Burnham
Dear Customer
Dear Margaret

G Complimentary close (UK)

Yours faithfully/sincerely
(Yours faithfully is rarely used now)
Yours sincerely, Kind regards
Yours sincerely
Best regards, Kind regards,
Best wishes

Salutation (USA and Canada)

(Ladies and) Gentlemen:
To whom it may concern:
Dear Mr O'Reilly:
Dear Sean:

Complimentary close (USA and Canada)

Sincerely, Very truly yours,
Sincerely, Sincerely yours,
Yours truly, Sincerely, Sincerely yours,
Regards, Cordially,

If at all possible you should address the person you are writing to by name. "Dear Sirs" or "Gentlemen:" is only used when you do not have a name to write to. Traditionally salutation and complimentary close should be in line with each other.

H Body of the letter

Note that in English the first word of a business letter starts with a capital letter.

I Subject line

may be preceded by the words "Subject" or "Re" and should be as specific as possible. Do not just write **"Your offer"** but **"Your offer for mouse pads of 23 May"**. In the UK subject lines are normally written below the salutation, in the USA above the salutation. They may be either underlined or typed in capital letters or bold type.

J Enclosure

Whenever enclosures are sent with a letter, a reference to the enclosure is required at the bottom of the letter. You may write "Enclosure(s)" or "Enc(s)".

K Signature block

In the UK – but not in the USA – the signature block often begins with the company's name. The signatory's name and title (or department) are typed below the signature. If somebody signs the letter on behalf of another person, the other person's name is typed below the signature, preceded by the word **"for"** or by the abbreviation **pp.** meaning "on behalf of".

NetOrbiter Ltd.

Maria Bertram

pp. Henry Crawford
Chief Information Officer

Fred Parry

for Betty Bickerton
Credit Manager

2 Work with a partner. Find the right order for these jumbled addresses.
Then dictate them to your partner.

UK	Ultimate IT Solutions Inc.	Attention: Tom Finch
Woodbridge	USA	4 Tamar Industrial Estate
Messrs Frost & Winter	Denver, CO 80121	UK
22 James Street	Barbara Goodyear	Finch Electronics Ltd.
Suffolk	1280 Mayflower Drive	PL3 7CT
IP3 7KL		Plymouth
Managerial Skills Training		

3 Seven elements are missing from this traditional business letter. Copy the letter
R/P and add the missing elements using your own imagination for details.

Superdress GmbH

Fritz-Walter-Str. 28, 80469 München
Tel. +49 89 4677524, Fax +49 89 4677625
www.superdress.munich.de

TS / is

Mr Tony Shaw
Wilson and Thatcher Ltd.
2 Brook Lane
Bristol
BS9 2ET

We are pleased to enclose our Spring Catalogue showing our absolutely fabulous
range of shirts. We feel sure that they will appeal to your young customers. If
you place an order within the next two weeks, you will be granted 3% early order
discount.

We look forward to welcoming you as a customer.

Resi Martl

B   Structure and style of business correspondence

1   Beginning, main part and end

Business correspondence must be well organised. The body of the correspondence should consist of three separate parts: the beginning, the main part and the end.

The **beginning** is either a single sentence or a short paragraph that states the reason why you are writing the correspondence. Example: I am going to be in Boston on May 20, and would like to meet you, if possible.

The **main part** contains the details. There should be a separate paragraph for every new idea. Example: Every now and then the new software does not provide the degree of protection against spam that we had expected. That is why I would like to discuss the problem with you personally.
A morning meeting would be best for me. Would 9 a.m. be convenient for you?

In the end section the writer sums up and underlines what he/she would like the recipient to do. Alternatively he/she may add a remark designed to create goodwill. Example: If this fits in with your schedule, please leave a message with my secretary. I look forward to seeing you in Boston.

Especially when you are writing to a customer it is advisable to end the communication on a friendly note.

> Business correspondence should meet the so-called ABC specifications:
> **Accurate** correct and complete as to facts
> **Brief**   short sentences, simple expressions, plain English
> **Clear**   easy, natural style, without formality or familiarity

Put the eight jumbled elements of this correspondence into the correct order and
R/P **write it out.**

> **1**   Furthermore, we would like to draw your attention to our latest development, small wind turbines for commercial and domestic use. Please see page 3 of our catalogue.

> **2**   Yours sincerely

> **3**   Should you need any further information please contact us at any time.

> **4**   As an attachment we are sending you our catalogue and price list. These already include a 25% trade discount. We also offer quantity discounts for major orders. Our terms of payment are 30 days net.

5   Dear Mr Wyndham

6   We look forward to receiving your first order which will be given top priority.

7   Your e-mail enquiry of 18 June

8   Thank you for your interest in our solar panels.

2   Linking words

Business correspondence is often made up of standard phrases. In order for the correspondence to read smoothly such individual text-building blocks ought to be connected by **linking words** like **also**, **as well as**, **both … and**, **in addition**, **moreover**, **further**, **firstly**, **secondly**, **finally** etc. which suggest a list. Example: **Finally**, we should like to confirm the date for next year's fashion show.

Other linking words imply a contrast: **whereas**, **while**, **in contrast to**, **however**, **although** etc. Example: Last month sales of DVD players rose by 3.5 per cent **whereas** sales of TV sets fell by 2.8 percent.

The following linking words indicate that an explanation is being given: **this is why**, **therefore**, **thus**, **as**, **because** etc. Example: We are most dissatisfied with your services. **This is why** we have decided to instruct a different company.

✳   **Translate the following sentences into German. Note particularly the linking words in bold type.**

M

1. He is very unhappy with the service. **This is why** he has stopped going to that restaurant.
2. Last year wages increased **whereas** retail sales stagnated.
3. **First**, delivery by road is quicker and **second**, it is more flexible.
4. We have decided not to place further orders **as** there have been so many delays.
5. **Both** our company **and** our suppliers have experienced strong growth this year.
6. We are prepared to place an order for 1000 notebooks. **However**, we expect a substantial quantity discount.
7. There has been severe flooding in this part of the country. **In addition**, we have been faced with prolonged electricity cuts.
8. **Although** we were not entirely satisfied with the execution of our previous order, we are prepared to give your company another chance.
9. Our canteen offers three different menus. We **also** serve vegetarian dishes.
10. **Finally**, we would like to thank you once more for making this concession.

Language and grammar 1
Decide which of the alternatives in brackets is correct.

1. I suggest (that you wait/to wait) for the outcome of the inspection.
2. We would appreciate (if you could/it if you could) let us have your confirmation by return.
3. We would appreciate (receiving/to receive) your prompt reply.
4. We would like to (excuse us/apologize) for not having reacted earlier.
5. Please (excuse/apologize) the inconvenience caused by this incident.
6. We look forward (to doing/to do) business with you.
7. We hope (to be entrusted/to being entrusted) with your order.
8. I would appreciate (to hear/hearing) from you soon.
9. We would suggest (to ring/ringing) Fisher's bookshop in Cambridge.
10. I would appreciate (it if you sent/if you sent) a driver to the airport.

✳ Language and grammar 2
Find the English equivalents of the following German phrases.

1. Wir möchten uns für die entstandenen Unannehmlichkeiten entschuldigen.
2. Wir sehen Ihrer baldigen Antwort mit Interesse entgegen.
3. Bitte entschuldigen Sie dieses Versehen.
4. Wir hoffen, bald wieder von Ihnen zu hören.
5. Wir schlagen vor, die Teile per Luftfracht zu schicken.
6. Wir möchten Ihnen vorschlagen, die Sache mit der Geschäftsleitung zu besprechen.
7. Wir wären Ihnen für eine ausführliche Beschreibung sehr dankbar.
8. Ich würde vorschlagen, ein Taxi zu nehmen.
9. Wir freuen uns, Ihren Auftrag in Kürze zu erhalten.
10. Für diese Verzögerung bitten wir um Entschuldigung.

Language and grammar:
Typical mistakes in business correspondence

Wer diese Verben korrekt verwendet, vermeidet die häufigsten Fehler, die Deutschen beim Verfassen englischer Geschäftskorrespondenz unterlaufen.

suggest (vorschlagen)
We suggest **repeating** the test.
We suggest **that you (we) repeat** the test.
falsch: We suggest to repeat the test.

appreciate (schätzen, begrüßen, dankbar sein, anerkennen)
(a) We would appreciate **it** if you could assist us.
(**"it"** is absolutely necessary here!)
(b) We would appreciate **receiving** the unit as soon as possible.
falsch: We would appreciate to receive the unit as soon as possible.

apologize (sich entschuldigen)
We **apologize for** the delay.
falsch: We ~~excuse us~~ for the delay.

excuse (verzeihen, entschuldigen)
Please **excuse** the delay.
falsch: Please ~~apologize~~ the delay.

look forward to (entgegensehen, sich freuen auf)
We look forward to **hearing** from you soon.
falsch: We look forward to ~~hear~~ from you soon.

hope (hoffen)
We hope **to hear** from you soon.
falsch: We hope to ~~hearing~~ from you soon.

Communicating across cultures:
The tone of English business correspondence

What is considered polite differs in different cultures. For example, one-word answers such as "ja", "nein" are not impolite in German. If I say: "Sollen wir ins Kino gehen?", you could answer "Ja" in German. In English people would be more inclined to say "Yes, that would be nice / great". Thus, German business correspondence tends to be factual and to the point. Polite phrases are often considered superfluous. While this abrupt tone is generally accepted in Germany, it may seem rude to English-speaking people or sound as though you are not interested. That is why you ought to aim to make frequent use of expressions like: **We would like to** (inform you); **I would be grateful** (if you could help me), **I am afraid** (the system is not running smoothly); **We are very sorry** (to inform you); **Would you be so kind as** (to inform us in time) in your English correspondence. Do not forget to insert the word **please** whenever you make a request, e.g.: If we can be of further assistance **please** do not hesitate to contact us.
Note: Please do not say: ~~We kindly ask you~~ …, say **We would like to ask you** … instead.

Logistics expert

1 A missing transport document

1
KMK **Robert Menz arbeitet in der Abteilung Seefracht von Rauch Transporte in Bad Hersfeld. Beim Abrufen seines E-Mail-Accounts findet er folgende E-Mail vor.**

From:	PakKairi@TransAsianBusan.com		
To:	IntDep@Rauchtrans.de	**Cc:**	
Sent:	201_-08-14 12:08	**Attachments:**	
Subject:	Delay consignment #584/040		

Dear Rauch Transporte
Unable to collect your above-mentioned consignment as customs authorities in Busan want certificate of origin which was not enclosed in the documentation. Please send missing document by return, if possible in Korean, as matter is urgent.
Kind regards
Pak Kairi
Operator Overseas Transactions

Beantworten Sie die E-Mail für Robert und verwenden Sie dabei folgende Angaben: `Phrases ▶`

- Bedanken Sie sich für die schnelle Information.
- Koreanische Fassung des Ursprungszeugnisses ist kurzfristig in Bad Hersfeld zu beschaffen.
- Dokument wird schnellstmöglich per Fax nach Busan übermittelt.
- Bitte um Angabe der Faxverbindung der örtlichen Zollbehörde.

2
P **Pak Kairi immediately sends Robert the fax number of the Busan Customs Office (+82 51 495999). After Robert has received the official Korean version of the certificate of origin, he has to send a fax to the customs office. Write the fax for him using the following information:** `Phrases ▶`

- use a reference line
- apologize for the missing certificate of origin
- a copy of the document is attached on page 2
- the original will be sent the same day by air mail
- use a polite closing phrase

Many East Asian names consist of the family name, followed by the given name. Generally, given names are used by family members and close friends. In Korea, for example, lots of people are named Kim, Lee, Choi or Pak. To manage the problem of having many people with identical family names, titles connected with profession, place of work and rank are often used. In large companies, staff are distinguished by their title (e.g. supervisor, manager) plus their department.

2 Solving transport problems

1 Sie arbeiten für die Spedition Transporte Leipzig und erhalten folgende E-Mail
KMK von der Firma Forlogistics in London.

From:	harry.dunhill@forlogistics.co.uk
To:	(your name)@transporteleipzig.com
Sent:	201_-07-10 15:22
Subject:	Incomplete delivery, HD6F 5686/3

Dear …
This morning we were supposed to collect six pallets for you with bathroom equipment from Felixstowe port. The consignment number is HDGF 5686/3, the consignor is Werner Grühe GmbH in Magdeburg and the pallets were to be delivered to Your Bath Ltd. in Birmingham, UK.
On unloading, we found that one pallet was missing. The question now is whether we should deliver the incomplete consignment or wait for the missing pallet? Please find out about the lost pallet as soon as possible so that we can instruct our driver without detention charges being incurred.
Thank you in advance for a quick response.
Regards
Harry

Sie setzten sich sofort mit dem Ladebüro in Bremerhaven in Verbindung und beantworten Harrys Mail unter Berücksichtigung der folgenden Angaben: `Phrases >`

- Sie haben den Fehler gefunden: Beim Verstauen in den Container in Bremerhaven sind die Waren aus Platzgründen von sechs auf fünf Paletten umgepackt worden; das ist aber in den Lieferpapieren nicht geändert worden.
- Die Sendung ist demnach vollständig und kann ausgeliefert werden.
- Ist die Sendung trotzdem pünktlich zustellbar? Es handelt sich um Terminfracht; ansonsten müssten Sie den Empfänger benachrichtigen.

2 Harry asks the lorry driver to change his tour so that the consignment will arrive
P on time in Birmingham. Then he sends an e-mail to Forlogistics, explaining the arrangement and assuring them of a punctual delivery. Write the e-mail for him. `Phrases >`

Phrases: Correspondence – E-mail, Letter, Fax

To refer to previous communication

Thank you very much for your letter **of** …	Wir danken Ihnen für Ihren Brief vom …
Many thanks for your e-mail/e-mail.	Vielen Dank für Ihre E-Mail.
We refer to your fax **of** …	Wir nehmen Bezug auf Ihr Fax vom …
Further to our discussion **on** 2 May …	Im Anschluss an unser Gespräch am 2. Mai …

To ask for something

Please let us have …	Wir bitten Sie um …
Would you please send us …	Bitte schicken Sie uns …
Please be so kind **as** to send us …	Wir bitten Sie höflich uns … zu schicken.
We **would** like to ask you for …	Wir möchten Sie um … bitten.
Please make sure that …	Bitte sorgen Sie dafür, dass …

To communicate good news

We are pleased to inform you that …	Wir freuen uns Ihnen mitteilen zu können, dass …
You will be pleased to hear that …	Sie werden sich bestimmt darüber freuen, dass …
It is particularly gratifying that …	Besonders erfreulich ist, dass …

To refuse something

I'm afraid I cannot agree **to** this proposal.	Leider muss ich diesen Vorschlag ablehnen.
I'm afraid that sounds quite unacceptable **to** us.	Das ist für uns leider völlig inakzeptabel.
Much as we regret it, we have to say no.	Zu unserem großen Bedauern müssen wir eine abschlägige Antwort geben.
We regret that we are unable to assist you.	Wir bedauern, Ihnen nicht behilflich sein zu können.

To apologize

We are very sorry but …	Es tut uns sehr leid, aber …
We **would** like to apologize for the delay.	Wir möchten uns für die Verspätung entschuldigen.

Please accept our apologies for this.	Wir entschuldigen uns dafür.
Please excuse the mix-up.	Bitte entschuldigen Sie die Verwechslung.

To make a suggestion

We would suggest that you send us a copy.	Wir schlagen Ihnen vor, uns eine Kopie zu schicken.
May we suggest that you inform the supplier.	Wir möchten vorschlagen, den Lieferanten zu benachrichtigen.
It would be advisable to send the details **by** fax.	Es wäre gut, wenn Sie uns die näheren Angaben faxen könnten.

To request that something is done by a certain date

We need the components **by** Friday **at** the very latest.	Wir benötigen die Teile spätestens Freitag.
Please make sure that they arrive **no** later **than** the end of April.	Bitte sorgen Sie dafür, dass sie spätestens Ende April ankommen.
Monday, 31 July, is the final deadline.	Montag, der 31. Juli, ist der letzte Termin.

To end a correspondence on a friendly note

We **look forward to hearing** from you.	Wir sehen Ihrer Antwort mit Interesse entgegen.
We **hope to hear** from you soon.	Wir hoffen, bald von Ihnen zu hören.
We look forward to a long and fruitful business relationship.	Wir freuen uns auf lange und lohnende Geschäftsbeziehungen mit Ihrer Firma.
We look forward to serving you again.	Wir freuen uns darauf, Ihnen wieder zu Diensten sein zu können.
We look forward to welcoming you as our customers.	Wir würden Sie gerne als neuen Kunden begrüßen.
We hope this proposal will be of interest **to** you.	Wir hoffen, dieser Vorschlag findet Ihr Interesse.
We hope this information **will** help you.	Wir hoffen, dass diese Auskunft hilfreich für Sie ist.
Thank you for your assistance.	Wir danken Ihnen für Ihre Bemühungen.

Unit 9
Enquiries

Business transactions often start with enquiries. **General enquiries** are requests for brochures, pricelists etc. and for information about business terms. **Specific enquiries** give particulars about the goods/ services requested and ask for detailed **quotations**.

The internet is now the most convenient way of locating possible suppliers and this is facilitated by the use of search engines. Traditional sources of information, such as chambers of commerce, yellow pages and trade associations have their own websites offering links to many potential suppliers. Trade fairs and exhibitions, visits by agents and advertising campaigns also provide information on new products.

Read the text above and translate the German sentences into English.

M

1. Die Suche nach Lieferanten im Internet wird durch Suchmaschinen sehr erleichtert.
2. Industrie- und Handelskammern, Gelbe Seiten und Branchenverbände geben auch über das Internet Auskunft.
3. Auch auf Messen und Ausstellungen sowie durch Werbekampagnen und den Besuch eines Vertreters werden neue Produkte bekannt gemacht.

Online-Link
808264-0009

A   Enquiries in writing

Sarah Brookfield, purchasing manager at SPORTS ISLAND, a British sports equipment chain, is interested in the latest running shoes presented by Herkules, the German manufacturers, on their website. She decides to make further enquiries by e-mail.

1 Study Sarah's e-mail enquiry and say which of the prepositions in brackets are
R   correct.

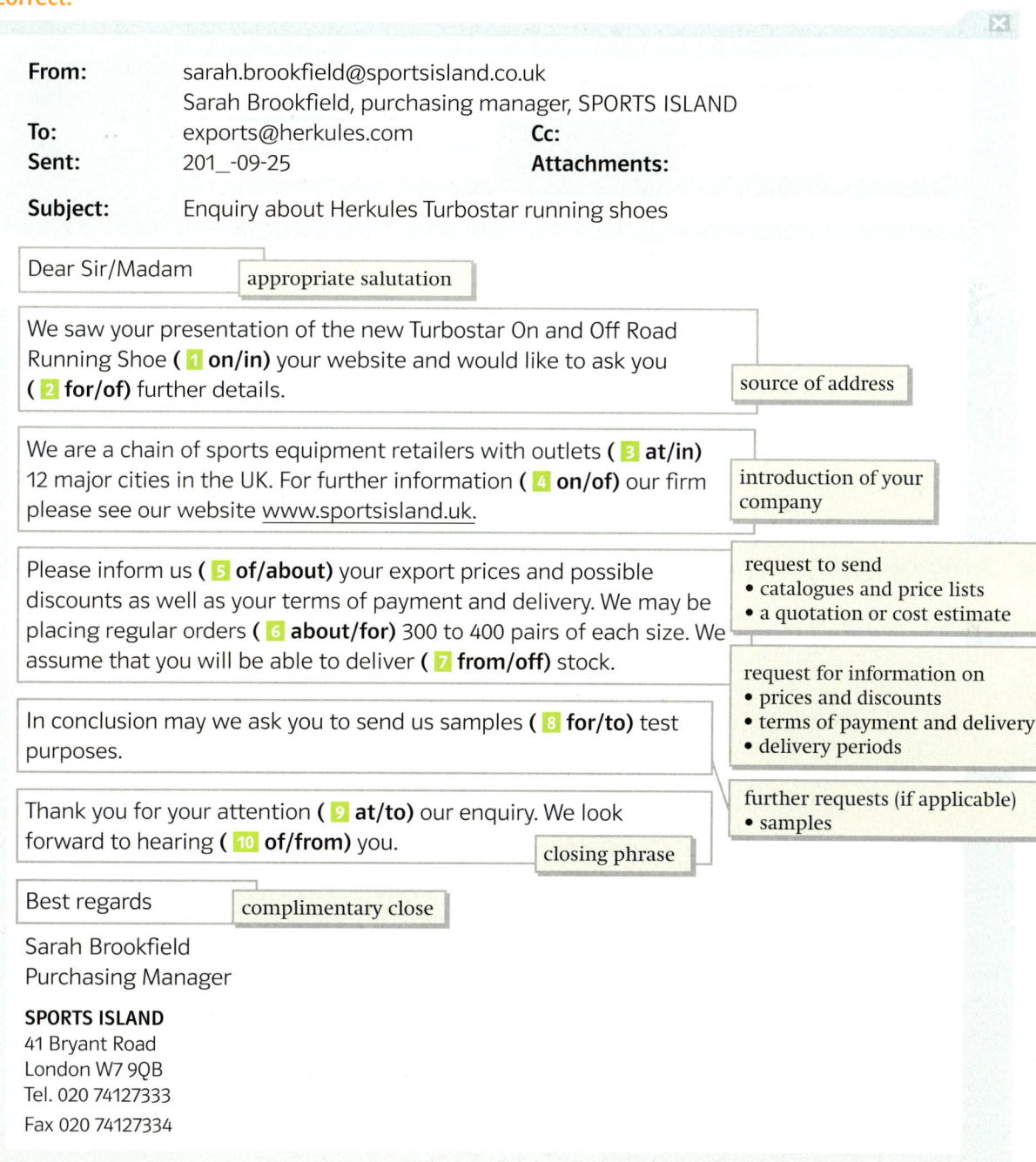

From:	sarah.brookfield@sportsisland.co.uk
	Sarah Brookfield, purchasing manager, SPORTS ISLAND
To:	exports@herkules.com **Cc:**
Sent:	201_-09-25 **Attachments:**
Subject:	Enquiry about Herkules Turbostar running shoes

Dear Sir/Madam   *appropriate salutation*

We saw your presentation of the new Turbostar On and Off Road Running Shoe (**1** on/in) your website and would like to ask you (**2** for/of) further details.   *source of address*

We are a chain of sports equipment retailers with outlets (**3** at/in) 12 major cities in the UK. For further information (**4** on/of) our firm please see our website www.sportsisland.uk.   *introduction of your company*

Please inform us (**5** of/about) your export prices and possible discounts as well as your terms of payment and delivery. We may be placing regular orders (**6** about/for) 300 to 400 pairs of each size. We assume that you will be able to deliver (**7** from/off) stock.

request to send
• *catalogues and price lists*
• *a quotation or cost estimate*

request for information on
• *prices and discounts*
• *terms of payment and delivery*
• *delivery periods*

In conclusion may we ask you to send us samples (**8** for/to) test purposes.

further requests (if applicable)
• *samples*

Thank you for your attention (**9** at/to) our enquiry. We look forward to hearing (**10** of/from) you.   *closing phrase*

Best regards   *complimentary close*

Sarah Brookfield
Purchasing Manager

SPORTS ISLAND
41 Bryant Road
London W7 9QB
Tel. 020 74127333
Fax 020 74127334

2 Cover up Sarah Brookfield's e-mail and complete these sentences on your own
R/P sheet of paper.

1. Sarah Brookfield saw a presentation of …
2. SPORTS ISLAND is a …
3. They would like to be informed about …
4. Their regular orders might comprise …
5. For test purposes they would like to have …
6. They look forward to …

3 Restore the correct order of these jumbled elements and rewrite the
R/P correspondence on your own sheet of paper.

1 We look forward to your early reply.

2 Please send us your price list and information on quantity discounts, terms of payment and delivery and indicate your shortest delivery time.

3 Subject: Topsweets Mint Bars

4 We are a German wholesaler specialising in confectionery for young people and are very interested in your Mint Bars as there is a rapidly growing market for British-type sweets here in Germany.

5 Yours sincerely
Zuckermann & Sacher GmbH

Dieter Sacher

6 We would appreciate it if you could send us samples for test purposes.

7 Dear Topsweets Ltd

8 We would then place a trial order. If the mint bars sell well, we expect to place regular orders in future.

9 We saw the advertisement for your Topsweets Mint Bars in the March issue of the International Confectionery Journal and our general manager tasted them at a reception in the British Embassy in Berlin.

4 Copy the e-mail form below. Use the above correspondence and the phrases at
P the end of the unit and write a detailed e-mail enquiry about the new innovative generation of tablet PCs. You saw their advertisement in the computer journal "IT.COM!". Address your e-mail to IT.COM, ITcom@aol.com, using your own name and a company name of your choice. Use your imagination for any details you may need.

Phrases ▶

From:

To:

Sent:

Cc:

Attachments:

Subject:

5

KMK

Sie arbeiten bei Getränke König, Am Sprudelbach 17, 06122 Halle, Tel. 03 45 78 56 34, Fax 03 45 78 56 35 im Einkauf. Ihre Firma möchte ihren guten Kunden zu Weihnachten ein besonderes Geschenk machen. Ihre Chefin, Nicole Sachse, hat auf der Hompage des irischen Glasherstellers Wexford Crystal plc, 1 Wexford Avenue, Sanditon, County Cork, Republic of Ireland, farbige Kristallgläser für Long Drinks im Geschenkkarton zu je drei Stück gesehen.

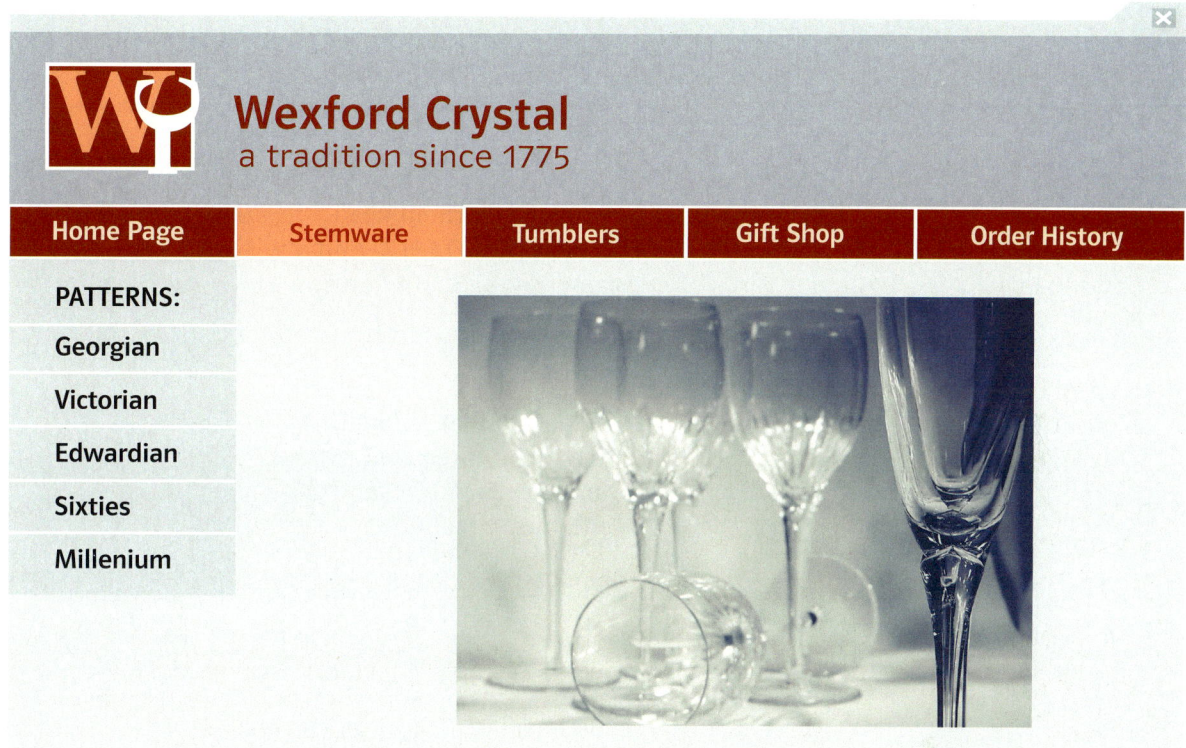

Sie bittet Sie eine Anfrage, die sie selbst unterschreiben wird, zu verfassen und dabei folgende Punkte zu berücksichtigen:

Phrases ▶

- Datum 1. September
- Betreff
- Bezug auf Internetseiten von Wexford Crystal
- Vorstellung Ihrer Firma als einer führenden Getränkegroßhandlung, Firmenbroschüre liegt bei
- Grund Ihrer Anfrage
- Bitte um Zusendung von Prospekten und Preislisten
- Bitte um Angabe der Lieferzeit
- Bitte um Angabe der Liefer- und Zahlungsbedingungen
- Sonderwunsch: nur je zwei Gläser pro Geschenkpackung
- Umfang eines möglichen Auftrags: 3 000 Sets
- Bitte um baldige Antwort
- Anlage: Firmenbroschüre

6 Your stressed out boss, a Canadian, feels he is in desperate need of a wellness holiday on a Caribbean island. Check out wellness holidays on the Caribbean Commonwealth island of Santa (or Saint) Lucia and make notes for him in English. Your boss is very demanding and only the best is good enough for him.

B Enquiries by phone

1 Restore the order of this jumbled dialogue. Match the numbers with the letters.

1. Calendars 4 U. Michael Bennet speaking. How can I help you?

2. Certainly. Please let me have your address.

3. Thank you. I'll post it today.

4. Yes of course. And full details of our generous discounts for volume orders.

5. My pleasure. Thank you for calling.

a. That's good. Thank you.

b. It's 30, Netherfield Road, Winchester SO2 9LZ. And my name is Jonathan Denny.

c. I take it the brochure contains a price list?

d. Hello. My name is Jonathan Denny. I'm interested in your animal calendars. Could you send me a brochure?

e. Goodbye.

2 Listen to the dialogue and check your work.

R

◎ A 1.22

◎ V 4 **Video lounge** General enquiries

This video shows an enquiry by telephone. Look out for the answers to the following questions:

1. Compare the appearance of the two women. Which do you find more appropriately/appealingly dressed?
2. What seems to be the secretary's main activity apart from answering the phone?
3. What is Purple Fashion enquiring about?
4. What kind of order does she wish to place first?
5. What discount does the manufacturer offer her? What discount does she want?
6. What is the final discount offered?
7. What is the total amount of the invoice?
8. How long does delivery take?

3 Working with a partner now create and act out a similar dialogue along the
I/P following lines.

Phrases ▶

A

Linda/Larry Lawson from the British language school Business Speak in Brighton gets a call.

Linda/Larry Lawson offers to send a detailed brochure and asks for the caller's address.

Linda/Larry Lawson promises to send the brochure by post the next morning and thanks the caller for his/her interest in their courses. He/she adds that he/she is convinced that the caller will find the appropriate course.

B

The caller introduces him/herself as Stefan/Stefanie Merz from Rostock, Germany. He/she is interested in crash courses in business English in the summer.

Stefan/Stefanie Merz spells his/her name and address, Ostseeallee 27, 66123 Rostock, Germany.

Stefan/Stefanie Merz thanks Linda/ Larry Lawson and says Good-bye.

✳ 4 Work with a partner, sit back to back and act out the following telephone
I conversation with the help of the role cards.

Phrases ▶

Role card: Partner A   **Role card partner B ⇨ page 256**

Torsten/Tanja Kirchner, Auszubildende/r bei Hammer Werkzeughandel, Remscheid, ruft auf Bitten des Chefs bei Powertools plc, Cardiff, UK, an. Torsten/Tanja bittet um Auskunft über die Werkzeugsätze für Heimwerker (household tool kits) von Powertools.
Die E-Mail-Adresse lautet: imports@hammerwerkzeughandel.de. Vor allem möchte man Näheres über Lieferzeiten und Mengenrabatte erfahren.
Torsten/Tanja beendet das Gespräch und dankt für die Bemühungen.

Info: Discounts

Granting discounts is an effective means of winning new or retaining old customers.
Trade discounts are granted to retailers.
Introductory discounts are granted to facilitate the introduction of new products or services.
Quantity discounts are granted for volume orders.
Early order discounts are granted for bookings/purchases made well in advance.
Cash discount is granted for early payment.

5 Copy the sentences and complete them on your own sheet of paper, inserting the
R appropriate type of discount.

1. In view of the size of your order we are prepared to grant you a **1** of 15%.
2. We are prepared to launch your new product on the Greek market, if you
   grant us a substantial **2**.
3. For payment within 7 days we grant 2% **3**.
4. Only registered businesses qualify for a **4**.
5. On bookings made 3 months in advance you will be granted 10% **5**.

6 Work with a partner. Partner A wishes to place an order with partner B, provided
I he/she is granted a discount. Use the ideas from the grid below to negotiate the
granting of a discount. Then change roles.

Phrases

Example:

A

B

I'd be quite willing to introduce your new software package CP36-97 to the German market. But I'm afraid that won't be so easy. There are a lot of competing programs. That's why I'd have to offer customers at least a 20% introductory discount.

Well, actually the package isn't exactly new. It's just an updated version of the previous one. So there isn't any real reason for granting an introductory discount.

I'm afraid we will have to offer **some** incentive to our customers. What would you say to 10% introductory discount?

I'd have to get back to my boss for that. I'll let you know in a few minutes.

Order for	Discount requested	Arguments	
		for	against
Hotel room for 3 nights	20% early order discount	booking made 2 months in advance	granted on bookings made 3 months in advance
200 Topsweets Mint Bars	30% trade discount	buyer is a retailer, has a small shop	quantity too small, trade discount only for business-size volumes
50 CD/radio/cassette stereo players	3% cash discount	payment made within 10 days	normally only 2%
75 kgs of Norwegian Smoked Salmon	5% quantity discount	price high compared to competitors' prices	quantity discounts start at 100 kgs.

Language and grammar
Copy the sentences and fill in the correct form, either the adjective or the adverb, and underline the word the adjective or adverb refers to.

Example:
(clear) We wish to point out **1** that this is the deadline.
We <u>wish to point out</u> *clearly* that this is the deadline.

(prompt) We would be grateful for a **2** reply.
(prompt) Thank you for replying **3** to our inquiry.
(strict) This information is given in **4** confidence.
(relative) This is a **5** minor problem.
(immediate) We must insist on **6** delivery.
(immediate) Please contact our representative **7**.
(comparative) Last year they placed **8** small orders with us.
(high) We are **9** dissatisfied with your services.
(fair) Their customers receive updates **10** regularly.
(considerable) Prices have increased **11** in the last few months.
(considerable) They have **12** funds at their disposal.
(approximate) What is the **13** arrival date of the vessel?
(approximate) We have received **14** seventy enquiries.
(definite) This car is **15** too small for me.
(definite) We will let you have our **16** decision by Wednesday.

Language and grammar: Adjectives and adverbs

Mit Adjektiven werden Substantive und das Verb "to be" näher bestimmt.

We expect to place **regular orders** in future.
"regular" ist ein Adjektiv und kennzeichnet das Substantiv "orders".

We **will be glad** to receive information on your discounts.
"glad" ist ein Adjektiv und gehört zu "will be", einer Form von "to be".

Mit Adverbien (adjective +ly) werden Verben, Adjektive und Adverbien näher bestimmt.

We assure you that your order **will be executed promptly**.
"promptly" ist ein Adverb und kennzeichnet das Verb "to execute".

There is a **rapidly growing** market for British sweets in Germany.
"rapidly" ist ein Adverb und kennzeichnet das Adjektiv "growing".

There is an **extremely rapidly** growing market for British sweets in Germany.
"extremely" ist ein Adverb und kennzeichnet das Adverb "rapidly".

Logistics expert

Dealing with transport enquiries

Oral or written customer communication is a crucial part of a forwarder's everyday routine. The foundation of every business partnership is the first contact, which often takes the form of an initial enquiry. The way you deal with this may not only influence your chances of success, it is also an opportunity to maximise your potential by presenting your company in the best possible light.

1 Do you agree with the statement that the good reputation of a company is a
P crucial element of its success? Give reasons for your opinion.

2 In order to submit an offer, a forwarder needs detailed information on the
P shipment. Rearrange the letters so that they make up elements of an enquiry.
Then add three more terms.

1. C E E G I N N O S
2. C E I M N O R S T
3. A I N Q T T U Y
4. A D E I I N N O S T T
5. A E E E M M N R S T U

3 Spedition GoGlobal, a Fulda-based forwarding agency, has been asked by
P Wehrmeyer & Co. in Hanover (Germany) to organise the transport of a waterslide
to an exhibition that will be held in Orlando (USA). How does such a transport
differ from normal import / export procedures? Discuss this in class, taking the
following aspects into consideration.

1. quantity of goods
2. punctuality
3. importance

Info: ATA Carnets

A carnet is a document allowing the temporary importation of certain goods without paying customs duty. Carnets for the Temporary Admission of Goods (ATA) make the importation of commercial samples, professional equipment and items for exhibitions and fairs easier. They simplify customs procedures as only a single document is needed for all customs transactions. Carnets cover virtually all goods, except consumable or disposable products (e.g. food).

4 Lisa Bechmann von der Spedition GoGlobal kontaktiert ihren amerikanischen
KMK Partner wegen der Anfrage von Wehrmeyer & Co. Hören Sie sich das Gespräch an
◇ A 2.10 und notieren Sie die wichtigsten Angaben auf Deutsch.

```
TELEFONNOTIZ

Nachricht aufgenommen von: Lisa Bechmann

Gesprächspartner:                    Firma:

Anliegen:
```

5 Shortly afterwards, Lisa Bechmann receives the following e-mail. Rewrite it using
P full words instead of the abbreviated forms.

From:	Howard Stone [mailto: h.stone@globaltransport.com]
To:	Lisa.Bechmann@goglobal.de
Sent:	Friday, August 27, 201_ 4:31 PM
Subject:	Orlando / Exhibition

Hello Lisa,

Tnx for yr call. Need acc addr of cnee in Orl., pls. We'll need approx 3ds for carnet clnce.
Can you pls adv if 3.00 is L/H/W?
B. rgds
Howard

6 Beantworten Sie Howards E-Mail für Lisa und berücksichtigen Sie dabei Folgendes: Phrases ▷
KMK
• Bedanken Sie sich für die schnelle Bearbeitung.
• Sie schicken die Empfängeradresse im angehängten Dokument.
• Machen Sie die Zusage für einen rechtzeitigen Flug zu sorgen.
• Die Länge der Wasserrutschbahnteile beträgt 3 m.
• Bitten Sie um baldige Zusendung eines Angebots.
• Finden Sie einen angemessenen Schlusssatz.

7 The original enquiry by Wehrmeyer & Co. has to be attached to this e-mail.
M Translate the following part of the enquiry into English.

Anfrage: Warentransport nach Orlando, USA
Wir nehmen am 2. November dieses Jahres an einer Messe in Orlando teil und möchten dafür
das Modell einer Wasserrutsche von unserem Werk in Hannover zum Ausstellungsgelände
versenden. Die Rutsche wird von uns zerlegt und in eine Kiste mit den Maßen 3 m × 1,8 m ×
1,8 m verpackt. Das Gesamtgewicht liegt bei ca. 850 kg. Die Sendung muss spätestens zwei Tage
vor Messebeginn vor Ort sein. Bitte unterbreiten Sie uns schnellstmöglich ein Angebot.

Phrases: Enquiries

To mention the source of address

We saw your advertisement for laser printers in the October issue of PC World.	Wir haben Ihre Anzeige für Laserdrucker im Oktoberheft der Zeitschrift PC World gesehen.
We have obtained your address **from** the Anglo-German Chamber of Commerce.	Wir erhielten Ihre Anschrift von der Deutsch-Britischen Handelskammer.
Your services have been recommended to us **by** a business partner, …	Ihre Dienstleistungen wurden uns von einem Geschäftspartner empfohlen, …
We have visited your website and …	Wir haben Ihre Webseite angeklickt und …

To introduce your company

We are a young and rapidly growing firm **specialising** in …	Wir sind ein junges, rasch wachsendes Unternehmen und sind auf … spezialisiert.
We are well-established manufacturers **of** …	Wir sind ein gut eingeführter Hersteller von …
Our firm is a leading importer of tools with excellent contacts **all over** the EU.	Unsere Firma ist ein führender Importeur von Werkzeugen mit ausgezeichneten Kontakten in der gesamten EU.

To say what you require

We are interested in …	Wir interessieren uns für …
Could you please let us have a brochure and a price list **for** the services you offer.	Wir bitten um einen Prospekt und eine Preisliste für die von Ihnen angebotenen Dienstleistungen.
Please enclose a catalogue **of** your latest products.	Bitte fügen Sie einen Katalog für Ihre neuesten Produkte bei.
Please send us a quotation **for** …	Bitte machen Sie uns ein (Preis-)Angebot über …
We would be grateful for a cost estimate **for** …	Für einen Kostenvoranschlag für … wären wir dankbar.
Please quote your lowest prices for …	Bitte nennen Sie uns Ihre günstigsten Preise für …
We need a further shipment **of** …	Wir benötigen eine weitere Lieferung …

We would be grateful for information **on** your terms of payment and delivery.	Wir bitten um nähere Angaben zu Ihren Liefer- und Zahlungsbedingungen.

Do you grant any quantity discounts?
    ... any early order discount?
    ... trade discount?
    ... introductory discount?
    ... cash discount?

Gewähren Sie Mengenrabatt?
    ... Frühbucherrabatt?
    ... Wiederverkaufsrabatt?
    ... Einführungsrabatt?
    ... Skonto?

Can you deliver ex stock?

Können Sie ab Lager liefern?

Please state your earliest delivery date.

Bitte geben Sie uns Ihr frühestes Lieferdatum an.

What is the minimum quantity **for** a trial order?

Was ist die Mindestmenge für einen Probeauftrag?

We would welcome a presentation of your services on our premises.

Wir wären dankbar für eine Präsentation Ihrer Dienstleistungen in unseren Geschäftsräumen.

A visit **by** your representative would be appreciated.

Wir wären dankbar für einen Besuch Ihres Vertreters.

We look forward to hearing from you soon.

Wir freuen uns darauf, bald wieder von Ihnen zu hören.

If your prices are competitive, we may be able to place substantial orders in future.

Wenn Ihre Preise konkurrenzfähig sind, werden wir Ihnen bald größere Aufträge erteilen können.

If the goods **meet with** our customers' approval, your products should sell well in this market.

Wenn die Ware unseren Kunden zusagt, dürften sich Ihre Erzeugnisse auf unserem Markt gut verkaufen lassen.

We hope to hear from you shortly.

Wir hoffen, bald wieder von Ihnen zu hören.

Unit 10
Offers

WORD BANK

offer • quotation • cost estimate • catalogue • brochure • price list • stock • sample • terms of delivery • INCOTERMS • terms of payment • options • solicited • unsolicited • valid • to offer • to quote • to process • to enclose • to attach

Offers are sent either in reply to an enquiry **(solicited offers)** or on the seller's own initiative in the form of sales communications to individuals or companies likely to be interested in the goods or services offered **(unsolicited offers)**. Detailed, specific offers are often called **quotations**. Offers for work to be done take the form of **cost estimates**.

By making an offer the seller declares his willingness to sell certain goods or perform certain services at a certain price and on certain terms.

Offers are binding on the person or firm making the offer unless it is expressly stated in the offer that

- the prices are subject to change without notice or that the offer is either
- without engagement or
- valid until a certain date or
- valid as long as stocks last.

Note that all enquiries should be answered, even those for goods or services your firm does not provide. Where possible, recommend an alternative supplier.

140

Online-Link
808264-0010

1 Study the text on offers on page 140 and match the expressions on the left with their German equivalents on the right.

1.	solicited offer	a.	freibleibend
2.	unsolicited offer	b.	gültig bis 31. Mai
3.	without engagement	c.	Preisänderungen vorbehalten
4.	valid until 31 May	d.	Kostenvoranschlag
5.	as long as stocks last	e.	solange Vorrat reicht
6.	prices are subject to change without notice	f.	unverlangtes Angebot
7.	cost estimate	g.	verlangtes Angebot

2 Übertragen Sie folgende Sätze ins Englische.

KMK

1. Ein verlangtes Angebot wird als Reaktion auf eine Anfrage abgegeben.
2. Viele Firmen schicken unverlangte Angebote an mögliche Interessenten für ihre Produkte.
3. Ein Kostenvoranschlag ist ein Angebot für eine Arbeit, die ausgeführt werden soll.
4. Dieses Angebot ist freibleibend.
5. Unsere Preise gelten nur bis zum 31.07.201_.
6. Preisänderungen bleiben vorbehalten.
7. Solange der Vorrat reicht, bieten wir Ihnen wie folgt an: …

Info: Successful offers

Effective offers are decisive for the success of your business. When making an offer you should
- answer an enquiry promptly
- whenever possible personalise the salutation
- thank the enquirer for his interest in your goods or services
- if you cannot provide all the information right away let the prospective customer know that his enquiry will be processed as soon as possible
- be as helpful and polite as possible
- give all the information required
- provide additional information that might be useful
- refrain from making promises you cannot keep
- say something positive about your firm and / or your products
- conclude your offer with a phrase designed to make the customer feel positive towards your firm

---

3 Work in pairs. Close the book. Write down as many of the above recommendations as you remember. Then compare your list with your neighbour's list.

P

A   Offers in writing

In reply to her enquiry about running shoes Sarah Brookfield from SPORTS ISLAND has received the following e-mail offer from Herkules.

1   Study the e-mail offer and find the missing nouns from the box.

R

attachment • business • delivery period • discount • enquiry • orders • position • sample • stock

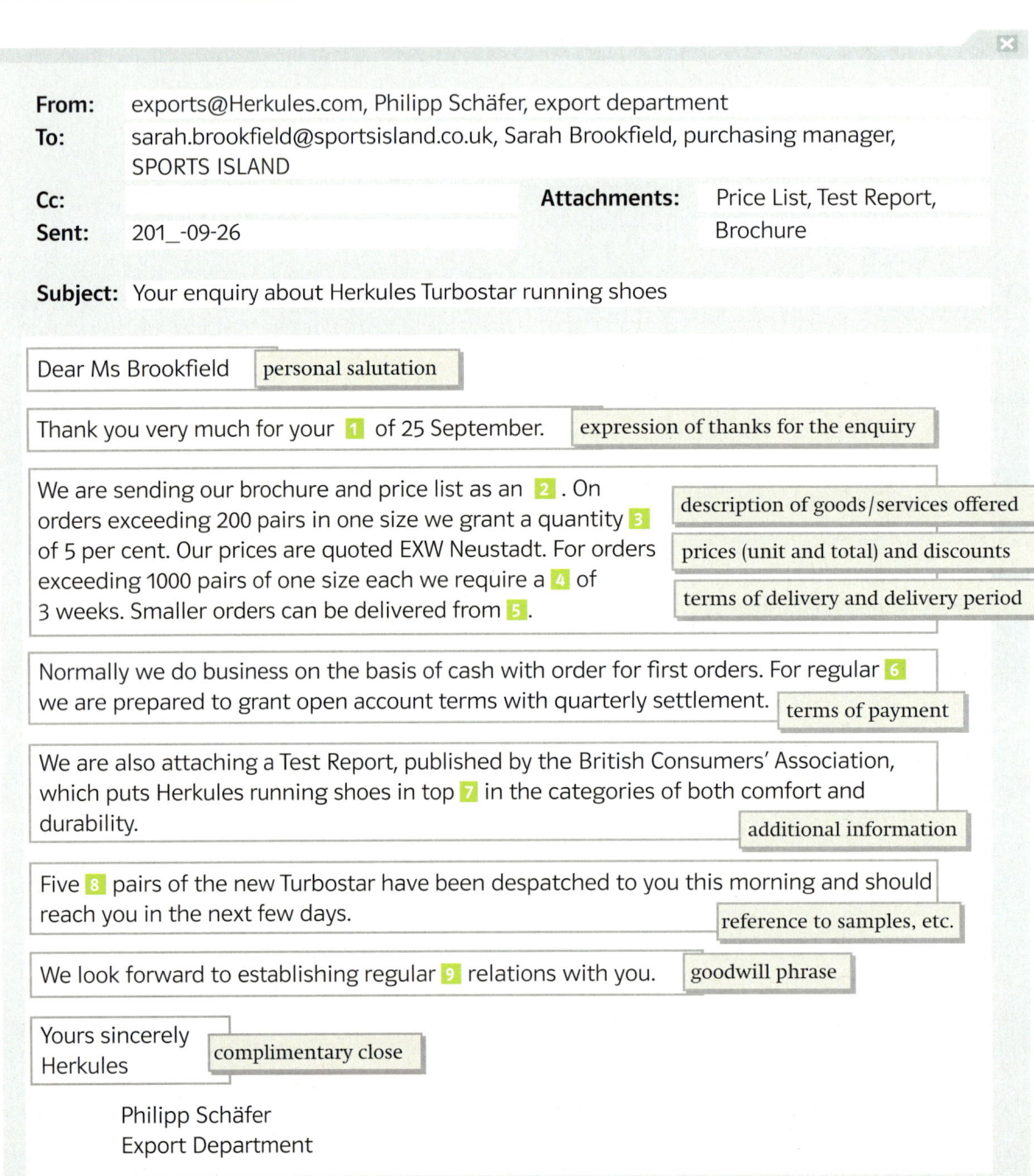

From: exports@Herkules.com, Philipp Schäfer, export department

To: sarah.brookfield@sportsisland.co.uk, Sarah Brookfield, purchasing manager, SPORTS ISLAND

Cc: **Attachments:**   Price List, Test Report, Brochure

Sent: 201_-09-26

Subject: Your enquiry about Herkules Turbostar running shoes

Dear Ms Brookfield | personal salutation

Thank you very much for your **1** of 25 September. | expression of thanks for the enquiry

We are sending our brochure and price list as an **2** . On orders exceeding 200 pairs in one size we grant a quantity **3** of 5 per cent. Our prices are quoted EXW Neustadt. For orders exceeding 1000 pairs of one size each we require a **4** of 3 weeks. Smaller orders can be delivered from **5** .

| description of goods/services offered
| prices (unit and total) and discounts
| terms of delivery and delivery period

Normally we do business on the basis of cash with order for first orders. For regular **6** we are prepared to grant open account terms with quarterly settlement. | terms of payment

We are also attaching a Test Report, published by the British Consumers' Association, which puts Herkules running shoes in top **7** in the categories of both comfort and durability. | additional information

Five **8** pairs of the new Turbostar have been despatched to you this morning and should reach you in the next few days. | reference to samples, etc.

We look forward to establishing regular **9** relations with you. | goodwill phrase

Yours sincerely
Herkules | complimentary close

Philipp Schäfer
Export Department

2

R/P

Restore the correct order of these jumbled elements and rewrite the correspondence on a piece of paper.

1 We look forward to welcoming you as our customers.

2 Topsweets Mint Bars

3 For first orders our terms of payment are cash with order. For regular customers our terms are 30 days net.

4 Our prices are quoted DAP to your premises. On orders for more than 100 kgs we grant 10 % discount. The mint bars can be delivered within 2–4 weeks from receipt of order, depending on the volume of the order.

5 We are pleased to send you enclosed our brochure describing our whole range of products and our special folder on Topsweets Mint Bars as well as our latest price list.

6 Dear Mr Sacher

7 To enable you to convince yourself of the superior taste of Topsweets Mint Bars we are sending you by separate post samples together with an assortment of our other products. We are sure that you will be delighted with our sweets that are very popular among discerning customers all over the world.

8 Encls. Brochure, folder, price list

9 Yours sincerely
Topsweets Ltd.

Martha Creams

10 Thank you very much for your recent enquiry.

3 You work in the export department of a German wholesaler for electronic
P   equipment. Your boss, Cornelia Klinkenberg, has received the following e-mail
enquiry. Reply to this enquiry taking your boss's notes into account.

Phrases ▶

From:	james.leigh@leigh.co.uk
To:	cornelia.klinkenberg@topelektronik.de
Cc:	
Sent:	201_-08-02 **Attachments:**
Subject:	SomeThing Mp3 Players

Dear Ms Klinkenberg

Please quote us your best prices for the following
SomeThing Mp3 players:

vorrätig, Stückpreis EURO 83,50

500 units   article No. 487-13, 8 GB,
with backlit LCD display

700 units   article No. 487-26, 16 GB 3D,
USB, extremely compact in size

*nur 400 vorrätig, Stückpreis EURO 32,80
Lieferzeit für die restlichen 300 Stück 6 Wochen
als Ersatz Artikel 487-15 vorschlagen, gleiches Modell,
aber Lebensdauer der Batterie 30 statt 24
Stunden, Stückpreis EURO 45,90*

300 units   article No. 487-45, 1.5 GB,
with SD-card slot

vorrätig, Stückpreis EURO 85,30

As the goods are urgently required for a new store to
be opened by the end of next month, we would ask
you to indicate your earliest date of delivery.

*20 % Mengenrabatt für gesamten
Auftrag einräumen*

*Versand kann drei Tage
nach Auftragseingang erfolgen*

We assume that the usual terms of payment and
delivery will apply.

richtig

Thank you for your prompt attention to our enquiry.

Yours sincerely

James Leigh
Leigh & Co. Ltd.
17 Camden Place
Bristol
BS6 6HR
Tel. 0117 4430030

bitte meinen Namen darunter setzen

Danke Klinkenberg

* 4
KMK Sie sind Susan/James Vernon und arbeiten im Verkauf bei Powertools plc, Snowdon Industrial Estate, Cardiff CA4 9ZB. Torsten/Tanja Kirchner von der Firma Hammer Werkzeughandel, Lehmkuhle 104, 42896 Remscheid, hat um eine schriftliche Bestätigung des Angebots gebeten, das Sie ihm/ihr heute früh telefonisch gemacht haben.

Verfassen Sie dieses Schreiben (in englischer Sprache) und berücksichtigen Sie dabei Folgendes:

- Datum von heute
- Betreff: Angebot Nr. TK/234
- Bezug auf Telefongespräch
- Angebot für 1000 Stück 9-teiliger Haushalts-Werkzeugsatz (9-piece household tool kit), Artikel Nr. HTK-9
- Listenpreis pro Stück: €4,99, FCA Cardiff, Incoterms 2010, einschließlich Verpackung, abzüglich 30% Händlerrabatt
- Gesamtpreis nach Abzug des Händlerrabatts: €3.493,00.
- Zahlungsbedingungen: innerhalb von 30 Tagen netto, innerhalb von 10 Tagen 2% Skonto (cash discount)
- Lieferzeit: 3 Wochen
- 2 Muster-Werkzeugsätze werden heute an Hammer Werkzeughandel zu Testzwecken geschickt
- Dank für das Interesse an den Produkten von Powertools plc
- Zusicherung sorgfältiger Ausführung des Auftrags

B Offers by phone

1 Edward Ferrars from Norland Industries in Southampton, Great Britain, gets a
R phone call from an overseas customer.
A1.23 **Read the statements first. Then listen to the dialogue and mark on your own
sheet of paper whether the statements are TRUE or FALSE.**

1. Tom De Boer is calling from South America.
2. He has no Norland colour printers left in his stock.
3. He wishes to order 200 units of the colour printer CP 150.
4. The terms of delivery are FOB Durban.
5. Last year's model CP 100 cost GBP 72.50.
6. There is increasing competition from Japan.
7. 30% trade discount will be granted on all future orders.
8. The customer asks for an offer in writing.

2 Copy Mr Ferrars' quotation and insert the missing expressions from the box.
R

from receipt of order • look forward to • pleased to • Referring to • within 30 days

---

Dear Mr De Boer

Norland Colour Printers CP 100 and 150 – Quotation no. CP-2024

1 your enquiry of 2 Feb. 201_ we are **2** inform you that we can quote as
follows

Quantity	Description	Unit Price	Total
500	Norland Colour Printer CP 100	GBP 75.50	GBP 37,750.00
200	Norland Colour Printer CP 150	GBP 85.20	GBP 17,040.00
			GBP 54,790.00
	less 30 % trade discount		GBP 16,437.00
TOTAL			**GBP 38,353.00**

Delivery: within four weeks **3** , CIF Durban.

Payment: net cash **4** from receipt of invoice.

We **5** receiving your order.

Yours sincerely
Edward Ferrars
Norland Industries

C Comparing options

1
KMK Ihre Firma plant, 5 Mitarbeiter aus dem Export für eine Woche zu einem Intensiv-Sprachkurs nach England zu schicken. Zwei Angebote wurden in die engere Wahl gezogen. Verschaffen Sie sich einen Überblick über diese beiden Angebote, indem Sie die Tabelle auf Seite 148 (kopieren und) in deutscher Sprache vervollständigen.

THE DORSET SCHOOL OF ENGLISH

The DORSET SCHOOL OF ENGLISH offers you a tailor-made study programme for your staff at any time you wish, except in August. Our offer includes a one-week intensive course, 6 hours of tuition a day (except Sundays), focussing on general business English and on specific export terminology.

Our language school is situated in Lyme Regis, the pearl of Dorset, a traditional seaside resort on the English Channel, made famous by the celebrated novelist Jane Austen.

Your staff will be placed with English business and professional families and there will never be another student of your native language in the same family.

The sports programme (tennis, swimming, surfing and sailing), which is free of charge, takes the learning experience outside the classroom.

Lyme Regis is rich in fossils. We offer fossil hunting trips as a special treat for our students.

Excursions to Exeter, Dartmoor and Bath can be booked at short notice.

Tuition fees: £400 per week
For more than 10 participants from one firm we offer a 15 % discount.
Accommodation and full board in host families: £490 per week.

Booking fee, to be paid when booking: £50. Full payment to be made 6 weeks before the course begins.

Contact: Brian Hill, THE DORSET SCHOOL OF ENGLISH, The Cobb, Lyme Regis, EX3 5AN

BUSINESS SPEAK

BUSINESS SPEAK is an international language school for business people, located in Brighton on the South Coast. Brighton is a vibrant seaside resort and conference centre, just one hour's train journey from London.

Our business English intensive courses which take place four times a year (September 2–8, October 14–20, February 10–16 and May 21–27) would suit your staff's needs admirably. These intensive courses consist of 5 hours of tuition in the mornings and four study visits to British firms in the afternoons.

Maximum number of participants: 8.

Our students live either at an exclusive private hotel or with carefully selected English host families.

We offer a wide range of sports activities, such as golf, riding, surfing, sailing and fishing. Equipment can be hired at a small charge.

Course fees: £480 per week
Accommodation and half board:
Private hotel: £90 per day
Host family: £450 per week

To confirm the booking a deposit of £75 per person must accompany the booking form. The balance is required no later than eight weeks before the course commencement date.

Please contact:
Mrs Pam Robinson • BUSINESS SPEAK • 120, Brunswick Square • Brighton • BN1 9PH

	Anbieter A	Anbieter B
Veranstalter	Dorset School of English	
Kursort		
Teilnehmerkreis und -zahl	speziell unsere Gruppe	
Schwerpunkt		
Unterrichtsstunden pro Tag		
Unterbringung		
Exkursionen		
Freizeitangebot		
Kurstermine		
Preis für Unterkunft und Verpflegung		
Kursgebühren		
Anzahlung		
Auskunft		

✳ **2** Make up your mind which of these two offers you would prefer to accept. Then write a short memo for your US parent company's personnel department, giving at least two reasons for your choice.

MEMO
From: (your own name)   Date:
To: Personnel Department, Headquarters USA
Subject: Intensive language course in the UK

3 Your boss has asked you to look up Business English courses in Poole / Bournemouth on the south coast of England. Make notes on two or three that seem suitable and write a memo in English giving names and important details.

D INCOTERMS® (Terms of delivery)

The Incoterms are a set of nationally and internationally accepted rules defining the obligations of the seller and the buyer as regards the tasks, costs and risks involved in the transport of goods. They were first drawn up by the International Chamber of Commerce in Paris in 1936 and were last updated in 2010.

The Incoterms 2010 are grouped in two categories:
- rules for any mode or modes of transport
- rules for sea and inland waterway transport

The Incoterms 2010 consist of 11 rules, two of which are new:
- DAT (Delivered at Terminal) replaces the former DEQ rule
- DAP (Delivered at Place) replaces the former rules DAF, DES and DDU

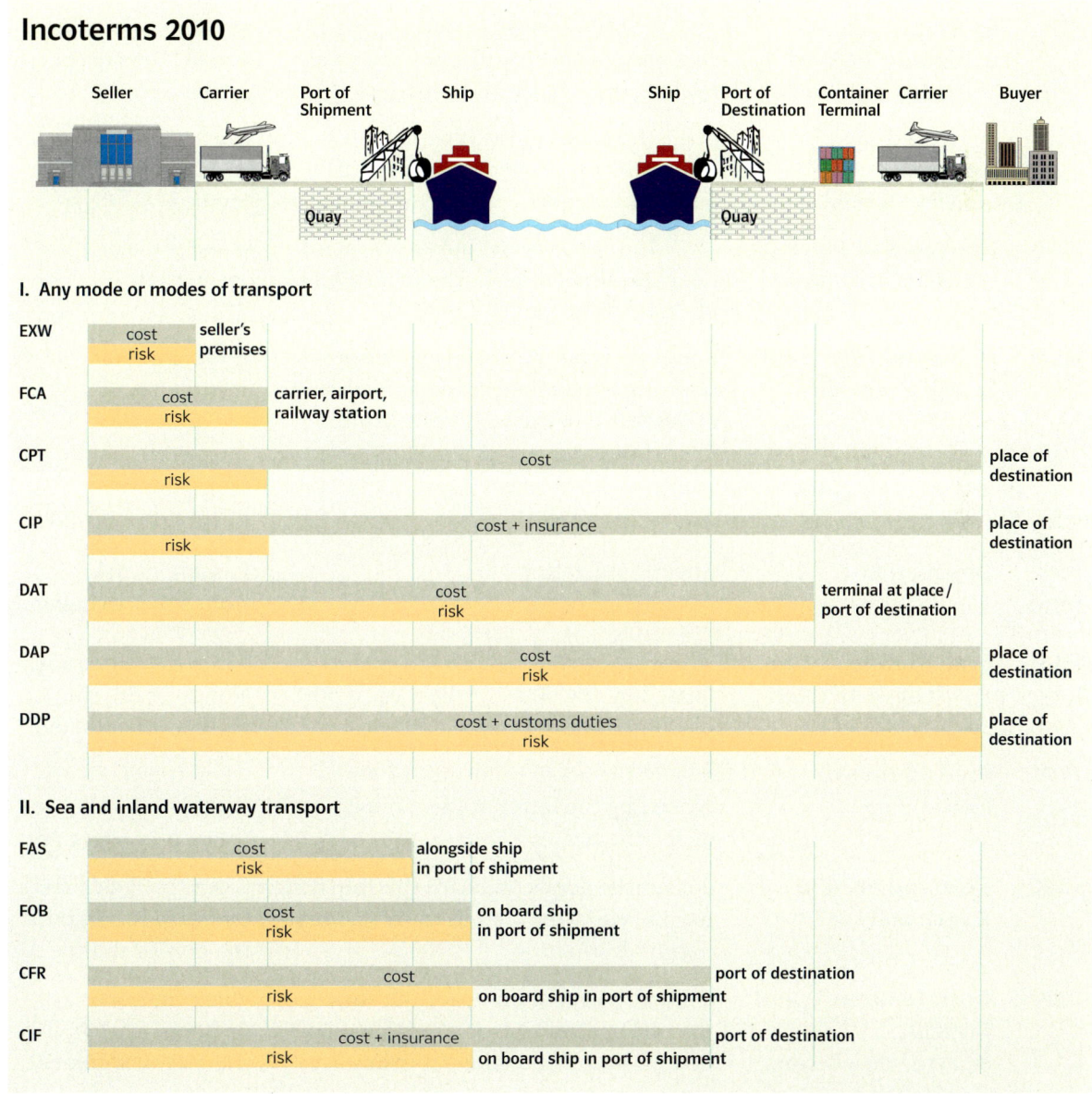

® International Chamber of Commerce, ICC

Rules for any mode or modes of transport

Incoterms® 2010

Inco-term	Designation	Seller's obligations	Passing of risk from seller to buyer
EXW	**Ex Works** Ab Werk	place the goods at the disposal of the buyer at the seller's premises (factory, warehouse etc.)	at the seller's premises
FCA	**Free Carrier** Frei Frachtführer	deliver the goods to the carrier named by the buyer	when the goods are handed over to the carrier
CPT	**Carriage Paid to** Frachtfrei	deliver the goods to the carrier and pay the cost of carriage to the named place of destination	when the goods are handed over to the carrier
CIP	**Carriage and Insurance Paid to** Frachtfrei versichert	deliver the goods to the carrier, pay the cost of carriage and take out insurance to the named place of destination	when the goods are handed over to the carrier
DAT	**Delivered at Terminal** Geliefert Terminal	place the goods at the buyer's disposal, unloaded, at a named terminal at a named place/port	when the goods have been unloaded at the terminal
DAP	**Delivered at Place** Geliefert benannter Ort	place the goods at the buyer's disposal, ready for unloading, at the named place of destination	at the place of destination
DDP	**Delivered Duty Paid** Geliefert verzollt	place the goods at the buyer's disposal, ready for unloading, at the named place of destination, carry out all customs formalities and pay import duty, if any	at the place of destination

Rules for sea and inland waterway transport

Incoterms® 2010

Inco-term	Designation	Seller's obligations	Passing of risk from seller to buyer
FAS	**Free Alongside Ship** Frei Längsseite Schiff	deliver the goods alongside the ship named by the buyer at the named port of shipment	when the goods are alongside the ship in the port of shipment
FOB	**Free on Board** Frei an Bord	deliver the goods on board the ship named by the buyer at the named port of shipment	when the goods are on board the ship in the port of shipment
CFR	**Cost and Freight** Kosten und Fracht	deliver the goods on board the ship and pay the costs and freight to the named port of destination	when the goods are on board the ship in the port of shipment
CIP	**Cost, Insurance and Freight** Kosten, Versicherung und Fracht	deliver the goods on board the ship; pay the costs and freight to the named port of destination and take out insurance for the transport	when the goods are on board the ship in the port of shipment

® International Chamber of Commerce, ICC

Under all clauses the seller must deliver the goods to the buyer at the named place and the buyer must take delivery of the goods *(Ware abnehmen)*. The seller must procure *(beschaffen)* or help to procure the transport documents and pack the goods, if customary *(handelsüblich)*.

Note that under the Incoterms CPT, CIP, CFR and CIF the seller bears the risks only up to the place of delivery, i.e. until the goods are handed over to the (first) carrier or have been loaded on board ship in the port of shipment. Under these terms the seller must, in addition, contract *(Vertrag abschließen)* and pay for the carriage to the place or port of destination.

1 **Read the business transactions and complete them with the right Incoterms.**
R

1. Jennings Food Ltd. has bought five colour printers from Norland Industries. Jennings Food's driver picks up the colour printers at Norland Industries' production plant. The printers have been sold on the basis of …?

2. Powertools plc, Cardiff, has received a large export order from a Brazilian customer. Powertools plc pays for the goods to be taken to the docks in Cardiff and for the loading on board the vessel "Southern Cross". The terms of delivery are …?

3. International Snacks GmbH, a German food processing company, usually delivers its snacks by lorry to Global Catering's premises in Manchester, assuming all costs and risks for the entire transport and dealing with any border formalities that may arise. Their terms of delivery are most likely …?

4. Herkules is processing a major order for running shoes and tennis shoes from a Japanese customer. Herkules arranges and pays for the transport of two 20 ft containers to the container terminal at the Japanese port of Yokohama. Herkules delivers on the basis of …?

2

M

Study the Incoterms 2010 on page 149 and 150 and find the English equivalents
for the following German expressions.

1. Geschäftsräume des Verkäufers
2. Frachtführer
3. vom Käufer benannt
4. Gefahrenübergang
5. Beförderungskosten
6. Versicherung abschließen
7. entladebereit
8. Bestimmungsort
9. dem Käufer zur Verfügung stellen
10. Verschiffungshafen
11. sich an Bord befinden
12. Einfuhrzoll

Language and grammar
Complete these sentences with "some" or "any".

1. He says he has lived in the UK for … years.
2. Fortunately we did not have … trouble getting an import licence.
3. When we finally managed to go the cafeteria there was hardly … food left.
4. I don't think he will complete … of these tasks in time.
5. Could you lend me … of your knives and forks for the party?
6. I couldn't think of …thing else to buy.
7. Scarcely …body turned up for the meeting.
8. …body must help me with this update.
9. We doubt that …body could have solved that problem without help
   from the experts.
10. We will send you … samples by parcel post.
11. Has …body seen my car keys?
12. …body must have copied the data.
13. I wonder whether …body will bother to return the questionnaire.
14. There are scarcely … funds left for this project.

Language and grammar: some and any	
"Some" steht • in **bejahten Aussagen** und • in Fragen, auf die eine **positive Antwort** erwartet wird.	Examples: Here are **some** brochures for you. Can you give us **some** of these folders?
"Any" steht • in **verneinten Aussagen** und • in Fragen, auf die eine **negative Antwort** erwartet wird, • bei **"hardly", "scarcely"** oder **"barely"** (deutsch: kaum), • in **Bedingungssätzen** und • nach Ausdrücken des **Zweifels**.	Examples: I am afraid there aren't **any** mint bars among the samples TOPSWEETS sent us. Are there **any** of those delicious ginger cookies left? There can hardly be **any** doubt about it. If you have **any** problems, let me know. I wonder whether **any** of the students will be satisfied with this reply.

Logistics expert

1 Offering transport service

Choosing the right mode of transport, quoting accurately and completely as well as good pricing are three critical elements in selling transport services. Of the three, pricing can be the most problematic. For example, prices for goods sent as less than container loads (LCL) differ from those for consolidated shipments that make up a full container load (FCL). Moreover, prices cannot be set without evaluating competitors' pricing policies.

1
KMK Lisa Bechmann von GoGlobal hat von Wehrmeyer & Co. eine Anfrage für einen Warentransport zu einer Messe in Orlando, Florida, erhalten. Sie kontaktierte daraufhin Howard Stone von Global Transport Inc., der den Transport innerhalb der USA organisieren soll. Kurz darauf erhält Lisa ein Angebot von Global Transport.

Übertragen Sie das folgende Angebot für Wehrmeyer & Co. ins Deutsche. `Phrases ▸`

From:	h.stone@globaltransportusa.com
To:	Lisa.Bechmann@goglobal.de
Sent:	Monday, August 30, 201_ 3:42 PM
Subject:	Orlando / Exhibition

Hi Lisa,

The rates based on the general zip code for Orlando airport are as follows
(all prices quoted in US$):

Customs work – $120.00
Reforwarding – $35.00
Courier fee – $30.00 (if carnet is sent to us)
Delivery – $300.00
Waiting time – first 30 minutes free of charge, $70.00 per h thereafter
EXCL transport insurance / storage / certificates or permits / labelling

Rates are valid for 30 days and subject to change.

Best regards,

Howard

2 After having been informed about the complete transport rate Wehrmeyer & Co.
R   asks for a review of the offer. So Lisa phones Howard again to discuss the matter.
A 2.11   Listen to the conversation and answer the following questions.

1. How does Howard react to Lisa's request to reduce the transportation costs?
2. Why does Lisa want to keep that customer?
3. What does Howard first suggest to reduce the price?
4. Why does Lisa not agree with Howard's first suggestion?
5. What do they agree on in the end? For which reasons?

3 Wehrmeyer & Co. stimmt dem Vorschlag zu und verspricht andere Aussteller   Phrases ▶
KMK   zu kontaktieren. Lisa möchte Howard über die neue Absprache informieren.
Verwenden Sie folgende Angaben und schreiben Sie Howard ein Fax.

- Kunde versucht Aussteller zu finden, die ebenfalls Ware nach Orlando
  transportieren lassen.
- Kunde wird uns bis Ende der Woche Bescheid geben.
- Habe schon mal einen LD 6 Container in der Maschine am 28. Oktober
  reserviert.
- Hoffe, dass ihr flexibel auf Transport der Sammelladung reagieren könnt.
- Rufe am Freitag, den 1. Oktober wieder an.

✳ **4** As promised, Lisa phones Howard on Friday after speaking to Wehrmeyer & Co.   Phrases ▶
I   again. Complete Lisa's part of the dialogue below using your own ideas. Then act
out the conversation with a partner.

Howard: Good morning, Global Transport, Howard Stone
speaking.

Lisa: **1**

Howard: Hi, Lisa. Could your customer convince some
more people to have their goods shipped with
us?

Lisa: **2**

Howard: Three more? Wow, that is good news. Have
you already got information on the nature and
dimensions of the consignments?

Lisa: **3**

Howard: Don't worry – as long as none of the three crates
are bigger than an elephant we won't have a
problem.

Lisa: **4**?

Howard: Sure. I know one of the guys from customs
clearance. He'll have all the necessary
documents ready within three days.

Lisa: **5**

Howard: You're welcome. Bye for now.

2 International packaging regulations

With increasing global commerce, interest in sustainability has grown, as have the by-products of trade. To reduce the environmental impact of packaging, many countries have implemented packaging requirements.

1 Discuss the messages of the photos above in class. Make suggestions about how
P to solve the problems connected with the growing amount of waste.

2 Read the text and complete it with the correct words from the brackets.
R

WHAT YOU NEED TO KNOW ABOUT PACKAGING

Companies selling goods on (**1** **alien**/**foreign**) markets face a growing range of packaging regulations. (**2** **Failure**/**Loss**) to adhere to these rules may lead to poor performance abroad, a bad public (**3** **image**/**imagination**) or even enforcement measures.

Traditionally, disposing or recycling (**4** **waste**/**dirt**) had to be managed and paid for by the state in which a product was being used. However, today countries are no longer willing to (**5** **carry**/**bear**) the increasing costs alone. This is reflected in a fee system that punishes companies for using environmentally unfriendly packaging. Generally, fees for a (**6** **special**/**particular**) form of packaging are determined by its weight. Depending on the nature of the packaging material, this fee can (**7** **easily**/**simply**) exceed the actual cost of producing it. In this way companies are being (**8** **discouraged**/**encouraged**) to reduce packaging or change the material used. In Central Europe, for example, fees on plastics are several times higher (**9** **than**/**then**) those on glass or paper.

All companies selling products in the EU must (**10** **complain**/**comply**) with the European Directive on Packaging and Packaging Waste to prevent their products from being removed from the market. Moreover, a growing number of countries have banned certain materials because they are (**11** **hazardous**/**perishable**). In particular, the packaging of toys, food or child care products is (**12** **closely**/**hardly**) monitored. Finally, companies must (**13** **also**/**although**) strive not to exceed empty space limits, as some countries allow no more than 10–35 % of the volume of a single product to be concealed empty space.

3 Read the text on page 155 again and summarize the main points in German.

M

4 Da einige amerikanische Kunden Einfuhrprobleme wegen Verstößen gegen die
KMK Europäische Verpackungsrichtlinie hatten, soll Lisa eine Kurzinformation über
die wichtigsten Bestimmungen an die Partner in den USA schicken.

**Fassen Sie für diesen Zweck, unter Zuhilfenahme eines Wörterbuches,
den folgenden Text auf Englisch zusammen.**

Die Europäische Verpackungsrichtlinie

1. Firmen müssen nachweisen, dass sie ihre Verpackungen so weit wie möglich
   reduziert haben. Sie müssen nachweisen, aus welchen Gründen (z.B. Produkt-
   schutz, Käuferakzeptanz, etc.) eine weitere Verringerung des Gewichts oder
   des Volumens der Verpackungselemente unmöglich ist.
2. Die Verpackungskomponenten müssen durch eine der folgenden
   Möglichkeiten weiterverwendet werden können: zur Energieerzeugung
   (z.B. durch Verbrennung), Kompostierung oder Materialrückführung.
3. Die Verpackung darf nur als „wiederverwendbar" gekennzeichnet werden,
   wenn sie die dafür definierten Standards voll erfüllt.
4. Der Schwermetallanteil (z.B. von Blei oder Quecksilber) einer Verpackung darf
   den EU-Grenzwert nicht überschreiten.
5. Substanzen, die als schädlich gelten (z.B. Zink) dürfen nur in geringster Menge
   enthalten sein, falls sie durch Verbrennung freigesetzt werden könnten.

3 Incoterms® 2010

1 Read the following statements and decide which Incoterm applies to them.
R There may be more than one applicable Incoterm.

1. Shipper: "As soon as the consignment is loaded onto the vessel we can no longer be held responsible."

2. Consignee: "I bought some rather expensive machines overseas. But at least there weren't any further expenses involved for me."

3. Shipper: "Paying the duty? No, we've already paid the rest."

4. Consignee: "Do I understand you correctly, you pay for the transport but we have to insure the consignment?"

＊ **2** Make similar statements for the following situations:
P

1. Consignee: EXW agreed
2. Consignee: CIP agreed
3. Shipper: FAS agreed
4. Shipper: FCA agreed

Phrases: Offers

To say thank you for an enquiry

Many thanks for your enquiry **of** 2 October **about** our new range of …	Wir danken Ihnen vielmals für Ihre Anfrage vom 2. Oktober wegen unseres neuen Sortiments von …
We **were** pleased to hear that you are interested in our …	Wir freuen uns über Ihr Interesse an unseren …

To make an offer and to refer to prices and discounts

As requested, we are sending you enclosed our latest catalogue and price list.	Wie gewünscht, fügen wir unseren neuesten Katalog und unsere Preisliste bei.
We are pleased to quote as follows:	Wir freuen uns, Ihnen hiermit folgendes Angebot machen zu können:
We would now like to make the following quotation:	Wir möchten Ihnen nun folgendes Angebot unterbreiten:
… **at** a unit price of € …, including packing.	… zum Stückpreis von € … einschließlich Verpackung.
… less 30 % trade discount.	… abzüglich 30 % Händlerrabatt.
We can offer a 10 % quantity discount **on** orders **for** at least 500 units.	Für Aufträge über mindestens 500 Stück wird 10 % Mengenrabatt gewährt.
May we draw your attention **to** our special offer for …?	Dürfen wir Sie auf unser Sonderangebot für … aufmerksam machen?
We grant 2 % cash discount **for** payment within 10 days.	Für Barzahlung innerhalb von 10 Tagen gewähren wir 2 % Skonto.
We take pleasure **in** submitting the following cost estimate:	Wir freuen uns Ihnen folgenden Kostenvoranschlag zu unterbreiten:

To state your terms of delivery and payment

Our prices are quoted CIF Singapore.	Unsere Preise verstehen sich CIF Singapur.
Terms of delivery: EXW Neustadt	Lieferbedingungen: EXW (Ab Werk) Neustadt
Our usual terms of payment are: cash **with** order cash **on** delivery 30 days net, 10 days 2 % **by** irrevocable and confirmed letter of credit	Normalerweise lauten unsere Zahlungsbedingungen: Barzahlung bei Auftragserteilung Barzahlung bei Lieferung 30 Tage netto, 10 Tage 2 % Skonto durch unwiderrufliches und bestätigtes Akkreditiv

Regular customers are granted open account terms.	Unseren Stammkunden gewähren wir offenes Zahlungsziel.
We would request payment **by** bank transfer **to** our account **with** ABC bank.	Wir bitten um Zahlung per Banküberweisung auf unser Konto bei der ABC Bank.

To refer to the delivery time

The delivery period is 6 weeks.	Die Lieferzeit beträgt 6 Wochen.
Delivery can be made ex stock.	Die Lieferung kann ab Lager erfolgen.

To inform the customer how long the offer is valid

The offer is firm **until** 31 March. without engagement. valid **as long as** stocks last.	Das Angebot ist fest bis 31. März. unverbindlich. gültig solange der Vorrat reicht.
The prices are **subject to** change without notice.	Preisänderungen bleiben vorbehalten.
The offer is **subject to** prior sale.	Zwischenverkauf vorbehalten.

To create goodwill

I hope this quotation will find your approval.	Ich hoffe, dieses Angebot sagt Ihnen zu.
We look forward to welcoming you as our customers.	Wir freuen uns darauf, Sie als Kunden begrüßen zu dürfen.
We assure you that your order **will be** dealt with promptly and carefully.	Wir sichern Ihnen eine rasche und sorgfältige Erledigung Ihres Auftrags zu.
Should you have any further queries, our staff **will be** pleased to assist you **at any** time.	Sollten Sie nun weitere Fragen haben, stehen Ihnen unsere Mitarbeiter jederzeit gerne zur Verfügung.

Unit 11
Orders

WORD BANK

initial order • trial order • standing order • repeat order • order on call • order form • quantity • description • item • article • sample • pattern • terms and conditions • unit price • total price • to choose • to order • to place an order • to process • to deliver

Orders are placed either in response to an offer or on the buyer's own initiative. A first order is also called an **initial order**. A **trial order** is placed for a small quanity to test the merchandise or service. **Repeat orders** cover goods or services ordered before. **Standing orders** ensure that identical quantities are supplied at regular intervals. **Orders on call** are placed for large quantities, called for at irregular intervals. They play an important role within the concept of just-in-time delivery.

1 Read the text. Then cover it up and complete the sentences.

R / P

1. A first order is also called …
2. A trial order is placed for a small quantity to test …
3. Repeat orders cover goods or services …
4. Standing orders ensure that identical quantities are supplied at …
5. Orders on call are placed for large quantities, called for at …

2 Translate the text above.

M

Online-Link
808264-0011

A Orders in writing

Sarah Brookfield has studied Herkules' offer for Turbostar running shoes and has read the attached test report. As she is favourably impressed by this report and by the results of the durability tests Sports Island conducted on the sample pairs, she decides to place a trial order.

1 Study Sarah Brookfield's order letter and the order form on the next page and choose the correct prepositions from the box.

R

by • for • from • of • to • with (2x)

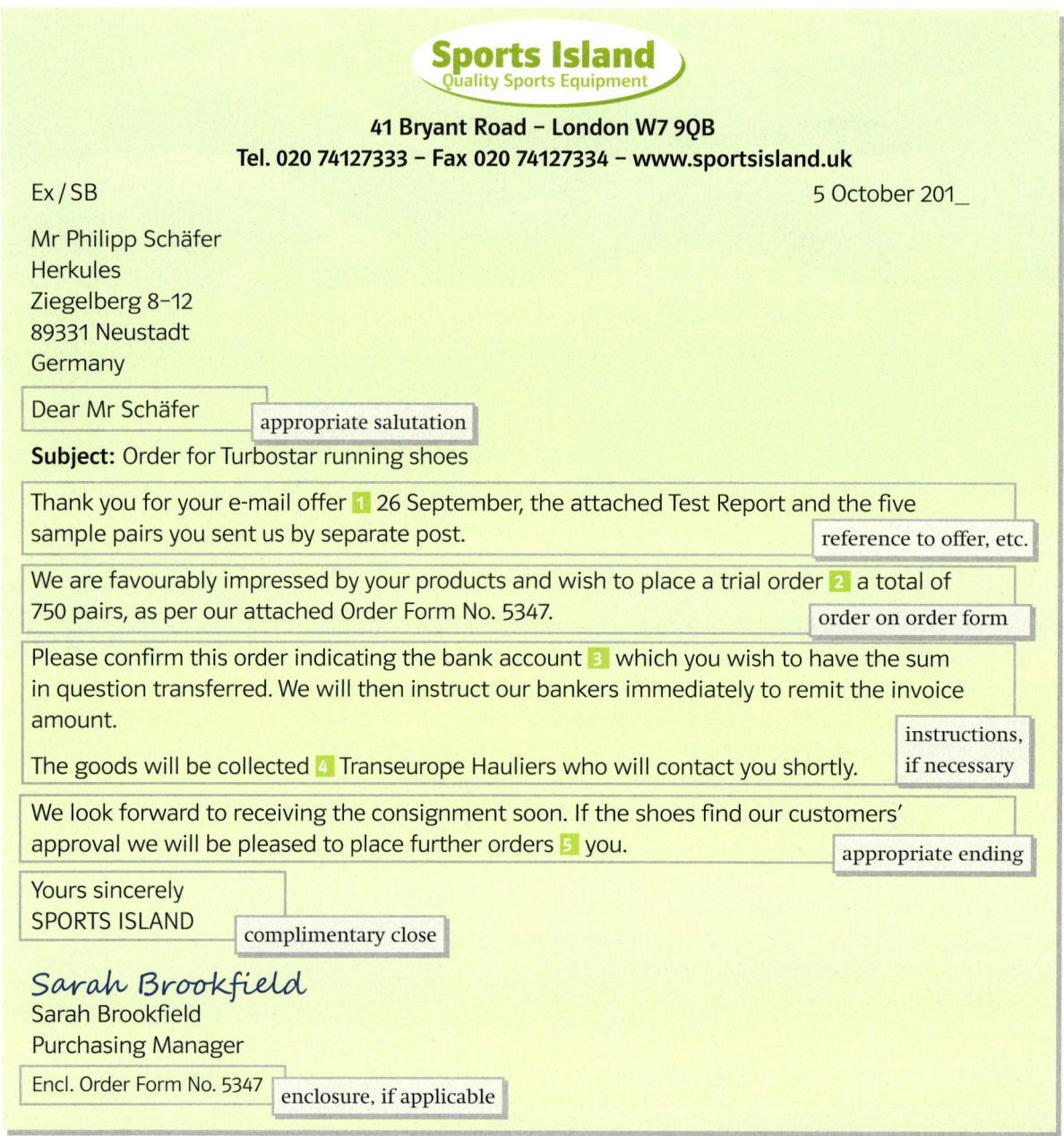

Sports Island
Quality Sports Equipment

41 Bryant Road – London W7 9QB
Tel. 020 74127333 – Fax 020 74127334 – www.sportsisland.uk

Ex / SB   5 October 201_

Mr Philipp Schäfer
Herkules
Ziegelberg 8–12
89331 Neustadt
Germany

Dear Mr Schäfer   `appropriate salutation`

Subject: Order for Turbostar running shoes

Thank you for your e-mail offer **1** 26 September, the attached Test Report and the five sample pairs you sent us by separate post.   `reference to offer, etc.`

We are favourably impressed by your products and wish to place a trial order **2** a total of 750 pairs, as per our attached Order Form No. 5347.   `order on order form`

Please confirm this order indicating the bank account **3** which you wish to have the sum in question transferred. We will then instruct our bankers immediately to remit the invoice amount.

The goods will be collected **4** Transeurope Hauliers who will contact you shortly.   `instructions, if necessary`

We look forward to receiving the consignment soon. If the shoes find our customers' approval we will be pleased to place further orders **5** you.   `appropriate ending`

Yours sincerely
SPORTS ISLAND   `complimentary close`

Sarah Brookfield
Sarah Brookfield
Purchasing Manager

Encl. Order Form No. 5347   `enclosure, if applicable`

Order form

Sports Island
Quality Sports Equipment

41 Bryant Road – London W7 9QB
Tel. 020 74127333 – Fax 020 74127334 – www.sportsisland.uk

ORDER NO. 5347

5 October 201_

Herkules
Ziegelberg 8–12
89331 Neustadt
Germany

Please supply

order (on order form, if appropriate)
– quantity
– description (article No.)
– unit price, total price

Quantity	Item	Sizes	Unit Price	Total Price
25 pairs each	Turbostar Running Shoes	5, 5 ½ ,11, 12	€ 40.50	€ 4,050.00
50 pairs each		6, 6 ½, 7, 7 ½, 10	€ 40.50	€ 10,125.00
100 pairs each		8, 8 ½, 9, 9 ½	€ 40.50	€ 16,200.00

Terms of delivery: EXW Neustadt   terms of delivery

Terms of payment: Cash **6** order   terms of payment

Delivery: **7** stock   delivery time

Sarah Brookfield

Sarah Brookfield
for Sports Island

2 Restore the correct order of these jumbled elements and rewrite the
R/P correspondence on a sheet of paper.

1　We have studied the enclosed spring catalogue and have chosen two models:

2　Dear Ms Martl

3　I would like to stress that this is a trial order. If we are satisfied with your shirts you may expect regular repeat orders.

4　Thank you very much for your letter of 11 November.

5

Quantity	Article No.	Description	Colours	Sizes	Unit price
50 each	334 053 R	Sports Shirt	Canyon Red	L and XL	€17.50
50 each	334 062 T	Dress Shirt	White	L and XL	€21.70

6　We look forward to receiving the goods as soon as possible.

7　We would like to point out that this order qualifies for 3% early order discount, as mentioned in your letter.

8　Yours sincerely
Tony Shaw

Wilson & Thatcher Ltd.

9　This order is placed subject to the terms and conditions specified in your catalogue.
Payment will be made by bank transfer on receipt of your invoice.

10　Subject: Trial order for shirts

3 You work in the purchasing department of the German stationery shop,
P Papier Gehrke, Bahnhofsallee 27, 19053 Schwerin, Tel. 0385 467095, e-mail
m.gerke@papier-gehrke.de. Your boss, Martin Gehrke, has put this leaflet
with his handwritten notes on your desk and has asked you to e-mail an order
to Calendars 4 U.

Phrases ▶

Calendars 4 U
proudly presents its multilingual animal calendar range

Kittens
You're certain to
be smitten
12" x 12" wall calendar

$11.99

*gehen besonders gut!
30 Stück bestellen*

Tigers **!new!**
Spectacular photos
12" x 12" wall calendar

$11.99

*sehr interessant,
20 Stück bestellen*

Puppies
Bright-eyed and
ready to romp
8" x 8" wall calendar

$9.99

*fragen, ob auch in
"12 x 12" erhältlich,
wenn ja 20 Stück,
sonst nur 10 Stück*

Horses
Superb photos
capture
their nobility
12" x 12" wall calendar
$11.99

nicht bestellen

We offer special rates for orders of 200+ items.
Please call us: 800/752-3326.

Calendars 4 U
100 Dolphin Way
San Sebastian, CA 94901
info@calendars4U.com
www.calendars4U.com

*auf sofortige Lieferung per
Luftpost drängen
Zahlung, wie üblich, durch Überweisung bei Erhalt
der Rechnung
um kurze Auftragsbestätigung bitten
E-Mail in meinem Namen an Cyrus B. Reid
senden: cb.reid@calendars4U.com*

B Orders by phone

Kirsty Burnham from Global Catering in Manchester has received an order from an upmarket chain of delicatessens. She rings International Snacks in Düsseldorf and places an order with them.

1 Kopieren Sie das Bestellformular und füllen Sie es aus, während Sie das Telefonat zweimal hören.

KMK

◎ A1.24

Portionen	Code-Nr.	Artikel	Preis pro Portion
	PSF 135	Schwäbischer Wurstsalat	€ 0,55
	PSF 136	Schinkenröllchen mit Spargel	€ 0,45
	PSF 137	Salami-Aufschnitt auf Roggentaler	€ 0,60
	PSF 138	kleine Frankfurter Würstchen mit Senf	€ 0,45
	PSF 139	Mini-Frikadellen mit Kartoffelsalat und fettarmer Yoghurtsoße	€ 1,05
	PSG 234	Putencocktail in Melone	€ 0,85
	PSG 235	Geflügelsalat Hawaii	€ 0,75
	PSM 311	Räucherlachs auf Pumpernickel mit Meerrettich	€ 0,95
	PSM 312	Bismarckhering, gerollt mit Gürkchen	€ 0,35
	PSM 313	Matjesfilet mit Remoulade	€ 0,65
	PSM 314	Anchovisfilet, gerollt mit gefüllten Oliven	€ 0,85
	PSM 315	Eismeerkrabben-Cocktail	€ 1,15
	PSD 408	Früchtequark	€ 0,45
	PSD 409	Rote Grütze mit Vanillecreme	€ 0,45

Transportart:	Liefertag und -zeitpunkt:	Lieferort:	Rechnung an:

2 Schreiben Sie als Marcel Krenz die im Telefonat mit Kirsty Burnham angekündigte KMK E-Mail als Auftragsbestätigung (siehe ausgefülltes Bestellformular) mit Versandanzeige.

Absender: marcel.krenz@internationalsnacks.de
Empfänger: burnham.globalcateringuk@aol.com
Sie haben inzwischen folgende Einzelheiten zum Versand geklärt:
- Versand per Luftfracht durch Spedition Fuhrmann & Söhne, Düsseldorf
- Flug-Nr. LH 3697, Abflug: Flughafen Düsseldorf, 13:05 Uhr deutsche Zeit
- Ankunft Manchester Airport, Freight Terminal, 13:25 Uhr britische Zeit

Language and grammar
Rewrite the following text, using capital letters where necessary.

the organisation of petroleum exporting countries (opec) was formed in 1960 with five founding members: iran, kuwait, saudi arabia and venezuela. by the end of 1971 six other nations had joined the group: qatar, indonesia, libya, united arab emirates, algeria and nigeria. since then opec has been trying to control crude oil prices by setting quotas for production. some major oil exporting countries such as russia, norway and mexico have remained outside opec. the british analyst jonathan baker writing in the june edition of the trade journal "global oil" says that oil prices are highly cyclical and are supported by high demand from south east asia, especially china and india.

Language and grammar: Use of capital letters

Geographische Eigennamen werden groß geschrieben. Im Gegensatz zum Deutschen werden im Englischen auch geographische Adjektive groß geschrieben.

We have customers in **N**ew **S**outh **W**ales in **A**ustralia.
Our **B**ritish and **I**talian subsidiaries are quite successful.

Wochentage, Monate und Feiertage werden groß geschrieben.

The meeting will be held next **F**riday / in **S**eptember / before **C**hristmas.

Vorangestellte Titel, die Teil des Namens bilden, schreibt man groß. Nachgestellte Titel werden meist klein geschrieben.

The report was presented by **V**ice-**P**resident Brian Laurel.
John Hardy, chairman of Media Clusters, agreed to the proposal.

Die Namen von Ministerien, Behörden etc. werden groß geschrieben.

The **F**ederal **C**ommunications **C**ommission ruled that the deal was illegal.
The **D**epartment of **T**rade and **I**ndustry provides help for start-ups.

◉ V5 Video lounge Manufacturing

BBC Motion Gallery

You are about to see a video about a company based on the Isle of Wight (small island off the south coast of England). Watch the video, then answer the following questions:

1. What does the company manufacture?
2. What industry do orders for these products come from?
3. How are the products transported to customers?
4. What other industry on the Isle of Wight is mentioned?

Logistics expert

Importing goods

1 Complete the text with the words in the box.
R / M There are more words than you need. Then read
the text aloud and translate it into German.

> arrival • carrier • consignee • consignments • containerisation • customer •
> export • forwarding agent • import • shipper

For the forwarder, the hard work starts when the **1** has placed an order.
Each transport job poses a new challenge. The **2** and the **3** are often located
thousands of kilometres away from each other. Different kinds of **4** require
specific forms of storage, **5** and labelling and, depending on the country, special
regulations may apply for the **6** of goods from abroad.

2 Restore the correct order of the steps that have to be taken when importing
R goods by plane. Then organise the steps in the form of a diagram.

> - forwarder informs partner in shipping country about order
> - shipment is made ready for dispatching
> - customer gives order
> - partner contacts shipper of goods
> - partner informs forwarder about flight dates
> - forwarder informs customer about estimated time of arrival
> - flight
> - delivery at consignee
> - partner issues documents and organises pre-carriage and flight
> - customs clearance

3 Match the statements (1.–7.) to the diagram you made in Exercise 2.
R

1. I've arranged a flight
via Shanghai to Frankfurt
which arrives earlier than
the one via Peking.

2. Can you make
sure that there are
identical markings on
all packages, please?

3. I'd like to book an LD 7
container for the next
flight to Frankfurt.

7. The cargo will arrive
at Frankfurt airport on
16 September and will be
forwarded directly to you.

4. Please present the
documents to the
officer in room 122.

5. We've got cargo
to be shipped from
Shenzhen next week.

6. When can we
collect the shipment
from your warehouse?

4

KMK GoGlobal hat den Auftrag von der Firma Weihler & Söhne bekommen, Waren aus China zu importieren. GoGlobal lässt den Transport innerhalb Chinas durch ihren Partner TransAsian organisieren. Übertragen Sie zur Weiterleitung des Auftrags an TransAsian den folgenden Faxauszug ins Englische.

```
+ + + + + + + + + + + + + + + + FAX + + + + + + + + + + + + + + + + + + + + + +

Betreff: Warenimport von Shenzhen nach Berlin

Sehr geehrte Damen und Herren,

hiermit beauftragen wir Sie mit dem Import von 20 Kisten mit Plastikrohren aus
Shenzhen (China) nach Berlin in unsere Niederlassung.

Die Kisten haben die Maße 120 cm × 60 cm × 40 cm und wiegen jeweils ca. 30 kg.
Verpackung und Kennzeichnung wird durch den chinesischen Partner vorgenommen.
Informieren Sie bitte Herrn Xiao Wang (E-Mail: xiaowang@plastic.com,
Tel.: +86 832 529918), wann die Ware im Werk der Firma Plastics & More (110 Fuhua
Road, Futian, Shenzhen, China 528022) abholbereit sein soll.

Bitte kümmern Sie sich um alle notwendigen Dokumente und informieren Sie uns
schnellstmöglich über den voraussichtlichen Liefertermin.

Mit freundlichen Grüßen

Valentina Silva

Versandabteilung
Weihler & Söhne
```

5

P On the day the shipment was meant to be loaded at Shenzhen airport, Lisa from GoGlobal receives a fax from their partner TransAsian. As there is a problem with the printer, some words can hardly be read. Fill in the missing letters.

S▮ment of ▮ds impo▮! We have pr▮ms with the ▮pper. We need all do▮ts from the Ge▮ ▮nee. Pl▮ con▮ me as ▮n as ▮ble.

✶ 6

KMK Lisa telefoniert mit Su Ling, die den Auftrag in China bearbeitet. Führen Sie in Partnerarbeit dieses Telefongespräch mithilfe der Rollenkarten.

> Phrases ▷

Role card: Partner A   Role card partner B ⇨ page 257

Sie sind Lisa Bechmann von GoGlobal. Sie rufen Su Ling von TransAsian wegen der Probleme bei der Ausfuhr der Ware für Weihler & Söhne an.

- Begrüßen Sie Su Ling und fragen Sie, welche Probleme aufgetreten sind.
- Fragen Sie, ob Plastics & More trotzdem die bestellten Waren liefern kann.
- Erkundigen Sie sich, ob Su Ling den gebuchten Frachtcontainer stornieren konnte.
- Sagen Sie, dass Plastics & More für diesen Schaden aufkommen muss.
- Danken Sie Su Ling für die gute Arbeit und bitten Sie um Bestätigung, wenn alles geklärt ist.
- Verabschieden Sie sich angemessen.

Phrases: Orders

To refer to previous contacts and place an order

We have studied your quotation and enclose Purchase Order No. …	Wir haben Ihr Angebot genau durchgesehen und fügen unsere Bestellung Nr. … bei.
Please supply the following items **on** the terms stated below:	Bitte liefern Sie uns folgende Positionen zu den unten genannten Bedingungen:

To confirm prices and discounts

We would like to order model AC **at** the price of € … less 5 % introductory discount.	Wir möchten Modell AC zum Preis von € …, abzüglich 5 % Einführungsrabatt, bestellen.
We would like to confirm that the prices are taken **from** your price list **of** 1 September.	Wir möchten bestätigen, dass die Preise Ihrer Preisliste vom 1. September entnommen sind.

To confirm the method of payment and the terms of delivery and the delivery time

As agreed, we will effect payment **by** bank transfer 30 days **from** date of invoice.	Wie vereinbart werden wir die Zahlung 30 Tage nach Rechnungsdatum per Banküberweisung vornehmen lassen.
Payment will be made **by** irrevocable and confirmed letter of credit.	Die Zahlung erfolgt durch unwiderrufliches und bestätigtes Akkreditiv.
Your above-mentioned prices are quoted CIF Hamburg.	Ihre oben genannten Preise verstehen sich CIF Hamburg.
Delivery **is to** be made DAP Stuttgart.	Die Lieferung soll DAP Stuttgart erfolgen.
Complete delivery **by** … is a firm condition of this order.	Vollständige Lieferung bis … stellt eine feste Bedingung für diesen Auftrag dar.
Please note that the goods must reach us **by** 1 March at the latest.	Wir weisen darauf hin, dass die Ware bis spätestens 1. März hier eintreffen muss.

To give instructions and ask for confirmation

Please arrange for transportation **by** Eurotrans Ltd.	Bitte veranlassen Sie, dass der Transport von Eurotrans Ltd. durchgeführt wird.
Please make sure that the figurines are packed with the utmost care.	Bitte sorgen Sie dafür, dass die Figürchen äußerst sorgfältig verpackt werden.
Please acknowledge this order promptly.	Bitte bestätigen Sie diesen Auftrag umgehend.

To close the correspondence

We look forward to receiving the goods **in** time and to doing further business with you.	Wir sehen dem rechtzeitigen Eintreffen der Ware entgegen und freuen uns auf weitere Geschäfte mit Ihnen.

Unit 12
Transport and logistics

WORD BANK

transport · logistics · shipping · forwarding · cargo · freight · door-to-door delivery · modes of transport · types of packing · dispatch advice · waybill · consignment note · bill of lading · certificate of origin · packing list · insurance policy/certificate · to confirm · to acknowledge · to send · to ship · to transport · to pack · to wrap · to deliver

CONTAINER SHIPPING

World trade is forecast to continue growing strongly over the next decade. Today roughly 90 % of non-bulk cargo is
5 transported in containers stacked on transport ships. Cargo is also transported via roll on/roll off (ro-ro) ferries that offer easy loading and
10 unloading. New cars, for instance, are simply driven on and off massive car carriers that hold thousands of vehicles. Ports such as Felixstowe
15 in East Anglia are being deepened to accommodate the new generation of massive container ships.

The fact that the average consumer appears to have no idea how running shoes, washing machines, coffee or tonnes of toys arrive in the shops from all over the world is a constant source of irritation to the shipping world. "The global economy only exists thanks to shipping, in particular container shipping," says one industry analyst. The long-term downward trend in shipping costs has facilitated economic growth worldwide.

At the present time China clearly dominates world trade flows both in terms of exports of finished goods and imports of raw materials. However,
36 shipping is a highly cyclical business reflecting growth and stagnation in the world economy. Carriers, ship-owners and
40 terminal operators have constantly to invest in new ships and facilities. But they do not have a good record of getting the supply/demand ratio
45 right and have often ended up either with inadequate or excess capacity.

Online-Link
808264-0012

1 Beantworten Sie folgende Fragen zu vorstehendem Zeitungsartikel auf Deutsch.

R

1. Welches sind die größten und wichtigsten Transportmittel für den Welthandel?
2. Weswegen ist die Schifffahrtsbranche verärgert?
3. Wodurch wurde das rasche Wachstum des Welthandels erst ermöglicht?
4. Wie zeigt sich, dass die Schifffahrtsbranche von der Konjunktur abhängt?

✶ 2 Work in groups. Each group translates one paragraph from the text on page 169

M in writing. Present your result to the class.

3 Use the internet to find out the percentages of goods transported by a. road and b. rail in the EU.

A Modes of transport

Tobias Krabbe from the German company Form und Raum GmbH has been asked to collect first-hand information on the various modes of transport. He interviews Marie Boucher from the freight forwarding company FranceTransports which handles most of Form und Raum's international shipments.

1 Listen to the interview with Marie Boucher twice and complete the grid on a

KMK separate sheet of paper. Then add whatever other advantages, disadvantages and

A 1.25 suitable cargoes you can think of. Compare your result with that of your neighbour.

	Road	Rail	Air	Sea / Inland Waterways
Advantages	door-to-door delivery, flexible timetables			
Disadvantages		unless a firm has its own private siding, goods must be transported to and collected from the station		slow; seaworthy packing required
Suitable cargoes			light, urgently required, perishable or valuable goods	

2 Work in groups. Choose one of the goods mentioned below and explain to your group which mode(s) of transport you would use, giving reasons for your choice. Use the expressions in the bubbles.

Example: "I'd send the wine by road from Spain to Poland because door-to-door delivery by lorry is probably faster than rail transport."

"I wouldn't transport … because …"

"I'd rather send …"

"It would not be a good idea to ship … considering that …"

"I'd definitely not use … as …"

"In my opinion it would be best to choose …"

"There's no doubt that … should be transported by …"

"I think it would be better to …"

"I suggest we send … either by … or by …"

"I'd suggest sending …"

Urgent medical supplies from Leipzig, Germany, to Wellington, New Zealand

Laptops from a port in South Korea to Berlin

A large printing press from Mannheim in Germany to the port of Jeddah in Saudi Arabia

Tropical fruit from Brazil to Sweden

Designer shoes from Italy to Denmark

Furniture from a manufacturer in Westphalia to a hotel in Austria

Wine in bottles from Spain to Poland

50 cars from a plant in Munich to a car dealer in Lisbon, Portugal

B Packing

Adequate packing is essential to ensure that goods arrive in perfect condition, regardless of the distance they have travelled.

1 Match the German terms (see photos above) with their English equivalents.

1. Eisenfass, Trommel	a. bale
2. Holzkiste	b. bundle with steel strapping
3. Fass	c. coil on euro-pallet
4. folienumwickelter Karton	d. container
5. Rolle, Coil auf Europalette	e. crate
6. Kunststoffbox mit Formeinlagen	f. drum
7. Container	g. foil-wrapped cardboard box
8. Ballen	h. plastic box with mouldings
9. Bündel mit Stahlbandumreifung	i. one-way pallet
10. Lattenkiste, -verschlag	j. sack
11. Einwegpalette	k. wooden case
12. Sack	l. barrel

2 The following sentences do not make much sense. Rearrange the words to form
R/P meaningful sentences.

1. The fruit will be packed in 15 bundles with steel strapping.
2. The pure new wool will be sent in a crate.
3. The steel rods will be shipped in bales.
4. The replacement Mp3 player will come on a reusable pallet.
5. The printing machine will be packed in a cardboard box.
6. The engine will be sent in a plastic gift box with mouldings.

C Dispatch advice

As soon as the goods are ready for dispatch it may be necessary to inform the customer that the goods can either be collected at the seller's premises or that they have been handed over to the carrier – depending on the Incoterms agreed upon in the sales contract. Remember that you are communicating with a customer and be as friendly and helpful as possible.

1 Dispatch advice in writing

Topelektronik has received an order for a total of 1,500 SomeThing Mp3 players from the British company Leigh & Co. Ltd. Cornelia Klinkenberg, head of sales at Topelektronik, informs James Leigh that the goods have now been shipped to the UK.

1 Complete Cornelia's e-mail using the verbs from the box.

R

| accompanied • arrive • attached • delivered • given • packed • picked up • pleased • reach |

From:	cornelia.klinkenberg@topelektronik.de
To:	james.leigh@leigh.co.uk
Cc:	

Sent: 201_-08-14   **Attachments:**   Invoice No. 149 / 08 / 1_

Subject: Your order dated 7 August for 1,500 SomeThing Mp3 Players

Dear Mr Leigh

We are **1** to inform you that the consignment has today been **2** by our forwarders, Transcontinental Logistik, to be **3** by road to your warehouse in Bristol.
The forwarders have **4** us the assurance that the goods will **5** you by Friday afternoon, at the latest.

The Mp3 players are **6** in 15 triple-walled cardboard boxes on one pallet.
The consignment is **7** by the required documents (consignment note, packing list and commercial invoice). A copy of the invoice is **8**.

Thank you once more for this order. We hope the goods will **9** safely and in good time. We look forward to serving you again.

Kind regards

Cornelia Klinkenberg
Topelektronik
Am Osthang 37
09114 Chemnitz
Tel. +49 371 460873
Fax. +49 371 460874

2
P

Mr Kunal Mahajan, export manager at India Sports, has been processing an order for T-shirts from the German firm Herkules. He now sends them a dispatch advice. Write his fax, using the following prompts:

- reference to their order of 20 Jan. and their letter of 1 Feb.
- consignment packed in one 20 ft container
- markings on the container: HKS, 3479, Antwerp
- yesterday loaded on board MV Maharani in the port of Mumbai
- expected time of arrival at Antwerp: on or about 12 March
- friendly closing phrase

India Sports

112 Delhi Road, Meerut–250 001
Uttar Pradesh, India
Fax +91 121 2512275
Tel. +91 121 2512270

Telefax

To :	Herkules Ziegelberg 8–12 89331 Neustadt, Germany	**Attention:**	Ms Laura Bayerle
		Fax:	+49 8358 88820
From:	Kunal Mahajan, Export Manager		
Date:	15 Feb 201_	**Pages (incl. this one):**	1
Subject:	Your order No. ABF / 16 of 20 January and 1 February		

✱ **3**
KMK

Sie (eigener Name) arbeiten bei der Münchner Firma Superdress GmbH, E-Mail: sales@superdress.munich.de. Ein britischer Kunde, Richard Knight, Einkäufer bei der Warenhauskette Hamilton's, E-Mail: richard.knight@ hamiltons.co.uk, hatte bei Ihnen eine Sendung Herrenhemden bestellt, die dringend für eine Modeschau benötigt werden.

Schreiben Sie eine E-Mail als Versandanzeige und berücksichtigen Sie dabei Folgendes:

- Bezug auf Auftrag vom 18. August
- Sendung heute der Spedition Kleine zum Transport per Luftfracht übergeben
- British Airways Flug Nr. BA 777
- Abflug: Flughafen München, 22 August, 11:35 Uhr,
  Ankunft: Manchester Airport, 12:55 Uhr
- Erwartung, dass Hemden rechtzeitig für die Modeschau eintreffen
- nochmaliger Dank für den Auftrag

2 Order confirmation and inquiry concerning transport by phone

1
R
A 1.26
Thomas Krabbe from Form und Raum has received an order from a British customer. He confirms the order and the transport arrangements by phone. Listen to the dialogue and answer the following questions.

1. What is the name of Jennifer Ashley's firm?
2. Has Tobias spoken to Jennifer before?
3. When did Jennifer place the order?
4. How many Hermes standard lamps, Odin uplighters and Bauhaus coffee tables were ordered?
5. What are the first and the last order numbers, the second being O160u?
6. When is the consignment expected to arrive?

2
I
Cornelia Klinkenberg from Topelektronic in Chemnitz had promised James Leigh from Leigh & Co. Ltd in Bristol, UK, that the Mp3 Players he had ordered would arrive by Friday afternoon at the latest. It is now 4 pm on Friday (local time) and the lorry has not yet arrived. James Leigh rings Cornelia Klinkenberg.

Act out their dialogue with your neighbour using the prompts below.

Phrases ▶

James Leigh	Cornelia Klinkenberg
	Topelektronik, Klinkenberg
James Leigh/Leigh & Co., Bristol/ Mp3 players/not yet arrived/ now 4 pm	
	Try to reach driver on his mobile phone/hold line?/ring back?
hold/urgent	
	spoken to driver/driver on motorway M4/ 20 miles away
here/next half hour?	
	driver confident/arrive before 5 pm/ reason for delay/held up in Channel Tunnel/ security check/false alarm/explosives in a van on the train/took almost 3 hours
glad to hear/arrive this afternoon/thanks	
	lucky still in office/5 pm in Germany
e-mail/as soon as goods have arrived/ nice weekend/Bye	
	too/Goodbye

D Documents in foreign trade

Waybills, also called **consignment notes, (Frachtbriefe)** are used in road, rail or air transport. They are contracts between the sender of the goods and the carrier (Frachtführer) and provide detailed information about the consignment and the transportation.

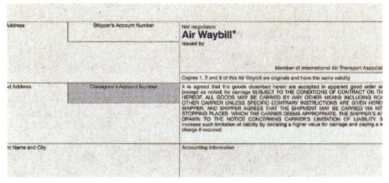

The **Bill of Lading** (B/L) **(Konnossement)** is the freight document in sea transport and when the transportation involves several modes of transport. It is a document of title (Eigentumsurkunde), which means that any lawful holder of the B/L is the rightful owner of the goods. Bills of Lading must be **clean (rein)**, that is to say the carrier (e.g. the captain of the ship) must have signed the B/L **without** making a note on it that the consignment shows signs of a defect or damage from the outside.

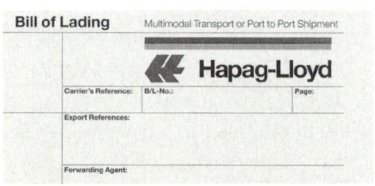

A **Certificate of Origin (Ursprungszeugnis)** shows the country of origin of the goods or the country where they were mainly produced. There is a common EU Certificate of Origin. Certificates of Origin are usually legalized by a chamber of commerce.

The **Packing List (Packliste)** is a detailed statement of the goods supplied in a particular consignment.

Commercial Invoice (Handelsrechnung) and Proforma Invoice (Proforma-Rechnung) see Unit 13.

Insurance Policy/Certificate (Versicherungspolice/-schein) see Info-Box on page 177.

Export documents are available as standard paper forms. Increasingly, however, such documents are created by computer software and forwarded via the internet.

1 Compare the translation with the above text on the Bill of
R Lading and find the missing words from the box.

> Beschädigung • Eigentümer • Kapitän • Seetransport • Sendung

Das Konnossement (B/L) ist das Frachtpapier für den **1** und für Transporte, bei denen mehrere Transportarten zum Einsatz kommen. Es ist eine Eigentumsurkunde, d. h. jeder rechtmäßige Inhaber der B/L ist rechtmäßiger **2** der Ware. Konnossemente müssen rein sein, das heißt, der Frachtführer (z. B. der **3** des Schiffes) muss die B/L unterschrieben haben, ohne einen Vermerk anzubringen, der besagt, dass die **4** äußerlich Zeichen eines Mangels oder einer **5** aufweist.

2 Edward Ferrars from Norland Industries in Southampton ships 700 colour printers
P to a customer in Durban, South Africa. Study his quotation in Unit 10 and fill in
the details missing from the B / L (on a separate sheet of paper).

SHIPPER Norland Industries, 39 Marchwood Industrial Park, Southampton SO11 3DG	CUSTOMER NO. MSA-24	REF. NO. CP 100 / 150	B/L NO. 428 379 421
CONSIGNEE	LINER BILL OF LADING		

SHIPPER	CUSTOMER NO.	REF. NO.	B/L NO.
Norland Industries, 39 Marchwood Industrial Park, Southampton SO11 3DG	MSA-24	CP 100 / 150	428 379 421
CONSIGNEE	**LINER BILL OF LADING**		
NOTIFY De Boer Office Equipment Pty., 422 Drakens Road, Durban 4051, SA	568 HARBOUR STREET, SOUTHAMPTON, SO4 3DL UNITED KINGDOM		
LOCAL VESSEL	FROM Southampton	GENERAL AGENTS WORLD WIDE **WORLDCARGO**	
OCEAN VESSEL Santa Maria	PORT OF LOADING		
PORT OF DISCHARGE	FINAL DESTINATION	FREIGHT PAYABLE AT Southampton	NUMBER OF ORIGINAL B/L three
MARKS & NUMBERS	NUMBER OF PACKAGES/DESCRIPTION OF GOODS	GROSS WEIGHT Kos.	MEASUREMENT Cbm.
MOE, 18/18 Durban	18 pallets containing	6.1 t	600 x1200 x215 each

FREIGHT AND CHARGES
GBP 1145.30

Shipped on board in apparent good order and condition, weight, measure, marks, numbers, quality, contents and value unknown, for carriage to the port of discharge or so near thereunto as the Vessel may safely get and lie always a oat, to be delivered in the like good order and condition at the aforesaid Port unto Consignee or their Assigns they paying freight as per note on the margin plus other charges incurred in accordance with the provisions contained in this Bill of Lading.
In accepting this Bill of Lading the Merchant expressly accepts and agrees to all its stipulations on both pages, whether written, printed, stamped or otherwise incorporated as fully as if they were all signed by the Merchant.
One original Bill of Lading must be surrendered duly endorsed in exchange for the goods or delivery order.
IN WITNESS whereof the Master of the said Vessel has signed the number of the original Bills of Lading stated above, all of this tenor and date, one of which being accomplished, the others to stand void.

PLACE AND DATE OF ISSUE
SOUTHAMPTON
SIGNED FOR THE MASTER BY:

Info: Insurance Policy / Certificate

Exports shipments are usually insured **"against all risks"**, which covers a wide
range of risks, from sinking to theft. The contract between the sender and the
insurance company is called a **policy**. Whenever an open policy, covering a
certain lump sum or valid for a certain period, has been taken out, the insurance
company issues an insurance **certificate** for an individual shipment. The **premium**
is the sum payable by the insured to the insurance company at regular intervals.

✳ **3** Translate the text above into German. Use the words from the box.
M

abdecken · abschließen · ausstellen · Diebstahl · Generalpolice ·
Pauschalsumme · Police · Prämie · Untergang · Versicherungsnehmer ·
Versicherungszertifikat

Language and grammar
Translate the statements into English.

1. Ich arbeite in einem Warenhaus und möchte Einzelhandelskaufmann werden.
2. Mein Chef ist leider ziemlich selbstbewusst und nicht sehr sympathisch.
3. Auf Seite 3 unseres Prospekts finden Sie Berichte unserer Kunden, die den Erfolg unserer Methode beweisen.
4. Ich bekomme ungefähr 50 E-Mails pro Tag.
5. Unsere Firma beobachtet die aktuellen Trends auf dem Markt sehr genau.
6. Diese Rechnungen müssen noch einmal geprüft werden.
7. Dieses System wird eventuell in unserem Büro eingeführt.

Language and grammar: False friends

Einige deutsche Wörter werden oft mit englischen Wörtern verwechselt, die etwas ganz anderes bedeuten

deutsches Wort	englische Bedeutung	nicht zu verwechseln mit	deutsche Bedeutung
aktuell	current(ly), topical	actual	tatsächlich, wirklich
bekommen	to get	to become	werden
Billion	trillion	billion	Milliarde
Chef*	boss	chef, chief	(Chef-)koch, Häuptling
eventuell	perhaps, possibly	eventual	schließlich
Fabrik	factory, works	fabric	Stoff
Gymnasium	grammar school	gym(nasium)	Sporthalle
Prospekt	brochure	prospect	Aussicht
Provision	commission	provision	Vorsorge
prüfen	to check, examine	to prove	beweisen
übersehen	to overlook	to oversee	überwachen
Warenhaus	department store	warehouse	Lagerhaus

*Ausnahme: Zusammengesetzte Begriffe wie chief accountant, chief executive officer

---

⊚ V6 Video lounge IT

BBC Motion Gallery

This video illustrates important IT applications.
Look out for the answers to the following questions:

1. What are the duties of the three staff members shown in the video?
2. Give a brief description of any one of them.
3. Why is it important to check everything carefully?
4. What possible problems do they have to watch out for?

Logistics expert

1 Growing transport markets

1
P
Use the word cloud to describe the journey of a product from the raw materials until the final product reaches the end-user. Compare your notes with a partner's.

Phrases

2
R
Read the following text and answer the questions below.

A number of innovations have changed the transport market in the past few years. Carriers can cut down transit times and reach almost any destination thanks to growing containerisation and new high-tech telecommunication networks. The growth of the European Single Market has made the distribution of goods among most European countries easier and faster. The production strategies of multinational concerns have created a high degree of specialisation, dependent on the labour costs in different countries and technological standards of production. International division of labour and the global search for resources need integrated transport solutions which make use of all means of transport and ensure reliability.

These factors have led to a growing demand for transport of all kinds. Forwarders and carriers have become global players who offer and supervise complete transport chains (e.g. road-sea-rail) rather than just one means of transport (e.g. port-to-port transport). When deciding on the best means of transport within this chain, they have to consider: type of goods, cost, urgency, distance and ecological aspects. So the forwarder's job is to decide on a suitable means of transport, while the client chooses the freight forwarder or carrier who offers the best integrated system for a consignment. The main question is: How do I get the right item in the right quantity to the right place at the right time at the right price?

1. Why do forwarders nowadays have to transport consignments worldwide?
2. What is meant by "integrated transport solutions"?
3. Which factors must be considered for finding the best means of transport?
4. From the forwarder's point of view, what is a "right price"?
5. What are the advantages of an international division of labour?

2   Handling air freight

1   Work in groups and find examples of typical air freight goods. Make a list giving
P   details of their countries of origin, their features, special transport requirements
and typical destinations. Choose one particularly interesting example and present
it in class.

Phrases ▶

2   Sie arbeiten in einem internationalen Luftfrachtunternehmen und haben im
KMK   Internet folgenden Text gefunden. Lesen Sie den Text aufmerksam durch und
beantworten Sie die Fragen dazu auf Deutsch.

Lufthansa Cargo flies in tokens of love for Valentine's Day

Lufthansa Cargo will be transporting millions of love tokens over the next few days. By
Valentine's Day on 14 February, the logistics services provider will have delivered around
850 tonnes of roses to Europe on board its freighters or in the belly holds of Lufthansa
passenger aircraft. That's about 24 million roses, or ten full MD-11 freighters, for lovers to
express their feelings.

Kenya is one of the world's biggest rose producers. From Nairobi alone, Lufthansa Cargo
flies in more than 280 tonnes of roses each year for Valentine's Day. The flowers are
picked at rose farms in the Kenyan uplands in the morning and transported during the
day to the Kenyan capital to be loaded in the late evening onto a Lufthansa Cargo MD-11
freighter. Efficiency is at a premium because flowers in their full glory as messages of love
are perishable products. The logistics chain, from the rose farm in Africa to the florist in
Hamburg or Munich, has to function reliably. Fast transport at a constant temperature
of between 2 and 3 degrees Celsius is absolutely essential. After touch-down at Frankfurt
airport, the Valentine roses are quickly conveyed to the nearby Perishables Centre, the
largest of its kind in Germany, keeping transit through the airport to a minimum. From
the Frankfurt cargo hub, the roses are shipped out mostly on the same day to all corners
of Germany to ensure that High Street florists have them in stock when the Valentine
cavaliers call in.

In addition to Kenya, Ecuador, Colombia and Ethiopia also rank as principal suppliers.
Overseas rose producers benefit from a crucial competitive advantage over European flower-
growing regions. In the uplands of South America and Africa, long-stemmed roses thrive
in a tropical climate all year round, and their production, even with air transport, is more
environment-friendly. Unlike European roses, which have to be cultivated in heated and
artificially lighted greenhouses, the roses grown in regions on the equator normally need
no artificial irrigation or additional heating and consequently generate less CO_2 than their
European siblings.

(Quelle: LH Cargo Website)

1. Wie viele Rosen werden jedes Jahr zum Valentinstag aus Kenia importiert?
2. Warum werden Rosen per Luftfracht transportiert?
3. Welche Transportbedingungen gewährleisten, dass die Blumen frisch bleiben?
4. Weshalb werden in den äquatorial gelegenen Ländern viele Blumen angebaut?

3 Eine Auszubildende kommt neu in die Luftfrachtabteilung Ihres Unternehmens.
KMK Fassen Sie den folgenden Text für sie auf Deutsch zusammen, damit sie sich
schnell in der Abteilung einarbeiten kann.

TACT

The **A**ir **C**argo **T**ariff (TACT) is the most important reference for all International
Air Transport Association (IATA) agents and can be consulted online or offline
when bought on CD or in print from the IATA. TACT is updated every year and
provides different types of cargo rates and charges based either on the weight or
the volume of the consignment. Here are the basic rates:

– **Minimum Charges (M):** Under no circumstances shall the charge for any
  consignment be less than the minimum charges shown in the *TACT-Rates* book.
– **General Cargo Rates (GCR):** General Cargo Rates apply to all goods which
  are not covered by a specific rate. They are divided into the Normal General
  Cargo Rates (N) for consignments up to 45 kg and the Quantity General Cargo
  Rates (Q) for consignments weighing more than 45 kg.
– **Special Rates (S/W):** These are based on the Normal General Cargo Rates
  and apply to a few commodities within, or between, certain designated
  areas. There are reductions (S) for consignments comprising newspapers or
  magazines, for example, and surcharges (W) for valuable goods or livestock.

The invoice amount is the chargeable
weight multiplied by the applicable rate.
The real weight of the packed goods
is rounded up; the unit of weight for
normal cargo is 0.5 kg, for valuable cargo
(VAL) it is 0.1 kg. The space (volume)
needed to transport the goods has to be
considered, too. The volume weight is
calculated using the following formula:
length (cm) × width (cm) × height (cm)
× number of packages / 6,000. Then the
chargeable weight is compared with the
volume weight and the higher weight is
invoiced.

4 Complete the table using the information above. Then write at least six sentences
R comparing the products (1.–6.) in terms of their weight and volume.

Phrases

Description of goods	Weight (incl. packing)	Chargeable weight	Volume (l/w/h)	Volume weight	Applicable freight rate
1. high pressure cleaner	33.51 kg		40 × 40 × 80		
2. 18th century painting	47.1 kg		100 × 80 × 20		
4. fashion magazines	12.3 kg		20 × 30 × 40		
5. engine spare parts	88.5 kg		60 × 50 × 30		
6. sparkling wine	25.55 kg		40 × 50 × 30		

3 Dealing with maritime transport

1 Try to identify the vessels in the photos. Use the internet to check your answers and find the English names for the vessels. Then write one sentence about each vessel describing its typical characteristics.

P

2 Harald Keller, who works for a logistics company specialising in sea freight, and
R   Luano Santos, a client from Brazil, are sitting in a café in Schulau near Hamburg.
⊚ A 2.12 Listen to their conversation and take notes on the ships that are mentioned.

1. Type of ship	2. Transported goods	3. Other details

3 Work with a partner and think of other typical goods that are transported on   Phrases ▶
P   the types of ships mentioned above. Find other types of merchant ships on the
internet and add them to the table in Exercise 2. Compare your findings in class.

4 Match the English terms (1.–9.) to their German equivalents (a.–i.).
Use a dictionary, if necessary.

1. berth
2. container crane
3. container storage area
4 customs office
5. feeder road
6. floating crane
7. gantry crane
8. packing centre
9. shunting yard

a. Containerkran
b. Containerlager
c. Liegeplatz
d. Packzentrum
e. Portalkran
f. Schwimmkran
g. Verschiebebahnhof
h. Zollamt
i. Zubringerstraße

5 Look at the picture below and say which means of transport it shows. Then assign
R the terms 1.–9. in Exercise 4 to the letters in the picture.

Ian Wilders, a trainee from Ireland, works at Embrosius Logistics in Erfurt. He
has just changed to the sea freight department and his boss wants him to get
an overview of the procedures in a container port. With Xaver Stein, one of the
company's drivers, Ian goes to the container terminal. Xaver has six euro-pallets
with car parts on his truck that have to be transported to Liverpool. Together
they follow the consignment through the port until it is loaded onto the ship.

✳ 6 Collect ideas in class about the stages the consignment has to go through in the
P port and put them in chronological order. Then write Ian's report of his visit to the
container terminal.

4   Ordering containers

1
R / P
Work with a partner and match the illustrations (A.–E.) to the container types mentioned in the table below. Compare the containers with regard to their capacity and suitability for certain goods.

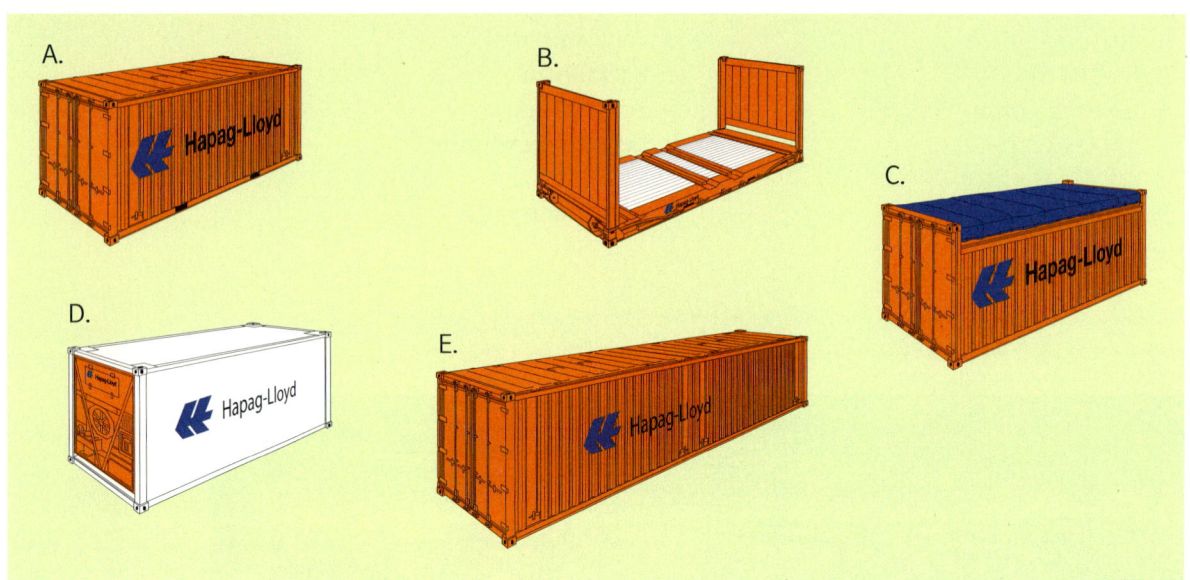

Type	Payload (cu. ft.)	Payload (lbs)	Door width (inch)	Door height (inch)	Length interior (inch)	Width interior (inch)	Height interior (inch)
1. 20' Standard	1,140	47,711	90.7	89.6	233.0	91.7	92.8
2. 40' Standard	2,362	58,036	91.7	89.7	473.0	91.7	94.1
3. 40' High cube	2,705	57,288	92.1	102.0	473.7	92.5	106.1
4. 20' Insulated reefer	928,8	39,934	87.9	81.5	223.5	88.0	81.8
5. 20' Open top	1,140.7	39,908	91.3	89.5	231.7	91,3	93.1
6. 40' Open top	2,355.5	58,366	91.9	90.0	473.1	91.8	91.3
7. 20' Flat rack	1,147.7	46,420	–	–	232.3	94.4	90.7
8. 40' Flat rack	2,295.4	57,816	–	–	473.8	91.9	91.1

Info: Containers

Containers are reusable transport and storage units for transporting raw materials or products. A typical container has doors at one end and is made of corrugated steel. The size of container ships and the costs for transport are calculated in twenty-foot equivalent units (TEU). Containers can be used in a variety of transport modes such as ship, rail, road or air and can carry up to 25 tonnes. Every container has a BIC code on the outside for identification.

2 Choose a suitable type of container for the following consignments and give
P reasons for your decision.

1. 65 m³ cardboard boxes with electric appliances
2. 60 plastic tubes, each 10 m long, weighing 40 kg
3. 16,200 kg of frozen beef
4. 66.8 m³ bales of cotton

3 Sie arbeiten bei der Spedition Krügard in Nordhorn. Ihre Chefin, Frau Krügard
KMK gibt Ihnen die folgende Telefonnotiz und bittet Sie Herrn Matthew per E-Mail ein
Angebot auf Englisch für eine entsprechende Containererstellung zu schicken.

Phrases

```
TELEFONNOTIZ

Von:      Frau Krügard

An:       (Name)

Betreff:  Angebot für Containererstellung

* Anruf von Baumaschinen AG (Hauptsitz: Emden),
  Vertriebsbüro: Nordamerika, Chicago, IC (USA)

* Potentieller neuer Großkunde für Radlader in Boston (MA), USA

* Probelieferung (Emden – Boston) von 4 Radladern mit folgenden Abmessungen:
  - Typ WL 1000: 8,37m x 2,22m x 2,35m, Gewicht: 13,45t
  - Typ WL 1500: 8,78m x 2,33m x 2,47m, Gewicht: 15,39t
  - Typ WL 2000: 9,52m x 2,33m x 2,90m, Gewicht: 16,57t
  - Typ XWL-CR: 11,99m x 2,78m x 3,10m, Gewicht: 20,08t

* Passende Container für die Radlader anbieten

* E-Mail an: matthew@baumasch-emd.usa
```

5 Bill of lading, air waybill and certificate of origin

1 Use the following details to fill in the bill of lading on page 177 of your book.
R Write on a separate piece of paper.

- six euro-pallets with car parts weighing 90 kg each
- transportation via Hamburg to Liverpool
- sender: Union-Autoteile Eisenach (Wartburgstraße 18, 99817 Eisenach)
- Midland Logistics (5 Houghton Road, Oldbury A53 7CR, UK) will pick up the
  consignment from Liverpool docks for on-carriage to CarComponents Ltd.
  (248 Kirkstall Street, Leeds, LS5 6QD, UK)
- carrier: Embrosius Logistics (Frischmarkt 18, 99251 Erfurt)
- the pallets will be transported on board MS Ålesund
- invoice amount for car parts: €19,225.00
- use today's date

2 **The following form is an example of an air waybill. Use the information below to complete the form in English on a separate sheet of paper.**

1. Abflughafen: Frankfurt
2. Währung: USD
3. Absender: Bürowelt GmbH, Den Haager Str. 33, 60327 Frankfurt am Main
4. Empfänger: Executive Furnishings, 875 Spring St, Newark, N. J. 07205, USA
5. Beförderer: Lufthansa, Frankfurt
6. Zielflughafen: Newark International Airport
7. Deklarierter Zollwert: NCV
8. Anzahl der Frachtstücke: 32
9. Bruttogewicht: 972,4 kg
10. Zu berechnendes Gewicht: 972,4 kg
11. Deklarierter Transportwert: NVD
12. Art und Anzahl der Ware: 24 Bürostühle aus Leder, 12 Besucherstühle aus Holz, 8 Archivschränke, 4 Prospektständer

Shipper's Name and Address		Shipper's Account Number		Not negotiable **Air Waybill*** Issued by

Member of International Air Transport Association

Copies 1, 2 and 3 of this Air Waybill are originals and have the same validity

Consignee's Name and Address		Consignee's Account Number	It is agreed that the goods described herein are accepted in apparent good order and condition (except as noted) for carriage SUBJECT TO THE CONDITIONS OF CONTRACT ON THE REVERSE HEREOF. ALL GOODS MAY BE CARRIED BY ANY OTHER MEANS INCLUDING ROAD OR ANY OTHER CARRIER UNLESS SPECIFIC CONTRARY INSTRUCTIONS ARE GIVEN HEREON BY THE SHIPPER, AND SHIPPER AGREES THAT THE SHIPMENT MAY BE CARRIED VIA INTERMEDIATE STOPPING PLACES WHICH THE CARRIER DEEMS APPROPRIATE. THE SHIPPER'S ATTENTION IS DRAWN TO THE NOTICE CONCERNING CARRIER'S LIMITATION OF LIABILITY. Shipper may increase such limitation of liability by declaring a higher value for carriage and paying a supplemental charge if required.

Issuing Carrier's Agent Name and City	Accounting Information

Agent's IATA Code	Account No.

Airport of Departure (Addr. of First Carrier) and Requested Routing

To	By First Carrier	Routing and Destination	To	By	To	By	Currency	CHGS Code	WT/VAL PPD COLL	Other PPD COLL	Declared Value for Carriage	Declared Value for Customs

Airport of Destination	Flight/Date	Amount of Insurance	INSURANCE – If Carrier offers insurance, and such insurance is requested in accordance with the conditions thereof, indicate amount to be insured in figures in box marked 'Amount of Insurance'

Handling Information

SCI

(For U.S.A. use only) These commodities licensed by USA for ultimate destination .... Diversion contrary to USA law prohibited.

No. of Pieces RCP	Gross Weight	kg lb	Rate Class / Commodity Item No.	Chargeable Weight	Rate / Charge	Total	Nature and Quantity of Goods (incl. Dimensions or Volume)

Prepaid	Weight Charge	Collect	Other Charges

Valuation Charge	

Tax	

Total Other Charges Due Agent	Shipper certifies that the particulars on the face hereof are correct and that insofar as any part of the consignment contains dangerous goods, such part is properly described by name and is in proper condition for carriage by air according to the applicable Dangerous Goods Regulations.

Total Other Charges Due Carrier	

3 Look at the example of a certificate of origin. Match the German terms (a.–r.) to the terms used on the form.

a. Anzahl und Art der Pakete
b. Artikelnummer
c. ausgestellt in (Land)
d. Beschreibung der Waren
e. Bruttogewicht oder andere Mengenangabe
f. Erklärung und Zeugnis kombiniert
g. Für den Dienstgebrauch
h. Handelskammer
i. Kennzeichnung und Anzahl der Pakete
j. Kopie
k. null und nichtig
l. Rechnungsnummer und -datum
m. Referenznummer
n. Siehe Anmerkungen auf der Rückseite
o. Transportmittel und Route (sofern bekannt)
p. Ursprungskriterium
q. Waren versandt an
r. Waren versandt von

COPY

1. **Goods consigned from** (exporter's business name, address, country)	Reference No **257967**
	GENERALIZED SYSTEM OF PREFERENCES **CERTIFICATE OF ORIGIN** (Combined declaration and certificate) **FORM A**
2. **Goods consigned to** (consignee's name, address, country)	issued in _____ Taiwan _____ (country) See notes overleaf

3. **Means of transport and route** (as far as known)	4. **For official use**

5. **Item number**	6. **Marks and numbers of packages**	7. **Number and kind of packages; description of goods**	8. **Origin criterion** (see notes overleaf)	9. **Gross weight or other quantity**	10. **Number and date of invoice**

This certificate shall be considered null and void in case of any alteration.
It is hereby certified that the goods described in this certificate originate in Taiwan.

Chamber of Commerce of Taichung City, Taiwan

6   Trade documentation

✳ ▮ Sie arbeiten bei einer Spedition und Ihre Vorgesetzte hat Sie gebeten, einem
KMK Praktikanten einige Handelsdokumente zu erklären. Verfassen Sie mithilfe des
folgenden Textes eine Zusammenfassung der einzelnen Dokumente auf Deutsch.

Ticking the right boxes

Anyone who works in international trade will tell you that shipping consignments around the world involves filling in a lot of forms. If you want to avoid fines, delayed shipments and trouble with customs officials, it is important to tick the right boxes and file the appropriate paperwork. *Silk Road Journal's* **guide to trade documentation continues this month with six new documents.**

As the name suggests, a **consular invoice** is a specific invoice that is issued by the consulate of the importing country. A large number of countries have completely phased out this document. The consular invoice is used for customs clearance and other purposes. Any errors or missing information on the document are likely to lead to problems and possibly fines at customs in the importing country.

The **customs invoice** is used for customs purposes in place of the commercial invoice in a few importing countries. Nevertheless, the importer is often required to present a commercial invoice, too. Like the consular invoice, the customs invoice contains largely the same information as the commercial invoice and the packing list, but in a different format. In some countries importers are required to provide a completed customs invoice for customs clearance.

An **export declaration** form is a required document which acts as a formal statement made to the customs officials at the place of exit, declaring full details of the goods being exported. It is used for goods shipped to countries outside the EU which are worth €1,000 and more.

The **EUR1 movement certificate** is for goods which are produced in the EU. These goods are subject to cheaper rates of duty or may be completely duty free, providing they were manufactured in a member country. By completing an EUR1 certificate the manufacturer certifies the origin of the goods.

A **certificate of analysis** is required by some countries as proof of the quality of certain food products, such as grain, health foods, fruits & vegetables and pharmaceutical products. The required analysis may be made by either a governmental or private health agency. The **certificate of inspection** is a similar form, required for the shipment of industrial equipment and meat products.

Phrases: Transport and logistics

To give particulars about packing

The goods are packed in …	Die Ware ist verpackt in …
• polythene bags.	• Plastikbeutel.
• 20 bales weighing 50 kgs per bale.	• 20 Ballen zu je 50 kg.
• one 20 ft container.	• einem 20-Fuß-Container.
• fibreboard boxes with steel bands.	• Hartfaserkisten mit Stahlbändern.
The goods will be shipped …	Die Ware wird …
• **in** sturdy crates.	• in stabilen Lattenkisten
• **on** reusable pallets.	• auf Mehrwegpaletten
	versandt.

To say that the goods are ready for collection

We are pleased to inform you that the keyboards can now be collected **at** our plant in Leeds.	Wir freuen uns Ihnen mitteilen zu können, dass die Keyboards jetzt in unserem Werk in Leeds abgeholt werden können.

To give particulars about the transport

The consignment has today been handed over to the freight forwarders **for** transportation **to** Warsaw by lorry.	Die Sendung wurde heute der Spedition zur Beförderung nach Warschau per LKW übergeben.
Yesterday the machine was loaded **on board** MS Seagull in Bremerhaven.	Die Maschine wurde gestern in Bremerhaven auf die MS Seagull verladen.
The spare parts will be sent **by** air freight **on** Air Canada flight No. AC 442, arriving **at** Toronto airport at 11:55 **on** 25 September.	Die Ersatzteile werden per Luftfracht mit Air Canada, Flug Nr. AC 442 verschickt. Ankunft: Flughafen Toronto, 25. Sept., 11:55 Uhr.

To close on a friendly note

We hope the goods will arrive punctually and in good condition.	Wir hoffen, die Ware kommt pünktlich und in gutem Zustand bei Ihnen an.
We trust that the quality of our garments will meet your expectations.	Wir sind überzeugt, dass die Qualität unserer Bekleidungsartikel Ihren Erwartungen entspricht.
We feel sure that your customers will be pleased with our new range of …	Wir sind sicher, dass unser neues Sortiment von … Ihren Kunden gefallen wird.

Unit 13
Payment and reminders

CURRENCY QUIZ

Questions:

1. Which is the youngest of the currencies shown above?
2. Which is the oldest of these currencies?
3. Which of these currencies is the most widely used in international business transactions?
4. Which of these currencies do most individuals use for their daily purchases?

1. The Euro. Euro banknotes and coins replaced 12 former European currencies on 1 January 2002.
2. The Pound Sterling. It has been in use since the Middle Ages. The US Dollar was introduced in 1785, (the Swiss Frank in 1798 and the Yen in 1871).
3. The US Dollar. On a global scale the US-Dollar is still the most widely used currency in business transactions.
4. The Euro. The number of inhabitants in the Euro zone (EU without Denmark, Sweden and the United Kingdom) is estimated at 325,7 million, approx. 306 million people live in the USA.

Online-Link
808264-0013

A The invoice

The **commercial invoice** (Handelsrechnung) is sent by the seller to the buyer and provides full details on the transaction, such as names, dates, numbers, descriptions, quantities, prices, discounts, terms, taxes (VAT) etc. When making out an export invoice you should make sure that it includes your company's IBAN and your bank's BIC.

A **proforma invoice** (Proformarechnung) contains all the details of the eventual commercial invoice. It may serve as a quotation or be required to apply for an import licence.

1 The above text contains three abbreviations. Study their German translations and
R find the words that have been left out in the full English expressions.

VAT   Value-added **1** = Mehrwert**steuer**
IBAN   International Bank **2** Number = Internationale **Konto**nummer
BIC   Bank Identifier **3** = Internationaler Bank-**Code**.

2 Philipp Schäfer is processing the trial order for Turbostar Running shoes which
R his company, Herkules, has received from Sports Island, a major British chain of sports equipment retailers. (See Unit 11, A). The necessary arrangements for transportation having been made Philipp Schäfer now confirms the order by e-mail and sends the invoice as an attachment.

Study Philipp Schäfer's e-mail and decide which of the tenses in brackets is correct.

Dear Ms Brookfield

Thank you very much for your above-mentioned order.

We are pleased to inform you that the consignment **1 is picked up / will be picked up** by Transeurope Hauliers for transportation to the UK in two days' time, that is to say on Wednesday, 10 October. The forwarders **2 have given / had given** us the assurance that the running shoes **3 will be delivered / will have been delivered** to your premises in London on the following Friday, 12 October, between 9 and 11 a.m. your time.

Since this is a first order we **4 were sending / are sending** you our invoice No. GB113-14 as an attachment and would appreciate it if you **5 instructed / have instructed** your bankers at your earliest convenience to remit the sum of € 30,375.00 to our account with Bayernbank. For particulars see the attached invoice.

We **5 feel / felt** sure that your customers **6 will be pleased / are pleased** with the Turbostar running shoes as they are not merely comfortable, serviceable and durable but stylish as well. We look forward to receiving further orders from you in the near future.

Herkules
the global sports brand
Ziegelberg 8–12
89331 Neustadt
Tel. +49 8358 888-0
Fax +49 8358 88820
www.Herkules.com

USt. ID No. DE 812 039 979

INVOICE No. GB113-14

Sports Island
41 Bryant Road
London W7 9QB
UK

VAT No. 186 4405 32

Customer No. UK 22267

Date: 8 Oct 201_
Your Order No. 5347 of 5 Oct 201_

Person in charge: Mike Kappler
Tel.: +49 8358 888 317
Fax: +49 8358 888 300
E-Mail: accounts@herkules.com

Quantity	Item	Sizes	Unit Price	Subtotal
25 pairs each	Turbostar Running Shoes	5, 5 ½ ,11, 12	€ 40.50	€ 4,050.00
50 pairs each		6, 6 ½, 7, 7 ½, 10	€ 40.50	€ 10,125.00
100 pairs each		8, 8 ½, 9, 9 ½	€ 40.50	€ 16,200.00

Total Price € 30,375.00

tax-exempt intra-Community delivery

Terms of delivery: EXW Neustadt
Terms of payment: Cash on receipt of invoice

Please instruct your bank to forward the payment order through

Bank:	Bayernbank AG
BIC:	BABADET TS08
In favour of:	Herkules AG
Bank account number:	214365987
IBAN:	DE49 2006 0460 0214 3659 87

3 Study the invoice and find words and expressions for the following German
R equivalents.

1. Gesamtpreis 4. Artikel 7. Menge
2. Preis pro Einheit/Stückpreis 5. Lieferbedingungen 8. Rechnung
3. Zahlungsbedingungen 6. Größen 9. Zwischensumme

✳ 4 Study the invoice again and draw up the invoice Cornelia Klinkenberg sent James
P Leigh on 14 August. Use your imagination for the missing details and refer back to:

1. the enquiry James Leigh sent Cornelia Klinkenberg (Unit 10, A)
2. the dispatch advice Cornelia Klinkenberg sent James Leigh (Unit 12, C)
3. James Leigh's reply to Cornelia Klinkenberg's reminder (Unit 13, C).

B Means and terms of payment

1 Means of payment in trade

A **credit card** (Kreditkarte) issued by a major credit card
company is widely accepted as a means of payment all over the
world. The amount to be paid is advanced by the credit card
company and debited to the cardholder's account at a later date.

A **debit (or bank) card** (Bankkarte) is issued by a bank. The
account-holder may use it to pay for goods and services in shops
without handling cash. It differs from credit cards in that the
customer's account is immediately debited with the amount of
the transaction. Bank cards can also be used to withdraw money
from cash points (ATMs). The German EC card is a debit card.

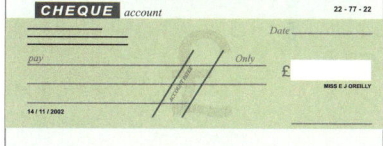

A **cheque** (Scheck) is a written order to a bank to pay a sum of
money to a named person or to the bearer (Überbringer) of the
cheque. Crossed cheques (Verrechnungsschecks) require the
sum to be paid into a bank account. In the UK cheques are still
widely used in private and business transactions.

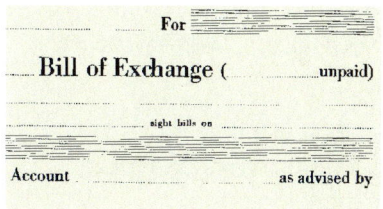

A **bill of exchange** (Wechsel) is a written order telling one
person to pay a certain sum of money to a named person on
demand or at a certain time in the future. Nowadays bills of
exchange are used mainly in foreign trade. If the exporter
wishes payment to be made immediately, he orders the
importer to pay the invoice amount on demand, or "at sight",
that means on presentation of the bill of exchange (B/E). Should
the exporter be obliged to grant the importer credit, he will
order him to pay the invoice amount at a certain time in the
future, e.g. 60 days after the date of the B/E.

1 Match the following expressions with their German equivalents.

1. to accept a credit card	a. Geld abheben
2. to advance an amount	b. eine Kreditkarte annehmen
3. to debit an account	c. eine Bankkarte ausstellen
4. to grant credit	d. ein Konto belasten
5. to issue a bank card	e. Kredit gewähren
6. to withdraw money	f. einen Betrag vorschießen

✳ **2** Study the text on the bill of exchange on page 193 and translate the following
M text.

Mittels eines Wechsels kann der Verkäufer den Käufer auffordern, eine
bestimmte Summe zu einem bestimmten Zeitpunkt an eine bestimmte Person
zu zahlen. Der Verkäufer könnte auf dem Wechsel auch vorschreiben, dass
der Käufer den Betrag „auf Verlangen" zahlt. Die entsprechende Formulierung
wäre dann „zahlbar bei Sicht", d. h. bei Vorlage des Wechsels.

✳ **3** Übersetzen Sie nachstehenden Text zum Einsatz von Kreditkarten in
KMK Großbritannien ins Deutsche. Im Internet haben Sie Übersetzungen für
folgende Ausdrücke gefunden:

overindebted – überschuldet; to turn down an application – einen Antrag
ablehnen; debit card – Bankkarte; cashback – Auszahlung von Bargeld;
debt levels – Ausmaß der Verschuldung; check-out – Ladenkasse

Payment by plastic cards

In the UK payment by plastic cards overtook cash payments several years ago as
consumers use credit or debit cards more frequently. The vast majority of retail outlets
accept these cards as a matter of course and supermarkets offer cashback*. Adults now
have an average of 4 cards each and this is expected to rise to 5 cards by 2013. Last year
the number of credit cards issued rose by 13 per cent and the number of debit cards rose
by 6 per cent. Well over half of all debit card holders use their cards on a regular basis
when shopping.

Recently banks and other credit card providers have come in for criticism because of
fears that consumers are becoming over-indebted. A spokesman for the banks said that
between 40 and 50 per cent of all credit card applications were turned down. Debt levels
were a problem only for 4 per cent of households.

Plastic cards are essential for e-commerce. Four out of five adults who have access use the
internet for online shopping. A third of all online purchases are made from work and top
sites include major supermarkets and a well-known young people's fashion chain.

* If the customer wishes, they provide a sum in cash at the check-out, as stipulated by the customer.

4 Use the internet to find statistics on the preferred payment methods – cash, credit card, debit card, cheque, bank transfer – in Germany and the UK.

2 Terms of payment in foreign trade

The terms of payment chosen in an international transaction will depend on the size of the order, the creditworthiness of the customer and the banking system and political situation in the customer's country.

Payment in advance (Vorauszahlung) provides maximum security for the seller, e.g. when the goods have to be manufactured to the buyer's specifications. Payment in advance may also be part of staggered payment, e.g. ⅓ with order, ⅓ on delivery, ⅓ 30 days after delivery.

If **Cash on delivery (COD)** (Zahlung durch Nachnahme) has been agreed upon, the carrier (e.g. the postman) will hand over the goods to the buyer against payment or against written proof by the bank that payment has been effected.

Open credit (Zahlung gegen einfache Rechnung) terms are terms like "30 days net, 10 days 2 %", which means that the buyer has to remit the invoice amount within 30 days. If he pays the amount within 10 days he will be entitled to deduct 2 % cash discount from the invoice amount. Open credit terms provide little security for the seller but are widely used in transactions involving comparatively small sums and/or trusted customers.

In long-standing business relations it is customary to trade on **open account** terms (offenes Zahlungsziel). This means that the buyer does not pay individual invoices, but waits for the monthly statement of account.

A **letter of credit (L/C)** (Akkreditiv) is a promise made by the importer's bank to pay a certain sum to the exporter on presentation of specified documents, the most important of which is a clean bill of lading (see Unit 12). Nowadays L/Cs are irrevocable (unwiderruflich) that means they cannot be revoked without the consent of all parties concerned. As the L/C offers maximum security for both buyer and seller it has become one of the most widely used methods of payment in foreign trade. The exporter can be sure to receive payment as he can rely on the promise made by the importer's bank (the opening bank) – and in the case of a confirmed (bestätigtes) L/C – also on the promise of a bank in his own country (the confirming bank). The importer can be sure to receive the goods as the bank(s) will only advance the money against presentation of the shipping documents which prove that shipment has been effected.

1
R / M
Study the paragraph on the Letter of Credit on page 195. Choose the correct prepositions from the box for the following text. Then translate the text into German.

> at • by • in • until

In a major export transaction the terms of payment may read as follows: **Terms of payment:** Payment **1** irrevocable and confirmed letter of credit, to be opened **2** our favour, payable **3** a German bank and valid **4** 31 July.

2
R
Complete the following business transactions by matching the terms of payment from the box with the numbers.

> cash on delivery • letter of credit • open account terms • open credit • payment in advance

Wilson & Thatcher Ltd, a British retailer, also sells its high-quality shirts and blouses via the Internet. As a means of payment the firm accepts all major credit cards. For customers who refuse to disclose their credit card details on the internet, the retailer's terms of payment are **1** which means that the postman will collect the amount due.

International Snacks GmbH, a German food processing company, gets a phone call from its long-standing customer, Global Catering in Manchester, asking for another 500 tins of mini smoked sausages. These two business partners most likely trade on **2** .

Powertools plc from Cardiff has received an enquiry from a new German customer who wishes to have 10,000 drill heads (Bohrköpfe) manufactured to the German firm's specifications. As Powertools would be unable to sell these drill heads to another customer if the deal broke down, Powertools will insist on **3** .

Norland Industries made an offer for colour printers to De Boer Office Equipment in Durban, South Africa. The terms of payment stipulated were: net cash within 30 days from receipt of invoice. Such terms of payment are referred to as **4** .

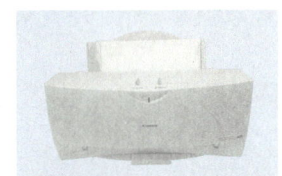

At Herkules, a German manufacturer of sports shoes and bags, the managers in charge of exports are discussing the terms of payment for a substantial order for sports bags from a firm in Bolivia they do not know. They decide to demand payment by **5** .

C Reminders

There are times when bills go unpaid and steps must be taken to collect the invoice amount. One or several reminders may have to be sent, with the requests for payment becoming increasingly insistent. At first a copy of the invoice or statement of account is sent suggesting that the invoice may have been overlooked. If further reminders by telephone, e-mail, fax, or letter have failed to produce the desired reaction, the seller will threaten to charge interest on arrears and to take legal steps unless payment is received by a certain deadline.

On 18 August the British department stores Hamilton's placed an urgent order for men's shirts with Superdress GmbH. Payment was to be effected 30 days after date of invoice. The goods were shipped by air and must have arrived at Manchester Airport on 22 August. It is now 10 October and no communication from Hamilton's has been received. Bastian Schneider, who is in charge of accounts at Superdress GmbH, decides to send a first polite reminder by fax.

1 **Complete Bastian Schneider's fax using the words from the box.**

R

above • aware • dated • due • grateful • immediate

$\mathcal{Superdress}$ GmbH

Fritz-Walter-Str. 28, 80469 München
Tel. +49 89 4677524, Fax +49 89 4677625
www.superdress.munich.de

Telefax Message

Date: 10 Oct 201_

To: Hamilton's Department Stores
Hamilton House
Beaumont Rd
Bolton
BL3 4TA

Sender: Bastian Schneider, Accounts

Attention: Richard Knight

Fax : +44 161 234 57799

Pages : 1 (including this)

Re: Our invoice no. OHGB / 42778 **1** 21 August

reference to invoice

Dear Mr. Knight

According to our records the **2** invoice, which was **3** on 21 September, has not been settled.

I wonder whether the invoice has been overlooked or if there has been a problem with this order of which we are not **4** ?

request for explanation

We should be **5** for an **6** settlement and look forward to serving you again.

request for settlement

Yours sincerely
Superdress GmbH

2
P
You are Richard Knight, purchasing manager at Hamilton's Department Stores, e-mail: richard.knight@hamiltons.co.uk. You have just received the fax on page 197 from Superdress GmbH.

Send Mr Schneider, whose e-mail address is b.schneider@superdress.munich.de, an e-mail:

- thanks for fax
- apologize for the delay in payment
- reason: new software in accounts department faulty
- operations now running smoothly at last
- bank instructed to remit invoice amount
- further orders probably next month

3
R
Restore the correct order of these jumbled elements of a final request for payment.

1 I still hope that you will make this action unnecessary by remitting the amount in full within the next seven days.

2 Dear Mr Clarke

3 This account has now remained unpaid for eight weeks and I cannot allow this state of affairs to continue. I regret that I will have to take legal steps unless payment is received in the course of one week.

4 Yours sincerely

Barbara Bruno
Legal Department

5 I am surprised to have received no reply to our previous e-mails and faxes asking for immediate settlement of the attached statement of account.

6 Re: Our statement of account number NZ / 7034 of 9 December 201_

■ **Language and grammar**
Translate the following sentences.

1. Wir machen Sie darauf aufmerksam, dass die Zahlung per Kreditkarte erfolgen soll.
2. Das Unternehmen soll in 5 selbstständige Geschäftseinheiten aufgeteilt werden.
3. Sollen wir Ihnen die Preisliste per E-Mail zukommen lassen?
4. Soll die Rechnung Nr. ABC/1234 storniert werden?
5. Die neue Geschäftsleitung soll weiteren Stellenabbau planen.
6. Die neue Autobahn soll von einem privaten Unternehmen betrieben werden.
7. Der neue Exportleiter soll sehr tüchtig sein.

Language and grammar:
How to translate the German word "sollen"

Wendungen mit **sollen** werden von Deutschen häufig ungeschickt wiedergegeben.

Die direkte Entsprechung **shall** passt nur bei • Fragen • und juristischen Texten	Shall I help you? The parties to this contract shall notify the administrator within 24 hours.
should bedeutet **sollte (eigentlich)**:	You should put more emphasis on this point.
sollen kann im Geschäftskontext in Fragen mit **do you want me / us to . . .?** übersetzt werden: Sollen wir diese Teile zurückschicken?	Do you want us to return these components?
to be to . . . ist eine passende Übersetzung für **sollen** im Sinne einer Anordnung oder einer Absicht bzw. eines festen Planes: Die Bauarbeiter sollen sofort anfangen. Das Problem soll durch weitere Verhandlungen gelöst werden.	The builders are to start work immediately. The problem is to be solved by further negotiations.
Im Falle einer Absicht / eines Plans kann **to be to . . .** durch **to be intended to / planned to . . .** präzisiert werden: Die Erhöhung der Mehrwertsteuer soll den Haushalt ausgleichen. Die Ausstellung soll Anfang nächsten Jahres stattfinden.	The increase in VAT is intended to balance the budget. The exhibition is planned to take place early next year.
to be said to . . . bedeutet **sollen** im Sinne von **es heißt, man sagt**: Die Firma soll sich in Schwierigkeiten befinden.	The company is said to be in trouble.

Logistics expert

1 Organising international payment

For business transactions with overseas customers, especially for first business contacts, the safest method is payment by letter of credit (L / C).

1 **Heike Krull, management assistant in freight forwarding at Spezialmaschinenbau**
R **Hoffmann in Berlin, is talking on the phone to Pat Wills, a friend in Leeds, about the latest export contract her company has won. Read the dialogue aloud in class.**

Heike: … and I had already given up hope, when the fax finally arrived yesterday. It was time to go home, but when I saw that they had ordered four bottling machines, I knew it would mean long hours for me again.

Pat: Where did you say the guys are from? Saudi Arabia?

Heike: No, the company's in Qatar. It's called Al Mazayah and it's based near Doha. They make ketchup and all sorts of other sauces.

Pat: And how can you be sure you'll get your money?

Heike: Well, in the sales contract they agreed on payment by letter of credit. This means that the money is safe with their bank. The invoice amount is paid into a kind of special account and Al Mazayah can't have it back for some time.

Pat: So you'll have to do the business with the bank in Qatar?

Heike: No, our bank in Berlin is in contact with the Qatari bank. Once we've dispatched the machines, we'll hand the transport documents and all the other paperwork to our bank. They check if delivery was made on time and if the forwarder has received the consignment in good condition. Then they'll send the papers to their colleagues in Qatar.

Pat: And they'll still have the money down there, won't they?

Heike: Yes. The Qatari bank will check the documents again and if they're OK, they'll remit the invoice amount to our bank, who will credit it to our account.

Pat: But the ketchup company doesn't have the machines yet, does it?

Heike: No, the Qatari bank has the documents which makes them the owners of the machines. As soon as we get the money Al Mazayah will get the documents, in particular the bill of lading, which they will need to collect the machines when they've arrived in Doha.

Pat: I'm so happy I earn my living in a less complicated job.

Heike: I wouldn't change my work for yours either.

2 **Work with a partner and take notes on the steps of the L / C transaction described**
R **in the dialogue above.**

200

✷ 3 Look at the illustration below and number the different steps. Then use your notes
P from Exercise 2 and the illustration to explain how an L/C works.

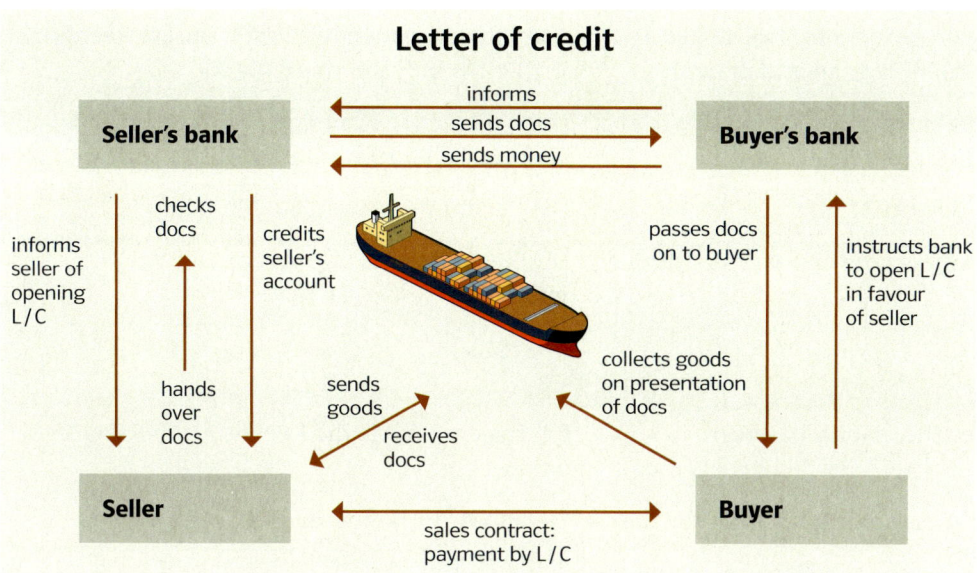

Letter of credit

| Seller's bank | informs ⟵ sends docs ⟶ sends money ⟵ | Buyer's bank |

informs seller of opening L/C

checks docs

credits seller's account

passes docs on to buyer

instructs bank to open L/C in favour of seller

hands over docs

sends goods

receives docs

collects goods on presentation of docs

| **Seller** | sales contract: payment by L/C | **Buyer** |

2 Problems with payment

KMK Sie betreuen den Kunden Hochstraate in Belgien. Bisher hat die Firma
stets pünktlich bezahlt, aber heute haben Sie die folgende E-Mail erhalten.
Beantworten Sie diese unter Berücksichtigung der unten stehenden Punkte.

Phrases ▸

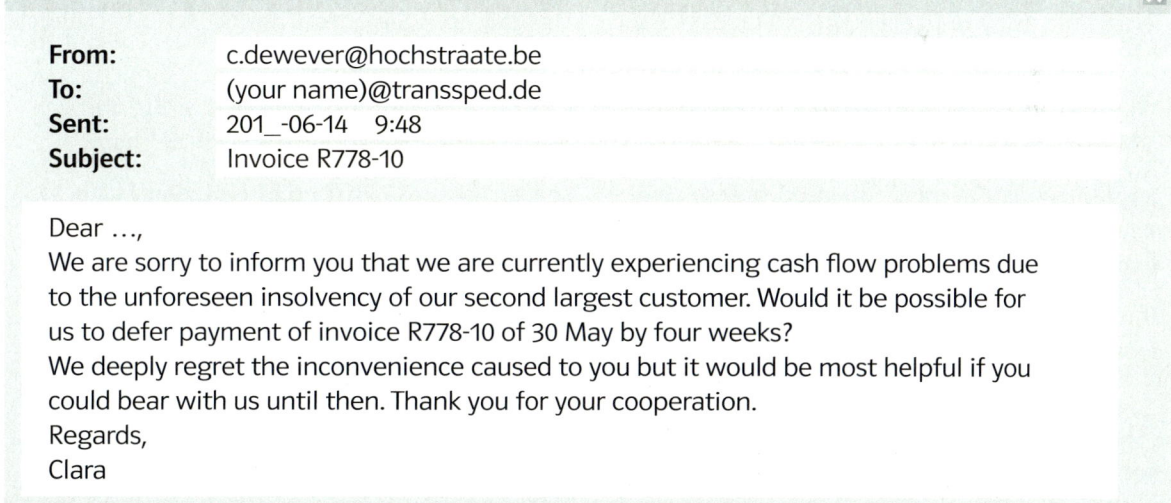

From:	c.dewever@hochstraate.be
To:	(your name)@transsped.de
Sent:	201_-06-14 9:48
Subject:	Invoice R778-10

Dear …,
We are sorry to inform you that we are currently experiencing cash flow problems due
to the unforeseen insolvency of our second largest customer. Would it be possible for
us to defer payment of invoice R778-10 of 30 May by four weeks?
We deeply regret the inconvenience caused to you but it would be most helpful if you
could bear with us until then. Thank you for your cooperation.
Regards,
Clara

- Äußern Sie Ihr Bedauern, dass Hochstraate Schwierigkeiten hat.
- Rechnung R778-10 beläuft sich auf eine beträchtliche Summe und ihre Firma
  muss auch ihren Verpflichtungen nachkommen.
- Vorschlag: ⅓ sofort per Überweisung, ⅓ in zwei Wochen, Rest in einem Monat.
- Bitte um schriftliche Bestätigung, wenn Hochstraate einverstanden ist.

Phrases: Invoices and reminders

To refer to the invoice or statement of account

We are sending you our invoice No. 43-298 **amounting to** €304.75 as an attachment.	Als Anhang senden wir Ihnen unsere Rechnung Nr. 43-298 in Höhe von €304,75.
The enclosed statement of account shows a balance of €5,402.90 **in** our favour.	Der beiliegende Kontoauszug weist einen Saldo von €5.402,90 zu unseren Gunsten auf.
The invoice was due **on** 31 July.	Die Rechnung war am 31. Juli fällig.
The invoice amount is now four weeks overdue.	Der Rechnungsbetrag ist nun vier Wochen überfällig.

To suggest an oversight or demand an explanation

I wonder whether the invoice has been overlooked.	Ich frage mich, ob die Rechnung übersehen wurde.
You have not given us any explanation for the delay **in** payment.	Sie haben uns keinerlei Erklärung für den Zahlungsverzug gegeben.

To demand payment and to point out consequences of non-payment

Please remit the amount due immediately.	Bitte überweisen Sie den fälligen Betrag umgehend.
We should be grateful for an early settlement of our statement of account.	Für baldigen Ausgleich unseres Kontoauszugs wären wir dankbar.
We would ask you to clear the balance without further delay.	Wir möchten Sie bitten, den Saldo unverzüglich auszugleichen.
We must insist that you make payment **by** 5 May at the latest.	Wir müssen darauf bestehen, dass Sie die Zahlung bis spätestens 5. Mai vornehmen.
Should you fail to meet this deadline we shall have no option **but** to change our terms of payment.	Sollten Sie diese Frist nicht einhalten, bleibt uns keine andere Wahl als unsere Zahlungsbedingungen zu ändern.
If we do not receive payment **by** the end of the week, we will have to stop further deliveries.	Wenn Ihre Zahlung nicht bis Ende der Woche hier eingeht, müssen wir die Belieferung einstellen.
I will have to take legal steps if you do not settle the account within 7 days.	Ich werde juristische Schritte einleiten müssen, falls Sie die Rechnung nicht innerhalb von 7 Tagen begleichen.
Unless you remit the amount **in** time, we will hand the matter over to a collection agency.	Wenn Sie den Betrag nicht rechtzeitig überweisen, übergeben wir die Angelegenheit einem Inkassounternehmen.

To close the reminder

If payment has already been effected in the meantime, please disregard this letter.	Sollte die Zahlung inzwischen erfolgt sein, betrachten Sie diesen Brief bitte als gegenstandslos.
We should be sorry to lose a long-standing customer and would ask you to contact us immediately.	Wir würden einen langjährigen Kunden nur ungern verlieren, setzen Sie sich deshalb bitte sofort mit uns in Verbindung.
We are looking forward to an early settlement.	Wir erwarten Ihre baldige Zahlung.

To reply to a reminder

We have instructed our bank to transfer the sum of €7,455 **to** your account **with** Sachsenbank.	Wir haben unsere Bank angewiesen, den Betrag von €7.455 auf Ihr Konto bei der Sachsenbank zu überweisen.
We have received your letter **of** 2 July and thank you for your patience.	Wir haben Ihr Schreiben vom 2. Juli erhalten und danken Ihnen für Ihre Geduld.
We assure you that payment will be effected in full as soon as our computers are operational again.	Wir versichern Ihnen, dass die Zahlung in voller Höhe erfolgt, sobald unsere Rechner wieder funktionieren.
We are deeply sorry that the invoice has become overdue.	Es tut uns sehr leid, dass die Rechnung überfällig wurde.
We apologize for the delay **in** payment.	Wir entschuldigen uns für den Zahlungsverzug.
The delay was due to • an oversight. • a breakdown of our computer system. • an error **by** our bank.	Der Grund für den Zahlungsverzug war • ein Versehen. • eine Störung unserer EDV-Anlage. • ein Irrtum unserer Bank.
We are afraid we must ask you **for** an extension of 4 weeks.	Wir müssen Sie leider um einen Aufschub von 4 Wochen bitten.
We suggest that we pay **in** 3 instalments **of** $30,330.	Wir schlagen vor, dass wir in 3 Raten von $30.330 zahlen.
We are prepared to pay 7% interest on arrears.	Wir erklären uns bereit, Verzugszinsen in Höhe von 7% zu entrichten.
We hope you will understand our difficult situation and grant us this concession.	Wir hoffen, Sie haben Verständnis für unsere schwierige Lage und machen uns dieses Zugeständnis.

Unit 14
Complaints and adjustments

WORD BANK

complaint • inconvenience • transaction • explanation • adjustment • solution • replacement • substitute • discount • compromise • faulty • damaged • too late • defective • wrong • justified • unjustified • to complain • to insist on • to cancel • to return • to apologize • to grant • to repair • to replace • to take back

A Making complaints

Even though in business transactions not "everything that can go wrong, will" – as the saying goes – it will sometimes be necessary to make a complaint. Goods or services may have been supplied too late, goods may be faulty or damaged, services may prove unsatisfactory, the wrong goods or the wrong quantities may have been delivered etc. In such cases the customer must promptly notify the seller of the problem in writing, especially if a complaint by telephone has not brought the desired result. A complaint should not be written to express anger, but to get results. It should be calm and polite but also firm. In your written complaint you should

- give all the necessary details of the transaction (order No., date of delivery, etc.)
- describe the problem clearly (327 mugs broken, hotel noisy, etc.)
- stress the inconvenience caused
- suggest a solution (replacement, discount, etc.)
- ask for immediate action

Online-Link
808264-0014

✳ 1 Übertragen Sie den Text auf Seite 204 ins Deutsche.

KMK

2 Match the causes for complaint on the left with the suggested solutions on the right. Sometimes several solutions may be appropriate.

1. delay in delivery
2. faulty goods
3. goods damaged
4. services unsatisfactory
5. the wrong goods
6. wrong quantity

a. grant a price reduction
b. improve the service rendered
c. repair the goods
d. replace the goods
e. send the goods by air freight
f. send the missing quantity
g. take back the goods
h. take back the surplus goods
i. send a credit note

3 Describe to your class a recent experience when you had reason to complain or

P actually made a complaint. If you can't think of any, use the prompts below.

flight overbooked

hairdresser ruined your hair

noisy building site next to the beach

had to wait 50 minutes for a meal at a restaurant

beetle found in soft drinks bottle

car repair costs not refunded by insurance company

pages in detective novel were missing

new camera did not work

soles came off new shoes after 4 weeks

bank debited your account with the wrong amount

1 Complaints in writing

The British chain of sports equipment, SPORTS ISLAND, has just received a consignment of polo shirts from a new supplier in India. Unfortunately their Incoming Goods Control has found that most of the polo shirts are not correctly labelled. Sarah Brookfield, the purchasing manager, decides to complain by e-mail.

From:	sarah.brookfield@sportsisland.co.uk
To:	mahajan@indiasports.id
Cc:	

Sent: 201_-01-31   **Attachments:**

Subject: Polo shirts, our purchase order No. PH / 346 / 06 of 18 Dec 201_

Dear Mr Mahajan

> detailed reference to order

The consignment of 5,000 polo shirts under our above-mentioned purchase order arrived yesterday in due course.

However, when our Incoming Goods Control checked the merchandise we were dismayed to find that most of the polo shirts are not labelled correctly. The sizes printed on the inside tags sewn onto the shirts do not correspond to the actual sizes of the garments. Needless to say, the polo shirts cannot be sold with these incorrect tags.

> description of problem

As it would be rather time-consuming to return the goods to you at your expense and wait for a replacement delivery, I would like to suggest that we commission a local firm to remove the tags and replace them with the right ones. You would, of course, have to bear the costs for the reworking and send us the required number of tags by air as soon as possible.

> solution suggested

We are disappointed at the way you have handled our first order and look forward to receiving your comments on this matter in the very near future.

> request for prompt adjustment

Best regards

Sarah Brookfield
Purchasing Manager

SPORTS ISLAND
41 Bryant Road
London W7 9QB
Tel. 020 74127333
Fax 020 74127334

1 Read Sarah Brookfield's e-mail several times. Then cover it up and complete these
R sentences on your own sheet of paper.

1. The consignment of polo shirts arrived yesterday **1**.
2. We were dismayed to find that most of the polo shirts **2**.
3. **3** the polo shirts cannot be sold with these incorrect tags.
4. As it would be **4** to return the goods to you at your expense …
5. You would, of course, **5** for the reworking …
6. We are disappointed **6** our first order …

2 Restore the correct order of these jumbled elements of a complaint about a delay
R in delivery.

1 This matter is causing us great inconvenience and we hope you will do your
utmost to deliver the tool kits without any further delay.

2 On 31 July we placed the above mentioned order with you which you
confirmed the next day assuring us of delivery within 3 weeks.

3 Subject: Delay in delivery of our order No. W-549 / 07 for 1000 household
tool kits

4 We hope to receive your comments by return.

5 Dear Mr Vernon

6 Since then 5 weeks have passed and we have neither received the tool
kits nor heard anything from you.

7 Yours sincerely
Hammer Werkzeughandel

8 Tanja Kirchner
Purchasing Department

9 As our own customers are getting impatient we must insist on immediate
delivery. Should you fail to deliver by the end of next week we are afraid that
we shall have no option but to cancel the order and seek another supplier.

3
P

You (Markus Reber) work in the personnel department of Otto Greiling GmbH (e-mail: personnel@ottogreiling.aol.com), a major supplier to the car industry. For several years your firm has been sending junior executives to a language school in Brighton, UK, for intensive coaching in business English. This year's two participants were, however, not completely satisfied with the language school's services when they attended the course from October 14 to 20.

Send the principal an e-mail. (E-mail: pam.robinson@businessspeak.co.uk)

- Point out the following shortcomings:
  - accommodation at private hotel inadequate – central heating system out of order
  - participants' needs (the language of export procedures) not properly taken into account
  - one morning teacher did not turn up, took school three hours to organise replacement
  - golf course closed for refurbishment.
- Ask for refund of part of the course fees.
- Ask the school to take up the matter with the hotel.
- Close on a friendly note considering your long business relationship.

✳ 4
KMK

Sie sind Christiane Sauer und sind bei Ihrer Firma, Zuckermann & Sacher, Farinweg 19, 73979 Suessen, für den Einkauf von Büromaterial zuständig. Seit 4 Jahren beziehen Sie jedes Quartal Drucker- und Kopierpapier sowie Umschläge aller Art von der britischen Firma East Anglia Stationery Ltd., 6 Malvern Business Park, Ely, CB6 4JR, UK. In der letzten Zeit hat Ihnen dieser Lieferant wiederholt Anlass zur Unzufriedenheit gegeben.

Schreiben Sie einen förmlichen Beschwerdebrief an den Geschäftsführer, Charles Bingley, und führen Sie dabei Folgendes an:

- Datum: 30 Juli
- In den ersten Jahren keine Beanstandungen
- Seit letztem Jahr allmähliche Verschlechterung des Service:
  - Ware häufig nicht vorrätig
  - Lieferzeiten immer länger
  - keine prompte Reaktion auf E-Mails und Faxe
  - stets wechselnde Ansprechpartner am Telefon
  - dieses Jahr schon einmal zu viel und einmal zu wenig geliefert
- Mängel bei der heutigen Lieferung:
  - 150 000 Umschläge DIN A3 nicht selbstklebend (self-adhesive), (Auftrag Nr. 200-5437 vom 23. Juni)
  - Muster der beanstandeten Umschläge beigefügt
  - Bitte um Abholung der beanstandeten Umschläge bei nächster Gelegenheit
  - sofortiger Ersatz erforderlich
- Drei Monate Frist für Verbesserung des Service
- Andernfalls keine Verlängerung des Liefervertrags
- Anlage

2 Complaints by telephone

1

R

Maria Sanchez from Papier Gehrke in Schwerin has placed an order for multilingual wall calendars with the US firm Calendars 4 U. Two weeks after the date the calendars should have arrived in Germany she rings Joan Reid at Calendars 4 U, whom she knows very well from numerous previous transactions.

Restore the order of their jumbled dialogue. Match the numbers with the letters.

Joan	Maria
1. Calendars 4U. Joan speaking. How can I help you?	a. Certainly. It is 4900/312 dated 18 July.
2. Hi Maria. Can you give me the order number and date?	b. You're welcome. Good bye Joan.
3. Here it is on my monitor. Is there a problem?	c. Yes, there certainly is. The calendars have not arrived yet. They ought to have been here two weeks ago.
4. I see that they should arrive in Germany any day now. We dispatched them a week ago by air-mail.	d. You could have mailed me.
5. I am very sorry about this. I was going to call you but whenever I got around to it, it seemed to be the wrong time of day in Europe.	e. Hello Joan, this is Maria Sanchez from Papier Gehrke in Schwerin, Germany. I'm calling about our order for calendars.
6. That's true. I am so sorry. I promise it won't happen again.	f. Well, as long as the calendars arrive in the next few days, no harm will be done.
7. Thank you very much for your patience.	g. Why didn't you let us know that delivery would be made two weeks later?
8. Bye Maria.	

✱ **2** Work with a partner. Draw up a similar dialogue about a delay in delivery.
l   Then act it out with your partner.

Phrases ▶

3 Kirsty Burnham of Global Catering in Manchester asks Kevin Sears to ring an
R Italian firm about their consignment of Italian speciality convenience foods.
A1.28

Listen to the dialogue and answer the following questions.

1. Which firm does Kevin Sears work for?
2. What is Chiara Durini's position at Buongusto Italiano?
3. What is the problem with the sell-by date of the Parma ham and the mortadella antipasti?
4. Would it help if Chiara Durini gave Global Catering a discount?
5. By which means of transport is Chiara Durini going to send the replacement delivery?

4 **You are Kevin Sears. First copy the form below. Then listen to the conversation**
R/P **again and write a memo in English for your boss, Kirsty Burnham.**
A1.28

```
TELEPHONE MEMO

For:      _____

From:     _____

Date:     _____

Caller:   _____

Subject:  _____
```

5 Nicole Sachse from Getränke König in Halle, Germany, had ordered 3000 sets of long drink glasses from Wexford Crystal in Sanditon, County Cork, Ireland. The consignment arrived punctually, but inspection has revealed that some glasses are broken und some are smaller than the others. Nicole rings Sean O'Sullivan at Wexford Crystal.

Act out their dialogue with your neighbour using the prompts below.

Nicole Sachse	Sean O'Sullivan
	Wexford Crystal/Exports/Sean O'Sullivan
Nicole Sachse/Getränke König/Halle, Germany/order of 10 September/3000 sets of long drink glasses	
	on monitor/colours red, blue and green/arrived?
arrived punctually/inspection/disappointed/one box damaged/50 sets of green glasses broken	
	sorry to hear/all sets checked before dispatch/must have happened in transit/contact forwarders immediately
terms of delivery DAP Halle/Wexford Crystal deal with forwarder and/or insurance company/need replacements urgently	
	send replacements/by air/this afternoon
transport free of charge/confirmation by fax	
	certainly/once more apologies
afraid/must mention/roughly ⅓ of the glasses/slight differences in height/about 1mm shorter	
	easy to explain/glasses pipe-blown by hand/differences inevitable/sign of hand-made glass/much more valuable/machine-made glasses always identical
sounds plausible/customers may not notice	
	pleased with the sets?
yes/colours brilliant/crystal glass clear/remind of replacements/good-bye	
	promise immediate dispatch/again sorry thanks for call/bye

✳ **6** Work with a partner. Sit back to back and act out the telephone conversation
I   using the prompts on the role cards. Then change roles.

Role card: Partner A (buyer)   **Role card partner B ⇨ page 257**

Sie haben über das Internet ein überaus preiswertes Skateboard gekauft und
mit Kreditkarte bezahlt. In der Beschreibung des Skateboards auf der Webseite
des Verkäufers war als zulässiges Höchstgewicht für den Benutzer 70 kg
angegeben. Als das Skateboard wie versprochen nach 3 Tagen ankommt,
müssen Sie feststellen, dass auf dem englisch beschrifteten Karton ein
zulässiges Höchstgewicht von (nur) 90 lbs (= 40,8 kg) aufgedruckt ist. Sie
rufen die Firma an und verlangen Rücknahme des Skateboards.

7 Communicating across cultures
M   Drücken Sie folgende Aussagen in (möglichst höflichem) Englisch aus:

1. Wir teilen Ihnen hiermit mit, dass wir mit Ihrem Kundendienst sehr
   unzufrieden sind.
2. Die Farbe entspricht nicht dem Muster.
3. Wir bestehen darauf, dass Sie uns den vollen Kaufpreis erstatten.

Communicating across cultures:
Complaining about products or services

In Germany correspondence in connection with complaints tends to be direct,
stating the facts bluntly and requiring adjustment in no uncertain tones. This is
the accepted usage here and nobody takes offence at the curt and no-nonsense
style of German complaints. In the English-speaking world, on the other hand,
complaints are formulated in a different way. The style is much more indirect,
polite and conciliatory as nothing would be gained by antagonizing the other
party; he / she would simply be less cooperative. So remember to express your
complaint in a friendly and understanding manner.

Do not say:	**Say instead:**
I want to complain about …	I'm afraid I have to raise the matter of …
The glasses are broken.	Unfortunately, the glasses are broken.
You have made a mistake.	There must have been an error on your part / There seems to have been a mix-up somewhere.
You are wrong.	I'm afraid I cannot quite agree.
We expect you to send replacements.	We would be grateful if you would send replacements.
Therefore, we request a discount of 20%.	We think a discount of 20% would be appropriate.

 8 Use the Internet to find other examples of cultural differences or problems of
intercultural communication. Make notes and compare your findings with the
group.

B   Adjusting complaints

It is much easier to hold on to existing customers than to find new ones, so it is essential to manage customer complaints well. Remember, disgruntled customers are twice as likely as satisfied customers to tell others about their experience with your firm. When dealing with customer complaints you should

- thank the customer for making you aware of the problem
- treat the customer with courtesy and patience and tell him that you are sorry
- respond to the complaint quickly, telling the customer what will happen next
- if possible, give an explanation for what has happened
- involve the customer in the process of finding a solution
- suggest a compromise that meets the customer halfway if the complaint is not wholly justified
- ensure that all action promised is executed promptly
- explain the reasons before saying no, if the complaint is unjustified.

✳ 1 **Study the text above and translate the following recommendations**
M   **taken from a textbook.**

21

Die Erledigung von Reklamationen muss mit großer
Sorgfalt geschehen, um den Kunden nicht zu
verlieren. Zunächst sollten Sie dem Kunden dafür
danken, dass er Sie auf ein Problem aufmerksam
5   gemacht hat, und ihn dann in die Suche nach einer
Lösung einbeziehen.
Beschwerden müssen umgehend beantwortet und
der Kunde über den Fortgang der Erledigung auf
dem Laufenden gehalten werden. Wenn möglich,
10 sollten Sie dem Kunden erklären, wie es zu der für
ihn unbefriedigenden Situation kommen konnte.
Zudem müssen Sie den Kunden davon überzeugen,
dass Sie Maßnahmen treffen werden oder schon
eingeleitet haben, die sicherstellen, dass sich
15 solche Vorfälle nicht wiederholen.
Falls die Reklamation nur teilweise begründet ist,
sollten Sie versuchen, sich mit dem Kunden auf
einen Kompromiss zu einigen. Sind Sie gezwungen,
die Reklamation als völlig unbegründet
20 zurückzuweisen, empfiehlt es sich zuerst die
Gründe zu erläutern, bevor die Absage erteilt wird.

2
R

Restore the correct order of these jumbled elements of a reply to a complaint about a delay in delivery.

1   We are, therefore, prepared to release you from the contract.

2   Dear Ms Kirchner

3   We have not contacted you before because we were hoping to locate another manufacturer willing to supply similar tool kits at short notice. So far, however, we have not met with success.

4   Yours sincerely
James Vernon
Export Manager

5   Please accept our sincere apologies. We hope to be of service to you at another time in the future.

6   Re: Your order no. W-549 / 07

7   I'm afraid we are after all unable to execute your order for 1000 household tool kits for the time being as our own supplier, our parent company, has become insolvent.

8   Thank you for your e-mail.

3 You are Pam Robinson, principal of BUSINESS SPEAK, the language school
P in Brighton which 2 junior executives from Otto Greiling GmbH, Germany, attended for a week's intensive coaching in business English. Markus Reber from their human resources department has sent you an e-mail complaining about some shortcomings concerning the course from October 14 to 20:

- accommodation at private hotel inadequate – central heating system out of order
- participants' needs (the language of export procedures) not properly taken into account
- one morning teacher did not turn up, took school three hours to organise replacement
- golf course closed for refurbishment

Reply by e-mail, bearing in mind that Markus Reber has been sending staff to your courses for several years.

- spoken with hotel manager, hotel prepared to reduce price by ⅓, cheque under way by post
- export procedures dealt with as always, never any complaint about this before
- apologies for teacher not turning up one morning, had a fall in the bathroom, had to be taken to hospital, you did your best to organise replacement
- participants informed in advance that the golf course would be out of use
- very sorry that participants should be dissatisfied
- sent them each a copy of "Doing Business in the UK" in compensation
- hope that cordial relations will not be affected

✳ 4 Sie sind Henry Crawford, der neue Geschäftsführer von East Anglia Stationery
KMK Ltd., 6 Malvern Business Park, Ely CB6 4JR, UK. Die deutsche Firma Zuckermann & Sacher, Farinweg 19, 73979 Suessen, bezieht von Ihnen seit Jahren Drucker- und Kopierpapier sowie Umschläge. Christiane Sauer, zuständig für den Einkauf von Büromaterial, ist inzwischen mit Ihrem Service unzufrieden und hat sich bei Ihnen in einem förmlichen Schreiben beschwert (siehe S. 208).

Beantworten Sie ihren Brief in Englisch unter Berücksichtigung folgender Punkte:

- Datum: 5. August
- Vorstellung Ihrer Person
- Ihr Vorgänger, Charles Bingley, nach längerer Krankheit im Ruhestand
- Beanstandete Unzulänglichkeiten verursacht durch Mr. Bingley's Abwesenheit
- Radikale Maßnahmen eingeleitet
- Service in Kürze wieder einwandfrei
- Entschuldigung
- Ersatzlieferung Umschläge bereits unterwegs
- 20 % Rabatt auf diesen Auftrag
- Beanstandete Umschläge werden kommenden Mittwoch abgeholt
- Hoffnung auf weitere gute Beziehungen

Language and grammar
Find the correct form of the verbs in brackets.

1. We will grant you 10% quantity discount if you (order) at least 500 units.
2. We would place a substantial order if you (can promise) delivery within one week.
3. We would not have dispatched the goods if they (not be) in perfect condition.
4. We (be glad) if you looked into the matter without delay.
5. Unless you instruct us to the contrary, shipment (be effected) on receipt of new supplies.
6. It (be) most helpful if the sets could reach us before the end of the month.
7. You would be taking a great risk if you (invest) your money in that project.
8. Should you be uncertain about any aspect of it, please (not hesitate) to give me a call.
9. If we (accept) their order we would have to recruit three additional workers.
10. If she had worked harder she (not fail) the exam.

Language and grammar: Conditional clauses

Bedingungssätze (conditional clauses) werden im Englischen nach einem relativ festen Schema gestaltet. Es gibt drei Grundtypen von Bedingungssätzen:

Hauptsatz	Nebensatz der Bedingung
We will take the goods back (FUTURE) (wir **werden** …)	if you return them at your expense. (PRESENT TENSE)
We would grant you a discount (CONDITIONAL) (wir **würden** …)	if you increased your order. (SIMPLE PAST)
He would have taken part in the meeting (CONDITIONAL PERFECT) (er **hätte** …)	if he had not been away on a business trip. (PAST PERFECT)

Das Schema gilt auch dann, wenn der Nebensatz der Bedingung vor dem Hauptsatz steht:

If it is fine on Friday	we will have the office party in the park.
If you applied	you would get the job.
If you had applied	you would have got the job.

Ferner gilt das Schema, wenn der Nebensatz durch eine andere Konjunktion eingeleitet wird: wie z. B. unless (wenn nicht, außer wenn), provided (that) (vorausgesetzt, dass), on condition (that) (unter der Bedingung, dass):

They will not place any further orders	unless you offer a satisfactory solution.
Employees may smoke	provided they go out into the courtyard.

Eine besondere Form stellt der Bedingungssatz ohne Konjunktion dar:

Should you have any further questions	please do not hesitate to ask.
But for John helping out (If John had not helped out …)	we would never have coped with the sudden demand.

Eine Ausnahme von diesem Schema bildet die höfliche Bitte in der Geschäftskorrespondenz:

We would be grateful	if you would grant us a respite of 4 weeks.

Logistics expert

Cargo insurance

It is a common wish of the consignor, forwarder and consignee that all goods are delivered safely and on time. However, it is impossible to prevent all risks on the way. Cargo insurance should therefore be arranged to protect against loss or damage of goods while they are being transported.

1
P
What do you think has happened to the ship in the photo? Suggest possible reasons for the incident and its consequences for all the parties involved. Then make a list of things that can go wrong in road, air and sea transport. Discuss which measures must be taken in such a situation.

2
R
The vessel Morning Star, carrying about 1500 containers of mixed cargo, was on its way from China to Australia when it struck ground. As it was chartered by the German forwarding agency GoGlobal the captain's report on the accident is sent to them. Use the sentences (A–G) to restore the chronological order of events.

A   At the moment we are taking measures to get the vessel afloat again.

B   Due to the collision, water got into the hull on the port side.

C   Fearing that the vessel could capsize, I beached it in Hong Kong waters the following day.

D   I left 980 of the containers for interim storage at the port of distress.

E   On examining the other 530 containers, we found the cargo considerably damaged by sea water. Those containers remained on the beached ship.

F   The tank room and three cargo holds flooded, leading to a dangerous tilt of the boat.

G   We struck ground 230 miles off Hong Kong on 13 August 2011 shortly after midnight.

3
M
Write a summary of the incident in German to keep the customer informed.

4 GoGlobal had also arranged insurance and agreed on the terms of "limited cover".
R / M Read the following extract from the DTV Cargo Insurance Conditions and check
the meaning of the words in bold print with the help of an online dictionary.

The German DTV Cargo Insurance
Conditions 2000/2008 comprise the
following two types of coverage:
1. **"All risks"** applies unless any other
   form of **coverage** is agreed upon. The
   insurance covers loss of or damage to the
   goods insured as a consequence of a risk
   insured against.
2. **"Limited cover"** is the most common
   restricted coverage and is considerably
   cheaper than full coverage. The insurance
   covers loss or damage to the goods as a
   consequence of:
   - An accident involving the means of
     transport carrying the goods.
   - An accident is also said to exist
     when the vessel carrying the goods
     is **stranded**, **strikes ground**, **runs
     aground**, **capsizes**, sinks, **founders**,
     or is damaged by ice.

- **Collapse** of warehouse buildings.
- Fire, **lightening**, explosion,
  earthquakes, **seaquakes**, volcanic
  eruptions, and other natural **disasters**,
  strike or **crashing** of a flying object,
  parts thereof including its cargo.
- **Jettison**, washing overboard or
  otherwise being lost overboard as a
  result of heavy weather.
- **General average sacrifice**.
- Discharging, **interim storage** and
  loading of goods at a **port of distress**
  entered as a result of an insured event.
- Total loss of entire packages during
  loading onto or unloading from
  a means of transport, or during
  transshipment to or from a means of
  transport.

5 Discuss in groups in how far GoGlobal can make an insurance claim. Then search
P the internet for reports by major insurance companies specialising in marine
insurance. Present one incident you found to your class.

6 GoGlobal kontaktiert den Kapitän der Morning Star, um mit ihm das weitere
KMK Verfahren zu besprechen. Führen Sie einen Dialog mithilfe der Rollenkarten.

Role card: Partner A   **Role card partner B** ⇨ page 257

Sie arbeiten für GoGlobal. Rufen Sie den Kapitän der Morning Star an, um ihn
über das weitere Vorgehen zu informieren.

- Nennen Sie Ihren Namen und fragen Sie den Kapitän nach seinem Befinden.
- Sagen Sie, dass Sie dem Kapitän Hinweise zum weiteren Ablauf geben wollen.
- Bitten Sie ihn, einen baldigen Besichtigungstermin mit dem örtlichen
  Versicherungsvertreter zu vereinbaren.
- Fotos müssen gemacht werden. Bitten Sie ihn, alle wichtigen Dokumente, wie
  Frachtschein, Packlisten und Versicherungsschein, bereitzuhalten.
- Sagen Sie, dass Sie darüber entscheiden werden, wenn die Versicherung den
  Schaden begutachtet hat.

Phrases: Complaints and adjustments

To start a complaint

We are writing **with** reference to our order no …	Wir nehmen Bezug auf unseren Auftrag Nr. …
We regret to report that we have not yet received the goods ordered **on** 18 May.	Wir bedauern, Ihnen mitteilen zu müssen, dass wir die am 18. Mai bestellten Waren noch nicht erhalten haben.

To give reasons for your complaint

On unpacking the cases our Incoming Goods Control discovered that 15 items are missing.	Beim Auspacken der Kisten stellte unsere Warenannahme fest, dass 15 Positionen fehlen.
We are afraid that several units are – seriously damaged/defective. – broken/badly scratched/stained.	Leider sind mehrere Teile – schwer beschädigt/schadhaft. – zerbrochen/stark zerkratzt/verschmutzt.
The goods should have arrived a week **ago**.	Die Waren hätten schon vor einer Woche eintreffen sollen.
We are sorry to point out that the repair work has been poorly executed.	Wir müssen leider darauf hinweisen, dass die Reparatur schlecht ausgeführt wurde.

To mention likely reasons for the problem

We believe that the damage may be due to rough handling **in** transit.	Wir glauben, dass der Schaden auf unsachgemäße Behandlung beim Transport zurückzuführen ist.
Apparently, our order was **mixed up** with another customer's order.	Unser Auftrag wurde anscheinend mit einem anderen verwechselt.

To inform the seller what you expect him to do and what steps you are taking

Please arrange **for** the immediate dispatch of the missing items.	Bitte sorgen Sie dafür, dass die fehlenden Artikel sofort abgeschickt werden.
We would ask you to – replace the faulty goods **at** your expense. – have the defective articles collected **at** our warehouse. – grant us a price reduction **of** 20%. – cut the price **to** €780.	Wir möchten Sie bitten, – die mangelhafte Ware auf Ihre Kosten zu ersetzen. – die schadhaften Artikel von unserem Lager abholen zu lassen. – uns einen Preisnachlass von 20% zu gewähren. – den Preis auf €780 zu senken.

To demand prompt adjustment

We expect that you will settle this matter speedily and **to** our entire satisfaction.	Wir erwarten, dass Sie die Sache rasch und zu unserer vollen Zufriedenheit regeln.

To refer to a complaint received

Thank you for your e-mail drawing a serious problem **to** our attention.

Danke für Ihre E-Mail, mit der Sie uns auf ein ernstes Problem aufmerksam gemacht haben.

To apologize

We wish to apologize for this mistake.

Wir bitten für diesen Fehler um Entschuldigung.

We are extremely sorry **for** the poor service you have received.

Es tut uns außerordentlich leid, dass Sie so schlecht bedient wurden.

To explain the problem or promise to investigate it

The damage was caused **by** a software failure.

Der Schaden wurde durch fehlerhafte Software verursacht.

We will investigate the matter thoroughly and inform you of the steps taken.

Wir werden die Angelegenheit gründlich untersuchen und Sie über die Schritte informieren, die wir unternommen haben.

To suggest a solution and inform the buyer what you expect him to do

We are pleased to say that replacements are now **on** their way to you.

Wir freuen uns, Ihnen mitteilen zu können, dass Ersatz bereits unterwegs ist.

Please return the faulty items **at** our expense.

Bitte senden Sie die mangelhaften Artikel auf unsere Kosten zurück.

We are prepared to reduce the price **by** 15 % if you decide to keep the goods.

Wir sind bereit, den Preis um 15 % zu senken, wenn Sie sich entschließen, die Ware zu behalten.

To reject an unfounded claim

After careful examination of the case we must say that the order was carried out in accordance with the contract.

Nach gründlicher Untersuchung des Falles müssen wir festhalten, dass der Auftrag vertragsgemäß ausgeführt wurde.

As we are **in no way** to blame we have no alternative but to reject your claim.

Da uns keinerlei Schuld trifft, bleibt uns nichts anderes übrig, als Ihre Reklamation zurückzuweisen.

To close on a note designed to promote goodwill

We hope that this proposal will find your approval.

Wir hoffen, dieser Vorschlag findet Ihre Zustimmung.

We trust that the solution suggested will help to settle the matter **to** the satisfaction of all parties concerned.

Wir hoffen, dass die vorgeschlagene Lösung dazu beiträgt, die Angelegenheit zur Zufriedenheit aller Beteiligten zu erledigen.

Unit 15
Marketing products and services

Marketing includes a wide range of activities. Even when a product or service is still at the idea or design stage, companies set about finding out what sort of a market exists – for instance, what age group they should aim at and how likely people in this age group are to buy this product or service. When a company is planning a new product they need to decide on the "marketing mix" or 4Ps (product, price, place, promotion) – i.e. what kind of product to develop, what price to charge and what channels to sell it through – cheap chain or exclusive boutique, for instance. Finally, they will have to decide how and where to advertise.

1 Life cycle of a product

Products may be thought of as having a life cycle with five phases – introduction, growth, maturity, decline and phasing out. The focus of marketing changes, depending on the phase.

Online-Link
808264-0015

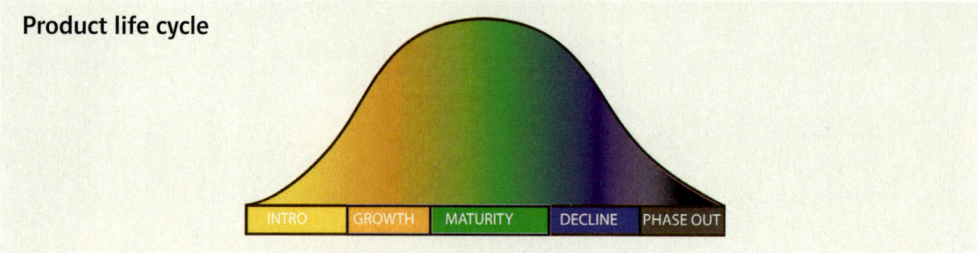

Product life cycle

INTRO | GROWTH | MATURITY | DECLINE | PHASE OUT

1 Study the text on page 221 and the illustration above and decide whether the
R following statements are TRUE or FALSE.

1. Marketing is the same as advertising.
2. Marketing includes advertising.
3. Companies first design and produce a product and then see whether there's a
   market for it or not.
4. It is important for a company to have a clear idea of what group it is targeting.
5. Marketing is the same as selling.
6. It is always best to sell as cheaply as possible.
7. A product has a life cycle of six phases.
8. Sales reach a peak in the last phase.

2 Use the internet to select what you consider to be the five leading brands in the
UK. Make a few notes on what is associated with the brands and discuss your
results with the group.

2 Market research

Companies conduct market research to find out what people think about them and
their products. They also try to establish what needs or desires a particular target
group may have and how able or willing they will be to pay for a particular product
or service. This may involve "desk" research (e.g. statistics) or "field research".
The following is an example of field research.

Listen to the interview. The interviewer is ringing a random sample of people
R taken from the local telephone book. Complete the following sentences.
A1.29

1. Could you possibly spare a few minutes **1**?
2. I am actually in a bit **2**.
3. We are doing a market survey **3**.
4. I tend to book flights and holidays **4**.
5. We are particularly interested in **5**.
6. Do you buy these articles regularly and how much do you **6**?
7. I can do my shopping when I **7**.
8. Prices are often more **8**.
9. I often give up in **9**.
10. Would you visit the website more often if it were **10**?

Distribution channels

Manufacturer → Wholesaler ← Retailer / Retailer / Retailer

Distribution is also a part of marketing. Traditionally, wholesalers are the link between manufacturers and retailers. Manufacturers generally sell goods in large quantities to wholesalers who sell them on in smaller quantities to retailers (= "breaking bulk"). Retailers sell them to end users.

1   Retailers, wholesalers and agents

Retailers
Retailers ensure a supply of goods to the general public. There is a wide variety of retail outlets, starting with small specialist shops such as independent chemists, beauty consultants, opticians and exclusive fashion boutiques. Most High Street stores are, however, major chains with branches in a large number of towns and often in several countries. Supermarkets generally belong to one of a small number of major chains. Department stores sell many different kinds of goods under one roof. Large retailers, who buy in bulk, may order directly from manufacturers without involving a wholesaler.
Recently, online retailing has become the fastest growing segment.

Wholesalers

Wholesalers provide a range of services from which both manufacturers and retailers benefit. They may have a sales force to keep contact to their customers, they have warehousing facilities, offer a range of products from a number of manufacturers, and may offer credit facilities to their customers. Finally, they provide advisory services. However, wholesalers charge for their services and are, therefore, also a cost factor (putting up the price).

Agents

In foreign trade manufacturers often appoint an agent in the foreign country. This has a number of advantages. The agent speaks the language, he is familiar with the foreign market and will have the necessary contacts. He has an office and possibly warehousing facilities. He is usually paid on a commission basis which means he receives a percentage (say 3%) on sales. He is thus only paid when he succeeds in selling something. His principal has therefore few overheads.

1 Übertragen Sie folgende Sätze ins Deutsche.

KMK

1. Wholesalers are the link between manufacturers and retailers.
2. They may offer credit facilities to their customers.
3. Supermarkets belong to a small number of major chains.
4. Wholesalers charge for their services and are therefore a cost factor.
5. Wholesalers generally have warehousing facilities.

2 Answer the following questions.

1. In what way do wholesalers make life easier for manufacturers?
2. Why does a small retailer (e.g. a 24-hour mini-market or a small fashion boutique) need wholesalers?
3. Why may large retailers try to cut out the wholesaler?
4. Give examples of independent retailers (not part of chains).
5. What is the characteristic feature of a department store?

✳ **3** Übertragen Sie den obigen Text über „Agents" ins Deutsche.

KMK

4 Decide whether the following statements are TRUE or FALSE.

R

1. Agents are paid a commission whether they sell anything or not.
2. Wholesalers generally have warehousing facilities.
3. Retailers sell to end users.
4. Retailers buy in bulk and sell to wholesalers.
5. Wholesalers perform a useful service both for manufacturers and retailers.

5 Describe briefly the activities of retailers, wholesalers and agents.

P

6 Listen to the following statements in which young people taking part in a training seminar describe their place of employment. Take notes.

R

A 1.30

7 Now listen to the statements again, use your notes and answer the following questions in writing.

R / P

A 1.30

1. Does speaker 1 work for a wholesaler?
2. Does speaker 2 work for a retailer?
3. What does speaker 3 mean by "retail customers"?
4. Does speaker 4 work for a retailer or a wholesaler?
5. What sort of a company does speaker 5 work for?
6. What kind of customers help the shop of speaker 6 to survive?
7. Who does the company of speaker 7 sell its products through?
8. What kind of an organisation does speaker 8 work for?

2 E-commerce

1 Complete the following text using words from the box.

R

outlets • major • credit cards • retail • via • online • charges • customers •
facilities • wholesalers

An important development at the present time is the rapid growth of e-commerce. This is revolutionising some **1** sectors. Internet retailing operations are growing faster than traditional retail **2**. Shopping and booking flights, hotels and holidays **3** the internet is becoming more and more popular. Some **4** supermarkets have large internet operations. You can do your shopping **5** and have the goods delivered.

Airlines offer online booking **6**, which makes it easy to compare prices and avoid paying travel agents' **7**.

Wholesalers may also offer their **8** internet facilities (Business to Business – B2B – services) to enable them to do their ordering at any time of the day or night. However, internet exchanges are making **9** superfluous in some fields.

E-commerce is at present the fastest growing retail segment paralleled by a rapid increase in the number of **10**.

2 Beantworten Sie die Fragen zum folgenden Zeitungstext schriftlich in deutscher
KMK Sprache.

1. Warum mussten Online-Einzelhändler ihren Service stark verbessern?
2. Welche Vorteile bietet das Internet beim Preisvergleich?
3. Welche Möglichkeiten gibt es im Internet, sich über Produkte zu informieren?
4. Warum mussten Firmen neue Strategien in der Werbung und im Marketing
   entwickeln?
5. Welche Altersgruppe soll besonders durch die Internet-Werbung angesprochen
   werden?

E-Commerce takes off

Consumers love to shop on the internet. After initial problems leading websites now offer an excellent service. Competition on 5 the web is fierce and many sites have had little choice but to raise service levels, often far above those of offline retailers. Price transparency is the great advantage for the 10 consumer. It is possible to check the price offered by hundreds of merchants with a couple of mouse clicks. Consumers also have access to an unprecedented amount of inform- ation, not just from manufacturers' 15 websites but also from online reviews written by other customers. To reach online customers companies have had to look at new and different advertising and marketing 20 strategies. This is why firms pay for sponsored links to appear on search sites like *Google* and *Yahoo!*. It has become one of the most effective marketing tools, especially for 25 people who spend as much time on the internet as watching television, such as teenagers.

◎V7 **Video lounge** Retailing

You are about to see a video on retail marketing.
Watch it carefully and then answer the following questions:

1. Describe the marketing expert.
2. The video speaks of "sales consultants" and "professional
   friends". How is this different from the traditional sales
   assistant?
3. What method is used to show them how NOT to approach
   the customer?
4. What is meant by "linked selling"?
5. What are the rewards of successful customer care for the
   "consultants"?
6. Would you like to be served by this kind of assistant?

Language and grammar
Choose the correct form of the adjective or adverb in brackets.

1. Our elegant sofas are the (good) value ever.
2. We are the market leaders because we have reacted (swiftly) to changing markets.
3. This company has expanded (dramatic) than its competitors over the past year.
4. Last year the winter was (severe) than this year.
5. These are the (late) designer furnishings from Milan.
6. This is the (expensive) holiday I have booked so far.

Language and grammar: Comparatives and superlatives

Adjektive, meist in Form von Komparativen oder Superlativen, spielen in der Werbung eine große Rolle.

Einsilbig gesprochene Adjektive bilden Komparativ und Superlativ durch Anhängen von *-er*, *-est* an das Adjektiv.

bright – brighter – brightest
This car has **smoother** handling than any other car in its class.

Drei- oder mehrsilbige Adjektive bilden Komparativ und Superlativ durch Voranstellen von *more* und *most* vor das Adjektiv.

interesting – more interesting – most interesting
This is the **most sophisticated** MP3 player available today.

Zweisilbige Adjektive werden entweder wie einsilbige oder wie mehrsilbige gesteigert: Adjektive, die auf *-er*, *-ow*, *-y* oder *-le* enden, hängen *-er*, *-est* an. Vor Adjektive, die auf *-ful* oder *-re* enden, wird *more* oder *most* gesetzt.

clever – cleverer – cleverest	narrow – narrower – narrowest
pretty – prettier – prettiest	noble – nobler – noblest
careful – more careful – most careful	obscure – more obscure – most obscure

This is a **most restful** way of spending a weekend abroad.

Einige englische Adjektive besitzen die Wirkung von Superlativen.
Cutting-edge* technology goes into this stereo system.
Get this **state of the art** handset at all authorised dealers.
Get the coolest, **up to the minute**, **must-have** accessories at all our boutiques.
This car has **superb** handling.

Auch Adverbien können gesteigert werden. Komparativ und Superlativ von Adverbien wird durch Voranstellen von *more* und *most* gebildet.
quickly – more quickly – most quickly
They dealt with our order **more efficiently** than we had expected.
Technology is changing **more and more rapidly** (= immer schneller).

* Diese Wendungen können sowohl mit als auch ohne Bindestriche geschrieben werden.

Logistics expert

1 Transport and environment

1 Read the text and complete it with the words from the box.

R

alternatives • atmosphere • button • cell • climate • comparable • disease • emissions •
locomotives • monitor • renewable • sail • shipping companies • transmitted • winds

There is strong evidence that human activities have a negative influence on the global **1**.
Catastrophic weather events, variable climates that affect food and water supplies, and new
infectious **2** outbreaks are all connected with **global climate change**. Climate and weather are
subject to the so-called "greenhouse effect", when gases like carbon dioxide (CO_2) or methane
(CH_4) accumulate in the **3** and change the world's climate. As a consequence we will have to
decrease the use of fossil fuels and look for **4**.

Germany is a world leader in **5** energy technology. According to the *Frankfurter Allgemeine
Sonntagszeitung*, around one third of all water-power installations in the world are produced
by German firms, while every other wind turbine and every third solar **6** are German-made.
But these **innovative technologies** do not help the logistics industries to present a greener
balance sheet. Powerful diesel engines in lorries, **7**, jet engines and in particular ships' engines
still contribute their share towards making our planet warmer. There are nearly 100,000 ocean
ships sailing worldwide, and the **8** use a kind of fuel which would have long been banned
ashore: heavy oil. While the emissions of cars, lorries and planes are subject to more and more
regulation, no government or any other authority has placed restrictions on **9** from ships.

This is where a Hamburg-based firm comes in. It has developed **SkySails** – an innovative
system designed to save on ship fuel. It consists of three main components: 1. a towing kite
with rope, 2. a launch and recovery system, and 3. a control system for automatic operation.
Instead of a traditional **10** fitted to a mast, SkySails uses large towing kites to drive the ship.
Their shape is **11** to that of a paraglider. The towing kite is made of high-strength, weather-
proof textiles and can operate at altitudes between 100 and 300 m, where stronger and more
stable **12** blow. With dynamic flight manoeuvres (e.g. the figure 8), SkySails produce five to
25 times more power per square metre of sail than conventional sails. The towing forces are **13**
to the ship via a tear-proof, synthetic rope. The crew can operate the system from the bridge.
Emergency actions can be taken at the push of a **14**. An automatic system controls the towing
kite and adjusts its flight path. All information on the operational status is displayed in real-
time on the **15** of the SkySails workstation.

2 Complete the sentences with information from the text on page 228.

R

1. Many people believe that thunderstorms, floods and droughts are signs of a … in the world climate.
2. Inside greenhouses it is … than outside.
3. Oil and natural gas can be classified as … fuels.
4. Most lorries are powered by … engines.
5. SkySails can help … on ship fuel.
6. Kites only fly when a strong … is blowing.
7. The … of a ship is the captain's workplace.
8. Wind and rain cannot damage the kite because it is …

3 Read the text on page 228 again and decide if the following statements are

R TRUE or FALSE. Correct the false statements.

1. The control panel for the kite is located in the ship's engine room.
2. In a heavy storm, the rope of the kite may tear.
3. Conventional sails produce less power than the SkySails kite.
4. The wind blows stronger at an altitude of 250 metres than at sea level.
5. Sails are usually fitted to a mast.
6. The SkySails system consists of four main components.
7. Each year, there are stricter regulations on emissions from cars and planes.
8. Heavy oil is so dirty that it may not be used ashore.

✳ **4** Explain in German how the SkySails system works.

M

👤 **5** Work in small groups and search the internet to find out how the logistics
P industry can help to protect the environment. Choose one particularly interesting example and present it to your class.

Phrases ▸

2 Innovative products in logistics

1 Work in pairs and list the benefits of using tracking systems a. for the company
P management and the drivers, b. for the environment. Compare your findings in class.

✳ **2** Read the following text about a new tracking system and complete the list you
R   have made in Exercise 1. Then draft a flyer in English, advertising the Easytrack
system. Use the information from your list and the text.

New product launch – Easytrack

Easytrack is based on a combination of GPS, GSM and VHF radio technology and gives fleet owners detailed real time information on the whereabouts of their vehicles and containers. Moreover, **Easytrack** provides peace of mind in the event of theft or loss.

The producer, TRACKER plc in Leeds, claims that a fleet tracking system should be accurate, reliable and informative as well as flexible, easy to use and proven on fleets of all sizes. They also believe that it should be backed up with the sort of dedicated customer service you can only get from a market leader.

While other tracking companies have come and gone in the past few years, TRACKER's success has come from listening to customers and constantly developing new products to ensure that they always meet their customers' changing needs. We have asked some companies where TRACKER systems have been in use for some time about their experience.

Mark Yates, of Caledonian Hauliers comments: "We've used TRACKER appliances for the last two and half years and it has greatly improved the utilisation and efficiency of our fleet of vehicles. One of the key benefits is the real-time reporting, which allows us to accurately record how long a job has taken. This is very important as a lot of our jobs are paid based on the time they take,

so we can ensure that we are invoicing for the correct time and the customer knows exactly what time they have been charged for. Also, on the rare occasion when we do receive a complaint about late arrivals, the reporting function allows us to check exactly what time the vehicle arrived at its destination."

Andy Stokes, Fleet Controller, says: "As a 24-hour service provider, our drivers' safety is of great importance. When staff are out at night, we're able to track exactly where they are and to monitor their driving times. In this way we ensure drivers work their proper hours."

Bob Cowan, Head of Fleet Services at South Staffordshire Water PLC, says: "The competent management of our fleet of vehicles makes a significant contribution to the overall success of our business. So it is vital for us to constantly review and improve our working practices.

TRACKER has not only brought improved efficiency, but has also enabled us to make important financial savings which are crucial in today's economic climate. The service we provide to our customers has also improved, with shorter emergency response times. If a driver gets lost or encounters a problem, assistance can be given immediately, ensuring that the driver is properly looked after and the customer is not kept waiting unnecessarily for long periods of time." ■

3 Sie arbeiten für ein Logistikunternehmen in München. Ihre Chefin hat Ihnen die
KMK folgende Werbebroschüre mit einer Notiz auf den Schreibtisch gelegt. Fassen Sie
die wesentlichen Inhalte für Ihre Chefin auf Deutsch zusammen.

BIOpal – the first plastic half-pallet

BIOpal is the new plastic half-pallet that offers an alternative to the old-style wooden Dusseldorfer type of pallet, which does not always meet the high standards of hygiene and durability required in pallet exchange pools. The revolutionary load carrier **BIOpal** is designed for universal use in the whole supply chain, from the manufacturer via the distributor to the retailer. **BIOpal** combines several advantages which together give it great durability in pallet logistics through the whole distribution process. Moreover, it is reliable and safe to use with all types of handling equipment.

BIOpal is designed to give long service life with both roller and chain conveyor systems. With dimensions of just 800 mm × 600 mm × 160 mm, **BIOpal** features non-slip stoppers on the top and the underside of the deck to ensure safety in transportation by fork-lift trucks. In addition, the patented interlocking "Lego structure" makes safe stacking of empty pallets easier.

In an age of diminishing raw materials, there is a growing need for an alternative that offers greater durability and functionality than the wooden half-pallet. We are breaking new ground in production, for example through the careful use of resources and the controlled use of recyclable materials. Traceability of pallet movements by means of RFID technology ensures reliable data management, and thus better cost control.

> Ist das etwas für uns?
> Bitte Zusammenfassung
> der wichtigsten Punkte.
> Danke!
>   Carola Rank

4 Is this new type of pallet really environmentally friendly? Read the text again and
P make a list comparing the older type of pallet with the new BIOpal. Then discuss
the pros and cons of the different pallet types in class.

Phrases

Dusseldorfer pallet	BIOpal
– made of wood	– plastic material

Phrases: Advertising

This state-of-the-art mobile phone is easy to operate with its simple slide-out keyboard.	Dieses Handy, das auf dem neuesten technischen Stand ist, hat eine leicht zu bedienende ausziehbare Tastatur.
It has an easy to use touch screen.	Es hat einen leicht zu bedienenden Touch-Screen.
This must-have versatile gizmo includes all the latest features.	Dieses vielseitige Hi-Tech-Spielzeug, das man unbedingt haben muss, hat all die neuesten Funktionen.
You'll love its slim compact shape.	Die schlanke, kompakte Form wird Sie begeistern.
You'll be bewitched by the dazzling designs of our new collection.	Lassen Sie sich verführen von den bestechenden Designs unserer neuen Kollektion.
The ultimate **in** costume jewellery.	Der ultimative Modeschmuck.
We use a minimum of packaging to minimise the environmental impact.	Wir verwenden ein Minimum an Verpackung, um die Auswirkungen auf die Umwelt so gering wie möglich zu halten.
Your finger-nails will look flawless and perfectly cared **for**.	Ihre Fingernägel sehen makellos und perfekt gepflegt aus.
… subdued autumnal colours …	… dezente Herbstfarben …
This is a portable stereo-system **of** truly diminutive dimensions.	Es handelt sich um eine tragbare Super-Mini-Stereoanlage.
This hand-crafted leather bag combines perfect chic with amazing capacity.	Diese handgearbeitete Ledertasche ist superschick und dabei unglaublich geräumig.
We rely **on** tried and tested craftsmanship.	Wir verlassen uns auf unser erprobtes handwerkliches Können.
Weekends feel simply wonderful in our silky soft-touch tops.	Erleben Sie romantische Wochenenden mit unseren flauschig-kuscheligen Tops.
This downy soft luxury scarf will go with all your winter garments.	Dieser daunenweiche Luxusschal passt zu Ihrer gesamten Wintergarderobe.
… ideal for sensitive skins …	… ideal für die empfindliche Haut …

Unit 16
Job applications in Germany and the EU

The first thing is to find a vacancy. Companies advertise openings in newspapers on certain days which differ from place to place and country to country and also from sector to sector. Job exchanges on the Internet have become an important source of information. Often, it is possible to type in your job specification and receive notification by e-mail when anything suitable turns up. Job centres may be able to assist in the search for a suitable position and provide research facilities such as directories and internet access. Finally, there are private sector recruitment agencies which specialise in a particular sector. People often send unsolicited applications to major organisations on the off-chance that they are looking to recruit people.

1 Tell the class how you found your job / apprenticeship. Discuss which of the above are the most effective ways of looking for a job. Give reasons to support your answers.

Online-Link
808264-0016

THE CARING COMPANY
NATURAL BEAUTY
first-rate natural products for hair and skin care

We are seeking young persons from the Continent to

assist our Birmingham-based sales team

REF.: NB 605

We offer employment in a challenging, fast-paced environment where enthusiasm is the norm.

Successful applicants will have
- sales experience
- good English language skills
- native speaker competence in Italian, French or German

Successful applicants will be
- PC literate, including Excel
- able to meet deadlines
- self-motivated and hard-working

We offer an attractive salary and will help you with finding accommodation.

If you are interested please send your CV with a covering letter to

Catherine Bennet ▪ Recruitment Officer ▪ NATURAL BEAUTY ▪ 17 Laura Place ▪ Birmingham ▪ BI2 1AC

Automotive Services Ltd

Wholesaler and Importer of Automotive Parts

REF.: JR 673

In view of our rapidly growing business with Continental Europe
we are looking to recruit bilingual assistants (German-English or French-English)
to work in our import department.

Applicants should be fluent in German or French and have a good command of English. Office skills and familiarity with import procedures are essential. Must enjoy working in a team.

Send application enclosing CV and certificates in English to:

Jennifer O'Rourke (Mrs) | Automotive Services Ltd | 103 Selsdown Drive | London E14 9LA

Small Tour Operator

Requires well-organised full-time travel consultant with admin and accounts background and fluent German and/or French. Hotel or travel experience desirable, but not essential. Must be team worker and have MS Office and typing skills.

Send CV and letter of application by e-mail to jobs@dreamworldholidays.com or by post to:

 Dreamworld Holidays

28 Percival St
London
WIT 1DW

Quote ref.: DH 15 Pw

2
R
Read the advertisement on page 234 (Natural Beauty) and formulate the questions to which the following statements are the answers. The elements suggesting the question word are in bold type.

Example:
Answer: 1. Natural Beauty is based **in Birmingham**.
Question: 1. **Where** is Natural Beauty based?

Answers

1. Natural Beauty is based **in Birmingham**.
2. Natural Beauty is seeking **young persons**.
3. Successful applicants will have **good English language skills**.
4. Successful applicants' mother tongue will be **Italian, French or German**.
5. **The following qualifications** are essential: PC-literacy, ability to work hard and meet deadlines.
6. **Natural Beauty** will help you with finding accommodation.
7. Your CV should be sent **to Catherine Bennet**.

3
I
Discuss with a partner what German qualifications would equip you for the jobs advertised in the three advertisements on page 234.

4
P
Describe your (future) qualifications (school leaving certificate, e.g. Abitur, apprenticeship, traineeship etc, language certificates) and state briefly what kind of job you would like. For job titles refer back to UNIT 1.

Example:
"I have just completed my training as a publisher's assistant and would like to work in a publishing house in or around Cologne. I spent a year in the United States and attended High School there, so I'd welcome the opportunity to use my English in my job."

5
KMK
Stellen Sie einem Freund / einer Freundin die Stellenanzeigen auf der Seite 234 auf Deutsch vor. Beachten Sie dabei folgende Punkte:

- Firma bzw. Branche
- Anforderungen an Bewerber
- Gehalt
- Sonstige Leistungen der Firma
- Standort des Arbeitsplatzes
- Gewünschte Art der Kontaktaufnahme

A Letter of application

Your letter of application should be set out clearly and include the points below:

Thomas Seegers
Georg Weerth Str. 46
40545 Duesseldorf
Tel. +49 211 370 311
thomasseegers@t-online.de

your address and contact details

25 September 201_

date

Mrs Emily Ferguson
Anglo-Hibernian Bank
12 Bishop's Close
London
EC24 3FT
UK

address and name of person to contact, where given

Dear Mrs Ferguson

I saw your advertisement for a bilingual bank clerk for the foreign trade department of your bank on the www.jobsunlimited.co.uk website and should like to apply for this position.

say where you saw the ad

After taking my Abitur (= A-levels), I completed a traineeship at Deutsche Handelsbank in Frankfurt two years ago.

state qualifications

Since then I have been working at the main branch of the same bank in Hamburg. I have specialised in banking services for exporters and have a good knowledge of this segment. For this reason I feel well-qualified for the position advertised.

give details of experience

I have a good command of English. I had eight years of English at school, have visited London several times and spent two months on a placement at Silverstein Merchant Bank in London. I also have a good knowledge of Spanish.

mention other qualifications

I enclose my CV and certified translations of my certificates. I should be pleased to supply names of referees if required.

send CV and copies of certificates

I look forward to hearing from you. I would very much welcome the opportunity of working for a bank in Britain.

closing remarks

Yours sincerely

Thomas Seegers

Enc.

1 Übertragen Sie die folgenden Sätze ins Deutsche.

KMK

1. I have decided to apply on the off-chance.
2. I am interested in applying for this vacancy.
3. I know you are recruiting staff at present.
4. I feel I am suitably qualified for this position.
5. I have completed a traineeship as an export clerk.

2 Complete the following letter of application as the applicant using one of the

P advertisements on page 234.

(Your address etc)

(Company address)

Reference no. (given in advertisement)

Dear Sir/Madam

I saw your **1** in the **2** yesterday and am interested in **3** this position.
I have now completed a **4** as an export clerk. My experience is limited to the **5**
of my present firm.
I have a good **6** of English and Spanish and am keen **7** these languages.
I **8** my curriculum vitae and copies of certificates. Please let me know if you **9** the
names and addresses of referees.

I look forward to **10** you soon.

With best regards*
(Your name and signature)

Enclosures: CV, certificates

* "Yours sincerely" is also possible. "Yours faithfully" is very formal and is hardly
  used nowadays.

B Curriculum Vitae (CV)

A neatly arranged CV is an essential part of any application. The following are two German CVs with paraphrases in English. As indicated in UNIT 1 German job titles often have no direct equivalent in English. It is important that you paraphrase your job title (e.g. Industriekaufmann, Hotelfachfrau etc.) in such a way that a potential employer has a clear and realistic impression of your training and experience. When applying for a job in English – and there is an increasing number of companies in continental Europe whose company language is English – it is important to be aware of differences. In an English CV do not give details of your parents' profession, your religious denomination, or the number of your brothers and sisters. International CVs do not include a photograph. Modern CVs often reverse the chronological order and start with the most recent developments in your career.

1 **Study the following CVs of Fatma Gülsuyu and Daniel Paulat with a suggested paraphrase in English.**

German CV I

Tabellarischer Lebenslauf

Persönliche Angaben

Name	Fatma Gülsuyu
Adresse	Dülkener Str. 5, 40235 Düsseldorf
	Tel.: 0211 571364, E-Mail: fatmaguelsuyu@t-online.de
Staatsangehörigkeit	türkisch
Geburtstag	23.01.89
Geburtsort	Düsseldorf
Familienstand	ledig

Schulbildung

1995–1999	Grundschule Niederkassel
1999–2007	Schiller-Gymnasium, Düsseldorf
2007	Abitur (Leistungskurse: Englisch, Mathematik, Grundkurse: Sozialwissenschaften, Türkisch, Gesamtnote: 2,2)

Tätigkeiten

August 2005–Juli 2006	Hausaufgabenhilfe im „Lernzentrum", Düsseldorf
August 2006–Juni 2007	Aushilfstätigkeit im Reisebüro „Evren", Düsseldorf
seit September 2007	Ausbildung als Kauffrau für Bürokommunikation im Reisebüro „Evren"

Sprachkenntnisse

Deutsch: wie Muttersprache
Türkisch: Muttersprache
Englisch: gut in Wort und Schrift
Italienisch: Grundkenntnisse

PC-Kenntnisse Windows, Excel, Powerpoint

Interessen Musik (Saz spielen, im Chor singen), Volleyball

English paraphrase CV I

Curriculum Vitae

Personal details

Name and address

Fatma Gülsuyu
Dülkener Str 5
40235 Düsseldorf, Germany
Tel. + 49 (0)211 571364
E-mail: fatmaguelsuyu@t-online.de

Nationality	Turkish
Date of birth	23 January, 1989
Place of birth	Düsseldorf, Germany
Marital status	single

Education

1995–1999	Primary School Niederkassel
1999–2007	Schiller Gymnasium Düsseldorf (grammar school)
2007	Abitur (= A-Levels) Major subjects: English, Mathematics
	Basic courses: Social Sciences, Turkish
	Overall grade: 2.2 (= good = B)

Job experience and other activities

August 2005 to July 2006	Assisting pupils with homework at the Lernzentrum (Learning Centre) in Düsseldorf
August 2006–June 2007	Temporary employment at the "Evren" travel agency in Düsseldorf
from September 2007	Traineeship as office communications clerk/office management assistant at the "Evren" travel agency

Languages

German: native command
Turkish: mother tongue
English: good command of both spoken and written English
Italian: basic knowledge

Computer skills

Windows, Excel, Powerpoint

Hobbies

Music (playing saz, singing in a choir), volleyball

German CV II

Tabellarischer Lebenslauf

Persönliche Angaben

Name	Daniel Paulat
Adresse	44369 Dortmund
	Servatiusstr. 37
	Tel. 0231 4669834
	E-Mail: danielpaulat@aol.com
Staatsangehörigkeit	deutsch
Geburtstag	17.1.1990
Geburtsort	Hagen
Familienstand	ledig

Schulbildung

1996–2000	Grundschule Haspe, Hagen
2000–2004	Albert-Einstein-Realschule, Hagen
2004–2006	Gesamtschule am Teich, Dortmund
	Abschluss: Fachoberschulreife
2006–2008	Höhere Handelsschule, Kaufmännische Schule II,
	Dortmund
	Abschluss: Fachhochschulreife

Ausbildung

2009–2012	Ausbildung zum Industriekaufmann bei Kabel AG,
	Leverkusen
	Schwerpunkte: Rechnungswesen, Einkauf
2011	Zertifikatsprüfung Englisch für kaufmännische und
	verwaltende Berufe, Niveau I
voraussichtlich Mai 2012	Abschlussprüfung

Tätigkeiten

2006–2008	Aushilfstätigkeit als Fahrradkurier
2008–2009	Zivildienst in einer Behindertenwerkstatt

Sonstige Kenntnisse

MS Office, Linux
Englisch fließend, Spanisch ausbaufähig

Interessen

Fitness, Fußball, Fantasy-Literatur

English paraphrase CV II

Curriculum Vitae

Personal details

Name	Daniel Paulat
Address	44369 Dortmund, Germany
	Servatiusstr. 37
	Tel.: +49 (0)231 4669834
	E-mail: danielpaulat@aol.com
Nationality	German
Date of birth	17 January, 1990
Place of birth	Hagen (North Rhine-Westphalia)
Marital status	single

Education/Training

1996–2000	Primary school Haspe, Hagen
2000–2004	Albert Einstein Realschule (= higher secondary school), Hagen
2004–2006	Gesamtschule am Teich (comprehensive), Dortmund School-leaving certificate: Fachoberschulreife (= certificate enabling student to continue education at higher vocational school)
2006–2008	Höhere Handelschule, Kaufmännische Schule II (higher commercial college), Dortmund Final examination: Fachhochschulreife (examination enabling student to enrol at a polytechnic university)
2009–2012	Traineeship as an industrial clerk/industrial business management assistant at Kabel AG, Leverkusen
2011	Special subjects: accounting, purchasing Zertifikatsprüfung (state examination)
probably May, 2012	English for clerical and administrative professions, Level I Final examination traineeship

Job activities

2006–2008	Temporary employment as cycle courier
2008–2009	Social service (in lieu of military service) in a workshop for handicapped people

Other skills

MS Office, Linux/Fluent English, basic Spanish

Personal interests

Working out, football, fantasy literature

✱ **2** Now write your own CV in English using the examples above and referring back to
P UNIT 1 for job titles. Use a dictionary if necessary.

Phrases ⟩

3 You have applied for a job with GlaxoSmithKline (UK). You feel you have a good
chance of being invited to an interview. Research the company and its products
and make brief notes in English.

4 Daniela Zeischegg sent off an application three weeks ago to the British company
I Tolaron plc in reply to an advertisement in which the company was looking for
a German mother-tongue export clerk. Since she has not received a reply she
decides to ring the company. Roleplay the dialogue below.

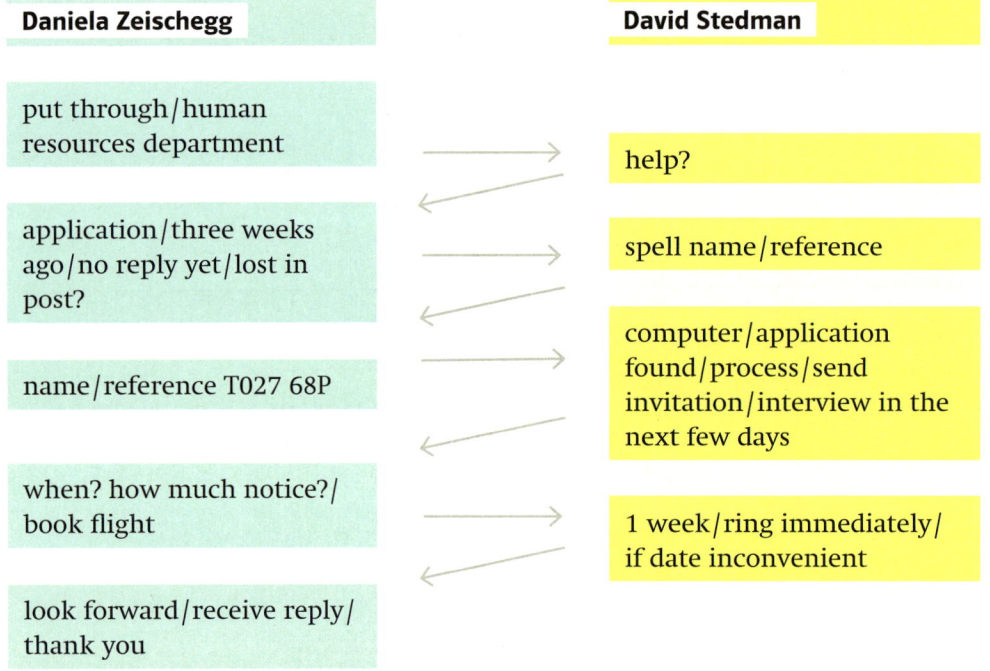

Daniela Zeischegg	David Stedman
put through/human resources department	help?
application/three weeks ago/no reply yet/lost in post?	spell name/reference
name/reference T027 68P	computer/application found/process/send invitation/interview in the next few days
when? how much notice?/ book flight	1 week/ring immediately/ if date inconvenient
look forward/receive reply/ thank you	

⊚ V8 **Video lounge** Travel and Tourism

BBC Motion Gallery

You are about to see a video on the travel and tourist industry.
Read through the questions below and listen for the answers
as you watch the video:

1. What kind of tour operator does the young man work for?
2. Try and list as many of the qualifications and characteristics
   that are mentioned as desirable in a tour leader.
3. What kind of person is likely to apply for a job as a tour
   leader?
4. How did he prepare for his job in Egypt?
5. What sort of disadvantages does life as a tour leader have?

C Interviews

If your application meets with the approval of the company or its personnel department, your name will be put on a shortlist and you will be invited to an interview.

How can you prepare for the interview?

It is important to find out as much as you can about the company, its products and the image it projects so that you make an informed impression and demonstrate that you are interested in the company.

Think beforehand of any questions you would like to ask if they are not covered by the interviewer, e.g. location, type of work, starting salary, opportunities for further training, opportunities to use your language skills, catering arrangements, company pension scheme, how big is the office you will be working in? Will you have contact with customers or is it a back office?

What are your other interests? Think carefully about this. If you say "cinema" expect to be asked about the last film you saw. If you mention an interest in your CV, e.g. working out at a gym, you should think in advance what you would say if asked about it.

Finally, do not underestimate the importance of so-called "soft skills" – a neat, clean appearance, shirt tucked neatly into trousers, polished shoes with laces tied, hair neatly cut and combed, etc. Women should go for a suit or skirt or trousers and jacket. Don't risk wearing jeans and a T-shirt.

1 **Answer the following questions on the text above.**

R

1. What may happen if the company has a lot of applications and you are one of the fortunate ones?
2. Why is it a good idea to know something about the company?
3. What questions might you want to ask if the interviewer doesn't cover them?
4. What interests or hobbies would you mention?
5. What is meant by the term "soft skills"?

2 Choose what you regard as appropriate from this list of do's and don'ts.

R

1. Your first question should be about annual holidays.
2. You should dress smartly.
3. You should take some gum with you to chew to help you relax.
4. The interviewer can't expect you to know much about the firm before you even work there.
5. You should feel free to tell the interviewer that you are bored with your present job.
6. You should be prepared (and able) to talk about any interests you mention.
7. You should make eye contact with the interviewer, smile and nod to express agreement or ethusiasm.
8. You should tell the interviewer straight away that you are applying for other jobs at the moment.
9. You should refuse to describe your strengths and weaknesses.

3 Send an encouraging e-mail to an anxious friend who has an interview in a couple of days. Make sentences by matching the bubbles with suitable parts from the list below.

P

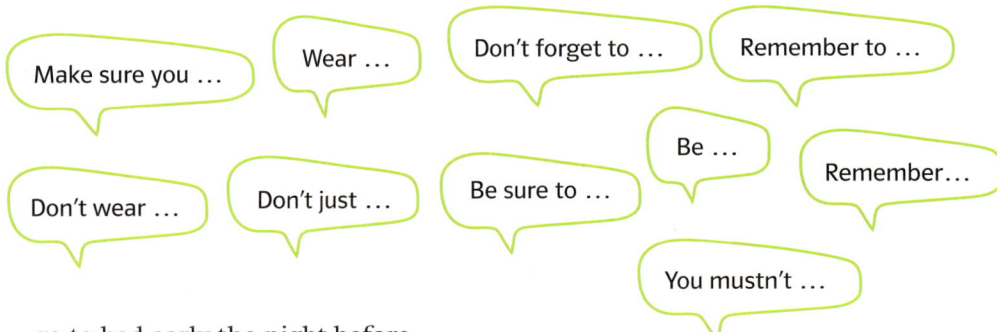

... go to bed early the night before.
... go to the hairdresser's beforehand.
... put on a clean set of clothes.
... a sweatshirt or fleece (boy)/see-through top or mini-skirt (girl).
... a smart costume (girl)/jacket (boy).
... wear sneakers.
... have a look at the firm's website before the interview.
... get there on time.
... yourself and act naturally.
... answer "yes" or "no". Take the initiative and volunteer information.
... that there are other fish in the sea.

4 Daniela Zeischegg has been invited to an interview at Tolaron plc's head office in Croydon, South London. She takes an early flight from Cologne-Bonn airport to London Gatwick. She takes the train from Gatwick to South Croydon and presents herself at Tolaron at 11 am. She wears a neatly tailored suit in navy blue and a white blouse.

R
◎ A1.31

Listen to the interview and write down the job details mentioned.

5 **Listen to the interview again and translate the following sentences into English.**

R / M
A 1.31

1. Sie haben eine Ausbildung bei einem großen Kölner Unternehmen der verarbeitenden Industrie gemacht.
2. Wir benötigen jemanden, der Deutsch spricht, weil wir eine große Anzahl von Kunden in Deutschland und Österreich haben.
3. Leider können wir Ihnen bei der Suche nach einer Unterkunft nicht behilflich sein.
4. Müsste ich am 1. August anfangen, wie in der Anzeige angegeben?
5. Ich habe mich gefreut, Sie kennen zu lernen. Sie werden von mir hören.

6 **Match these 10 questions with the answers given below.**

R

1. Why do you wish to leave your present position?
2. What would you say are your strengths and weaknesses?
3. Why would you like to work for this company?
4. Which animal do you most readily identify with?
5. What are your professional aims?
6. What are your expectations as far as salary is concerned?
7. What would you say was your advantage compared with other applicants?
8. What did you find most satisfying in your previous jobs?
9. What three positive things would your previous boss say about you?
10. What reasons would you give why we should employ you?

A. I particularly like lions/monkeys/elephants.
B. I don't know the other applicants. All I know is that I am highly motivated and keen to do this job.
C. Eventually I would like to be an export manager/head of department/set up in business on my own.
D. I am very enthusiastic and have all the necessary qualifications plus good references.
E. I have always enjoyed dealing with people. I liked being in the front office. I had a good rapport with customers.
F. I like my present job and the people I work with but it doesn't give me any opportunity to use my languages/I have no contact with clients.
G. My previous boss would probably say I had a good sense of humour, was good at working to deadlines and that I had a good manner with customers.
H. My strengths are that I'm good at working with clients, deadlines don't faze me. My weaknesses – I need praise and to feel that I'm needed. My motivation level drops if I feel unloved or unappreciated.
I. The company has a very good reputation for well-designed products and a positive approach to the environment. I also know that you have a good reputation as an equal opportunities employer.
J. From advertisements for similar positions I know that the usual starting salary is about Euro 2000. I would be happy with this salary but would hope that the career structure makes promotion possible.

✳ **7** **Work with a partner. Prepare and act out the following interview as a role play in English using the prompts on the role cards.**

Phrases ⟩

Role card: Partner A (interviewer)	**Role card partner B** ⇨ **page 258**

Sie sind Jennifer O'Rourke von Automotive Services Ltd., London, oder deren Kollege John Middleton. Mittels einer Stellenanzeige haben Sie eine/n zweisprachige/n Mitarbeiter/in für die Importabteilung gesucht. Ein/e Bewerber/in kommt zum Vorstellungsgespräch.

Beginnen Sie das Gespräch mit allgemeinen Fragen z. B. nach:
- Flug
- Heimatstadt des Bewerbers
- Wetter

Fassen Sie die Anforderungen kurz zusammen:
- zweisprachig
- teamfähig
- vertraut mit Einfuhrformalitäten

Fragen Sie nach Berufserfahrung:
- Dauer
- Arbeitsgebiete
- Software-Kenntnisse

Erkundigen Sie sich nach den Gründen für den Wunsch in GB zu arbeiten.

Fragen Sie nach den Gehaltsvorstellungen.

Gehen Sie auf das im CV genannte Interesse an Tennis ein:
- Sie spielen selbst.
- Ihre Firma besorgt für die Mitarbeiter Karten für Wimbledon.

Versprechen Sie in einer Woche Bescheid zu geben.

Verabschieden Sie den Bewerber freundlich.

D Employment in the EU

One of the central principles of the EU is the free movement of labour. This means that in principle any EU citizen can look for a job in any EU member country without having to apply for permits etc. An EU citizen also has the right to take up residence in any EU country.

1
R
A1.32
Jonathan Oxfurt, a 23-year-old German from Quedlinburg who has recently completed an apprenticeship as an export clerk, is thinking of looking for a job in another European country. He is talking on the telephone to an English friend, Daniel Peterson, whom he met while on a work placement in England and who is working in Bracknell at the logistics and warehousing operation of a major supermarket.

Listen to the conversation and decide whether the following statements are TRUE or FALSE.

1. Jonathan has sent off lots of applications.
2. He would need a green card to work in Britain.
3. A lot of companies have their head offices in Bracknell.
4. Jonathan's certificates do not need to be translated into English.
5. Jonathan could stay for a while with Daniel.
6. Daniel suggests he should apply to the export department.

2
R
A1.33
Marcel Krenz has seen that Global Catering are looking for an assistant to the export manager who speaks French and German. Kirsty Burnham has been promoted and the new export manager is Zoe Lovegrove. Marcel is excited about the job and would love to work in Manchester. He decides to ring Kirsty Burnham.

Listen to the dialogue and complete the following sentences.

Would you **1** for a moment, please?
As you know, **2** are now the big thing.
I have seen that your company is advertising for **3** who can speak German.
Of course, it will have to go through **4** .
Tell Herr Diepholz this is **5** for you.
I'll get **6** off right away.

3 Listen to the dialogue again and translate the following sentences into German.

R / M
A1.33

1. Kirsty Burnham has been promoted.
2. Global Catering are looking for an assistant to the export manager.
3. We are in the process of acquiring a US chain of organic snack outlets.
4. I would be able to involve you in the US projects.
5. I am dreading telling Herr Diepholz.
6. Keep your fingers crossed!

Communicating across cultures: Job applications

You should NOT include references from previous employers in your application when applying in Britain. You will usually be asked to give the names and addresses of possible referees so that the company can approach them direct. In your covering letter you may indicate that you are prepared to provide names of referees on request.

It is obviously a good idea to ask possible referees beforehand whether they are happy to provide a reference.

You should NOT include a photo in your application when applying in the USA or Britain nor make any reference to your religion or race, unless specifically asked to do so.

Info: EU-Facts and figures

EU member countries (27 at present):

Austria, Belgium, Bulgaria, Cyprus, Czech Republic, Denmark, Estonia, Finland, France, Germany, Greece, Hungary, Ireland, Italy, Latvia, Lithuania, Luxemburg, Malta, The Netherlands, Poland, Portugal, Romania, Slovakia, Slovenia, Spain, Sweden, United Kingdom

Total area: 4,324,782 sq. km.

Total population: c. 501.26 million

Total GDP: between $14 and $16 trillion

Languages: There are over 20 official languages. English is spoken by 34% of European citizens – the most widely spoken foreign language.

Logistics expert

1 Finding the right job

1

R / P Make up a chart of your priorities when looking for your future job. Then read the job advertisement below and tick which of your expectations are met by it. Would you apply for this job or not? Give reasons for your decision.

WATER IS OUR ELEMENT – SHIPPING IS OUR BUSINESS

Bremen-based carrier Orca Shipping GmbH is one of the world's leading companies in the niche segment project and heavy-lift shipments. Conducting logistically challenging transportation projects is our core business.

Thanks to richness of ideas, innovative spirit, commitment and competence plus a modern, powerful fleet of multi-purpose heavy-lift project carriers we safely and efficiently realise complex transportation solutions to the greatest possible customer satisfaction.

For strategic reasons, we intend to strengthen the transport engineering division at our Bremen headquarters as soon as possible with two

Cargo Superintendents (m/f)

The candidate's role and tasks will be:
- Taking responsibility for cargo quality issues (damage prevention), stowage planning and monitoring vessels' performance
- Supervising local load and discharge operations
- Attending technical meetings with customers

The successful candidate will bring along the following qualifications:
- At least 3 years training / experience in sea freight business
- Interpersonal and teamwork skills
- Computer literacy, preferable with AutoCAD and Excel

The position requires expertise in the specific field of work, strong commitment, flexibility and leadership qualities. We offer excellent career prospects, competitive salary and fringe benefits.

If you are interested in this job, please apply with a covering letter, CV and information on your earliest possible entry date to: career@orca-group.com.

2

R Read the job advertisement above again and complete the sentences with information from the text.

1. Orca Shipping is specialised in …
2. The company's principles together with … are the key to Orca's success.
3. The applicant will be responsible for …
4. The candidate should be able to …
5. The application has to consist of …

3 What do the following terms from the job advertisement on page 249 mean?
R Choose the right definitions. Sometimes more than one answer is correct.

1. **interpersonal skills**
   a. cooperating well with others
   b. knowledge of cultural differences
   c. the ability to work independently

2. **competitive salary**
   a. as good as in other companies
   b. depending on performance
   c. salary to be negotiated

3. **career prospects**
   a. brochures on future jobs
   b. good chances to advance in a job
   c. possibility to earn more money

4. **fringe benefits**
   a. company car
   b. expense account
   c. specific pension programmes

2 Applying for a job in logistics

1 Three people are interested in the jobs advertised by Orca Shipping. Listen to
R what they say about themselves. Decide who the most suitable candidate is and
A 2.14 give reasons for your choice.

2 Translate the following sentences into English.
M

1. Ich habe mit einer kurzen Unterbrechung vier Jahre lang in einer internationalen Spedition gearbeitet.
2. Meine Hauptaufgaben umfassten das Zusammenstellen der Fracht und die Bereitstellung der notwendigen Papiere.
3. Gerne arbeite ich im Team, bin aber auch daran gewöhnt selbstständig Entscheidungen zu treffen.
4. Ich verfüge über gute Englisch- und grundlegende Spanischkenntnisse.
5. Meine weiteren Qualifikationen können Sie dem Lebenslauf und den beiliegenden Zeugnissen entnehmen.

3 Listen again and take notes of all the information
R / P the applicant of your choice gives about his / her
A 2.14 personal and professional qualifications for the job.
Write a letter of application to Orca Shipping using
this information.

Phrases ▶

✳ **4** Make a list of six questions an interviewer for the
I advertised job might ask. Have a partner answer
them. Then change roles.

Phrases ▶

Phrases: Applications

To refer to the source of address

I saw your advertisement **in** …	Ich habe Ihre Anzeige in … gesehen.
I saw this vacancy advertised **on** the … website.	Ich habe diese Stellenanzeige auf der … Webseite gefunden.
I should like to apply for the position advertised in the …	Ich möchte mich für den in der … ausgeschriebenen Posten bewerben.
I have been given your address **by** … who told me that you have a vacancy **for** …	Ich habe Ihre Anschrift von … bekommen, der mich darauf aufmerksam machte, dass bei Ihnen die Stelle eines … frei geworden ist.
I am applying on the off-chance that you may have a vacancy.	Ich erlaube mir, Ihnen eine Initiativbewerbung zu schicken, für den Fall, dass bei Ihnen eine Stelle frei ist.

To give reasons for applying

I am particularly attracted **to** this position as …	Ich bin an dieser Stelle besonders interessiert, weil …
I have just completed a traineeship **at** …	Ich habe gerade meine Ausbildung bei … abgeschlossen.
I completed an apprenticeship two years ago.	Vor zwei Jahren haben ich meine Ausbildung abgeschlossen.
I have some experience in the export trade.	Ich habe Erfahrungen im Außenhandel.
I am familiar **with** this kind of work.	Mit dieser Tätigkeit bin ich vertraut.
I am used to working with people.	Ich bin es gewohnt mit Menschen zu arbeiten.
I enjoy working with people.	Ich arbeite gern mit anderen Menschen zusammen.
I enjoy working in a team.	Ich arbeite gern im Team.
I would welcome the opportunity to …	Ich würde mich über die Möglichkeit freuen …
I am keen to use my knowledge **of** English and French.	Ich möchte sehr gerne meine Englisch- und Französischkenntnisse anwenden.

To refer to your German school career

From … to … I attended … comparable **to** • primary (UK)/elementary (USA) school • grammar school (UK) • higher secondary school • secondary modern school	Von … bis … besuchte ich • die Grundschule • das Gymnasium • die Realschule • die Hauptschule

• comprehensive (school) • high school (USA) • vocational school • commercial school • business college • polytechnic university, university of applied sciences	• Gesamtschule (Einheitsschule für die Sekundarstufe) • die Berufsschule • die Höhere Handelsschule • das Berufskolleg • die Fachhochschule
In … I obtained the • certificate enabling a student to continue education at higher vocational school • German higher education entrance qualification • German university entrance qualification	Im Jahre … erwarb ich das Zeugnis der • Fachoberschulreife • Fachhochschulreife • allgemeine Hochschulreife (Abitur)
In … I passed the • state examination in English for clerical and administrative professions • Chamber of Commerce examination – "Certified Foreign Language Correspondent" – "English for Commercial Trainees"	Im Jahre … legte ich die … • Zertifikatsprüfung Englisch für kaufmännische und verwaltende Berufe (KMK-Zertifikat) • IHK-Prüfung – „Geprüfte/r Fremdsprachen-korrespondent/in" – „Zusatzqualifikation Englisch für kaufmännische Auszubildende" ab.

To refer to qualifications

I **took** my Abitur two years ago.	Vor zwei Jahren machte ich das Abitur.
My main subjects included English and Maths.	Meine Leistungskurse waren Englisch und Mathematik.
I have trained **as a** …	Ich bin gelernte/r …
I have completed an apprenticeship **in** …	Ich habe eine Ausbildung als … abgeschlossen.
I did my apprenticeship **with** the … company.	Ich habe eine Ausbildung bei der Firma … gemacht.
I spent two months in St. Albans **on** a placement.	Ich war zwei Monate zu einem Praktikum in St. Albans.
I have done a practical **with** a small travel operator.	Ich habe ein Praktikum bei einem kleinen Reiseveranstalter gemacht.
I have good admin and bookkeeping skills.	Ich verfüge über gute Kenntnisse und Fertigkeiten, was Organisation und Buchhaltung angeht.

To refer to certificates and references

I enclose certified copies of my certificates.	Als Anlage übersende ich Ihnen beglaubigte Zeugniskopien.
I enclose certified translations of …	Ich füge beglaubigte Übersetzungen von … bei.
I should be happy to provide the names of referees.	Ich würde Ihnen gerne Referenzen angeben.

To refer to starting date and relocation

I would be able to start **at** short notice.	Ich kann kurzfristig anfangen.
I would have to give the usual notice **at** my present firm.	Ich müsste die übliche Kündigungsfrist einhalten.
I could start **on** 1 August.	Ich könnte am 1. August anfangen.
I would be prepared to move **to** …	Ich wäre bereit nach … umzuziehen.

To close the letter

I look forward to hearing from you.	Ich sehe Ihrer Antwort mit Interesse entgegen.
I should be grateful if you would consider my application.	Ich würde mich freuen, wenn Sie meine Bewerbung berücksichtigen.
I hope that you will consider my application suitable and give me the opportunity to present myself **at** an interview.	Ich hoffe, dass Sie meine Bewerbung in Betracht ziehen und mir die Möglichkeit geben, mich Ihnen persönlich vorzustellen.

Role cards Partner B

Unit 5 C 5

Role card: Partner B   **Role card partner A ⇨ page 71**

1. 0033 (0) 4 92 04 89 20
2. 12 Gansevoort Street New York, NY 10014 USA Tel.: 001-212-2422455 info@usatech.com,
3. www.visitengland.com
4. e-mail: info@shanghai-cd.com, phone: 86-21-5365-8941
5. address: 12J-1 Golden Bell Plaza 18 Huaihai Zhong Lu Shanghai 200021 China

Unit 5 C 8

Role card: Partner A / B

Persons for whom the message is intended:	Possible contents of message:
Mr. Collins	Mr. Campbell ill with the flu / can't take part in the conference
Sales Manager	Meeting on Wednesday scheduled from 1:00 pm to 3:30 pm / 15 participants
Miss Otway in Purchasing	Proposal accepted / further details tomorrow
Dr. Temme	New deadline for application 16 October, must be kept whatever happens
Frau Sabine Johänntges	Flight delayed by one hour / arrival now at 10:15 London Heathrow

Unit 6 A 8

Role card partner A ⇨ page 88

Role card: Partner B

Sie sind James Critchley von der Firma SmartMart Ltd. und wollen für eine Geschäftsreise in den USA ein Auto mieten. Jennifer Ainsworth von Saskatchewan Airlines hat Ihnen die Mietwagenfirma Excelsior Limos Inc. in Chicago empfohlen. **Rufen Sie dort an.**

- Auto vom 25. bis 30. Juni benötigt
- Abholung und Rückgabe am Flughafen O'Hare in Chicago
- Kleinwagen genügt/Preis für fünf Tage?/Versicherung inbegriffen?
- Zusatzversicherung für Selbstbeteiligung (excess coverage) erwünscht?
- Rabatt für Kunden der Saskatchewan Airlines?
- Gesamtpreis für eine Woche?
- Zahlung per Kreditkarte?
- Visa Nr. 4731 5026 7100 5314, gültig bis 07/14
- Adresse: Brunswick Avenue, Brighton BN3 1NA, UK

Unit 6 B1 1

Role card partner A ⇨ page 89

Role card: Partner B

Kirsty Burnham's appointment diary

Monday	**13 June**
9–11 am: meeting to discuss Madrid; 1 pm working lunch with John Markham from PolisMedia; 2.30 pm meeting at office with Barbara Lonsdale from Cosmopolitan Gourmet	
Tuesday	**14 June**
Wednesday	**15 June**
From 10 am: visiting suppliers in Birmingham	
Thursday	**16 June**
5 pm: work-out at Royal Gym with Laurie	
Friday	**17 June**
10 am: Leeds/Amanda Rees from Snack Attack/introduction of trial range 4 pm: hairdresser	

Unit 6 Logistics expert 2

Role card: Partner B   Role card partner A ⇨ page 95

Departure time FRA	Destination	Duration of flight	Arrival time
?	San Francisco	11:30 h	09.00 am
?	Cape Town	11:20 h	09.35 pm
10.45 am	Singapore	?	?
02.00 pm	Rio de Janeiro	?	?

Unit 6 Logistics expert 4

Role card: Partner B   Role card partner A ⇨ page 96

Sie arbeiten für die Firma Weigand. Sie wollen Waren von Frankfurt nach Kapstadt schicken und rufen deshalb die Spedition Nah & Fern an.

- Benennen Sie, welche Ware wohin transportiert werden soll (z. B. Lebensmittel, Maschinen).
- Beschreiben Sie den Umfang der Lieferung.
- Fragen Sie nach der jeweiligen Dauer des Transports.
- Erkundigen Sie sich bei Flugtransport nach Abflug- und Ankunftszeiten.

Unit 9 B 4

Role card: Partner B   Role card partner B ⇨ page 133

Jane/James Vernon from Powertools plc, Cardiff, gets a call.
He/she offers to send brochures, price lists and detailed technical descriptions by e-mail and asks for Hammer Werkzeughandel's e-mail address.
Details about delivery times, quantity discounts etc. are dealt with in the brochure.
Jane/James thanks the caller for his/her interest in Powertool's products.

Unit 11 Logistics expert 6

Role card: Partner B **Role card partner A ⇨ page 167**

Sie sind Su Ling von TransAsian. Lisa Bechmann von GoGlobal ruft Sie wegen der Probleme bei der Ausfuhr der Ware für Weihler & Söhne an.

- Begrüßen Sie Lisa Bechmann und erklären Sie ihr, dass es scheinbar bei Plastics & More eine Verwechslung mit einer anderen Bestellung aus Deutschland gab.
- Sagen Sie, dass Ihnen versichert wurde, dass die richtigen Waren innerhalb 48 Stunden versandfertig sein werden.
- Sagen Sie, dass eine Stornierung möglich war, aber dafür eine Gebühr anfiel.
- Sagen Sie, dass Sie Plastics & More darüber bereits informiert haben und die Firma natürlich auch alle weiteren entstehenden Kosten übernehmen wird. Sie haben schon vorsorglich Laderaum für den Flug übermorgen gebucht.
- Sagen Sie, dass Sie Lisa über jeden Schritt informieren werden.
- Verabschieden Sie sich angemessen.

Unit 14 A2 6

Role card: Partner B (seller) **Role card partner A ⇨ page 212**

You receive a call from a customer who had expected to be supplied with a skateboard for a maximum weight of 70 kg. On checking the package the customer has found that the maximum admissible weight is only 90 lbs. The price the customer paid is the price for this smaller model. However, on your website you had quoted this lower price for the bigger model by mistake. Apologize. Try to persuade the customer to keep the smaller skateboard – as a present for a kid? – and promise to let him have the bigger one half price. Should the customer refuse this generous offer you will have to agree to take back the small skateboard at your expense and refund the purchase price.

Unit 14 Logistics expert 6

Role card: Partner B **Role card partner A ⇨ page 218**

Sie sind Kapitän der auf Grund gelaufenen Morning Star und erhalten einen Anruf von GoGlobal wegen des weiteren Vorgehens in dem Fall.

- Begrüßen Sie Partner A und geben Sie Auskunft darüber, wie es Ihnen geht.
- Sagen Sie, dass Ihnen das Geschehen leidtue und Sie bei einer schnellen Regelung gerne behilflich sind.
- Sagen Sie, dass Sie sich gleich darum kümmern werden. Fragen Sie, ob Sie Fotos von der beschädigten Fracht machen sollen.
- Sagen Sie, dass Sie das schon getan haben. Fragen Sie, was Sie mit den Containern tun sollen, die Sie an Land haben bringen lassen.
- Bedanken Sie sich für den Anruf und versprechen Sie, sich um alles vor Ort zu kümmern.

Role card: Partner B (interviewee)   **Role card partner A** ⇨ **page 246**

Sie (eigener Name) haben sich bei Automotive Services Ltd., London, als zweisprachige/r Importsachbearbeiter/in beworben und sind zu einem Vorstellungsgespräch eingeladen worden. Sie sind 23 Jahre alt und haben vor einem Jahr ihre Ausbildung als Kaufmann/-frau im Groß- und Außenhandel beendet.

Beantworten Sie die allgemeinen Fragen zu Beginn ganz nach Wunsch
- Flug angenehm/unruhig
- Wetter heiter/wolkig
- einige Sätze zu ihrer Heimatstadt

Sie kennen die Anforderungen und glauben sie vollständig zu erfüllen
- Deutsch Muttersprache, Englisch gut: Insgesamt 9 Jahre in der Schule, 1 Jahr in USA
- arbeiten gern im Team
- mit allen Export- und Importverfahren vertraut

Berufserfahrung
- Ausbildung in verschiedenen Abteilungen eines Stuttgarter Automobilherstellers (Verkauf, Einkauf, Lagerhaltung, Rechnungs- und Personalwesen)
- nach Abschluss der Lehre ein volles Jahr bis jetzt in einer Importabteilung für elektronische Bauelemente
- vertraut mit SAP Office

Begründen Sie Ihre Absicht in GB zu arbeiten ganz nach Ihrer Wahl

Gehaltsvorstellung noch nicht konkret, in Deutschland ca. € 2000 pro Monat

Tennis
- Sie spielen für Ihren Klub in der Regionalliga
- Sie versuchen immer möglichst viel von Wimbledon im Fernsehen zu sehen

Bitten Sie um baldige Nachricht, weil Sie rechtzeitig kündigen müssen.

Videotraining: Englische Aussprache

Perfekte englische Aussprache leicht gemacht: Mit dem Lernprogramm zur englischen Lautschrift können Sie alle Laute einüben. Wählen Sie einfach in der Navigation rechts den entsprechenden Reiter (*Vowels* oder *Consonants*) aus und dann klicken Sie auf das gewünschte phonetische Symbol. Sprechen Sie die Wörter laut nach.
Unter www.klett.de geben Sie einfach den Online-Link 808201-1000 ein. Von dort aus können Sie die Webanwendung online starten.

Hinweis: Unitbegleitendes Vokabular zum Herunterladen über Online-Link 808264-0000.

(AE) = **American English**
(BE) = **British English**

A

to abbreviate [ə'bri:vɪeɪt] abkürzen 137
abbreviation [ə,bri:vɪ'eɪʃn] Abkürzung 111
ability [ə'bɪlətɪ] Fähigkeit 100
able to work in a team [ˌeɪbl tʊ ,wɜ:k ɪn_ə 'ti:m] teamfähig 246
above-mentioned [ə,bʌv'menʃnd] obengenannte/r/s 124
abroad [ə'brɔ:d] im/ins/aus dem Ausland 41
to absorb [əb'zɔ:b] aufnehmen 101
access ['ækses] Zugang 53
accessibility [æk,sesə'bɪlətɪ] Erreichbarkeit 95
accident ['æksɪdənt] Unfall 88
to accommodate [ə'kɒmədeɪt] aufnehmen, unterbringen, entgegenkommen 169
accommodation [ə,kɒmə'deɪʃn] Unterkunft, Wohnung 234
to accompany [ə'kʌmpənɪ] begleiten 173
according to [ə'kɔ:dɪŋ ˌtʊ] entsprechend, gemäß 101
account [ə'kaʊnt] Konto 191
accountant [ə'kaʊntənt] Buchhalter/in, Bilanzprüfer/in, Buchprüfer/in 58
account-holder [ə'kaʊnt,həʊldə] Kontoinhaber/in 193
accounting [ə'kaʊntɪŋ] Rechnungswesen 241
accounts [ə'kaʊnts] Buchhaltung, Rechnungswesen 65
to accumulate [ə'kju:mjəleɪt] sich konzentrieren, anhäufen 228
accurate(ly) ['ækjərət(lɪ)] genau, präzise, akkurat 69
to ache [eɪk] schmerzen, wehtun 65

a couple of [ə 'kʌpl əv] ein paar 226
to acquire [ə'kwaɪə] sich aneignen 100
actually ['æktʃʊəlɪ] eigentlich 222
additions [ə'dɪʃnz] Hinzufügungen 90
additional [ə'dɪʃnl] zusätzlich 74
additional / supplementary insurance [ə,dɪʃənl / ,sʌplɪməntərɪ ɪn'ʃɔ:rəns] Zusatzversicherung 88
addressee [,ædres'i:] Adressat, Empfänger 112
adequate ['ædɪkwət] angemessen 50
to adhere to [əd'hɪə tu:] sich an etwas halten 155
to adjust [ə'dʒʌst] anpassen, sich anpassen 146
adjustment [ə'dʒʌstmənt] Ausgleich, Bereinigung, Erledigung 204
admin and accounts [,ædmɪn ən_ ə'kaʊnts] Verwaltung und Rechnungswesen 234
administration [əd,mɪnɪ'streɪʃn] Verwaltung 58
administrator [əd'mɪnɪstreɪtə] Vergleichs-, Vermögensverwalter 199
admirable ['ædmərəbl] bewundernswert, ausgezeichnet 148
adult ['ædʌlt] Erwachsene/r 194
to advance [əd'va:ns] vorankommen 250
advanced [əd'va:nst] hoch entwickelt 49
advantage [əd'va:ntɪdʒ] Vorteil 226
advent ['ædvent] Ankunft 63
advertisement [əd'vɜ:tɪsmənt, 'ædvətaɪzmənt] Anzeige 130
advertising ['ædvətaɪzɪŋ] Werbung 164
advertising agency ['ædvətaɪzɪŋ ,eɪdʒənsɪ] Werbeagentur 8
advertising assistant ['ædvətaɪzɪŋ ə,sɪstənt] Kaufmann/-frau für Marketingkommunikation 8
advertising campaign ['ædvətaɪzɪŋ kæm,peɪn] Werbekampagne 128

to advise [əd'vaɪz] (be)raten; benachrichrigen 49
advisory services [əd'vaɪzərɪ ,sɜ:vɪsɪz] Beratungsdienst 224
to affect [ə'fekt] Einfluss haben (auf) 49
afloat [ə'fləʊt] seetüchtig 217
age group ['eɪdʒ ,gru:p] Altersgruppe 221
agenda [ə'dʒendə] Tagesordnung; Termine 85
agent ['eɪdʒənt] Handelsvertreter/in, Vertretung 223
a good command of English [ə ,gʊd kə,ma:nd əv 'ɪŋglɪʃ] gute Englischkenntnisse 234
air-conditioning ['eəkən,dɪʃənɪŋ] Klimaanlage 26
air freight ['eəfreɪt] Luftfracht 122
airline ['eəlaɪn] Fluggesellschaft 225
airy ['eərɪ] luftig 26
aisle [aɪl] Gang 31
alien ['eɪlɪən] fremd 155
altitude ['æltɪtju:d] (Flug-)Höhe 228
amateur chef [,æmətʊə 'ʃef] Hobbykoch 29
amazing [ə'meɪzɪŋ] erstaunlich 41
ambitious [æm'bɪʃəs] ehrgeizig, anspruchsvoll 104
among [ə'mʌŋ] unter 20
amount [ə'maʊnt] Betrag, Summe 175
ancient ['eɪnʃnt] (ur)alt 25
anger ['æŋgə] Zorn 204
annual holidays [,ænjʊəl 'hɒlɪdeɪz] Jahresurlaub 244
answering machine (BE), voice mail (AE) ['a:nsərɪŋ mə,ʃi:n, 'vɔɪs ,meɪl] Anrufbeantworter 64
to antagonize [æn'tægənaɪz] vor den Kopf stoßen 212
apart from [ə'pa:t frəm] abgesehen von 40
apology [ə'pɒlədʒɪ] Entschuldigung 92

to appeal to [ə'piːl tuː] ansprechen, gefallen; appellieren 119

appetising [ˈæpətaɪzɪŋ] schmackhaft 57

apple juice [ˈæpl ˌdʒuːs] Apfelsaft 21

appliance [əˈplaɪəns] Gerät; Anwendung 64

applicant [ˈæplɪkənt] Bewerber/in 234

application [ˌæplɪˈkeɪʃn] Bewerbung 233

applications [ˌæplɪˈkeɪʃnz] Anwendungen, Funktionen 64

to appoint [əˈpɔɪnt] ernennen, bestellen 224

appointment [əˈpɔɪntmənt] Termin 88

approach [əˈprəʊtʃ] Haltung, Herangehensweise, Ansatz 245

to approach [əˈprəʊtʃ] sich nähern, herangehen an, ansprechen 226

appropriate [əˈprəʊprɪət] geeignet, passend, angebracht 112

approval [əˈpruːvl] Billigung, Zustimmung, Beifall 160

to arouse [əˈraʊz] wecken *(Interesse, Gefühle)* 101

as a result of [əz ə rɪˈzʌlt əv] auf Grund 20

as a rule [əz ə ˈruːl] in der Regel 89

as a whole [əz ə ˈhəʊl] insgesamt 100

a set break [ə ˌset ˈbreɪk] eine Pause zu festgesetzter Zeit 57

ashore [əˈʃɔː] an Land 228

as long as stocks last [əz ˌlɒŋ əz ˌstɒks ˈlɑːst] solange Vorrat reicht 140

asparagus [əˈspærəgəs] Spargel 28

to assess [əˈses] *(hier:)* bewerten, einschätzen 104

to assist [əˈsɪst] helfen 233

assistance [əˈsɪstəns] Hilfe 91

association [əˌsəʊʃiˈeɪʃn] Vereinigung, Verband 142

assortment [əˈsɔːtmənt] Sortiment, Auswahl 19

to assume [əˈsjuːm] annehmen, von etwas ausgehen 113

assurance [əˈʃɔːrəns] Zusicherung, Versicherung 173

ATA Carnet [ˌeɪtiːˈeɪ ˌkɑːneɪ] Zollverfahren für die vorübergehende Wareneinfuhr oder -ausfuhr 136

at a premium [ət ə ˈpriːmɪəm] von höchster Priorität 180

athlete [ˈæθliːt] Sportler/in, Athlet/in 39

athletics [æθˈletɪks] (Leicht-)Athletik 43

ATM (automated teller machine) [ˌeɪtiːˈem, ˌɔːtəmeɪtɪd ˈtelə məˌʃiːn] Geldautomat 193

at short notice [ət ˌʃɔːt ˈnəʊtɪs] kurzfristig, ohne lange Voranmeldung 67

at sight [ət ˈsaɪt] bei Sicht/Vorlage 193

to attach [əˈtætʃ] anhängen *(Datei)*, befestigen, anbringen 111

attached [əˈtætʃt] angeschlossen 57

attachment [əˈtætʃmənt] Anhang *(E-Mail)* 94

to attempt [əˈtempt] versuchen, sich bemühen 38

to attend a course [əˌtend ə ˈkɔːs] an einem Kurs teilnehmen 208

to attend a fair [əˌtend ə ˈfeə] an einer Messe teilnehmen 85

at your disposal [ət ˌjɔː dɪˈspəʊzl] zu Ihrer Verfügung 101

at your earliest convenience [ət ˌjɔːr ˌɜːlɪəst kənˈviːnɪəns] so bald wie möglich 191

audience [ˈɔːdɪəns] Publikum 100

author [ˈɔːθə] *(hier:)* Urheber/in; Verfasser/in, Autor/in, 76

automobile sales management assistant [ˌɔːtəməʊbiːl ˌseɪlz ˈmænɪdʒmənt əˌsɪstənt] Automobilkaufmann/-frau 11

available [əˈveɪləbl] erhältlich, zur Verfügung stehend 163

average [ˈævrɪdʒ] Durchschnitt 194

average consumer [ˌævrɪdʒ kənˈsjuːmə] Durchschnittsverbraucher/in 169

average price [ˌævrɪdʒ ˈpraɪs] Durchschnittspreis 106

to avoid [əˈvɔɪd] vermeiden 225

to award points [əˌwɔːd ˈpɔɪnts] Punkte vergeben *(z. B. Wettbewerb)* 104

aware [əˈweə] bewusst 238

awful [ˈɔːfl] schrecklich, scheußlich 21

axle [ˈæksl] Achse 78

B

background [ˈbækgraʊnd] *(hier:)* Ausbildung, Erfahrung 234

backlit [ˈbæklɪt] von hinten/innen beleuchtet 144

back office [ˌbæk ˈɒfɪs] Büro ohne Publikumsverkehr 53

to bake [beɪk] backen, im Ofen braten 28

balance [ˈbæləns] Rest, Saldo; Gleichgewicht 148

to balance [ˈbæləns] ausgleichen, ins Gleichgewicht bringen 199

balanced [ˈbælənst] ausgewogen 26

balance sheet [ˈbæləns ˌʃiːt] Bilanz 228

bale [beɪl] Ballen 50

ballet [ˈbæleɪ] (klassisches) Ballett 8

to ban [ˈbæn] verbieten 155

bank business management assistant [ˌbæŋk ˌbɪznɪs ˈmænɪdʒmənt əˌsɪstənt] Bankkaufmann/-frau 9

bank clerk [ˈbæŋk ˌklɑːk] Bankkaufmann/-frau 8

banknote [ˈbæŋknəʊt] Geldschein 190

bank transfer [ˈbæŋk ˌtrænsfɜː] Banküberweisung 162

bar chart [ˈbɑː ˌtʃɑːt] Balkendiagramm 105

barman / barmaid [ˈbɑːmən / ˈbɑːmeɪd] Bedienung hinter der Theke 89

based in [ˈbeɪst ɪn] mit Sitz in 235

basically [ˈbeɪsɪkli] im Grunde 164

battery [ˈbætəri] Batterie 144

Bavarian cuisine [bəˌveərɪən kwɪˈziːn] bayerische Küche 85

to be able [bɪˈeɪbl] in der Lage sein 222

to beach [biːtʃ] (absichtlich) auf den Strand setzen, stranden 217

bean [biːn] Bohne 28

bearer [ˈbeərə] *(hier:)* Überbringer/in 193

to bear with someone, bore, born [beə ˈwɪð ˌsʌmwʌn, bɔː, bɔːn] *(hier:)* etwas Geduld haben; so lange warten *(am Telefon)* 65

beauty consultant [ˈbjuːti kənˌsʌltənt] Kosmetiker/in 223

to be aware of a problem [bɪ ˌəˈweər ˌəv ə ˈprɒbləm] sich eines Problems bewusst sein 197

to become aware of [bɪˌkʌm əˈweə ˌəv] bewusst werden 103

to be cooperative [bɪ kəʊˈɒprətɪv] zur Zusammenarbeit bereit sein 212

to be destined [bɪ ˈdestɪnd] bestimmt sein 77

beef broth [ˌbiːf ˈbrɒθ] Fleischbrühe 28

to be entitled [bɪ ɪnˈtaɪtld] berechtigt sein, Anspruch haben 195

beetle [ˈbiːtl] Käfer 205

beforehand [bɪˈfɔːhænd] vorher 243

to be in a hurry [bɪ ˌɪn ə ˈhʌri] es eilig haben 222

to be inclined [bɪ ɪnˈklaɪnd] dazu neigen, geneigt sein 123

to be in demand [bɪ ɪn dɪˈmɑːnd] gefragt sein, nachgefragt werden 164

to be in line with [bɪ ɪn ˈlaɪn wɪð] übereinstimmen, im Einklang stehen mit 118

to be in trouble [bɪ ɪn ˈtrʌbl] in Schwierigkeiten sein 154

to be keen on something [bɪ ˈkiːn ɒn ˌsʌmθɪŋ] auf etwas erpicht sein 154

to be likely [bɪ ˈlaɪkli] wahrscheinlich sein, wahrscheinlich geschehen 109

belly hold [ˈbeli ˌhəʊld] Frachtraum *(bei Flugzeugen)* 180

bend [bend] Kurve 24

to benefit [ˈbenəfɪt] profitieren 224

to be on a familiar footing [bɪ ɒn ə fəˈmɪlɪə ˈfʊtɪŋ] auf vertrautem Fuße stehen 113

to be on hand [bɪ ɒn ˈhænd] zugegen sein, da sein 91

to be put on a shortlist [bɪ ˌpʊt ɒn ə ˈʃɔːtlɪst] in die engere Auswahl kommen 243

berry [ˈberi] Beere 29

berth [bɜːθ] Liegeplatz 183

to be stranded [bɪ ˈstrændɪd] auf Grund gesetzt, gestrandet sein 218

to be subject to [bɪ ˈsʌbdʒɪktˌtuː] unterliegen, abhängen von, unterworfen sein 140

beverage wholesaler [ˌbevərɪdʒ ˈhəʊlˌseɪlə] Getränkegroßhandlung 131

BIC (bank identifier code) [ˌbiːaɪˈsiː (ˌbæŋk aɪˈdentɪfaɪə ˌkəʊd)] internationaler Bank-Code 191

bilingual [baɪˈlɪŋgwəl] zweisprachig 234

bill [bɪl] Rechnung 90

bill of exchange [ˌbɪlˌəv ɪksˈtʃeɪndʒ] Wechsel 193

bill of lading (B / L) [ˌbɪlˌəv ˈleɪdɪŋ] Konnossement, Seefrachtbrief 176

biro [ˈbaɪrəʊ] Kugelschreiber 54

blank [blæŋk] unbeschrieben, leer 111

blunt(ly) [blʌnt(lɪ)] *(hier:)* unverblümt 212

board meeting [ˈbɔːd ˌmiːtɪŋ] Vorstandssitzung 102

body language [ˈbɒdɪ ˌlæŋgwɪdʒ] Körpersprache 103

to boil [bɔɪl] kochen, sieden 28

bold type [ˌbəʊld ˈtaɪp] Fettdruck 118

booking charge [ˈbʊkɪŋ ˌtʃɑːdʒ] Buchungsgebühr 73

booking reference [ˈbʊkɪŋ ˌrefrəns] Buchungsnummer 87

to bore [bɔː] langweilen 102

bored [bɔːd] gelangweilt 244

both ... and ... [bəʊθ ... ənd ...] sowohl ... als auch ... 115

brackets [ˈbrækɪts] Klammern 111

branch [brɑːntʃ] Filiale 19

brand [brænd] Marke, Markenartikel 225

breadcrumbs [ˈbredkrʌmz] Brotkrümel, Paniermehl 27

to break bulk [ˌbreɪk ˈbʌlk] Ware / Stückgut kommissionieren, große Gebinde aufbrechen 32

brewery [ˈbruːərɪ] Brauerei 25

brief(ly) [briːf(lɪ)] kurz 7

briefcase [ˈbriːfkeɪs] Aktentasche 102

bright [braɪt] hell, glänzend; klug 163

bright yellow [ˌbraɪt ˈjeləʊ] leuchtend gelb 25

to bring forward [brɪŋ ˈfɔːwəd] vorziehen, vorverlegen 115

brochure [ˈbrəʊʃə] Broschüre, Prospekt 39

Brussels sprouts [ˌbrʌslz ˈspraʊts] Rosenkohl 28

bubble [ˈbʌbl] Blase, Bläschen 19

budget [ˈbʌdʒɪt] (Staats-)Haushalt, Etat 199

building materials [ˈbɪldɪŋ məˌtɪərɪəlz] Baustoffe, -material 12

building site [ˈbɪldɪŋ ˌsaɪt] Baustelle 205

bulk goods [ˌbʌlk ˈgʊdz] Massen-, Schüttgüter 170

bulky [ˈbʌlkɪ] sperrig 49

bumpy [ˈbʌmpɪ] unruhig, holprig 20

bundle with steel strapping [ˌbʌndl wɪð ˌstiːl ˈstræpɪŋ] Bündel mit Stahlbandumreifung 172

business development [ˈbɪznɪs dɪˌveləpmənt] Firmenentwicklung 14

business relations [ˈbɪznɪs rɪˌleɪʃnz] Geschäftsbeziehungen 142

business section [ˈbɪznɪsˌsekʃn] Gewerbeteil 64

business terms [ˈbɪznɪs ˌtɜːmz] Geschäftsbedingungen 128

business unit, division [ˈbɪznɪs juːnɪt, dɪˈvɪʒn] Geschäftseinheit, Unternehmensbereich 199

business venture [ˈbɪznɪs ˌventʃə] geschäftliches Unternehmen 27

by means of [ˌbaɪ ˈmiːnzˌəv] mittels 194

by-product [ˈbaɪˌprɒdʌkt] (Abfall-) Nebenprodukt 155

by return [baɪ rɪˈtɜːn] umgehend 114

C

cabbage [ˈkæbɪdʒ] Kohl 27

calculator [ˈkælkjəleɪtə] Taschenrechner 54

calm [kɑːm] ruhig, gelassen 204

calorie count [ˈkælərɪ ˌkaʊnt] Kalorienangabe 57

to cancel an invoice [ˌkænsl ən ˈɪnvɔɪs] Rechnung stornieren 199

to cancel an order [ˌkænsl ən ˈɔːdə] einen Auftrag annullieren 207

canopy [ˈkænəpɪ] Überdachung 31

canteen [kænˈtiːn] Kantine 23

capable of [ˈkeɪpəblˌəv] in der Lage sein zu, fähig, tüchtig 41

to capitalize [ˈkæpɪtəlaɪz] in Großbuchstaben schreiben 113

to capsize [kæpˈsaɪz] kentern 217

to capture [ˈkæptʃə] (ein)fangen 163

carbon paper [ˈkɑːbn ˌpeɪpə] Kohlepapier 111

car carrier [ˈkɑː ˌkærɪə] Autotransporter, -transportschiff 169

cardboard box [ˌkɑːdbɔːd ˈbɒks] Pappkarton 31

cardholder [ˈkɑːdˌhəʊldə] Karteninhaber / in 193

care [keə] Sorgfalt 213

cargo [ˈkɑːgəʊ] (See-)Fracht, Ladung 33

cargo hold [ˈkɑːgəʊ ˌhəʊld] Frachtraum 217

cargo superintendent [ˈkɑːgəʊ suːˌpərɪnˌtendənt] Frachtaufseher / in 78

car hire / rental company [ˈkɑːˌhaɪə / ˌrentl ˌkʌmpənɪ] Mietwagenfirma 88

carnivorous [kɑːˈnɪvərəs] fleischfressend 27

carriage [ˈkærɪdʒ] Transport(kosten), Fracht(kosten) 150

carriage by sea [ˌkærɪdʒ baɪ ˈsiː] Seetransport 170

carrier [ˈkærɪə] Frachtführer / in 169

carrier's agent [ˈkærɪəz ˌeɪdʒənt] Beförderer 186

carrots [ˈkærəts] Möhren, Karotten 28

to carry out work [ˌkærɪ ˌaʊt ˈwɜːk] Arbeit ausführen 141

cart [kɑːt] Wagen 31

cash discount [ˌkæʃ ˈdɪskaʊnt] Skonto, Barzahlungsrabatt 195

cash on delivery [ˌkæʃ ɒn dɪˈlɪvərɪ] Zahlung durch Nachnahme / bei Lieferung 195

cash payment [ˌkæʃ ˈpeɪmənt] Barzahlung 194

cash point [ˈkæʃpɔɪnt] Geldautomat 193

cash with order [ˌkæʃ wɪð ˈɔːdə] Bezahlung bei Auftragserteilung, Vorkasse 142

casual [ˈkæʒjʊəl] zwanglos, leger 6

to catch, caught, caught [kætʃ, kɔːt, kɔːt] *(hier:)* mitbekommen 67

to cater for [ˈkeɪtə fɔː] *(hier:)* etwas bieten für 85

cauliflower [ˈkɒlɪˌflaʊə] Blumenkohl 28

caution mark [ˈkɔːʃn ˌmɑːk] Warnzeichen 51

celebrated [ˈseləbreɪtɪd] gefeiert 147

centre of gravity [ˌsentərˌəv ˈgrævətɪ] Schwerpunkt 51

certificate of analysis [səˌtɪfɪkətˌəv əˈnæləsɪs] Analysezertifikat 188

certificate of origin [səˌtɪfɪkətˌəv ˈɒrɪdʒɪn] Ursprungszeugnis 176

certified [ˈsɜːtɪfaɪd] beglaubigt, zertifiziert 236

chain [tʃeɪn] Kette 95

chair, chairperson [tʃeə, ˈtʃeəˌpɜːsn] Vorsitzende / r 92

chairman [ˈtʃeəmən] Vorsitzender 92

chairman of the board [ˌtʃeəmən əvˌðə ˈbɔːd] Vorstandsvorsitzender 58

challenging [ˈtʃælɪndʒɪŋ] herausfordernd 234

change [tʃeɪndʒ] Wechselgeld 90

changeable [ˈtʃeɪndʒəbl] wechselhaft 21

channel [ˈtʃænl] *(hier:)* Vertriebsweg 221

characters [ˈkærəktəz] *(hier:)* Buchstaben, Zeichen 111

characteristic feature [ˌkærəktərɪstɪk ˈfiːtʃə] typisches Merkmal 224

charge [tʃɑːdʒ] Belastung, Gebühr 147

to charge [tʃɑːdʒ] *(hier:)* berechnen 221

to charge for [ˈtʃɑːdʒ fɔː] bezahlen lassen 224

cheap chain [ˈtʃiːp ˌtʃeɪn] Billigladenkette 221

to check [tʃek] (über)prüfen 226

check-out [ˈtʃekaʊt] (Supermarkt-)Kasse 194

chemist [ˈkemɪst] Apotheker / in 223

cheque (BE), check (AE) [tʃek] Scheck 193

chicken ['tʃɪkɪn] Hähnchen, Hühnerfleisch 28

chief accountant [ˌtʃiːf əˈkaʊntənt] Leiter/in des Rechnungswesens 23

chief executive officer (CEO) [ˌtʃiːf ɪɡˌzekjətɪv ˈɒfɪsə] Firmenchef/in, Vorstandsvorsitzende/r 58

chilled [tʃɪld] eisgekühlt 27

chock [tʃɒk] Bremsklotz 78

to choose, chose, chosen [tʃuːz, tʃəʊz, ˈtʃəʊzn] wählen 87

to chop [tʃɒp] klein schneiden, hacken 28

to claim [kleɪm] behaupten 230

clean bill of lading [ˈkliːn ˌbɪl əv ˈleɪdɪŋ] reines Konnossement 195

(customs) clearance [ˌkʌstəmz ˈklɪərəns] (Zoll-)Abfertigung 32

clerical staff [ˈklerɪkl ˌstɑːf] Büropersonal, Sachbearbeiter 84

club [klʌb] Disko; Verein 20

coaching [ˈkəʊtʃɪŋ] Training 208

coaster [ˈkəʊstə] Küstenmotorschiff 182

coffee break [ˈkɒfi ˌbreɪk] Kaffeepause 57

coffee table [ˈkɒfi ˌteɪbl] Couchtisch 175

coil on euro-pallet [ˌkɔɪl ɒn ˈjuːrəʊˌpælɪt] Rolle, Coil auf Europalette 172

coin [kɔɪn] Münze, Geldstück 190

to collect [kəˈlekt] abholen 33

collection [kəˈlekʃn] Abholung 14

to collect the invoice amount [kəˌlekt ðɪ ˈɪnvɔɪs əˌmaʊnt] den Rechnungsbetrag eintreiben 197

colour printer [ˈkʌlə ˌprɪntə] Farbdrucker 146

to comb [kəʊm] kämmen 243

to combine [kəmˈbaɪn] kombinieren, verbinden 95

to come across [ˌkʌm əˈkrɒs] (hier:) wirken 73

comeback [ˈkʌmbæk] (hier:) Reaktion 65

comfort [ˈkʌmfət] Behaglichkeit, Komfort; Trost 142

comfortable [ˈkʌmftəbl] bequem 191

command [kəˈmɑːnd] (hier:) Beherrschung 239

commencement [kəˈmensmənt] Anfang, Beginn 148

commercial invoice [kəˌmɜːʃl ˈɪnvɔɪs] Handelsrechnung 173

to commission [kəˈmɪʃn] beauftragen 206

commission [kəˈmɪʃn] Provision 41

common [ˈkɒmən] normal, weit verbreitet 14

communication [kəˌmjuːnɪˈkeɪʃn] Nachricht, Mitteilung, Information 197

comparative(ly) [kəmˈpærətɪv(li)] verhältnismäßig 195

to compare [kəmˈpeə] vergleichen 225

comparing prices [kəmˌpeərɪŋ ˈpraɪsɪz] Preisvergleich 226

to compete [kəmˈpiːt] an einem Wettkampf teilnehmen, konkurrieren 39

competition [ˌkɒmpəˈtɪʃn] Konkurrenz, Wettbewerb 146

competitive [kəmˈpetɪtɪv] Wettbewerb-, konkurrenzfähig 77

competitive prices [kəmˌpetətɪv ˈpraɪsɪz] günstige, konkurrenzfähige Preise 222

competitor [kəmˈpetɪtə] Mitbewerber/in 94

complaint [kəmˈpleɪnt] Beschwerde, Beanstandung, Reklamation, Mängelrüge 204

to complete [kəmˈpliːt] abschließen 235

complimentary close [ˌkɒmplɪmentərɪ ˈkləʊz] Grußformel 110

to comply [kəmˈplaɪ] sich fügen, einhalten 155

to comply with regulations [kəmˌplaɪ wɪð ˌreɡjəˈleɪʃnz] Vorschriften einhalten 210

components [kəmˈpəʊnənts] Bestandteile 110

to comprise [kəmˈpraɪz] umfassen 130

computer projector [kəmˌpjuːtə prəˈdʒektə] Beamer 103

to conceal [kənˈsiːl] verdecken 155

concept [ˈkɒnsept] Konzept, Begriff, Auffassung 159

concerns [kənˈsɜːnz] (hier:) Sorgen, Fragen 90

concession [kənˈseʃn] Zugeständnis 121

conciliatory [kənˈsɪliətri] versöhnlich 212

concise [kənˈsaɪs] kurz und bündig 75

conclusion [kənˈkluːʒn] Schluss 101

to conduct [kənˈdʌkt] durchführen 222

to conduct a test [kənˌdʌkt ə ˈtest] einen Test durchführen 160

confectionery [kənˈfekʃənrɪ] Süßwaren 130

confident [ˈkɒnfɪdənt] selbstbewusst 103

to confirm [kənˈfɜːm] bestätigen 191

confirmation [ˌkɒnfəˈmeɪʃn] Bestätigung 87

consent [kənˈsent] Zustimmung, Einwilligung 195

to consider [kənˈsɪdə] erwägen, überlegen; ansehen als 123

considerably [kənˈsɪdərəblɪ] beträchtlich 217

consideration [kənˌsɪdəˈreɪʃn] Erwägung, Überlegung 26

consignee [ˌkɒnsaɪˈniː] Empfänger (einer Warensendung) 49

consignor [kənˈsaɪnə] Absender (einer Warensendung) 125

consignment [kənˈsaɪnmənt] Warensendung, Lieferung 15

consignment note [kənˈsaɪnmənt ˌnəʊt] Frachtbrief 173

consolidated shipment [kənˌsɒlɪdeɪtɪd ˈʃɪpmənt] Sammelladung 153

consolidation [kənˌsɒlɪˈdeɪʃn] Zusammenstellen von Transportgütern 15

conspicuous [kənˈspɪkjʊəs] auffällig 25

construction work [kənˈstrʌkʃn ˌwɜːk] Bauarbeiten 104

consular invoice [ˌkɒnsjələr ˈɪnvɔɪs] Konsulatsfaktura 188

consumer [kənˈsjuːmə] Verbraucher/in 226

contact person [ˈkɒntækt ˌpɜːsn] Ansprechpartner/in 208

to contain [kənˈteɪn] enthalten 120

content [ˈkɒntent] Inhalt 100

context [ˈkɒntekst] Zusammenhang, Kontext 109

contract [ˈkɒntrækt] Vertrag 109

convenience food [kənˈviːnɪəns ˌfuːd] Fertiggerichte 57

convenient [kənˈviːnɪənt] bequem, praktisch 128

conventional [kənˈvenʃənl] herkömmlich, traditionell 222

converted [kənˈvɜːtɪd] umgebaut 53

to convey [kənˈveɪ] transportieren 180

conveyor belt [kənˈveɪə ˌbelt] Förder-/ Fließband 31

to convince [kənˈvɪns] überzeugen 143

convincing [kənˈvɪnsɪŋ] überzeugend 44

cooking [ˈkʊkɪŋ] Art zu kochen, Küche 7

cooperation [kəʊˌɒpəˈreɪʃn] Zusammenarbeit, Mitarbeit; Hilfe 14

to cope with something [ˈkəʊp wɪð ˈsʌmθɪŋ] mit etwas fertig werden, etwas schaffen 216

copper [ˈkɒpə] Kupfer 104

cordial [ˈkɔːdɪəl] herzlich, freundlich 215

core [kɔː] Kern 95

corner stand [ˈkɔːnə ˌstænd] Eckstand 93

corn starch [ˈkɔːn ˌstɑːtʃ] Stärkemehl 29

corporate (e.g. culture) [ˈkɔːpərət] Unternehmens- (z. B. -kultur), bezogen auf Firmen/Unternehmen 102

corridor [ˈkɒrɪdɔː] Gang 18

corrugated [ˈkɒrəɡeɪtɪd] gewellt 184

cost estimate [ˈkɒst ˌestɪmət] Kostenvoranschlag 140

cost price [ˈkɒst ˌpraɪs] Selbstkostenpreis 26

cottage [ˈkɒtɪdʒ] (hier:) Ferienhäuschen 73

Could you tell me the way to . . . ? [kʊd jʊ ˌtel mɪ ðə ˈweɪ tʊ] Können Sie mir sagen, wie ich zu/nach … komme? 24

country of origin [ˌkʌntrɪ_əv ˈɒrɪdʒɪn] Herkunftsland, Ursprungsland 180

countryside [ˈkʌntrɪsaɪd] Landschaft, Gegend; ländliche Gegend 26

courier fee [ˈkʊrɪə ˌfiː] Zustellgebühr 153

court [kɔːt] Gericht(shof), Hof 109

courtesy [ˈkɜːtəsɪ] Höflichkeit 213

courtyard [ˈkɔːtjɑːd] Hof 216

to cover [ˈkʌvə] decken, abdecken 101

coverage [ˈkʌvərɪdʒ] Versicherungsschutz, Deckung 218

covering letter [ˈkʌvərɪŋ ˌletə] Begleitschreiben 234

covering page [ˈkʌvərɪŋ ˌpeɪdʒ] Deckblatt 114

crash course [ˈkræʃ ˌkɔːs] Kompaktkurs 133

crate [kreɪt] Kiste 34

to create [krɪˈeɪt] (er)schaffen, erzeugen, erstellen 38

credit note [ˈkredɪt ˌnəʊt] Gutschrift 205

creditworthiness [ˈkredɪtˌwɜːðɪnəs] Kreditwürdigkeit 195

crossed cheque [ˌkrɒstˈtʃek] Verrechnungsscheck 193

crowded [ˈkraʊdɪd] überfüllt 89

crucial [ˈkruːʃl] entscheidend 95

crude oil [ˌkruːd ˈɔɪl] Rohöl 170

crystal glass [ˌkrɪstl ˈɡlɑːs] Kristallglas 131

cucumber [ˈkjuːkʌmbə] Gurke 28

cues [kjuːz] Stichworte 101

currency [ˈkʌrənsɪ] Währung 190

current [ˈkʌrənt] laufend, gegenwärtig, derzeitig, aktuell 59

curt [kɜːt] knapp, schroff 212

to cushion [ˈkʊʃn] (aus)polstern 50

customary [ˈkʌstəmərɪ] üblich 195

customer service / relations [ˌkʌstəmə ˈsɜːvɪs] Kundendienst 58

customs [ˈkʌstəmz] Zoll 14

customs authorities [ˌkʌstəmz ɔːˈθɒrətɪz] Zollbehörden 124

customs duty [ˈkʌstəmz ˌdjuːtɪ] Zoll(abgabe) 136

customs formalities [ˈkʌstəmz fɔːˌmælətɪz] Zollformalitäten 150

customs invoice [ˌkʌstəmz ˈɪnvɔɪs] Zollfaktura 188

customs official [ˌkʌstəmz əˈfɪʃl] Zollbeamter, Zollbeamtin 188

to cut costs [ˌkʌt ˈkɒsts] Kosten einsparen 14

to cut off [ˌkʌt ˈɒf] (hier:) unterbrechen 67

to cut out [ˌkʌt ˈaʊt] (hier:) umgehen; ausscheiden 224

CV (curriculum vitae) [ˌsiːˈviː (kəˌrɪkjələm ˈviːtaɪ)] tabellarischer Lebenslauf 234

cycling [ˈsaɪklɪŋ] Radfahren 9

D

damage [ˈdæmɪdʒ] Beschädigung, Schaden 176

damage prevention [ˈdæmɪdʒ prɪˌvenʃn] Schadensverhütung 249

data processing, EDP [ˈdeɪtə ˌprəʊsesɪŋ, ˌiːdiːˈpiː] Datenverarbeitung, EDV 23

deadline [ˈdedlaɪn] letzte Frist, letzter Termin 135

debit card [ˈdebɪt ˌkɑːd] Bankkarte 193

to debit to an account [ˌdebɪt_tʊ_ən əˈkaʊnt] von einem Konto abbuchen 193

to debit to someone's account [ˌdebɪt_tʊ ˌsʌmwʌnz əˈkaʊnt] das Konto von jemandem belasten 175

debt level [ˈdet ˌlevl] Schuldenstand 194

decade [ˈdekeɪd] Jahrzehnt 169

to declare [dɪˈkleə] deklarieren 186

decline [dɪˈklaɪn] Rückgang 106

to decline [dɪˈklaɪn] sinken, zurückgehen 106

dedicated [ˈdedɪkeɪtɪd] (hier:) engagiert 230

to deduct [dɪˈdʌkt] abziehen 195

to deepen [ˈdiːpn] vertiefen, tiefer machen 169

deer [dɪə] Rotwild 27

defective [dɪˈfektɪv] schadhaft, beschädigt, unzulänglich 210

to defer [dɪˈfɜː] verschieben, aufschieben 201

definitely [ˈdefɪnətlɪ] auf jeden Fall 20

degree [dɪˈɡriː] Grad, Ausmaß; akademischer Grad 108

delay [dɪˈleɪ] Verzögerung 122

to delete [dɪˈliːt] löschen, tilgen, streichen 111

delicatessens [ˌdelɪkəˈtesənz] Feinkostgeschäfte 164

delighted [dɪˈlaɪtɪd] entzückt, begeistert 143

to deliver [dɪˈlɪvə] ausliefern 14

delivery [dɪˈlɪvərɪ] (hier:) das Halten (eines Vortrags); Lieferung, Auslieferung 100

denomination [dɪˌnɒmɪˈneɪʃn] Konfession (Religion) 238

department store [dɪˈpɑːtmənt ˌstɔː] Warenhaus, Kaufhaus 223

dependent [dɪˈpendənt] abhängig 179

depending on [dɪˈpendɪŋ ɒn] je nach, abhängig von 221

to depend on [dɪˈpend ɒn] abhängen von, sich verlassen auf 143

description [dɪˈskrɪpʃn] Beschreibung 161

to design [dɪˈzaɪn] entwerfen, erstellen 7

desirable [dɪˈzaɪərəbl] wünschenswert 234

desires [dɪˈzaɪəz] Wünsche 222

desk [desk] Schreibtisch 54

desk lamp [ˈdesk ˌlæmp] Schreibtischlampe 54

desk research [ˈdesk ˌriːsɜːtʃ] (Markt-)Forschung am Schreibtisch, Sekundärforschung 222

desk tidy [ˈdesk ˌtaɪdɪ] Stifteköcher 54

despair [dɪˈspeə] Verzweiflung 65

to despatch, dispatch [dɪˈspætʃ] (ab/ver)senden, (ab/ver)schicken 142

dessert [dɪˈzɜːt] Nachspeise 27

destination [ˌdestɪˈneɪʃn] Ziel; Bestimmung(sort) 24

destined [ˈdestɪnd] bestimmt 33

to destroy [dɪˈstrɔɪ] vernichten, zerstören 210

details [ˈdiːteɪlz] Einzelheiten 236

detailed [ˈdiːteɪld] ausführlich 122

detective novel [dɪˈtektɪv ˌnɒvl] Kriminalroman 205

detention charge [dɪˈtenʃn ˌtʃɑːdʒ] Standgeld 125

to determine [dɪˈtɜːmɪn] bestimmen 155

to develop [dɪˈveləp] entwickeln 226

development [dɪˈveləpmənt] Entwicklung 225

dialling tone [ˈdaɪəlɪŋ ˌtəʊn] Freizeichen 64

diameter [daɪˈæmɪtə] Durchmesser 77

diary [ˈdaɪərɪ] Terminkalender, Tagebuch 88

to differ [ˈdɪfə] unterschiedlich sein 233

directive [daɪˈrektɪv, dɪˈrektɪv] Richtlinie 155

directory [daɪˈrektərɪ, dɪˈrektərɪ] Nachschlagewerk, Verzeichnis 233

directory enquiries [daɪˌrektərɪ ɪnˈkwaɪərɪz, dɪˌrektərɪ ɪnˈkwaɪərɪz] Telefonauskunft 64

to direct someone [daɪˈrekt ˌsʌmwʌn, dɪˈrekt ˌsʌmwʌn] jemandem den Weg sagen/zeigen 23

disappointed [ˌdɪsəˈpɔɪntɪd] enttäuscht 49

discerning [dɪˈsɜːnɪŋ] anspruchsvoll, guten Geschmack besitzend 143

disclaimer [dɪˈskleɪmə] Haftungsausschluss, Widerruf 43

to disclose [dɪˈskləʊz] offenlegen, preisgeben 196

discount [ˈdɪskaʊnt] Rabatt, Nachlass 129

to discourage [dɪˈskʌrɪdʒ] entmutigen, abraten 155

disgruntled [dɪsˈɡrʌntld] verärgert, verstimmt 213

disgusting [dɪsˈɡʌstɪŋ] abscheulich 27

dish [dɪʃ] (hier:) Speise, Gericht 102

to dismantle [dɪsˈmæntl] zerlegen 77

dismayed [dɪsˈmeɪd] entsetzt 206

dispatch [dɪˈspætʃ] Versand, Lieferung 32

to dispatch [dɪ'spætʃ] versenden 166

dispatch advice [dɪ'spætʃ əd‚vaɪs] Versandanzeige 173

disposable [dɪ'spəʊzəbl] Wegwerf- 136

to dispose [dɪ'spəʊz] entsorgen 155

to distribute [dɪ'strɪbjuːt] verteilen 78

distribution [‚dɪstrɪ'bjuːʃn] Auslieferung; Vertrieb 14

distribution channels [dɪstrɪ'bjuːʃn ‚tʃænlz] Vertriebskanäle 223

to divide up [dɪ‚vaɪd 'ʌp] einteilen, aufteilen 101

diving ['daɪvɪŋ] Tauchen, Tauchsport 8

division of labour [dɪ‚vɪʒn əv 'leɪbə] Arbeitsteilung 49

to do a traineeship / an apprenticeship [duː ə ‚treɪ'niːʃɪp / ən ə'prentɪʃɪp] eine Ausbildung machen 7

dock [dɒk] Dock, Kai, Hafenbecken 151

docker ['dɒkə] Hafenarbeiter 51

document of title [‚dɒkjəmənt əv 'taɪtl] Eigentumsurkunde 176

domestic [də'mestɪk] Inland-, heimisch 95

domestic market [də‚mestɪk 'mɑːkɪt] Inlandsmarkt 103

dominant ['dɒmɪnənt] beherrschend, dominierend 40

dominated ['dɒmɪneɪtɪd] beherrscht, dominiert 25

to double ['dʌbl] (hier:) eine doppelte Funktion erfüllen 101

draft [drɑːft] Entwurf; Tratte 90

to draw up, drew, drawn [drɔː‚ 'ʌp, druː, drɔːn] zusammenstellen, verfassen 149

dreadful ['dredfəl] schrecklich 65

to dread something ['dred ‚sʌmθɪŋ] Angst vor etwas haben 248

dressing ['dresɪŋ] Salatsoße 29

drill head ['drɪl ‚hed] Bohrkopf 196

drizzle ['drɪzl] Nieselregen 21

to drop [drɒp] fallen 106

drop-off ['drɒpɒf] Liefer- 95

drought [draʊt] Dürre 229

drum [drʌm] Fass, Barrel 172

to dry [draɪ] abtrocknen 30

due [djuː] fällig 196

due to ['djuː tə] wegen 201

dumpling ['dʌmplɪŋ] Kloß, Knödel 27

durability [‚djʊərə'bɪlətɪ] Haltbarkeit 160

durable ['djʊərəbl] haltbar 191

duration [djʊə'reɪʃn] Dauer 95

duties ['djuːtɪz] (hier:) Aufgaben 58

duty ['djuːtɪ] (hier:) Zoll(gebühr) 150

E

early order discount [‚ɜːlɪ‚ɔːdə 'dɪskaʊnt] Frühbuchungsrabatt 119

to earn one's living [‚ɜːn wʌnz 'lɪvɪŋ] seinen Lebensunterhalt verdienen 42

earthquake ['ɜːθkweɪk] Erdbeben 218

e-commerce ['iː‚kɒmɜːs] Internethandel 194

economic growth [‚iːkənɒmɪk 'grəʊθ] Wirtschaftswachstum 169

effective [ɪ'fektɪv] wirksam 226

efficient [ɪ'fɪʃnt] leistungsfähig, wirksam, tüchtig 41

effort ['efət] Anstrengung, Bemühung 43

elderly person [‚eldəlɪ 'pɜːsn] ältere Person 58

electrical equipment [ɪ‚lektrɪkl ɪ'kwɪpmənt] Elektrogeräte 55

electrical goods industry [ɪ‚lektrɪkl 'gʊdz ‚ɪndəstrɪ] Elektroartikelbranche 10

electricity cut [elɪk'trɪsətɪ ‚kʌt] Stromsperre 121

electronic components [elek‚trɒnɪk kəm'pəʊnənts] elektronische Bauelemente 244

embarrassed [ɪm'bærəst] peinlich, verlegen 90

embarrassment [ɪm'bærəsmənt] Verlegenheit 65

embassy ['embəsɪ] Botschaft(sgebäude) 130

emergency [ɪ'mɜːdʒənsɪ] Notfall, Unfall 228

emphasis ['emfəsɪs] Nachdruck 199

to emphasise ['emfəsaɪz] betonen, hervorheben 38

to employ [ɪm'plɔɪ] beschäftigen, einstellen 33

employer [ɪm'plɔɪə] Arbeitgeber/in 14

employment [ɪm'plɔɪmənt] Beschäftigung 234

empty ['emptɪ] leer 210

to enable [ɪ'neɪbl] in die Lage versetzen 225

to enclose [ɪn'kləʊz] beifügen 234

enclosure [ɪn'kləʊʒə] Anlage (Brief) 109

to encourage [ɪn'kʌrɪdʒ] ermutigen 155

to end up [end 'ʌp] (hier:) landen 25

end user ['end ‚juːzə] Endverbraucher/in 223

energy content ['enədʒɪ ‚kɒntent] Brennwert (Energiegehalt) 57

enforcement [ɪn'fɔːsmənt] Erzwingung, Durchsetzung 155

engaged [ɪn'geɪdʒd] besetzt 64

engine ['endʒɪn] Motor 172

engine room ['endʒɪn ‚ruːm] Maschinenraum 229

enquiry (BE), inquiry (AE) [ɪn'kwaɪərɪ] Anfrage, Nachfrage 128

to enrol [ɪn'rəʊl] sich einschreiben 241

ensuite bathroom [ɒnswiːt‚'bɑːθruːm] eigenes Bad (Hotelzimmer) 86

to ensure [ɪn'ʃɔː] sichern, gewährleisten 223

to enter ['entə] eintreten, eintragen, eingeben 111

enterprise ['entəpraɪz] Unternehmen 63

to entertain [‚entə'teɪn] sich um jemanden kümmern, unterhalten 18

enthusiasm [ɪn'θjuːzɪæzm] Begeisterung 234

entire(ly) [ɪn'taɪə(lɪ)] ganz, gänzlich 121

to entrust [ɪn'trʌst] anvertrauen 122

entry date ['entrɪ ‚deɪt] Eintrittsdatum 249

envelope ['envələʊp] (Brief-)Umschlag 208

environment [ɪn'vaɪərənmənt] Umwelt, Umfeld 170

environmental [ɪn‚vaɪərən'mentl] Umwelt- 155

environmentally friendly [ɪn‚vaɪərən‚mentəlɪ 'frendlɪ] umweltfreundlich 103

equal opportunities employer [‚iːkwəl ɒpə'tjuːnətiz ɪm‚plɔɪə] Firma, der Chancengleichheit ein Anliegen ist 245

to equip [ɪ'kwɪp] (hier:) befähigen; ausstatten, ausrüsten 235

equipment [ɪ'kwɪpmənt] Geräte 54

equivalent [ɪ'kwɪvələnt] Entsprechung 14

error ['erə] Irrtum, Fehler 212

essential [ɪ'senʃl] wichtig, wesentlich 235

to establish [ɪ'stæblɪʃ] (hier:) feststellen 222

established [ɪ'stæblɪʃt] eingeführt, feststehend 114

estimated ['estɪmeɪtɪd] voraussichtlich, geschätzt 166

EUR1 movement certificate ['iːjuːɑː‚wʌn 'muːvmənt sə‚tɪfɪkət] Warenverkehrsbescheinigung EUR1 188

to evaluate [ɪ'væljʊeɪt] einschätzen, bewerten 153

evaluation scheme [ɪ‚væljʊ'eɪʃn ‚skiːm] Bewertungsschema 104

evenly ['iːvənlɪ] gleichmäßig 78

even though [‚iːvn 'ðəʊ] obgleich 204

event management assistant [ɪ‚vent 'mænɪdʒmənt ə‚sɪstənt] Veranstaltungskaufmann/-frau 10

eventual(ly) [ɪ'ventʃʊəl(ɪ)] letztendlich, mit der Zeit, schließlich 191

evidence ['evɪdəns] Beweis, Nachweis 109

to exceed [ɪk'siːd] übersteigen, überschreiten 142

excitement [ɪk'saɪtmənt] (hier:) Interesse 104

exclamation mark [‚eksklə'meɪʃn ‚mɑːk] Ausrufezeichen 113

to execute ['eksɪkjuːt] aus-, durchführen 135

execution [‚eksɪ'kjuːʃn] Aus-, Durchführung 121

executives [ɪgˈzekjətɪvz] leitende Angestellte 85

exhibition [ˌeksɪˈbɪʃn] Ausstellung 128

exhibition grounds [ˌeksɪˈbɪʃn ˌgraʊndz] Ausstellungsgelände 86

expenditure [ɪkˈspendɪtʃə] Ausgaben, Auslagen 41

expense account [ɪkˈspens əˌkaʊnt] Spesenkonto 250

expenses [ɪkˈspensɪz] (Un-)Kosten 156

experience [ɪkˈspɪərɪəns] Erfahrung 234

expertise [ˌekspɜːˈtiːz] Fachkenntnis, Kompetenz 14

expiry date [ɪkˈspaɪəri ˌdeɪt] Verfallsdatum *(bei Kreditkarten)* 88

exploration [ˌekspləˈreɪʃn] Erkundung neuer Lagerstätten, Probegrabungen/-bohrungen 104

export clerk [ˈekspɔːt ˌklɑːk] Exportkaufmann/-frau 7

export declaration [ˈekspɔːt ˌdekləˌreɪʃn] Ausfuhrerklärung 188

to express [ɪkˈspres] ausdrücken 65

expressly [ɪkˈspresli] ausdrücklich 140

extension [ɪkˈstenʃn] Durchwahl, Nebenstelle 65

F

fabulous [ˈfæbjələs] fabelhaft, sagenhaft, toll 119

to face [feɪs] gegenüberstehen 95

to facilitate [fəˈsɪlɪteɪt] ermöglichen, erleichtern 169

facility [fəˈsɪləti] Anlage, Einrichtung 14

factual [ˈfæktʃʊəl] sachlich, den Tatsachen entsprechend 123

fair [feə] Messe 15

familiarity [fəˌmɪliˈærəti] Vertrautheit 234

familiar with [fəˈmɪliə wɪð] vertraut mit 224

fare [feə] Fahrpreis 90

fashion [ˈfæʃn] Mode 43

fashion chain [ˈfæʃn ˌtʃeɪn] Kette von Modegeschäften 194

fast-paced [ˌfɑːstˈpeɪst] tempogeladen, hektisch 234

fault [fɒlt] Schuld, Fehler 49

faultless, perfect, unobjectionable [ˈfɒltləs/ˈfɔːltləs, ˈpɜːfɪkt, ˌʌnəbˈdʒekʃənəbl] einwandfrei 215

faulty [ˈfɒlti, ˈfɔːlti] fehlerhaft, mangelhaft 204

favourite (dish) [ˌfeɪvərɪt ˈdɪʃ] Lieblings(gericht) 29

to faze [feɪz] aus der Fassung bringen 245

feasibility study [ˌfiːzəˈbɪləti ˌstʌdi] Machbarkeitsstudie 41

feature [ˈfiːtʃə] Eigenschaft 103

to feature [ˈfiːtʃə] eine Rolle spielen, sich auszeichnen, kennzeichnen 39

fee [fiː] Gebühr, Honorar 147

feedback [ˈfiːdbæk] Rückmeldungen, Feedback 103

feeder road [ˈfiːdə ˌrəʊd] Zubringerstraße 183

fermented white cabbage [fəˌmentɪd ˌwaɪt ˈkæbɪdʒ] Sauerkraut 29

ferry [ˈferi] Fähre 169

field (of work) [fiːld (əvˌwɜːk)] Arbeitsgebiet 246

field research [ˈfiːld ˌriˈsɜːtʃ] Feldforschung, Primärforschung 222

fierce [fɪəs] *(hier:)* scharf 226

figures [ˈfɪgəz] Zahlen 92

file [faɪl] Akte, Datei 111

filing cabinet [ˈfaɪlɪŋ ˌkæbɪnət] Aktenschrank, Ablage 54

filled rolls [ˌfɪld ˈrəʊlz] belegte Brötchen 57

to finalise [ˈfaɪnəlaɪz] abschließen 26

fine [faɪn] Geldstrafe 188

first floor [ˌfɜːst ˈflɔː] erste Etage *(BE)*; Erdgeschoss *(AE)* 23

first name [ˌfɜːst ˈneɪm] Vorname 7

first-rate [ˌfɜːstˈreɪt] erstklassig 234

to fit in with [ˌfɪt ˈɪn wɪð] sich richten nach, übereinstimmen mit 88

fixed line set [ˌfɪkstlaɪn ˈset] Festnetzanlage 64

flat [flæt] flach 106

flat rack [ˌflæt ˈræk] Flatrack-Container *(ohne Dach und Seitenwände)* 184

fleet (of vehicles) [fliːt (əv ˈviːəklz)] Fuhrpark 14

to flood [flʌd] überfluten 217

flooding [ˈflʌdɪŋ] Überschwemmung 121

floor plan [ˈflɔː ˌplæn] Grundriss 23

flowchart [ˈfləʊˌtʃɑːt] Flussdiagramm 101

to fluctuate [ˈflʌktʃveɪt] schwanken 106

fluent [ˈfluːənt] fließend 234

focus [ˈfəʊkəs] Schwerpunkt 221

to focus [ˈfəʊkəs] (sich) konzentrieren, in den Mittelpunkt stellen 113

fog [fɒg] Nebel 22

foil-wrapped cardboard box [ˌfɔɪlˈræptˌkɑːdbɔːdˈbɒks] folienumwickelter Karton 172

folder [ˈfəʊldə] Falt-, Prospektblatt 143

follow-up order [ˌfɒləʊˌʌp ˈɔːdə] Folgeauftrag 164

food processing [ˈfuːd ˌprəʊsesɪŋ] Verarbeitung von Lebensmitteln 116

food processing company [ˈfuːd ˌprəʊsesɪŋ ˌkʌmpəni] Lebensmittel verarbeitendes Unternehmen 19

for approval [fər əˈpruːvl] zur Genehmigung 92

to forecast [ˈfɔːkɑːst] vorhersagen 169

foreign language correspondent/secretary with modern languages [ˌfɒrən ˈlæŋgwɪdʒ kɒrɪˌspɒndənt/ˌsekrətri wɪð ˌfɒrən ˈlæŋgwɪdʒɪz] Fremdsprachenkorrespondent/in 10

foreign trade [ˌfɒrən ˈtreɪd] Außenhandel 224

for instance [fər ˈɪnstəns] zum Beispiel 6

fork-lift truck [ˌfɔːklɪftˈtrʌk] Gabelstapler 31

form [fɔːm] Formular; Form 69

formal [ˈfɔːml] förmlich, formell 108

formal park [ˌfɔːml ˈpɑːk] Parkanlage 25

for the time being [fə ðə ˌtaɪm ˈbiːɪŋ] zurzeit, vorläufig 214

to forward [ˈfɔːwəd] weiterleiten, befördern, transportieren 111

forwarder [ˈfɔːwədə] Spedition 211

forwarding agent [ˈfɔːwədɪŋ ˌeɪdʒənt] Spediteur/in 14

forwarding company [ˈfɔːwədɪŋ ˌkʌmpəni] Spedition(sunternehmen) 14

fossil fuel [ˌfɒsl ˈfjʊəl] fossiler Brennstoff 228

fossils [ˈfɒsəlz] Fossilien, Versteinerungen 147

to found [faʊnd] gründen 40

foundation [faʊnˈdeɪʃn] Grundlage 136

to founder [ˈfaʊndə] untergehen 218

fragile [ˈfrædʒaɪl] zerbrechlich 50

free movement of labour [ˌfriːˌmuːvmənt əv ˈleɪbə] Freizügigkeit der Arbeitnehmer, freie Wahl des Arbeitsplatzes 247

free of charge [ˌfriːˌəv ˈtʃɑːdʒ] kostenlos, unentgeltlich 147

free port [ˌfriː ˈpɔːt] Freihafen 48

freighter [ˈfreɪtə] Frachtflugzeug, Frachter 180

freight forwarding and logistics services clerk [ˌfreɪt ˈfɔːwədɪŋ ənd ləˈdʒɪstɪksˈsɜːvɪsɪz ˌklɑːk] Kaufmann/-frau für Spedition und Logistikdienstleistung 9

freight forwarding company [ˌfreɪt ˈfɔːwədɪŋˌkʌmpəni] Spedition, Transportunternehmen 170

French fries [ˌfrentʃ ˈfraɪz] Pommes frites 28

frequent(ly) [ˈfriːkwənt(li)] häufig, oft 43

fridge [frɪdʒ] Kühlschrank 57

fried potatoes [ˌfraɪd pəˈteɪtəʊz] Bratkartoffeln 28

fringe benefit [ˈfrɪndʒ ˌbenəfɪt] Zusatzleistung 249

front office [ˌfrʌnt ˈɒfɪs] Büro mit Publikumsverkehr 53

full board [ˌfʊl ˈbɔːd] Vollpension 147

full container load (FCL) [ˌfʊl kənˈteɪnə ˌləʊd (ˌefsiːˈel)] Gesamtladung, Komplettladung 153

furnishings [ˈfɜːnɪʃɪŋz] Einrichtungsgegenstände 227

further training [ˌfɜːðə ˈtreɪnɪŋ] Weiterbildung 243

to fuse [fjuːz] verschmelzen 43

G

gale-force winds [ˌɡeɪlfɔːs ˈwɪndz] stürmische Winde 22

game [ɡeɪm] Wild 28

gantry crane [ˈɡæntrɪ ˌkreɪn] Portalkran 183

garlic [ˈɡaːlɪk] Knoblauch 27

garment [ˈɡaːmənt] Kleidungsstück 206

gathering [ˈɡæðərɪŋ] Versammlung 106

general average sacrifice [ˌdʒenrəl ˌævərɪdʒ ˈsækrɪfaɪs] große Havarie 218

general cargo [ˌdʒenrəl ˈkaːɡəʊ] Stückgut 48

generally [ˈdʒenrəlɪ] im Allgemeinen 223

general manager [ˌdʒenərəl ˈmænɪdʒə] Hauptgeschäftsführer/in 59

generous [ˈdʒenərəs] großzügig 146

Gents / Ladies [dʒents/ˈleɪdɪz] Herren-/ Damen-WC 23

germ [dʒɜːm] Bazillus, Keim 112

gestures [ˈdʒestʃəz] Gesten, Gestik 65

get [ɡet] *(hier:)* mitbekommen, hören 67

to get around to it [ɡet əˈraʊnd tʊ ɪt] dazu kommen, Zeit dazu haben 209

to get on well [ɡet ɒn ˈwel] gut miteinander auskommen 56

to get something over [ˌɡet ˈsʌmθɪŋ ˈəʊvə] etwas hinter sich bringen 103

ghastly [ˈɡaːstlɪ] entsetzlich 21

gift box [ˈɡɪft ˌbɒks] Geschenkkarton 131

gig [ɡɪɡ] Musikevent 20

ginger cookies [ˌdʒɪndʒə ˈkʊkɪz] Ingwerkekse 152

to give a refusal, to refuse a request [ˌɡɪv ə rɪˈfjuːzl, rɪˌfjuːz ə rɪˈkwest] Absage erteilen 213

to give notice [ˌɡɪv ˈnəʊtɪs] *(hier:)* im Voraus Bescheid sagen 242

to give someone a lift [ɡɪv ˌsʌmwʌn ə ˈlɪft] jemanden mitnehmen (im Wagen) 30

to give someone a ring [ɡɪv ˌsʌmwʌn ə ˈrɪŋ] jemanden anrufen 30

global economy [ˌɡləʊbl ɪˈkɒnəmɪ] Weltwirtschaft 169

to go clubbing [ɡəʊ ˈklʌbɪŋ] in die Disko gehen 9

to go for [ˈɡəʊ fə] wählen 243

good value [ˌɡʊd ˈvæljuː] preisgünstig 227

to go public [ɡəʊ ˈpʌblɪk] sich in eine Aktiengesellschaft umwandeln, an die Börse gehen 41

to go through the usual channels [ˌɡəʊ θruː ðə juːʒʊəl ˈtʃænlz] die üblichen Instanzen durchlaufen 248

to go window-shopping [ɡəʊ ˈwɪndəʊ ˌʃɒpɪŋ] einen Schaufensterbummel machen 8

gradual(ly) [ˈɡrædʒʊəl(ɪ)] allmählich 106

grain [ɡreɪn] Getreide 188

to grant [ɡraːnt] gewähren 133

to grant a discount [ˌɡraːnt ə ˈdɪskaʊnt] Rabatt einräumen 144

to grant credit [ˌɡraːnt ˈkredɪt] Kredit gewähren 193

graph [ɡraːf] Grafik 101

green card [ˌɡriːn ˈkaːd] *Arbeitserlaubnis für die USA* 247

grid [ɡrɪd] Raster 108

gross weight [ˌɡrəʊs ˈweɪt] Bruttogewicht 78

ground [ɡraʊnd] gemahlen 28

ground beef [ˌɡraʊnd ˈbiːf] Rindergehacktes 28

ground floor [ˌɡraʊnd ˈflɔː] Parterre, Erdgeschoss 23

groupage [ˈɡruːpɪdʒ] Sammelgut 14

growth [ɡrəʊθ] Wachstum 221

to guarantee [ˌɡærənˈtiː] garantieren 26

gym [dʒɪm] Turnhalle, Fitnessraum 7

H

haddock [ˈhædək] Schellfisch 28

half board [ˌhaːf ˈbɔːd] Halbpension 148

ham [hæm] Schinken 210

handicapped [ˈhændɪkæpt] behindert 241

to handle [ˈhændl] handhaben, erledigen, bearbeiten 170

handling [ˈhændlɪŋ] *(hier:)* Fahreigenschaften 227

harmful [ˈhaːmfəl] schädlich 170

to have access to [hæv ˈækses tuː] Zugang haben zu 226

to have little choice but [hæv ˌlɪtl ˈtʃɔɪs bət] keine andere Wahl haben als 226

to have the goods delivered [ˌhæv ðə ˌɡʊdz dɪˈlɪvəd] sich die Ware liefern lassen 225

hazardous [ˈhæzədəs] gefährlich 77

heading [ˈhedɪŋ] Rubrik 104

head of department [ˌhed əv dɪˈpaːtmənt] Abteilungsleiter/in 15

headquarters [ˌhedˈkwɔːtəz] Hauptverwaltung 85

health [helθ] Gesundheit 90

heavy-lift shipping [ˌhevɪlɪft ˈʃɪpɪŋ] Schwerladeverschiffung 77

height [haɪt] Höhe 211

helpful [ˈhelpfəl] hilfsbereit 18

heritage [ˈherɪtɪdʒ] Erbe 31

high cube [ˌhaɪ ˈkjuːb] High-Cube-Container 184

high street bank [ˌhaɪstriːt ˈbæŋk] Bank mit zahlreichen Zweigstellen 10

high street stores [ˌhaɪstriːt ˈstɔːz] Geschäfte in der Innenstadt 223

highway robbery [ˌhaɪweɪ ˈrɒbərɪ] Raubüberfälle auf Fernstraßen 170

hint [hɪnt] Hinweis, Andeutung 8

hit [hɪt] *(hier:)* Zugriff; Schlag, Stoß Treffer 41

to hold, held, held [həʊld, held, held] *(hier:)* warten 65

hook [hʊk] Haken 51

horseradish [ˈhɔːsˌrædɪʃ] Meerrettich 164

host family [ˈhəʊst ˌfæməlɪ] Gastfamilie 147

hot [hɒt] heiß, scharf 28

to house [haʊz] beherbergen 25

household tool kit [ˌhaʊshəʊld ˈtuːl ˌkɪt] Haushaltswerkzeugsatz 133

however [haʊˈevə] jedoch 108

how you come across [ˌhaʊ jʊ ˌkʌm əˈkrɒs] welchen Eindruck man macht 103

hub [hʌb] Basis, Zentrum 180

hull [hʌl] Schiffsrumpf 217

human resources department [ˌhjuːmən ˈriːsɔːsɪz dɪˌpaːtmənt] Personalabteilung 215

humorous [ˈhjuːmərəs] humorvoll 104

I

IBAN (international bank account number) [ˈaɪbæn, ˌaɪbiːeɪˈen (ˌɪntənæʃənl ˈbæŋk əˌkaʊnt ˌnʌmbə)] internationale Kontonummer 191

illegible [ɪˈledʒəbl] unleserlich 210

I'm afraid … [aɪm əˈfreɪd] Leider … 73

image [ˈɪmɪdʒ] Bild, Vorstellung 38

imagination [ɪˌmædʒɪˈneɪʃn] Phantasie, Vorstellungskraft 130

imaginative [ɪˈmædʒɪnətɪv] phantasievoll 102

immediate [ɪˈmiːdɪət] sofortig 65

I'm on a diet [aɪm ˌɒn ə ˈdaɪət] ich mache eine Diät 21

impact [ˈɪmpækt] Auswirkung 155

impatient [ɪmˈpeɪʃnt] ungeduldig 207

to implement [ˈɪmpləment] einführen 155

to imply [ɪmˈplaɪ] beinhalten, besagen, stillschweigend voraussetzen 121

impolite [ˌɪmpəˈlaɪt] unhöflich 73

import licence [ˈɪmpɔːt ˌlaɪsəns] Einfuhrgenehmigung, Importlizenz 191

to impress [ɪmˈpres] beeindrucken 160

impression [ɪmˈpreʃn] Eindruck 18

imprint [ˈɪmprɪnt] Impressum 43

to improve [ɪmˈpruːv] verbessern 226

inadequate [ɪˈnædɪkwət] unzureichend 169

in advance [ɪn ədˈvaːns] im Voraus 243

in bulk [ɪn ˈbʌlk] in großen Mengen 223

incentive [ɪnˈsentɪv] Anreiz 110

in charge of [ɪn ˈtʃaːdʒ əv] verantwortlich für 19

incident ['ɪnsɪdənt] Zwischenfall, Ereignis 122

to include [ɪn'klu:d] einschließen, beinhalten, umfassen 6

included in the price [ɪnˌklu:dɪd ɪn ðə 'praɪs] im Preis enthalten 88

incoming goods control [ˌɪnkʌmɪŋ 'gʊdz kənˌtrəʊl] Wareneingangskontrolle 206

incomplete [ˌɪnkəm'pli:t] unvollständig 125

in conclusion [ɪn kən'klu:ʒn] zum Abschluss, abschließend 129

in confidence [ɪn 'kɒnfɪdəns] vertraulich 135

inconvenience [ˌɪnkən'vi:nɪəns] Unannehmlichkeiten 122

inconvenient [ˌɪnkən'vi:nɪənt] unangenehm 49

to increase [ɪn'kri:s] zunehmen, steigern 106

increasing(ly) [ɪn'kri:sɪŋ(lɪ)] zunehmend 108

to incur [ɪn'kɜ:r] anfallen 125

independent [ˌɪndɪ'pendənt] unabhängig 76

to indicate ['ɪndɪkeɪt] angeben, andeuten 144

indicator ['ɪndɪkeɪtə] Anzeiger, Anzeigetafel 89

in due course [ɪn ˌdju: 'kɔ:s] fristgemäß 206

industrial business management assistant [ɪnˌdʌstrɪəl ˌbɪznɪs 'mænɪdʒmənt əˌsɪstənt] Industriekaufmann/-frau 7

industrial clerk [ɪn'dʌstrɪəl ˌklɑ:k] Industriekaufmann/-frau 7

industry analyst ['ɪndəstrɪ ˌænəlɪst] Branchenexperte/-expertin 169

I need to freshen up a bit [aɪ ˌni:d tə ˌfreʃn 'ʌp ə ˌbɪt] ich muss mich ein bisschen frisch machen 24

in full [ɪn 'fʊl] in voller Höhe 198

inhabitant [ɪn'hæbɪtənt] Einwohner/in 190

initials [ɪ'nɪʃlz] Initialen, Anfangsbuchstaben des Namens 117

initial [ɪ'nɪʃl] anfänglich 226

initial order [ɪˌnɪʃl 'ɔ:də] Erstauftrag 159

to initiate measures [ɪˌnɪʃɪeɪt 'meʒəz] Maßnahmen einleiten 215

in law [ɪn 'lɔ:] rechtlich, vor Gericht 92

in lieu of [ɪn 'lju:ˌəv] an Stelle von 241

in line with [ɪn 'laɪn wɪð] in Übereinstimmung mit, parallel zu 41

in our favour [ɪnˌaʊə 'feɪvə] zu unseren Gunsten 196

in principle [ɪn 'prɪnsɪpl] im Prinzip 90

to insert [ɪn'sɜ:t] einfügen, einlegen 12

to insist on [ɪn'sɪst ɒn] bestehen auf 196

insistent [ɪn'sɪstənt] nachdrücklich 197

insolvent [ɪn'sɒlvənt] zahlungsunfähig 214

inspection [ɪn'spekʃn] (Über-)Prüfung 32

in stock [ɪn 'stɒk] vorrätig, auf Lager 72

to instruct [ɪn'strʌkt] anweisen, unterweisen 191

to instruct to the contrary [ɪnˌstrʌkt tʊ ðə 'kɒntrəri] gegenteilige Anweisungen erteilen 216

insulated reefer [ˌɪnsjəleɪtɪd 'ri:fə] isolierter Kühlcontainer 184

insurance [ɪn'ʃɔ:rəns] Versicherung 14

insurance business management assistant [ɪnˌʃɔ:rəns ˌbɪznɪs 'mænɪdʒmənt əˌsɪstənt] Versicherungskaufmann/-frau, Kaufmann/-frau für Versicherungen und Finanzen 9

insurance certificate [ɪn'ʃɔ:rəns səˌtɪfɪkət] Versicherungsschein, -zertifikat 176

insurance claim [ɪn'ʃɔ:rəns ˌkleɪm] Schadensanspruch, Versicherungsfall 218

insurance clerk [ɪn'ʃɔ:rəns ˌklɑ:k] Versicherungskaufmann/-frau, Kaufmann/-frau für Versicherungen und Finanzen 9

insurance policy [ɪn'ʃɔ:rəns ˌpɒləsi] Versicherungspolice 176

insured [ɪn'ʃɔ:d] (hier:) Versicherungsnehmer/in, Versicherte/r 177

integration [ˌɪntɪ'greɪʃn] Eingliederung, Integration 88

interest ['ɪntrəst] Zinsen 197

interest on arrears [ˌɪntrəst ɒn ə'rɪəz] Verzugszinsen 197

interim ['ɪntərɪm] zwischenzeitlich, vorläufig 91

in terms of [ɪn 'tɜ:mzˌəv] in Bezug auf, was … betrifft 169

internet exchanges ['ɪntənet ɪksˌtʃeɪndʒɪz] Online-Börsen 225

to interpret [ɪn'tɜ:prɪt] dolmetschen 91

interpreter [ɪn'tɜ:prɪtə] Dolmetscher/in 93

to interrupt [ˌɪntə'rʌpt] unterbrechen, stören 115

interval ['ɪntəvl] Abstand 159

interview ['ɪntəvju:] Vorstellungsgespräch, Interview 39

in the course of [ɪn ðə 'kɔ:sˌəv] im Laufe von 90

in the foreseeable future [ɪn ðə fɔ:ˌsi:əbl 'fju:tʃə] in absehbarer Zukunft 104

in transit [ɪn 'trænzɪt] beim Transport 211

introduction [ˌɪntrə'dʌkʃn] Einführung; Vorstellung 221

introductory discount [ˌɪntrədʌktəri 'dɪskaʊnt] Einführungsrabatt 133

inventory ['ɪnventri] Lagerverzeichnis, Bestandsliste 31

investment portfolio [ɪn'vestmənt pɔ:tˌfəʊlɪəʊ] Bestand an Wertpapieren 104

invoice ['ɪnvɔɪs] Rechnung 15

to involve [ɪn'vɒlv] (hier:) einbeziehen 223

in working order [ɪn ˌwɜ:kɪŋ 'ɔ:də] funktionstüchtig 91

iron ore ['aɪənˌɔ:] Eisenerz 170

irrevocable [ɪrɪ'vəʊkəbl] unwiderruflich 195

irrigation [ˌɪrɪ'geɪʃn] Bewässerung 180

irritation [ˌɪrɪ'teɪʃn] Verärgerung 169

is paralleled by [ɪz 'pærəleld ˌbaɪ] geht einher mit 225

issue ['ɪʃu:] (hier:) Ausgabe, Heft 130

to issue ['ɪʃu:] ausstellen 49

item ['aɪtəm] Artikel, Gegenstand 78

IT specialist [ˌaɪ'ti: ˌspeʃəlɪst] Fachinformatiker/in 9

it tastes like … [ɪtˌteɪsts laɪk '…] es schmeckt wie … 28

J

jelly ['dʒeli] Götterspeise, Gelee, Aspik 29

to jettison ['dʒetɪsən] (Ballast) über Bord werfen 218

job exchanges ['dʒɒb ɪksˌtʃeɪndʒɪz] Job-, Stellenbörsen 233

job specification [ˌdʒɒb ˌspesɪfɪ'keɪʃn] Stellenbeschreibung 233

to join [dʒɔɪn] (hier:) sich jemandem anschließen, mitkommen 27

joint [dʒɔɪnt] gemeinsam 27

joint venture [ˌdʒɔɪnt 'ventʃə] Joint Venture (Gemeinschaftsunternehmen) 71

to jumble ['dʒʌmbl] durcheinander werfen/bringen 112

jumbled ['dʒʌmbld] durcheinander geworfen 21

to jump [dʒʌmp] springen, sprunghaft ansteigen 104

to jump by … from … to … ['dʒʌmp baɪ … frəm … tʊ …] sprunghaft ansteigen um … von … auf … 106

junction ['dʒʌŋkʃn] Kreuzung 24

junior executive [ˌdʒu:nɪər ɪg'zekjətɪv] Nachwuchsführungskraft 208

justified ['dʒʌstɪfaɪd] gerechtfertigt, berechtigt 213

justified complaint [ˌdʒʌstɪfaɪd kəm'pleɪnt] begründete Reklamation 213

K

keen [ki:n] sehr interessiert, eifrig 237

to keep an eye on [ˌki:p ən 'aɪ ɒn] aufpassen auf 30

to keep a record [ˌki:p ə 'rekɔ:d] aufzeichnen 84

to keep informed [ˌki:p ɪn'fɔ:md] auf dem Laufenden halten 213

to keep one's fingers crossed
[ˌkiːp wʌnz ˈfɪŋɡəz ˌkrɒst] den Daumen
halten 248

key [kiː] Schlüssel 100

keyboard [ˈkiːbɔːd] Tastatur 54

kitchenette [ˌkɪtʃɪˈnet] Kochgelegen-
heit; Teeküche 93

kitchen facilities [ˈkɪtʃɪn fəˌsɪlətiz]
Küchenanlagen 26

kitten [ˈkɪtn] Kätzchen 163

L

label [ˈleɪbl] Etikett, Aufkleber 26

to label, to provide with an inscription
[ˈleɪbl, prəˌvaɪd wɪð ən ɪnˈskrɪpʃn]
beschriften, etikettieren, kennzeichnen 206

labelling [ˈleɪblɪŋ] Etikettierung 32

labour costs [ˈleɪbə ˌkɒsts] Lohnkosten
179

laces [ˈleɪsɪz] Schnürsenkel 243

ladies' room *(AE)* [ˈleɪdɪz ˌruːm] Damen-
toilette 23

lamb [læm] Lamm 28

landlady [ˈlændˌleɪdɪ] Vermieterin 247

landline [ˈlændlaɪn] Festnetz(leitung)
64

largely [ˈlɑːdʒlɪ] weitgehend 92

lashing [ˈlæʃɪŋ] Befestigungsseil, Tau,
Verschnürung 77

lately [ˈleɪtlɪ] in letzter Zeit 20

launch [lɔːntʃ] Start 228

to launch [lɔːntʃ] (Produkt) einführen,
auf den Markt bringen; in die Wege
leiten 48

lawful holder [ˌlɔːfəl ˈhəʊldə] rechtmäßige Inhaber(in)/Besitzer(in) 176

layer [ˈleɪə] Schicht 77

layout [ˈleɪaʊt] Anordnung, Gestaltung
110

lbs (pounds) [paʊndz] *(englisches
Gewichts-)*Pfund *(453,59 g)* 212

leading [ˈliːdɪŋ] führend 131

to leave much to be desired [liːv ˌmʌtʃ
tʊ bɪ dɪˈzaɪəd] viel zu wünschen übrig
lassen 91

leeks [liːks] Lauch 27

legal [ˈliːgl] rechtlich, juristisch,
gesetzlich 58

to legalize [ˈliːgəlaɪz] beglaubigen;
legalisieren 176

legal steps [ˌliːgl ˈsteps] juristische
Schritte 197

leisure [ˈleʒə] Freizeit 102

lentils [ˈlentəlz] Linsen 29

less [les] abzüglich 145

less than container load (LCL) [ˌles ðən
kənˈteɪnə ˌləʊd (ˌelsiːˈel)] Teilladung 153

to let someone know [let ˌsʌmwʌn ˈnəʊ]
jemandem Bescheid sagen 30

letterhead [ˈletəhed] Briefkopf 117

letter of credit [ˌletər əv ˈkredɪt]
Akkreditiv 195

letting agent [ˈletɪŋ ˌeɪdʒənt] Makler/in
für Mietimmobilien, -wohnungen
244

lettuce [ˈletɪs] Kopfsalat 29

life [laɪf] Lebensdauer 144

lift [lɪft] Aufzug 23

lightening [ˈlaɪtnɪŋ] Blitzschlag 218

likewise [ˈlaɪkwaɪz] ebenfalls 88

limit [ˈlɪmɪt] Beschränkung 88

limited [ˈlɪmɪtɪd] begrenzt 218

line [laɪn] Verbindung 67

line graph [ˈlaɪn ˌgrɑːf] Liniendiagramm
105

liner [ˈlaɪnə] Linienschiff 177

lingua franca [ˌlɪŋgwə ˈfræŋkə] Ver-
kehrssprache 18

lining [ˈlaɪnɪŋ] (Unter-)Futter, Einlage
50

link [lɪŋk] Verbindung, Bindeglied 223

to link [lɪŋk] verbinden, verknüpfen
226

linking words [ˈlɪŋkɪŋ ˌwɜːdz] verbin-
dende Wörter 121

liquid [ˈlɪkwɪd] flüssig 182

livestock [ˈlaɪvstɒk] lebende Tiere 33

to load [ləʊd] beladen, einladen 169

loading dock [ˈləʊdɪŋ ˌdɒk] Ladebucht
31

local [ˈləʊkl] örtlich, ortsansässig,
hiesig 39

to locate [ləʊˈkeɪt] ausfindig machen,
lokalisieren 128

location [ləʊˈkeɪʃn] Standort 103

logistics and warehousing operation
[ləˌdʒɪstɪks ənd ˈweəhaʊzɪŋ ˌɒpəˌreɪʃn]
Logistik- und Lagerungsunter-
nehmen 247

long-distance running [ˌlɒŋdɪstəns
ˈrʌnɪŋ] Langstreckenlauf 8

long hours [ˌlɒŋ ˈaʊəz] Überstunden 200

to lose one's way, lost, lost [ˌluːz wʌnz
ˈweɪ, lɒst, lɒst] sich verirren, sich
verlaufen 23

low [ləʊ] Tief(punkt) 106

lump sum [ˌlʌmp ˈsʌm] Pauschalsumme
177

M

machinery [məˈʃiːnərɪ] Maschinen 39

magnificent [mægˈnɪfɪsənt] großartig,
prächtig 25

main branch [ˌmeɪn ˈbrɑːntʃ] Haupt-
filiale 236

main course [ˌmeɪn ˈkɔːs] Hauptgericht,
-gang 27

main entrance [ˌmeɪn ˈentrəns] Haupt-
eingang 23

main road [ˌmeɪn ˈrəʊd] Hauptstraße 24

major [ˈmeɪdʒə] groß, wichtig 223

to make an offer [ˌmeɪk ən ˈɒfə] ein
Angebot abgeben 141

to make someone feel welcome [ˌmeɪk
ˌsʌmwʌn fiːl ˈwelkəm] dafür sorgen,
dass sich jemand wohl fühlt 18

to make sure [meɪk ˈʃɔː] sich vergewis-
sern 103

to make up [meɪk ˈʌp] *(hier:)* erfinden
69

to manage complaints [ˌmænɪdʒ
kəmˈpleɪnts] Beschwerden bearbeiten
213

management [ˈmænɪdʒmənt] Geschäftsleitung 122

**management assistant for tourism
and leisure** [ˈmænɪdʒmənt əˌsɪstənt fə
ˌtʊərɪzm ən ˈleʒə] Kaufmann/-frau für
Tourismus und Freizeit 11

management assistant in advertising
[ˈmænɪdʒmənt əˌsɪstənt ɪn ˈædvətaɪzɪŋ]
Werbekaufmann/-frau 11

**management assistant in event
organisation** [ˈmænɪdʒmənt əˌsɪstənt ɪn
ɪˌvent ˌɔːgənaɪˈzeɪʃn] Veranstaltungs-
kaufmann/-frau 11

**management assistant in freight
forwarding** [ˈmænɪdʒmənt əˌsɪstənt ɪn
ˌfreɪt ˈfɔːwədɪŋ] Speditionskaufmann/
-frau 9

management assistant in informatics
[ˈmænɪdʒmənt əˌsɪstənt ɪn ˌɪnfəˈmætɪks]
Informatikkaufmann/-frau 11

**management assistant in office
communication** [ˈmænɪdʒmənt əˌsɪstənt
ɪn ˌɒfɪs kəˌmjuːnɪˈkeɪʃn] Kaufmann/-frau
für Bürokommunikation 11

management assistant in publishing
[ˈmænɪdʒmənt əˌsɪstənt ɪn ˈpʌblɪʃɪŋ]
Verlagskaufmann/-frau 9

**management assistant in retail
business** [ˈmænɪdʒmənt əˌsɪstənt ɪn
ˌriːteɪl ˈbɪznɪs] Kaufmann/-frau im
Einzelhandel 9

**management assistant in wholesale
and foreign trade** [ˈmænɪdʒmənt
əˌsɪstənt ɪn ˌhəʊlseɪl ənd ˌfɒrən ˈtreɪd]
Kaufmann/-frau im Groß- und
Außenhandel 9

managing director [ˌmænɪdʒɪŋ daɪˈrektə]
Geschäftsführer/in 14

manner [ˈmænə] Umgangsstil 245

manual [ˈmænjʊəl] Handbuch 78

manufacturer [ˌmænjəˈfæktʃərə] Herstel-
ler/in, Produzent/in 223

to manufacture to specification
[ˌmænjəˈfæktʃə tʊ ˌspesɪfɪˈkeɪʃn] als
Sonderanfertigung herstellen 195

manufacturing [ˌmænjəˈfæktʃərɪŋ] Ferti-
gung, Fabrikation 39

manufacturing industry
[ˌmænjəˈfæktʃərɪŋ ˌɪndəstrɪ] verarbeiten-
de Industrie 245

to marinate [ˈmærɪneɪt] marinieren,
einlegen 27

marital status [ˌmærɪtl ˈsteɪtəs] Familienstand 117

marketing tools [ˈmɑːkɪtɪŋ ˌtuːlz] Marketinginstrumente 226

market leader [ˌmɑːkɪt ˈliːdə] Marktführer 39

market research [ˌmɑːkɪt ˈriːsɜːtʃ] Marktforschung 222

market share [ˌmɑːkɪt ˈʃeə] Marktanteil 170

market survey [ˌmɑːkɪt ˈsɜːveɪ] Marktstudie, -untersuchung 222

marking [ˈmɑːkɪŋ] Markierung, Kennzeichnung 51

mart [mɑːt] Markt 41

mashed potatoes [ˌmæʃt pəˈteɪtəʊz] Kartoffelpüree 28

maturity [məˈtjʊərəti] Reife 221

maximum admissible weight [ˌmæksɪməm ədˌmɪsəbl ˈweɪt] zulässiges Höchstgewicht 212

means of payment [ˈmiːnz əv ˈpeɪmənt] Zahlungsmittel 193

measure [ˈmeʒə] Maßnahme 217

measurement [ˈmeʒəmənt] (hier:) Abmessungen 177

meat [miːt] Fleisch 28

meatball [ˈmiːtbɔːl] Frikadelle 28

medical supplies [ˌmedɪkl səˈplaɪz] Artikel zur medizinischen Versorgung 171

Mediterranean countries [medɪtərˌeɪnɪən ˈkʌntrɪz] Länder am Mittelmeer 8

to meet deadlines [miːt ˈdedlaɪnz] Termine/Fristen einhalten 234

to meet halfway [miːt ˌhɑːfˈweɪ] auf halbem Weg entgegenkommen 213

to meet someone [ˈmiːt ˌsʌmwʌn] jemanden kennenlernen, treffen 18

to meet with approval [ˌmiːt wɪð əˈpruːvl] auf Zustimmung stoßen 243

member [ˈmembə] Mitglied 165

memo [ˈmeməʊ] Aktennotiz 26

memory stick [ˈmemrɪ ˌstɪk] USB-Speicher 54

menu [ˈmenjuː] Speisekarte; Menü (Computer) 29

merchandise [ˈmɜːtʃəndaɪs] Ware, Gut, Handelsartikel 159

merchants [ˈmɜːtʃənts] Händler 226

merchant ship [ˈmɜːtʃənt ˌʃɪp] Handelsschiff 182

message [ˈmesɪdʒ] Nachricht, Botschaft 111

Middle Ages [ˌmɪdl ˈeɪdʒɪz] Mittelalter 190

mince(d) meat [ˈmɪns(t) ˌmiːt] Gehacktes 28

minor [ˈmaɪnə] gering(fügig) 135

mint bar [ˈmɪnt ˌbaː] Pfefferminzriegel 143

minute [maɪˈnjuːt] peinlich genau; winzig 43

minutes [ˈmɪnɪts] Protokoll 90

misunderstanding [ˌmɪsʌndəˈstændɪŋ] Missverständnis 108

mixed [mɪkst] gemischt 29

mix-up [ˈmɪksʌp] Verwechslung 212

mode of transport [ˈməʊd əv ˈtrænspɔːt] Transportart 48

moderate(ly) [ˈmɒdərət(li)] mäßig, maßvoll 106

modification [ˌmɒdɪfɪˈkeɪʃn] Änderung 85

to modify [ˈmɒdɪfaɪ] ab-, verändern 26

monitor [ˈmɒnɪtə] PC-Bildschirm 87

to monitor [ˈmɒnɪtə] überwachen 49

monotonous(ly) [məˈnɒtənəs(li)] eintönig 103

moreover [mɔːˈrəʊvə] überdies, außerdem 121

mother tongue [ˌmʌðə ˈtʌŋ] Muttersprache 235

motor-car mechanic [ˌməʊtəkaː məˈkænɪk] Kfz-Mechaniker/in 58

move [muːv] (hier:) Umzug 30

mug [mʌg] Becher 204

multilingual [ˌmʌltɪˈlɪŋgwəl] mehr-, vielsprachig 209

multi-modal transport [ˌmʌltɪˌməʊdəl ˈtrænspɔːt] Kombiverkehr 96

mushrooms [ˈmʌʃruːmz] Champignons, Pilze 27

mustard [ˈmʌstəd] Senf 164

N

named [neɪmd] namentlich genannt 193

native [ˈneɪtɪv] einheimisch, inländisch, Landes- 147

navy (blue) [ˌneɪvi (ˈbluː)] marineblau, dunkelblau 114

neat(ly) [niːt(li)] ordentlich, adrett 238

needs [niːdz] Bedarf, Bedürfnisse 222

to need, to require [niːd, rɪˈkwaɪə] benötigen 245

to negotiate [nɪˈgəʊʃɪeɪt] verhandeln 250

negotiation [nɪˌgəʊʃɪˈeɪʃn] Verhandlung 199

neighbouring [ˈneɪbərɪŋ] benachbart 39

net [net] netto 143

newsagent [ˈnjuːzˌeɪdʒənt] Zeitungshändler/in 21

nobility [nəʊˈbɪləti] Adel, Vornehmheit 163

noisy [ˈnɔɪzi] laut 22

non-attendance [ˌnɒnəˈtendəns] Fehlen, Abwesenheit 92

non-bulk cargo [ˌnɒnbʌlk ˈkaːgəʊ] Stückgutfracht 169

note pad [ˈnəʊtpæd] Notizblock 54

notification [ˌnəʊtɪfɪˈkeɪʃn] Benachrichtigung 233

to notify [ˈnəʊtɪfaɪ] benachrichtigen 199

novel [ˈnɒvl] Roman 9

novelist [ˈnɒvəlɪst] Romanschriftsteller/in 147

nowadays [ˈnaʊədeɪz] heutzutage 193

null and void [ˌnʌl ən ˈvɔɪd] null und nichtig 187

nutritionally conscious [njuːˌtrɪʃənli ˈkɒnʃəs] ernährungsbewusst 26

nutritional science [njuːˌtrɪʃənl ˈsaɪəns] Ernährungswissenschaft 26

O

obesity [əʊˈbiːsəti] Fettleibigkeit, klinisches Übergewicht 90

objective [əbˈdʒektɪv] Ziel 101

obligation [ˌɒblɪˈgeɪʃn] Verpflichtung, Verbindlichkeit 149

obscure [əbˈskjʊə] unbekannt 227

to observe [əbˈzɜːv] beachten 89

obvious(ly) [ˈɒbvɪəs(li)] offensichtlich 164

occasion [əˈkeɪʒn] Anlass, Gelegenheit 116

offer [ˈɒfə] Angebot 140

to offer credit facilities [ˌɒfə ˈkredɪt fəˌsɪlətiz] Kredite anbieten 224

office administration clerk [ˌɒfɪs ədˌmɪnɪˈstreɪʃn ˌklaːk] Bürokaufmann/-frau 7

office management assistant [ˌɒfɪs ˈmænɪdʒmənt əˌsɪstənt] Bürokaufmann/-frau 9

offshore [ˌɒfˈʃɔː] vor der Küste gelegen 77

old-established [ˌəʊldɪˈstæblɪʃt] alteingesessen 38

old-fashioned [ˌəʊldˈfæʃnd] altmodisch 64

to omit [əʊˈmɪt] aus-, weglassen 117

on a large scale [ɒn ə ˌlaːdʒ ˈskeɪl] in großem Stil/Umfang 40

on behalf of [ɒn bɪˈhaːf əv] im Auftrag von/für 84

on-carriage [ˈɒnˈkærɪdʒ] Weitertransport 32

on delivery [ɒn dɪˈlɪvəri] bei Lieferung 195

on demand [ɒn dɪˈmaːnd] auf Verlangen/Abruf 193

one-off [ˌwʌnˈɒf] Einmal- 146

onion [ˈʌnjən] Zwiebel 27

on presentation [ɒn ˌprezənˈteɪʃn] bei Vorlage 193

on request [ɒn rɪˈkwest] (hier:) wenn gewünscht; auf Anfrage 248

on the left / left-hand side [ɒn ðə ˈleft / ˌlefthænd ˈsaɪd] links 23

on the off-chance [ɒn ðɪ ˌɒftʃaːns] auf Verdacht 233

on / to the right [ɒn / tʊ ðə ˈraɪt] rechts 23

open account terms [ˌəʊpn əˌkaʊnt ˈtɜːmz] offenes Zahlungsziel 142

open credit [ˌəʊpn ˈkredɪt] Zahlung gegen einfache Rechnung 195

openings [ˈəʊpnɪŋz] offene Stellen 233

opening bank [ˈəʊpnɪŋ ˈbæŋk] ausstellende Bank 195

open-plan office [ˌəʊpnplæn ˈɒfɪs] Großraumbüro 23

open top [ˌəʊpn ˈtɒp] Open-Top-Container 184

to operate [ˈɒpəreɪt] bedienen 103

operations [ˌɒpəˈreɪʃnz] geschäftliche Aktivitäten; Betrief 14

opportunity [ˌɒpəˈtjuːnətɪ] Gelegenheit 12

opposite [ˈɒpəzɪt] gegenüber 24

opposite number [ˌɒpəzɪt ˈnʌmbə] Gegenüber, Kollege/Kollegin 85

optician [ɒpˈtɪʃn] Optiker/in 223

option [ˈɒpʃn] Wahl 14

oral [ˈɔːrəl] mündlich 100

order [ˈɔːdə] Auftrag, Bestellung 159

to order [ˈɔːdə] bestellen; anordnen 39

order confirmation [ˈɔːdə kɒnfəˌmeɪʃn] Auftragsbestätigung 163

order on call [ˈɔːdər ˌɒn ˈkɔːl] Abrufauftrag 159

or else [ˌɔːr ˈels] andernfalls, sonst 111

organic [ɔːˈgænɪk] biologisch, Bio- 26

organic foods [ɔːˈgænɪk ˌfuːdz] Bio-Lebensmittel 90

organisation [ˌɔːgənaɪˈzeɪʃn] Firma, Unternehmen, Organisation 225

original(ly) [əˈrɪdʒənl(ɪ)] ursprünglich 7

other business [ˌʌðə ˈbɪznɪs] Verschiedenes 90

outcome [ˈaʊtkʌm] Ergebnis 122

outlet [ˈaʊtlet] Verkaufsstelle, Vertriebsmöglichkeit 129

outload [ˈaʊtləʊd] ausgehende Sendung 33

out of order [ˌaʊt ˌɒv ˈɔːdə] kaputt, außer Betrieb 208

outsize [ˈaʊtsaɪz] übergroß 49

outskirts [ˈaʊtskɜːts] Außenbezirk 31

to outsource [ˈaʊtsɔːs] ausgliedern 14

overcast [ˈəʊvəkɑːst] bedeckt, bezogen (Himmel) 20

overheads [ˈəʊvəhedz] fixe Kosten 224

overindebted [ˌəʊvərɪnˈdetɪd] überschuldet 194

overload [ˈəʊvələʊd] Überladung, Übergewicht 78

to overlook [ˌəʊvəˈlʊk] übersehen; überblicken 197

overseas [ˌəʊvəˈsiːz] aus dem/ins Ausland, ausländisch 146

to oversee, oversaw, overseen [ˌəʊvəˈsiː, ˌəʊvəˈsɔː, ˌəʊvəˈsiːn] beaufsichtigen, leiten 85

oversight [ˈəʊvəsaɪt] Versehen 122

to overtake, overtook, overtaken [ˌəʊvəˈteɪk, ˌəʊvəˈtʊk, ˌəʊvəˈteɪkn] überholen 194

overview [ˈəʊvəvjuː] Überblick 101

overwhelmed [ˌəʊvəˈwelmd] überwältigt 41

owner [ˈəʊnə] Eigentümer/in 58

P

package tour [ˈpækɪdʒ ˌtʊə] Pauschalreise 110

packaging [ˈpækɪdʒɪŋ] Verpackung 49

packaging material [ˈpækɪdʒɪŋ məˌtɪərɪəl] Verpackungsmaterial 73

packing list [ˈpækɪŋ ˌlɪst] Packliste 173

pair of scissors [ˌpeər əv ˈsɪzəz] Schere 54

pallett [ˈpælɪt] Palette 31

pallett jack [ˈpælɪt ˌdʒæk] Palettenheber 31

palletised [ˈpælətaɪzd] auf Paletten 14

paper [ˈpeɪpə] (hier:) Vortrag 71

paragraph [ˈpærəgrɑːf] Absatz 120

paramount [ˈpærəmaʊnt] vorrangig 26

to paraphrase [ˈpærəfreɪz] umschreiben 13

parcel post [ˈpɑːsl ˌpəʊst] Paketpost 152

parent company [ˌpeərənt ˈkʌmpənɪ] Muttergesellschaft 214

parsley [ˈpɑːslɪ] Petersilie 29

participant [pɑːˈtɪsɪpənt] Teilnehmer/in 208

particular [pəˈtɪkjələ] besonders, speziell 38

partnership [ˈpɑːtnəʃɪp] Personengesellschaft 117

to pass a message on [ˌpɑːs ə ˈmesɪdʒ ɒn] eine Nachricht weitergeben 30

passing of risk [ˌpɑːsɪŋ əv ˈrɪsk] Gefahrenübergang 150

to pass on [pɑːs ˈɒn] weiterreichen, -geben 112

patience [ˈpeɪʃns] Geduld 67

patron saint [ˌpeɪtrən ˈseɪnt] Schutzheilige/r 25

to pause [pɔːz] eine Pause einlegen 75

payable at [ˈpeɪəbl ət] zahlbar bei 196

payable to [ˈpeɪəbl tuː] zahlbar an 73

to pay into a bank account [peɪ ˌɪntʊ ə ˈbæŋk əˌkaʊnt] auf ein Konto einzahlen 193

payload [ˈpeɪləʊd] Nutzlast 34

payment in advance [ˌpeɪmənt ɪn ədˈvɑːns] Vorauszahlung 195

payment, money transfer, remittance [ˈpeɪmənt, ˈmʌnɪ ˌtrænsfɜː, rɪˈmɪtəns] Überweisung 94

PC-literacy [ˌpiːsiːˈlɪtrəsɪ] PC-Kenntnisse 235

PC literate [ˌpiːsiːˈlɪtrət] PC-erfahren 234

peak [piːk] Gipfel, Höchststand 106

peak season [ˌpiːk ˈsiːzn] Hochsaison 73

pearl [pɜːl] Perle 147

pea soup [ˌpiː ˈsuːp] Erbsensuppe 28

peppers [ˈpepəz] Paprikaschoten 28

percentage [pəˈsentɪdʒ] Prozentsatz 224

perishable [ˈperɪʃəbl] (leicht) verderblich 170

perishables [ˈperɪʃəblz] verderbliche Waren 14

permit [ˈpɜːmɪt] Erlaubnis, Genehmigung 153

to permit [pəˈmɪt] erlauben 78

personal assistant [ˌpɜːsənl əˈsɪstent] Sekretär/in 58

personnel [ˌpɜːsənˈel] Personal 58

personnel department [ˌpɜːsənˈel dɪˌpɑːtmənt] Personalabteilung 208

person to contact [ˌpɜːsn tə ˈkɒntækt] Kontaktperson 236

to persuade [pəˈsweɪd] überreden 60

pharmaceuticals [ˌfɑːməˈsuːtɪklz] Arzneimittel 33

to phase out [feɪz ˈaʊt] allmählich vom Markt zurückziehen 221

to pick [pɪk] auswählen, zusammenstellen 31

to pick someone up [pɪk ˌsʌmwʌn ˈʌp] jemanden abholen 30

pick-up [ˈpɪkʌp] Lade- 95

picnic hamper [ˈpɪknɪk ˌhæmpə] Picknickkorb 112

pie chart [ˈpaɪ ˌtʃɑːt] Tortendiagramm 104

pile [paɪl] Stapel 182

pipe-blown by hand [ˌpaɪpbləʊn baɪ ˈhænd] mundgeblasen 211

to place an order [ˌpleɪs ən ˈɔːdə] einen Auftrag erteilen 129

placement [ˈpleɪsmənt] Praktikum 236

place of destination [ˌpleɪs əv ˌdestɪˈneɪʃn] Bestimmungsort 150

place of employment [ˌpleɪs əv ɪmˈplɔɪmənt] Arbeitsstätte 225

plaice [pleɪs] Scholle 28

plain [pleɪn] (hier:) ungemustert, einfarbig; schlicht, unscheinbar 114

plant [plɑːnt] Werk, Anlage; Pflanze 151

plastic box with mouldings [ˌplæstɪk ˈbɒks wɪð ˈməʊldɪŋz] Kunststoffbox mit Formeinlagen 172

platter [ˈplætə] Servierplatte, (Holz-)Teller 164

plausible [ˈplɔːzɪbl] plausibel, einleuchtend, glaubhaft 211

to point out [pɔɪnt ˈaʊt] hinweisen auf 162

polished [ˈpɒlɪʃt] mit Schuhcreme geputzt, poliert 243

polite [pəˈlaɪt] höflich 73

pollution [pəˈluːʃn] (Umwelt-)Verschmutzung 94

to pop into [ˌpɒp ˈɪntʊ] eben schnell hineintun 102

pork escalope [ˌpɔːk 'eskəlɒp] Schweine-schnitzel 29

port [pɔːt] Hafen 169

port of destination [ˌpɔːt əv ˌdestɪ'neɪʃn] Bestimmungshafen 150

port of discharge [ˌpɔːt əv 'dɪstʃɑːdʒ] Entladehafen 177

port of distress [ˌpɔːt əv dɪ'stres] Rettungshafen 217

port of shipment [ˌpɔːt əv 'ʃɪpmənt] Verschiffungshafen 150

port side [ˌpɔːt ˌsaɪd] Backbord 217

postcode (BE), postal code (BE), zip code (AE) ['pəʊstkəʊd, 'pəʊstl ˌkəʊd, 'zɪpkəʊd] Postleitzahl 69

to postpone [pəs'pəʊn] verschieben 71

potential customer [pəˌtenʃl 'kʌstəmə] Interessent in 141

pot plant ['pɒt ˌplɑːnt] Topfpflanze 54

poultry ['pəʊltrɪ] Geflügel 28

praise [preɪz] Lob 245

pre-carriage [ˌpriː'kærɪdʒ] Vorlauf 166

to precede [priː'siːd] vor(an)gehen, -stehen 118

precise(ly) [prɪ'saɪs(lɪ)] genau, exakt, präzise 69

precisely then [prɪˌsaɪslɪ 'ðen] gerade dann 67

preferably ['prefrəblɪ] vorzugsweise 103

preliminary [prɪ'lɪmɪnərɪ] vorläufig 110

premises ['premɪsɪz] Geschäftsräume, Firmengebäude, -gelände 143

premium ['priːmɪəm] Prämie 177

prerequisite [ˌpriː'rekwɪzɪt] Voraussetzung, Bedingung 103

prestigious [pres'tɪdʒəs] repräsentativ 53

pretzel ['pretsl] Brezel 25

to prevent [prɪ'vent] hindern, verhindern, vermeiden 111

previous ['priːvɪəs] früher, vorhergehend 245

price reduction ['praɪs rɪˌdʌkʃn] Preisnachlass 205

prices are subject to change without notice ['praɪsɪz ə ˌsʌbdʒɪkt ˌtʊ ˌtʃeɪndʒ wɪðˌaʊt 'nəʊtɪs] Preisänderungen vorbehalten 140

pricing ['praɪsɪŋ] Preisfestsetzung 153

principal ['prɪnsɪpl] (hier:) Schulleiter/in; Auftraggeber/in 208

printing press ['prɪntɪŋ ˌpres] Druckerpresse 171

priority [praɪ'ɒrətɪ] Priorität 249

privacy ['praɪvəsɪ] private Atmosphäre 56

private individual [ˌpraɪvət ˌɪndɪ'vɪdʒʊəl] Privatperson 41

procedures [prəˌsiːdʒəz] (Arbeits-)Abläufe, Verfahren 14

proceedings [prə'siːdɪŋz] (hier:) Ablauf der Konferenz 84

to process ['prəʊses] be-, verarbeiten 141

to procure [prə'kjʊə] besorgen 49

produce ['prɒdjuːs] (landwirtschaftliche) Erzeugnisse 26

production site [prə'dʌkʃn ˌsaɪt] Fertigungsstätte, Produktionsbetrieb 39

product range ['prɒdʌkt ˌreɪndʒ] Produktpalette 88

professional [prə'feʃnl] beruflich, professionell 6

proforma invoice [prəʊˌfɔːmər ˌ'ɪnvɔɪs] Proformarechnung 191

progress ['prəʊgres] Fortgang 213

to prohibit [prə'hɪbɪt] untersagen, verbieten 49

to project an image [prəˌdʒekt ən 'ɪmɪdʒ] ein Image projizieren 243

prolonged [prə'lɒŋd] langanhaltend 121

to promote [prə'məʊt] befördern 247

promotion [prə'məʊʃn] Aufstieg, Beförderung 12

prompt [prɒmpt] Hinweis, Stichwort 22

prompt cards ['prɒmpt ˌkɑːdz] Stichwortkarten 101

to pronounce [prə'naʊns] aussprechen 75

pronounced [prə'naʊnst] ausgeprägt 60

proof [pruːf] Beweis, Nachweis 195

proportion [prə'pɔːʃn] Anteil 104

proposal [prə'pəʊzl] Vorschlag 165

prospects ['prɒspekts] Aussichten 12

prospective [prəs'pektɪv] zukünftig, voraussichtlich, potentiell 141

to prosper ['prɒspə] gedeihen, florieren 39

protective software [prəˌtektɪv 'sɒftweə] Software zum Schutz 109

proud(ly) [praʊd(lɪ)] stolz 163

to prove [pruːv] beweisen, nachweisen 195

proven ['pruːvn] bewährt 230

to provide [prə'vaɪd] zur Verfügung stellen 224

provider [prə'vaɪdə] Dienstleister 14

public ['pʌblɪk] Öffentlichkeit 63

publisher's assistant ['pʌblɪʃəz əˌsɪstənt] Verlagskaufmann/-frau 235

publishing house ['pʌblɪʃɪŋ ˌhaʊs] Verlag 235

punch [pʌntʃ] Locher 54

punctual ['pʌŋktʃʊəl] pünktlich 21

to punish ['pʌnɪʃ] bestrafen 155

puppy ['pʌpɪ] Hündchen, Welpe 163

purchase order ['pɜːtʃɪs ˌɔːdə] Bestellung, Lieferungsauftrag 206

purchasing (department) ['pɜːtʃəsɪŋ (dɪˌpɑːtmənt)] Einkauf(sabteilung) 58

purchasing manager ['pɜːtʃəsɪŋ ˌmænɪdʒə] Einkaufsleiter/in 129

pure new wool [ˌpjʊə njuː 'wʊl] reine Schurwolle 172

purpose ['pɜːpəs] Zweck 49

purpose-built [ˌpɜːpəs'bɪlt] für bestimmten Zweck gebaut 53

to put someone through [pʊt ˌsʌmwʌn 'θruː] durchstellen, verbinden 65

Q

to qualify for ['kwɒlɪfaɪ fɔː] Voraussetzungen erfüllen für, Anspruch haben auf 162

quantity discount [ˌkwɒntətɪ 'dɪskaʊnt] Mengenrabatt 142

quarter finals [ˌkwɔːtə 'faɪnlz] Viertelfinale 20

quarterly ['kwɔːtəlɪ] vierteljährlich 142

quay [kiː] Kai, Dock, Anlegestelle 149

query ['kwɪərɪ] Anfrage 85

quota ['kwəʊtə] Quote, Rate, Kontingent, Anteil 165

quotation [kwəʊ'teɪʃn] Angebot mit Preisangabe 128

to quote [kwəʊt] Preis angeben; zitieren 142

R

rabbit ['ræbɪt] Kaninchen 28

rack [ræk] Ständer 31

rail siding ['reɪl ˌsaɪdɪŋ] Gleisanschluss 170

rail transport ['reɪl ˌtrænspɔːt] Schienentransport 170

to raise [reɪz] erhöhen 226

to raise a matter [ˌreɪz ə 'mætə] eine Sache ansprechen 212

random sample [ˌrændəm 'sɑːmpl] Zufallsprobe 222

range [reɪndʒ] Sortiment, Kollektion, Auswahl 163

to range from ... to ['reɪndʒ frəm ... tʊ] reichen von ... bis 100

range of products [ˌreɪndʒ əv 'prɒdʌkts] Produktpalette 39

rapid ['ræpɪd] schnell 104

rapport [ræ'pɔː, rə'pɔː] Verhältnis 245

raw materials [ˌrɔː mə'tɪərɪəlz] Rohstoffe 169

re [riː] bezüglich, wegen 214

receipt of order [rɪˌsiːt əv 'ɔːdə] Auftragseingang 143

to receive [rɪ'siːv] erhalten, empfangen 64

receiver [rɪ'siːvə] Hörer 64

recent ['riːsənt] nicht lange zurückliegend, vor kurzem geschehen 108

reception [rɪ'sepʃn] Empfang 130

receptionist [rɪ'sepʃənɪst] Rezeptionist/in, Mitarbeiter/in am Empfang 23

recipient [rɪ'sɪpɪənt] Empfänger 111

to recognize ['rekəgnaɪz] erkennen, anerkennen 109

to recommend [ˌrekəˈmend] empfehlen 93

record [ˈrekɔːd] Aufzeichnung 92

records [ˈrekɔːdz] Unterlagen, Verzeichnisse 197

to record [rɪˈkɔːd] aufzeichnen, eintragen 115

to recruit [rɪˈkruːt] einstellen 233

recruitment agencies [rɪˈkruːtmənt ˌeɪdʒənsɪz] Stellenvermittlungsagenturen 233

to redesign [ˌriːdɪˈzaɪn] neu-, umgestalten 26

to redirect [ˌriːdaɪˈrekt, ˌriːdɪˈrekt] umleiten 65

reefer ship [ˈriːfə ˌʃɪp] Kühlschiff 182

referee [ˌrefərˈiː] (hier:) jemand, der eine Empfehlung/ein Zeugnis schreibt 236

reference [ˈrefrəns] Bezug 145

to refer to [rɪˈfɜː tuː] ver-/hinweisen auf, sich beziehen auf 38

reforwarding [ˌriːˈfɔːwədɪŋ] Weitersendung 153

refreshments [rɪˈfreʃmənts] Erfrischung(en) 19

refrigerated [rɪˈfrɪdʒəreɪtɪd] (tief)gekühlt 31

refund [ˈriːfʌnd] Erstattung 208

to refund [ˌriːˈfʌnd] erstatten 205

refurbishment [ˌriːˈfɜːbɪʃmənt] Renovierung 208

regardless of [rɪˈɡɑːdləs əv] ungeachtet, trotz 172

to register [ˈredʒɪstə] eintragen, registrieren 134

regularly [ˈreɡjələlɪ] regelmäßig 222

regulations [ˌreɡjəˈleɪʃnz] Vorschriften, Verordnungen 116

to rehearse [rɪˈhɜːs] proben, einüben 103

to reinforce [ˌriːɪnˈfɔːs] verstärken 101

to reject [rɪˈdʒekt] zurückweisen 213

to release from a contract [rɪˌliːs frəm ə ˈkɒntrækt] von einem Vertrag entbinden 214

relevant [ˈreləvənt] wichtig, sachdienlich 69

reliable [rɪˈlaɪəbl] zuverlässig 38

relieved [rɪˈliːvd] erleichtert 71

to rely on [rɪˈlaɪ ɒn] sich verlassen auf, abhängen von 95

to remain unchanged [rɪˌmeɪn ʌnˈtʃeɪndʒd] unverändert bleiben 106

to remind [rɪˈmaɪnd] erinnern 103

reminder [rɪˈmaɪndə] (Zahlungs-)Erinnerung, Mahnung 190

to remit [rɪˈmɪt] überweisen 191

to remove [rɪˈmuːv] entfernen 206

to render a service [ˌrendər ə ˈsɜːvɪs] einen Dienst leisten, eine Dienstleistung erbringen 205

renewable [rɪˈnjuːəbl] erneuerbar 228

to renew a contract [rɪˌnjuːˌə ˈkɒntrækt] einen Vertrag verlängern 208

rent [rent] Miete 73

to rent [rent] mieten 39

repairs [rɪˈpeəz] Reparatur 43

repeat order [rɪˌpiːt ˈɔːdə] Folgeauftrag 159

to replace [rɪˈpleɪs] (hier:) auflegen; ersetzen 64

replacement [rɪˈpleɪsmənt] Ersatz 49

replacement Mp3 player [rɪˌpleɪsmənt ˌempiːˈθriː ˌpleɪə] Ersatz-MP3-Spieler 172

to report to [rɪˈpɔːt ˌtuː] unterstehen 58

representative [ˌreprɪˈzentətɪv] Vertreter/in 135

reputation [ˌrepjəˈteɪʃn] Ruf, Renommee 136

request [rɪˈkwest] Bitte 73

to request [rɪˈkwest] bitten um 90

to require [rɪˈkwaɪə] (hier:) verlangen, auffordern 100

research [ˈriːsɜːtʃ] Forschung 23

residence permit [ˈrezɪdəns ˌpɜːmɪt] Aufenthaltsgenehmigung 247

resort [rɪˈzɔːt] Urlaubs-, Badeort 147

resources [ˈrɪsɔːs] Ressourcen, Hilfsmittel 14

respite [ˈrespaɪt] Zahlungsaufschub 216

to respond [rɪˈspɒnd] antworten, reagieren 213

responsibility [rɪˌspɒnsəˈbɪlətɪ] Verantwortung, Zuständigkeit 14

responsible for [rɪˈspɒnsəbl fɔː] verantwortlich für 59

to restore [rɪˈstɔː] wiederherstellen, restaurieren 112

restricted [rɪˈstrɪktɪd] beschränkt 92

restriction [rɪˈstrɪkʃn] Einschränkung, Verbot 50

restroom (AE) [ˈrestˌruːm] Toilette 23

retail customer [ˌriːteɪl ˈkʌstəmə] Privatkunde (bei einer Bank) 225

retailer [ˈriːteɪlə] Einzelhändler/in 129

retailing operations [ˈriːteɪlɪŋ ˌɒpəreɪʃnz] Einzelhandelsgeschäftstätigkeit 225

retail outlet [ˌriːteɪl ˈaʊtlet] Einzelhandelsverkaufsstelle 194

retail sales [ˌriːteɪl ˈseɪlz] Umsatz im Einzelhandel 121

retail trade [ˈriːteɪl ˌtreɪd] Einzelhandel 164

to retain [rɪˈteɪn] halten, beibehalten 133

retirement [rɪˈtaɪəmənt] Ruhestand 215

retrieval [rɪˈtriːvl] Abruf 31

to return [rɪˈtɜːn] (hier:) zurückschicken 93

to reveal [rɪˈviːl] enthüllen, aufzeigen 211

to reverse [rɪˈvɜːs] umkehren 238

review [rɪˈvjuː] Überarbeitung, Prüfung 154

reviews [rɪˈvjuːz] Berichte, Besprechungen 226

to revoke [rɪˈvəʊk] widerrufen, annullieren, stornieren 195

reworking [ˌriːˈwɜːkɪŋ] Um-, Nacharbeitung 206

rice [raɪs] Reis 28

right away [ˌraɪtəˈweɪ] sofort 247

to rise, rose, risen [raɪz, rəʊz, rɪzn] steigen 106

rising demand for [ˌraɪzɪŋ dɪˈmɑːnd fə] steigende Nachfrage nach 104

road haulage [ˈrəʊd ˌhɔːlɪdʒ] Güterverkehr (auf den Straßen) 96

roast pork [ˌrəʊstˈpɔːk] Schweinebraten 28

roller door [ˌrəʊləˈdɔː] Rolltür 31

to romp [rɒmp] herumtollen 163

roof [ruːf] Dach 223

roro ship [ˌrəʊˈrəʊ ˌʃɪp] Ro-Ro-Frachter 182

rotor blade [ˈrəʊtə ˌbleɪd] Rotorblatt 77

roughly [ˈrʌflɪ] grob, rund, etwa 77

roughly one third [ˌrʌflɪ ˌwʌn ˈθɜːd] rund ein Drittel 211

roundabout [ˈraʊndəbaʊt] Kreisverkehr 24

to round up [raʊnd ˈʌp] aufrunden 90

rubber (BE), eraser (AE) [ˈrʌbə, ɪˈreɪzə] Radiergummi 54

rude [ruːd] grob, ungehobelt, unverschämt 123

rule [ruːl] Regel, Vorschrift 49

to rule [ruːl] entscheiden, verfügen, anordnen 165

ruler [ˈruːlə] Lineal 54

to run aground [ˌrʌn əˈɡraʊnd] auf Grund laufen 218

to run out of something [rʌn ˈaʊt əv ˌsʌmθɪŋ] ausgehen, zur Neige gehen 146

rush [rʌʃ] Ansturm 86

S

salary [ˈsælərɪ] Gehalt 234

sales (department) [ˈseɪlz (dɪˌpɑːtmənt)] Verkauf(sabteilung) 58

sales assistant [ˈseɪlz əˌsɪstənt] Verkäufer/in 226

sales consultant [ˈseɪlz kənˌsʌltənt] Verkaufsberater/in 226

sales force [ˈseɪlz ˌfɔːs] Vertreterstab 224

sales literature [ˈseɪlz ˌlɪtrətʃə] Prospektmaterial 38

sales representative [ˈseɪlz reprɪˌzentətɪv] Handelsvertreter/in, Außendienstmitarbeiter/in 110

salmon [ˈsæmən] Lachs 28

salutation [ˌsæljəˈteɪʃn] (hier:) Anrede; Begrüßung 110

sample [ˈsɑːmpl] Muster, Probestück 129

satisfaction [ˌsætɪsˈfækʃn] Zufriedenheit 210

to satisfy [ˈsætɪsfaɪ] zufrieden stellen 208

sausage [ˈsɒsɪdʒ] Wurst 28

savoury [ˈseɪvərɪ] herzhaft, pikant 28

scale [skeɪl] Maß, Maßstab 190

scarce(ly) [ˈskeəs(lɪ)] knapp; kaum 152

scared [skeəd] ängstlich 100

schedule [ˈʃedjuːl, ˈskedjuːl] Schema, Aufstellung, (Termin-/Fahr-)Plan 120

to schedule [ˈʃedjuːl] planen 95

school-leaving certificate [ˌskuːl ˈliːvɪŋ səˈtɪfɪkət] Schulabschlusszeugnis 235

Sci-Fi film [ˈsaɪfaɪ ˌfɪlm] Science-Fiction-Film 9

scope [skəʊp] Umfang, Bereich 58

scotch tape [ˌskɒtʃ ˈteɪp] Klebeband 54

sea and ocean freight [ˌsiː ənd ˈəʊʃn ˌfreɪt] Seefracht 14

to seal [siːl] versiegeln, (luft-/wasser-dicht) verschließen 50

seaquake [ˈsiːkweɪk] Seebeben 218

search engine [ˈsɜːtʃ ˌendʒɪn] Suchmaschine 128

seaworthy packing [ˌsiːwɜːðɪ ˈpækɪŋ] seetaugliche Verpackung 170

second floor [ˌsekənd ˈflɔː] zweite Etage (BE), erste Etage (AE) 23

sector [ˈsektə] Branche 225

secure [sɪˈkjʊə, sɪˈkjɔː] sicher 41

to seek, sought, sought [siːk, sɔːt, sɔːt] suchen 234

segment [ˈsegmənt] Marktsegment 223

selection [səˈlekʃn] Auswahl 103

sell-by date [ˈselbaɪˌdeɪt] Verfallsdatum (Lebensmittel) 210

to sell on [ˌsel ˈɒn] weiterverkaufen 223

to sell well [ˌsel ˈwel] sich gut verkaufen, gut gehen 163

semi-trailer [ˈsemɪˌtreɪlə] Sattelschlepper 31

senior [ˈsiːnjə] höherrangig 26

serviceable [ˈsɜːvɪsəbl] zweckdienlich, praktisch, strapazierfähig 191

service centre (BE) / center (AE) [ˈsɜːvɪsˌsentə] Kundendienst(zentrum) 212

to set [set] festsetzen, ansetzen, einrichten 165

to set about [set əˈbaʊt] sich daran machen 221

to settle an invoice [ˌsetl ən ˈɪnvɔɪs] eine Rechnung begleichen 197

settlement [ˈsetlmənt] Abrechnung, Bezahlung, Ausgleich, Erledigung 142

to settle the matter [ˈsetl ðə ˌmætə] die Angelegenheit erledigen 210

to set up in business on one's own [set ʌp ɪn ˈbɪznɪs ɒn wʌnzˌəʊn] eine eigene Firma gründen 245

severe(ly) [səˈvɪə(lɪ)] schwer, ernstlich, streng, hart 121

to sew, sewed, sewn [səʊ, səʊd, səʊn] nähen 206

shape [ʃeɪp] Form 228

share [ʃeə] Anteil 228

to share [ʃeə] teilen 14

sharp [ʃɑːp] scharf 24

shelf, (plural:) shelves [ʃelf; ʃelvz] Regal 31

to ship [ʃɪp] versenden, verschiffen 72

shipper [ˈʃɪpə] Spediteur/in, Befrachter/in 156

shipping [ˈʃɪpɪŋ] Seetransport, Verschiffung, Versand 169

shipping company [ˈʃɪpɪŋ ˌkʌmpənɪ] Reederei 228

shirt [ʃɜːt] (Herren-)Hemd 162

shoemaker [ˈʃuːˌmeɪkə] Schuhmacher/in, Schuster/in 39

shopping cart [ˈʃɒpɪŋˌkɑːt] Einkaufswagen 43

shortcomings [ˈʃɔːtˌkʌmɪŋz] Unzulänglichkeiten 208

shortly [ˈʃɔːtlɪ] in Kürze, bald 160

shunting yard [ˈʃʌntɪŋ jɑːd] Verschiebebahnhof 183

shuttle service [ˈʃʌtl ˌsɜːvɪs] Pendelbus 86

sibling [ˈsɪblɪŋz] Geschwisterkind 180

sights [saɪts] Sehenswürdigkeiten 24

signatory [ˈsɪgnətərɪ] Unterzeichner/in 117

signature [ˈsɪgnətʃə] Unterschrift 109

signature footer [ˈsɪgnətʃəˌfʊtə] Unterschriftsfußzeilen 110

significant(ly) [sɪgˈnɪfɪkənt(lɪ)] bedeutend 106

to simplify [ˈsɪmplɪfaɪ] vereinfachen 222

single [ˈsɪŋgl] ledig 239

single room [ˌsɪŋgl ˈruːm] Einzelzimmer 85

sister-in-law [ˈsɪstərɪnlɔː] Schwägerin 58

site [saɪt] Niederlassung, Gelände 14

size [saɪz] Größe 74

skill [skɪl] Fertigkeit 100

skin care [ˈskɪn ˌkeə] Hautpflege 234

to sleep [sliːp] (hier:) Schlafmöglichkeit bieten 73

slice [slaɪs] Scheibe, Anteil 104

slide [slaɪd] Folie 101

slight(ly) [slaɪt(lɪ)] gering(fügig), kaum merklich 106

slight drizzle [ˌslaɪt ˈdrɪzl] leichter Nieselregen 22

sling [slɪŋ] Schlinge 78

to sling, slung, slung [slɪŋ, slʌŋ, slʌŋ] in einer Schlinge hochziehen, aufhängen 51

to slump [slʌmp] stark fallen 106

smart [smɑːt] ordentlich, gepflegt, schick 244

smitten [ˈsmɪtn] hingerissen 163

smoked [sməʊkt] geräuchert 28

smoked salmon [ˌsməʊkt ˈsæmən] Räucherlachs 134

smooth(ly) [smuːð(lɪ)] glatt, reibungslos 121

smudged [smʌdʒd] verwischt, verschmiert 210

to soar [sɔː] sprunghaft steigen, in die Höhe schnellen 146

sociable [ˈsəʊʃəbl] gesellig, umgänglich 26

social service [ˌsəʊʃl ˈsɜːvɪs] Ersatzdienst 241

soft drinks [ˌsɒft ˈdrɪŋks] alkoholfreie Getränke 91

sole [səʊl] Sohle 205

solicited offer [səˌlɪsɪtɪd ˈɒfə] verlangtes Angebot 140

to some extent [tə ˌsʌm ɪkˈstent] in gewissem Maße 65

sophisticated [səˈfɪstɪkeɪtɪd] hoch entwickelt, technisch ausgefeilt 227

sour [saʊə] sauer 28

source [sɔːs] Quelle 233

spacing [ˈspeɪsɪŋ] Abstände, Abstandseinteilung 115

spacious [ˈspeɪʃəs] geräumig 53

to spare [speə] übrig haben 222

spare part [speə ˈpɑːt] Ersatzteil 96

sparing(ly) [ˈspeərɪŋ(lɪ)] sparsam, mäßig 113

sparkling mineral water [ˌspɑːklɪŋ ˈmɪnərəl ˌwɔːtə] Mineralwasser mit Kohlensäure 91

special features [ˌspeʃl ˈfiːtʃəz] besondere Eigenschaften 86

specialist shops [ˌspeʃəlɪst ˈʃɒps] Fachgeschäfte 223

special treat [ˌspeʃl ˈtriːt] besonderes Vergnügen, spezielles Extra 147

to spend, spent, spent [spend, spent, spent] (hier:) verbringen 226

spicy [ˈspaɪsɪ] würzig 27

spirits [ˈspɪrɪts] Spirituosen 225

spokesman [ˈspəʊksmən] Sprecher 194

square [skweə] Platz 25

to stack [stæk] stapeln 231

staff [stɑːf] Belegschaft, Personal 39

staff member [ˈstɑːfˌmembə] Mitarbeiter/in 178

stage [steɪdʒ] (hier:) Stadium 221

to stage [steɪdʒ] veranstalten 164

staggered payment [ˌstægəd ˈpeɪmənt] gestaffelte Zahlungsweise 195

to stagnate [stægˈneɪt] stagnieren 121

stagnation [stægˈneɪʃn] Stillstand 169

standard lamp [ˈstændəd ˌlæmp] Stehlampe 175

to stand in for someone [stænd ˈɪn fə ˌsʌmwʌn] jemanden vertreten 30

standing order [ˌstændɪŋ ˈɔːdə] Dauerauftrag 159

stapling machine / stapler [ˈsteɪplɪŋ məˌʃiːn/ˈsteɪplə] Tacker 54

starter ['stɑːtə] Vorspeise 27

start-up (business) ['stɑːtʌp (ˌbɪznɪs)] Neugründung, junges Unternehmen 41

statement ['steɪtmənt] Aussage, Äußerung 8

statement of account [ˌsteɪtmənt əv əˈkaʊnt] Kontoauszug 195

state of affairs [ˌsteɪt əv əˈfeəz] Zustand, Stand der Dinge 198

state-of-the-art [ˌsteɪtəvðɪˈɑːt] auf dem neuesten Stand (der Technik) 227

state rooms ['steɪt ˌruːmz] Empfangssäle 25

stationery ['steɪʃənrɪ] Büromaterial 208

steady, steadily ['stedɪ(lɪ)] stetig 106

steel [stiːl] Stahl 146

steel rods [ˌstiːl 'rɒdz] Stahlstäbe 172

stevedore ['stiːvədɔː] Stauer 51

stew, soup [stjuː, suːp] Eintopf 29

to stew [stjuː] kochen, dünsten, schmoren 28

to stipulate, to specify ['stɪpjəleɪt, 'spesɪfaɪ] vorschreiben 194

stock [stɒk] Vorrat, Lager(bestand) 140

to stock up on [stɒk 'ʌp ɒn] Lager(bestand) auffüllen 146

storage ['stɔːrɪdʒ] Lagerung 15

stowage ['stəʊɪdʒ] Verstauen, (Be-) Laden 50

straight away [ˌstreɪtəˈweɪ] sofort, unverzüglich 164

straightforward [ˌstreɪtˈfɔːwəd] einfach, unkompliziert 20

strapping ['stræpɪŋ] Riemen, Bänder 50

straw [strɔː] Stroh 49

strengths [streŋkθs] Stärken 244

to stress [stres] betonen 162

to strike ground [straɪk ˈɡraʊnd] auflaufen 217

striking ['straɪkɪŋ] auffallend 25

to strive [straɪv] streben 155

study group ['stʌdɪ ˌgruːp] Arbeitsgruppe 76

stuffed [stʌft] gefüllt 28

stylish ['staɪlɪʃ] schick, modisch 191

subject ['sʌbdʒɪkt] (hier:) Betreff; Gegenstand 110

subject matter ['sʌbdʒɪkt ˌmætə] Gegenstand, Thema 111

to submit [səbˈmɪt] unterbreiten 136

subsidary [səbˈsɪdərɪ] Tochtergesellschaft 48

substantial [səbˈstænʃl] erheblich, beträchtlich 196

substitute ['sʌbstɪtjuːt] Ersatz (durch Ähnliches) 144

suburb ['sʌbɜːb] Vorort, Stadtteil im Außenbezirk 71

to succeed in [səkˈsiːd ɪn] gelingen 224

sufficient(ly) [səˈfɪʃnt(lɪ)] genug, genügend, ausreichend 41

to suggest [səˈdʒest] (hier:) andeuten, zu verstehen geben 197

suggestion [səˈdʒestʃn] Vorschlag 164

suit [suːt] Kostüm (Damen), Anzug 243

suitable ['suːtəbl] geeignet 233

superb [suːˈpɜːb] hervorragend 21

superfluous [suːˈpɜːfluəs] überflüssig 225

superior [suːˈpɪərɪə] Vorgesetzte/r 58

superstructure ['suːpəˌstrʌktʃə] (Deck-) Aufbauten, Oberbau 182

to supervise ['suːpəvaɪz] beaufsichtigen 179

supplementary charge [ˌsʌplɪmentərɪ 'tʃɑːdʒ] Zuschlag 89

supplier [səˈplaɪə] Lieferant, Anbieter 128

supply [səˈplaɪ] Angebot 223

supply chain [səˈplaɪ ˌtʃeɪn] Versorgungskette 231

supply / demand ratio [səˌplaɪ dɪˈmɑːnd ˌreɪʃəʊ] Verhältnis zwischen Angebot und Nachfrage 169

to support [səˈpɔːt] unterstützen, helfen 7

to suppose [səˈpəʊz] vermuten 222

surcharge ['sɜːtʃɑːdʒ] Zuschlag, Aufschlag 181

surname ['sɜːneɪm] Familienname 8

surplus ['sɜːpləs] überschüssig 205

surprisingly [səˈpraɪzɪŋlɪ] überraschenderweise 20

to surround [səˈraʊnd] umgeben 26

to survive [səˈvaɪv] überleben 225

suspicious [səˈspɪʃəs] verdächtig 112

sustainability [səˌsteɪnəˈbɪlətɪ] Nachhaltigkeit 155

sweets [swiːts] Süßwaren, Süßigkeiten 130

swift(ly) ['swɪft(lɪ)] schnell 227

swivel chair [ˌswɪvl 'tʃeə] Drehstuhl 54

T

tag [tæg] Etikett, Anhängeschildchen 206

tailback ['teɪlbæk] Stau 22

tailored suit [ˌteɪləd 'suːt] Kostüm 244

tailor-made [ˌteɪləˈmeɪd] maßgeschneidert 147

to take [teɪk] (hier:) in Anspruch nehmen, dauern 20

to take a call [ˌteɪk ə ˈkɔːl] einen Anruf entgegennehmen 88

to take advantage of [ˌteɪk ədˈvɑːntɪdʒ ɒv] sich zunutze machen, ausnutzen 38

to take a message [ˌteɪk ə ˈmesɪdʒ] eine Nachricht entgegennehmen 69

to take down [teɪk ˈdaʊn] notieren 69

to take into account [teɪk ˌɪntʊ əˈkaʊnt] berücksichtigen 208

to take offence at something [teɪk əˈfens ət ˌsʌmθɪŋ] etwas übel nehmen 212

to take over [ˌteɪk ˈəʊvə] (eine Firma) übernehmen 39

to take part in [ˌteɪk ˈpɑːt ɪn] teilnehmen an 225

to take the minutes [ˌteɪk ðə ˈmɪnɪts] Protokoll führen 92

to take up [teɪk ˈʌp] aufnehmen, sich verlegen auf; hochheben 39

to take up residence [ˌteɪk ʌp ˈrezɪdəns] wohnhaft werden 247

tanker ['tæŋkə] Tankschiff 182

tare weight [ˌteə ˈweɪt] Leergewicht 78

to target ['tɑːgɪt] ansprechen, anpeilen 222

tart [tɑːt] herb, säuerlich 28

to taste [teɪst] schmecken 28

tax [tæks] Steuer 191

tax-exempt intra-Community delivery [ˌtæksɪgˈzempt ˌɪntrəkəˈmjuːnəti dɪˈlɪvərɪ] steuerfreie Innergemeinschaftslieferung (innerhalb der EU) 192

tear-proof ['teəpruːf] reißfest 228

tedious ['tiːdɪəs] langweilig, lästig 22

telephone directory ['telɪfəʊn daɪˌrektərɪ, 'telɪfəʊn dɪˌrektərɪ] Telefonbuch 64

telephony [təˈlefənɪ] Telefonverkehr 63

temporary ['tempərərɪ] vorübergehend, befristet 136

to tempt [tempt] in Versuchung führen 27

to tend to be ['tend tʊ biː] dazu neigen 123

to tend to book flights [ˌtend tʊ ˌbʊk 'flaɪts] Flüge häufig buchen 222

terminal operator ['tɜːmɪnl ˌɒpəreɪtə] Betreiber eines Terminals 169

terms of payment and delivery [ˌtɜːmz əv ˌpeɪmənt ənd dɪˈlɪvərɪ] Zahlungs- und Lieferbedingungen 129

terrible ['terɪbl] furchtbar 21

text-building block ['tekstbɪldɪŋ ˌblɒk] Textbaustein 121

theft [θeft] Diebstahl 49

thereof [ˌðeəˈrɒv] davon 218

to thicken ['θɪkn] eindicken 29

this is why [ˌðɪs ɪz ˈwaɪ] daher, deshalb, deswegen 121

those involved [ˌðəʊz ɪnˈvɒlvd] die Beteiligten 92

those present [ˌðəʊz ˈpreznt] die Anwesenden 92

to threaten ['θretn] drohen 197

to thrive [θraɪv] gedeihen 180

thus [ðʌs] daher 224

to tie [taɪ] binden 243

tilt [tɪlt] Neigung 217

time-consuming ['taɪmkənˌsjuːmɪŋ] zeitraubend 41

timetable ['taɪmˌteɪbl] Fahrplan 89

tip [tɪp] *(hier:)* Trinkgeld 90
token ['təʊkən] Zeichen, Symbol 180
tool [tuːl] Werkzeug 63
tool kit ['tuːl ˌkɪt] Werkzeugsatz 207
topics ['tɒpɪks] *(hier:)* Punkte, Themen 92
topic of conversation [ˌtɒpɪk əv ˌkɒnvə'seɪʃn] Gesprächsthema 21
touch-down ['tʌtʃdaʊn] Landung *(beim Flugzeug)* 180
tournament ['tɔːnəmənt] Turnier 22
tour operator ['tʊər ˌɒpəreɪtə] Reiseveranstalter 234
towering ['taʊərɪŋ] turmhoch, überragend 25
towing kite ['təʊɪŋ ˌkaɪt] Zugdrachen 228
town hall [ˌtaʊn 'hɔːl] Rathaus 24
traceability [ˌtreɪsə'bɪləti] Zurückverfolgbarkeit 231
to track [træk] verfolgen 43
trade association ['treɪd əsəʊʃiˌeɪʃn] Branchenverband 128
trade discount [ˌtreɪd 'dɪskaʊnt] Händler-, Wiederverkaufsrabatt 133
trade fair ['treɪd ˌfeə] (Fach-)Messe 128
trade flows ['treɪd ˌfləʊz] Handelsströme 169
trailer ['treɪlə] Anhänger 78
trainee [ˌtreɪ'niː] Auszubildende/r 10
training course ['treɪnɪŋ ˌkɔːs] Ausbildungslehrgang 12
train ride ['treɪn ˌraɪd] Zugfahrt 21
to transfer [træns'fɜː] überweisen, übertragen 160
transparencies [træn'spærənsiz] Folien 101
transport mode ['trænspɔːt ˌməʊd] Transportart 14
transshipment [trænz'ʃɪpmənt] Umladung 218
travel agency, travel agent ['trævl ˌeɪdʒənsi, 'trævl ˌeɪdʒənt] Reisebüro 8
travel consultant ['trævl kən'sʌltənt] Reiseverkehrskaufmann/-frau 8
tray [treɪ] Ablagekorb 54
trial order [ˌtraɪəl 'ɔːdə] Probeauftrag 159
tricky ['trɪki] kompliziert, schwierig 154
triple-walled cardboard box [ˌtrɪplwɔːld ˌkɑːdbɔːd 'bɒks] 3-wandiger Karton 173
trousers ['traʊzəz] Hose 243
trout [traʊt] Forelle 28
to trust [trʌst] vertrauen 195
to tuck into [ˌtʌk 'ɪntuː] hineinstecken in 243
tuition [tjʊ'ɪʃn] Unterricht, Unterweisung 147
turkey ['tɜːki] Pute, Truthahn 28
to turn down [ˌtɜːn 'daʊn] ablehnen 194
turnover ['tɜːnˌəʊvə] Umsatz 33

turn-taking ['tɜːnˌteɪkɪŋ] sich anstellen, warten bis man dran ist 89
to turn up [ˌtɜːn 'ʌp] auftauchen 233

U

unappreciated [ˌʌnə'priːʃieɪtɪd] nicht genügend geschätzt 245
unauthorised [ʌn'ɔːθəraɪzd] unbefugt 109
unavoidable [ˌʌnə'vɔɪdəbl] unvermeidlich 65
to undercut [ˌʌndə'kʌt] unterbieten 94
to underestimate [ˌʌndər'estɪmeɪt] unterschätzen 102
understanding [ˌʌndə'stændɪŋ] verständnisvoll 212
unemployment [ˌʌnɪm'plɔɪmənt] Arbeitslosigkeit 247
unforeseen [ˌʌnfə'siːn] unvorhergesehen 201
unique [ju'niːk] einzigartig 25
to unload [ʌn'ləʊd] entladen, löschen 169
unprecedented [ʌn'presɪdəntɪd] noch nie dagewesen 226
unreliable [ˌʌnrɪ'laɪəbl] unzuverlässig 109
unsatisfactory [ʌnˌsætɪs'fæktəri] unbefriedigend, ungenügend, unzureichend 109
unsolicited offer [ˌʌnsəlɪsɪtɪd 'ɒfə] unverlangtes Angebot 140
to update [ʌp'deɪt] aktualisieren 149
uplighter ['ʌplaɪtə] Deckenfluter 175
upmarket [ʌp'mɑːkɪt] im oberen Marktsegment 57
upper and lower case letters [ˌʌpər ən ˌləʊə keɪs 'letəz] Groß- und Kleinbuchstaben 101
up the hill [ʌp ðə 'hɪl] den Berg hinauf 24
urgency ['ɜːdʒənsi] Dringlichkeit 95
urgent ['ɜːdʒənt] dringend 49
usage ['juːsɪdʒ] übliche Praxis, Gepflogenheit 117
utilisation [juːtɪlaɪ'zeɪʃn] Auslastung; Verwendung, Nutzung 230

V

vacancy ['veɪkənsi] offene Stelle 233
valid (until) ['vælɪd (ʌnˌtɪl)] gültig (bis); bindend, rechtskräftig 140
valuable ['væljʊbl] wertvoll 77
van [væn] Kleintransporter 170
variety [və'raɪəti] Vielfalt 223
VAT (value-added tax) [ˌviːeɪ'tiː (ˌvæljuː ˌædɪd 'tæks)] Mehrwertsteuer 191
veal [viːl] Kalbfleisch 28
vegan ['viːgən] Veganer/in 27
vegetable(s) ['vedʒtəbl(z)] Gemüse 28
veggieburger ['vedʒɪˌbɜːgə] Gemüsebratling 27
vehicle ['vɪəkl] Fahrzeug 169

venison ['venɪsən] Hirsch, Rotwild *(als Fleisch)* 27
venue ['venjuː] Veranstaltungsort, Gerichtsstand 103
vessel ['vesl] Schiff 96
via [vaɪə; 'viːə] über 48
vibrant ['vaɪbrənt] lebendig 20
view [vjuː] *(hier:)* Ausblick 56
vinegar ['vɪnɪgə] Essig 29
virtually ['vɜːtʃʊəli] nahezu 136
visible ['vɪzəbl] sichtbar 89
visual aids [ˌvɪʒʊəl 'eɪdz] visuelle Hilfsmittel 101
vocational college [vəʊ'keɪʃənl ˌkɒlɪdʒ] Berufskolleg, Berufsfachschule 10
vocational school [vəʊ'keɪʃənl ˌskuːl] Berufsschule 7
volume order [ˌvɒljuːm 'ɔːdə] Großauftrag 132

W

waiter service ['weɪtə ˌsɜːvɪs] Bedienung 89
to wait one's turn [ˌweɪt wʌnz 'tɜːn] warten bis man an die Reihe kommt 27
wall calendar ['wɔːl ˌkæləndə] Wandkalender 209
warehouse ['weəhaʊs] Lager 224
warehousing ['weəˌhaʊzɪŋ] Lagerung 14
wastepaper bin ['weɪst'peɪpə ˌbɪn] Papierkorb 54
to watch [wɒtʃ] aufpassen auf 57
waterslide ['wɔːtəslaɪd] Wasserrutsche 136
to wave your arms around [ˌweɪv jɔːr 'ɑːmz əˌraʊnd] mit den Armen herumfuchteln 103
waybill ['weɪbɪl] Frachtbrief 176
weather forecast ['weðə ˌfɔːkɑːst] Wettervorhersage 21
well-substantiated [ˌwelsʌb'stænʃieɪtɪd] gut belegt 104
we've already met [ˌwiːv ɔːlredi 'met] wir kennen uns schon 19
whatever the price [wɒtˌevə ðə 'praɪs] ganz unabhängig vom Preis 210
What is the weather like …? [ˌwɒt ɪz ðə 'weðə ˌlaɪk …] Wie ist das Wetter …? 21
wheeled [wiːld] rollend, auf Rädern 182
whenever [wen'evə] immer dann, wenn 109
whereabouts ['weərəbaʊts] Position, Aufenthaltsort 230
whereas [weə'ræz] wohingegen, dagegen 117
wholesale and export clerk [ˌhəʊlseɪl ənd 'ekspɔːt ˌklɑːk] Kaufmann/-frau im Groß- und Außenhandel 8
wholesaler ['həʊlˌseɪlə] Großhändler 223

wide range [ˌwaɪd 'reɪndʒ] breite Palette 221

willing ['wɪlɪŋ] bereit 222

wind turbine ['wɪndˌtɜːbaɪn] Windkraft-anlage, -turbine 77

to withdraw money from an account, withdrew, withdrawn [wɪð'drɔː ˌmʌnɪ frəm ən ə'kaʊnt, wɪð'druː, wɪð'drɔːn] Geld von einem Konto abheben 193

with order [wɪð 'ɔːdə] bei Auftrags-erteilung 195

without engagement [wɪˌðaʊt ɪn'geɪdʒmənt] freibleibend 140

to wonder ['wʌndə] sich fragen 65

wooden case [ˌwʊdn 'keɪs] Holzkiste 172

wording ['wɜːdɪŋ] Formulierung 194

work contract ['wɜːkˌkɒntrækt] Arbeits-vertrag 15

workforce ['wɜːkfɔːs] Belegschaft, Gesamtheit der Mitarbeiter 39

to work on one's own [ˌwɜːk ɒn wʌnz 'əʊn] selbständig arbeiten 12

work-out ['wɜːkaʊt] Fitnesstraining 8

to work out [wɜːk 'aʊt] sich körperlich fit halten, trainieren 7

work placement ['wɜːk ˌpleɪsmənt] Praktikum 247

world championship [ˌwɜːld 'tʃæmpɪənʃɪp] Weltmeisterschaft 39

world leader [ˌwɜːld 'liːdə] (hier:) Welt-marktführer 228

written order [ˌrɪtn 'ɔːdə] schriftliche Anweisung 193

Z

zip code (AE) ['zɪpkəʊd] Postleitzahl 153

Communication
Written communication
Spoken communication
Collocations relating to communication
Information and communications technology (ICT)

Company organisation
Departments and functions
Jobs and responsibilities

Sales and distribution
Distribution channels
Terms of payment and delivery
Transport and shipping
Packing and labelling

Human resources
Hiring and firing
Wages and salaries
Training and assessment

Quality
Standards
Measures and approaches

International trade
Issues and policy
Documentation
Payment and delivery

Hinweis: Glossar zum Herunterladen über Online-Link 808264-0000.

Communication

Written communication
agenda Tagesordnung
application Bewerbung, Antrag
attach, to anhängen
attachment Anhang *(E-Mail)*
brochure Broschüre, Prospekt
catalogue *(BE)*, **catalog** *(AE)* Katalog
contract Vertrag
documents Unterlagen
draft Entwurf
enclosure Anlage *(Brief)*
enquiry *(BE)*, **inquiry** *(AE)* Anfrage
leaflet Flugblatt, Infoblatt, Prospekt
memo (*short for:* **memorandum**) interne Notiz, Vermerk
message Nachricht
minutes Protokoll
notice Aushang
paperwork Verwaltungsarbeit, Schreibarbeit
post-it note Haftnotiz, Klebezettel
report Bericht
sales literature Verkaufsliteratur
schedule (≈ **timetable**) Zeitplan, Fahrplan, Stundenplan
subject (*in a letter / email*) Betreff
offer Angebot
order Auftrag, Bestellung
paragraph Absatz, Paragraph
reminder (Zahlungs-)Erinnerung, Mahnung

Spoken communication
advice Rat, Ratschlag
advise, to beraten
announce, to ankündigen, bekannt geben, ansagen
apologise for something, to sich für etwas entschuldigen
apology Entschuldigung
available erhältlich, erreichbar, verfügbar
chat, to plaudern, schwätzen
controversy Kontroverse, Auseinandersetzung
debriefing Nachbesprechung
demonstration (to give / do a demonstration) Vorführung, Demonstration
dispute Streit
interview (to hold / give an interview) Interview, Vorstellungsgespräch
negotiate, to verhandeln
presentation (to give / do a presentation) Präsentation, Vortrag, Referat
rumour Gerücht
speech (to hold / give a speech) Rede
thank somebody for something sich bei jemandem für etwas bedanken

Collocations relating to communication
circulate the agenda, to die Tagesordnung verteilen
clarify a matter, to eine Angelegenheit klären
confirm an agreement, to eine Vereinbarung bestätigen
have an objection to something, to (= **to object to something**) Einwand gegen etwas erheben, etwas beanstanden
liaise with colleagues / business partners, etc., to zusammenarbeiten mit …, in Verbindung stehen mit …
make a complaint about something, to (= **to complain**) etwas reklamieren, sich über etwas beschweren
make an appointment, to einen Termin vereinbaren
make an enquiry, to (= **to enquire about something**) eine Anfrage machen
make an offer, to ein Angebot machen
make arrangements, to Vorkehrungen treffen
notify somebody of something, to jemanden über etwas informieren, jemandem Bescheid geben
place an order, to (**with a firm, for a product**) einen Auftrag erteilen

postpone an appointment, to einen Termin verschieben
solve a problem, to ein Problem lösen
update information, to Daten/Informationen aktualisieren

On the phone
"I'll put you through." „Ich stelle Sie durch."
"Speaking." „Am Apparat."
"The line is busy." / "The line is engaged." „Die Leitung ist besetzt."
answerphone, answering machine *(BE)*, **voice mail** *(AE)* Anrufbeantworter
bad line schlechte Verbindung
dial the wrong number, to sich verwählen
dial, to wählen
extension Durchwahl
hang up, to auflegen
hold the line, to am Apparat bleiben
landline phone Festnetztelefon
leave a message, to eine Nachricht hinterlassen
mobile phone *(BE)*, **cell(ular) phone** *(AE)* Mobiltelefon, Handy
put through, to durchstellen, verbinden
receiver Hörer
return a call, to zurückrufen

Information and communications technology (ICT)
cursor Cursor, Positionsmarke
click on something, to etwas anklicken
digital / computer projector Beamer
keyboard Tastatur
landline phone Festnetztelefon
screen Bildschirm
text message SMS

Company organisation

Departments and functions
accounts, accountancy Finanzbuchhaltung, Finanzabteilung
advertising Werbung
after-sales service Kundendienst
board of directors Direktion, Geschäftsleitung
customer service Kundendienst, Kundenbetreuung
department (dept.) Abteilung
distribution Vertrieb
executive board Vorstand
finance Finanz-
human resources / personnel Personal
legal department Rechtsabteilung
maintenance Wartung
marketing Marketing
organisation chart Organigramm
payroll Lohn- und Gehaltsabrechnung
PR (= public relations) Öffentlichkeitsarbeit
purchasing (≈ procurement) Einkauf, Beschaffung
quality assurance Qualitätssicherung
recruitment Personalbeschaffung
research and development (R&D) Forschung und Entwicklung

sales Verkauf
security Sicherheit
supervisory board Aufsichtsrat

Jobs and responsibilities
accountant Bilanzbuchhalter/in
administration Verwaltung
agent Vertreter/in *(auf Provisionsbasis)*
apprentice Lehrling, Auszubildende/r, Praktikant/in
automated teller machine (ATM) Geldautomat
billing clerk Sachbearbeiter/in Rechnungswesen
blue-collar workers Arbeiter *(in der Produktion)*
board (of directors) Geschäftsleitung, Vorstand
boss Chef/in
caretaker *(BE)*, **janitor** *(AE)* Hausmeister/in
Chief Executive Officer (CEO) Vorstandsvorsitzende/r, Hauptgeschäftsführer/in
Chief Financial Officer Leiter/in der Finanzabteilung
clerical staff Büroangestellte
co-worker *(AE)* Mitarbeiter/in
colleague Kollege/Kollegin
consultant Berater/in
director Mitglied des Vorstands/des Aufsichtsrats
employee Arbeitnehmer/in, Mitarbeiter/in
employer Arbeitgeber/in
executive leitende/r Angestellte/r
executive board Vorstand
facility / facilities manager Gebäudemanager/in
factory workers Fabrikarbeiter
foreman Vorarbeiter
founder Gründer/in
freelancer Freiberufler/in, freie/r Mitarbeiter/in
head of department, department head Abteilungsleiter/in
health and safety officer Arbeitsschutzbeauftragte/r
internee Praktikant/in
maintenance Wartung und Instandhaltung
maintenance engineer Wartungstechniker/in
management Geschäftsleitung
management assistant in freight forwarding *(etwa:)* Speditionskaufmann/-frau
management assistant warehousing and logistics *(etwa:)* Fachkraft für Lagerwirtschaft
managing director (MD) Geschäftsführer/in
owner Eigentümer/in, Besitzer/in
PA (= personal assistant) *(etwa:)* Chefsekretär/in
person responsible Verantwortliche/r
predecessor Vorgänger/in
procurement, purchasing Beschaffung, Einkauf
project manager Projektleiter/in, Projektmanager/in
research and development (R&D) Forschung und Entwicklung
sales representative Außendienstmitarbeiter/in, Vertriebsmitarbeiter/in
semi-skilled angelernt
skilled worker Facharbeiter/in
staff (= personnel) Personal
successor Nachfolger/in
supervisor Vorgesetzte/r, Betreuer/in, Aufseher/in, Kontrolleur/in
supervisory board Aufsichtsrat
team leader Teamleiter/in
technical support Technischer Dienst

temp (= temporary staff) Aushilfe, Zeitarbeiter/in
trainee Praktikant/in
trainer Ausbilder/in, Trainer/in
unskilled ungelernt
white-collar staff Büroangestellte
workforce Arbeiterschaft, Belegschaft

Sales and distribution

Distribution channels

break bulk, to größere Mengen teilen und weiterkaufen, große Gebinde aufbrechen
broker Makler/in
bulk delivery Großlieferung
buy in bulk, to in großen Mengen einkaufen
chain Kette, Ladenkette
commission Provision
contractual relationship Vertragsverhältnis
corner shop (BE), mom 'n pop store (AE) Tante-Emma-Laden
department store Kaufhaus
discount store Billigladen
distribution channels Vertriebswege
distributor Lieferant, Händler, Vertragshändler, Vertreiber
distribution chain Absatzkette, Verteilerkette
end user (≈ final customer) Endverbraucher/in
expenses, to incur Auslagen/Kosten übernehmen
factory outlet Direktverkauf, Fabrikverkauf
franchising Franchising (Vertriebsform)
intermediary (= middleman) Zwischenhändler
mail order Versandhaus
mall (AE), shopping centre (BE) Einkaufszentrum
outlet Verkaufsstelle
on one's own account auf eigene Rechnung
parallel import Fluss von Gütern über Vertriebswege, die nicht vom Hersteller autorisiert sind
principal (in an agency contract) Auftraggeber/in
representative Vertreter/in, Außendienstmitarbeiter/in
retail outlet Einzelhandelsgeschäft, Einzelhandelsverkaufsstelle
retailer Einzelhändler
retailing, retail Einzelhandel
retainer Vorschusshonorar
sales rep (= representative) Vertreter/in, Außendienstmitarbeiter/in
sell on one's own account, to auf eigene Rechnung verkaufen
speciality shop (BE), specialty store (AE) Fachgeschäft
supply chain Lieferkette
trader (= dealer) Händler
vendor Verkäufer, Anbieter, Lieferant
wholesale, wholesaling Großhandel

Terms of payment and delivery

at your expense auf Ihre Kosten
cash discount (= early-payment discount) Skonto
cash on delivery (= payment on delivery) Zahlung bei Lieferung
cash payment Barzahlung
cashpoint Geldautomat

cash with order Vorkasse
defer (payment) (Zahlung) aufschieben, verzögern
guarantee, to garantieren
handling charges Abladegebühren, Bearbeitungsgebühren
make an offer, to ein Angebot machen
place an order, to einen Auftrag erteilen, eine Bestellung aufgeben
purchase, to kaufen
remit, to (remittance) überweisen (Überweisung)
sales contract Kaufvertrag
staggered payment gestaffelte Zahlungsweise
to your premises an Ihre Firma/auf Ihr Firmengelände
transfer, to überweisen, übertragen
trial order Probeauftrag
warranty (= guarantee) Garantie

Transport and shipping

barge Kahn
batch Bündel, Stapel, Charge, Los
bonded warehouse Zolllager, Freilager
bulky goods sperrige Waren
cargo, (plural:) cargoes Fracht, Ladung
carrier Frachtführer
commodities Handelswaren, Rohstoffe
consignee Empfänger (einer Warensendung)
consignment Warensendung, Lieferung
consignor Versender (einer Warensendung)
consulate Konsulat
container Container (genormter Stahlbehälter)
  flat rack container Flatrack-Container (ohne Seiten- und Stirnwände)
  high cube container High-Cube-Container (mit größerer Kapazität als Standardcontainer)
  insulated reefer container isolierter Kühlcontainer, Tiefkühlcontainer
  open top container Open-Top-Container (mit Plane statt Dach)
  standard container Standardcontainer (Länge: 20 oder 40 Fuß)
  tank container Tankcontainer
country of destination Bestimmungsland
country of origin Ursprungsland, Herkunftsland
damage Beschädigung, Schaden
delayed verspätet
delivery van Lieferwagen
depot Lager, Warendepot
distance Entfernung
docks Hafen
embassy Botschaft
EU single market EU-Binnenmarkt
forklift truck Gabelstapler
freight train Güterzug
haulier, haulage company Lkw-Unternehmer, Lkw-Spediteur
incoming goods / goods inwards Wareneingang
in time rechtzeitig
in transit auf dem Transportweg
inland waterway Binnengewässer, Wasserstraße
merchandise Waren
on time pünktlich
outgoing goods / goods outwards Warenausgang
paperwork Formalitäten, Dokumentation

port of destination Bestimmungshafen
port of shipment Verschiffungshafen
receipt of delivery Empfangsbeleg, Wareneingang
road train (langer) Sattelzug, Lastwagenzug
ship, to versenden, transportieren
ship Schiff
  bulk carrier Massengutfrachter
  container ship Containerschiff
  LNG tanker (= liquid natural gas tanker) Flüssiggastanker
  oil tanker Öltanker
  reefer ship / vessel Kühlschiff
  roro ship / ferry (= roll on – roll off) Ro-Ro-Frachter / Fähre
shipment Warensendung, Lieferung
shipper Versender
shipping (= delivery) Verschiffung, Versand
shipping documents Versanddokumente
vehicle Fahrzeug
vessel (≈ ship) Schiff, Wasserfahrzeug
warehouse Lager (≠ Warenhaus)
warehousing Lagerung

Packing and labelling

bale Ballen
barrel Fass
bubble wrap Blisterfolie, Luftpolsterfolie
bundle Bündel
crate Lattenkiste
drum Trommel
foil-wrapped mit Folie umwickelt
inflammable entzündbar, brennbar, feuergefährlich
hazardous gefährlich
label Etikett, Bezeichnung
labelled beschriftet, gekennzeichnet, etikettiert, bezeichnet
packing (≠ packaging) Versandverpackung
packing list Packliste
padding Füllung
pallet Palette
polystyrene peanuts Schaum-Erdnüsse
protection Schutz
seaworthy packing seefeste Verpackung
sell-by-date Haltbarkeitsdatum
shrink wrap Schrumpffolie
sturdy robust
toxic giftig, schädlich

Human resources

Hiring and firing

applicant Bewerber / in
application form Bewerbungsformular
application letter Bewerbungsschreiben
apply for a job / a post, to sich bewerben
aptitude test Eignungstest
closing date for applications Bewerbungsschluss
covering letter (BE), cover letter (AE) Begleitbrief
CV (= curriculum vitae) (BE), résumé (AE) Lebenslauf
degree Hochschulabschluss
draw up a short-list, to eine Liste der aussichtsreichsten Bewerber / innen anfertigen

early retirement Frührente
entry requirments Zugangsvoraussetzungen
equal opportunities Chancengleichheit
fire (someone), to (jemanden) feuern, entlassen
give (someone) notice, to (jemandem) kündigen
hand in one's notice, to die Kündigung einreichen, kündigen
hire (someone), to (jemanden) einstellen
hiring freeze Einstellungssperre
interview Vorstellungsgespräch
job advertisement Stellenanzeige, Stellenausschreibung
job description Stellenbeschreibung
job vacancy offene Stelle
lay (someone) off, to (jemanden) entlassen
make (someone) redundant, to (jemanden) entlassen, freisetzen, überflüssig machen
period of notice Kündigungsfrist
recruit, to einstellen, anwerben, rekrutieren
recruitment Personalbeschaffung
reference (BE), testimonial (AE) Referenzschreiben, Zeugnis
rejection letter Absagebrief
replacement Vertretung, Nachfolger / in
take (someone) on, to jemanden einstellen
vacancy offene Stelle *(Arbeit)*
without notice fristlos

Wages and salaries

annual salary Jahresgehalt
benefits Zusatzleistungen, Sozialleistungen
bonus Gratifikation
commission Provision
fee (for a service) Honorar
golden handshake hohe Abfindung
holiday pay Urlaubsgeld
hourly rate Stundensatz
incentive Anreiz
lump sum payment Pauschalbetrag
minimum wage Mindestlohn
payment by seniority Zahlung nach Betriebszugehörigkeit
pay rise (BE), raise (AE) Gehaltserhöhung
pension Rente, Pension
performance-related pay leistungsorientierte Bezahlung
perks (= fringe benefits) Zusatzleistungen des Arbeitgebers *(außer Gehalt / Lohn)*
redundancy pay (BE), severance pay (AE) Abfindung
remunerate, to vergüten
salary Gehalt
unemployment benefit Arbeitslosengeld
wage Lohn

Training and assessment

appraisal Bewertung
apprentice Auszubildende / r
apprenticeship, traineeship Ausbildung, Lehre
assess, to bewerten, evaluieren
evaluate, to bewerten, evaluieren
induct, to einweisen, einführen
job satisfaction Zufriedenheit am Arbeitsplatz
peer pressure Gruppendruck
performance appraisal (= performance evaluation) Leistungsbeurteilung, Leistungsbewertung

promote, to befördern
skills Fertigkeiten, Fähigkeiten, Kompetenzen
track record Erfolgsbilanz, (gute) Leistungen am Arbeitsplatz
trainee Auszubildende/r, Praktikant/in, Lehrling
training course Ausbildung
vocational training berufliche Aus-/Weiterbildung, Berufsausbildung

Quality

Standards

below standard, to be unter dem Standard sein
compliance (with) Einhaltung, Übereinstimmung (mit)
comply with, to einhalten
conforming to specifications / requirements genau nach den technischen Vorgaben; den Vorschriften entsprechend
contaminated verseucht
cracked gesprungen, rissig
customer satisfaction Kundenzufriedenheit
defect Defekt
detect flaws, to Mängel entdecken
durable haltbar, robust
error Irrtum, Fehler
exacting / tight specifications genaue/strenge Vorgaben
exceed expectations, to die Erwartungen übertreffen
failure Versagen, Misserfolg,
fall short of expectations, to hinter den Erwartungen zurückliegen
fit for purpose, to be für eine besondere Verwendung geeignet sein
fitness for use Gebrauchstauglichkeit, einsatzgerechte Eignung
flaw Makel
flawed defekt
flawless makellos
flimsy schwach, dünn, nicht sehr stabil
fulfil a requirement, to (= to meet a need) eine Voraussetzung/Bedingung erfüllen
heavy-duty strapazierfähig
immaculate perfekt, makellos, vollkommen
imperfection Fehlerstelle, Mangel, Unvollkommenheit
improve (in quality), to (sich) verbessern
in compliance with entsprechend, gemäß, in Übereinstimmung mit
International Standards Organisation (ISO) ISO (Internationale Organisation für Normung)
latent defect verdeckter Mangel, verborgener Fehler
maintain standards, to Standards einhalten
non-compliance Nichteinhaltung
of (a) high / good / top quality, to be von hervorragender Güte (Spitzenqualität) sein
of (a) low / poor / varying quality, to be von minderwertiger Güte/Qualität sein
of a high standard, to be hohen Standard erfüllen
of a low standard, to be von niedrigem Standard sein
out of service außer Betrieb
pass inspection, to eine Kontrollprüfung überstehen
perfect einwandfrei
poorly-designed schlecht konstruiert sein

satisfy customers, to Kunden zufriedenstellen
scratched zerkratzt
set high standards, to hohe Anforderungen stellen
show a lack of quality, to zeigt Qualitätsmängel
tough, rigorous, exacting streng
up to standard, to be den Anforderungen entsprechen
value for money Preis-Leistungs-Verhältnis
waste Verschwendung

Measures and approaches

benchmarking Benchmarking, Vergleichstest
best practice optimaler Geschäftsablauf, bestes Verfahren
carry out checks, to Kontrollmaßnahmen durchführen, kontrollieren
certification Zertifizierung, Abnahme
corrective and preventive action Korrektur- und Vorbeugemaßnahme
customer feedback Kundenbewertung
investigate, to untersuchen, ermitteln
inspection Besichtigung, Prüfung, Kontrolle
measurable objective messbares Ziel
performance appraisal Leistungsbeurteilung
procedure Verfahren
quality audit Qualitätsaudit, Qualitätsmanagement
quality control Qualitätskontrolle
questionnaire Umfrage
random sample Stichprobe, Zufallsauswahl
spot check Stichprobe
verify, to auf Richtigkeit prüfen, kontrolliern
validation Gültigkeitsprüfung, Bewertung, Bestätigung
verification Nachweis, Nachprüfung, Feststellung der Richtigkeit

International trade

Issues and policy

apply for a licence, to eine Lizenz beantragen
arrange insurance, to eine Versicherung abschließen
bilateral trade bilateraler Handel
claim a customs refund, to eine Zollerstattung beantragen
deal with customs formalities, to Zollformalitäten bearbeiten
domestic trade Binnenhandel, inländischer Handel
exchange controls Devisenkontrolle
export ban, embargo Ausfuhrsperre, Embargo
export credit guarantee Exportkreditbürgschaft
fair trade fairer Handel
foreign trade Außenhandel
free trade Freihandel
free-trade agreement Freihandelsabkommen
import restriction Einfuhrbeschränkung
international trade Welthandel, Außenhandel, internationaler Handel
negotiate terms of payment and delivery Zahlungs- und Lieferbedingungen verhandeln
notify the exporter that the goods have arrived, to den Lieferanten über den Empfang der Waren informieren

open an L/C in favour of the supplier, to ein Akkreditiv eröffnen zugunsten des Lieferanten

protectionism Protektionismus, Schutzzollpolitik

quota Kontingent, Quote

sign the sales contract, to den Kaufvertrag unterschreiben

subsidy Subvention

tariff (Einfuhr-)Zoll

trade barrier Handelshemnnis, -schranke

trade term Handelsklausel

trade war Handelskrieg

transfer the invoice amount, to den Rechnungsbetrag überweisen

translate documents, to Unterlagen übersetzen

Documentation

air waybill Luftfrachtbrief

bill of lading (B/L) Konossement, Frachtbrief, Ladeschein

certificate of origin Ursprungszeugnis

commercial invoice Handelsrechnung

consignment note Frachtbrief, Ladeschein

consular invoice Konsulatsfaktura

customs declaration Zollerklärung

customs invoice Zollfaktura, Zollrechnung

dispatch advice Versandanzeige

export declaration Ausfuhrerklärung/-anmeldung

export/import licence *(BE)*, **export/import license** *(AE)* Export-/Importlizenz

in duplicate/ in triplicate in zweifacher/dreifacher Ausfertigung

insurance policy/certificate Versicherungspolice/ Versicherungsschein

marine insurance Seeversicherung

packing list Packliste

pro-forma invoice Proforma Rechnung

shipping documents Versanddokumente

Single Administrative Document (SAD) Einheitspapier

Payment and delivery

advance payment Vorauszahlung, Vorkasse, Vorschusszahlung, Anzahlung

bank guarantee Bankbürgschaft

bill of exchange (B/E) Wechsel

cancel an invoice, to eine Rechnung stornieren

cancel an order, to eine Auftrag stornieren

cash against documents (Bar-)Zahlung gegen Dokumente

compensate, to entschädigen

cost, insurance and freight (CIF) Kosten, Versicherung, Fracht

currency Währung

customs duty Zoll

documentary letter of credit (L/C) (Dokumenten) Akkreditiv

documents against acceptance (D/A) Dokumente gegen Akzept

documents against payment (D/P) Dokumente gegen Zahlung

exchange rate Wechselkurs

irrevocable and confirmed letter of credit unwiderrufliches, bestätigtes Akkreditiv

open account offenes Konto, laufende Rechnung

payment and delivery terms Zahlungs- und Lieferbedingungen

valid until gültig bis

VAT (= value added tax) Mehrwertsteuer

Acronyms and abbreviations

Abbreviation: shortened form of a word
Acronym: abbreviation formed from the first letters of each word in a term

Short form **Full form** German

a.m. / am ante meridian morgens / vormittags (24 Uhr – 12 Uhr)
approx. approximately ungefähr
asap as soon as possible so schnell wie möglich
ATM automated teller machine Geldautomat
Attn. for the attention of zu Händen (von)
B / E bill of exchange Wechsel
B / L bill of lading Konnossement, Frachtbrief
B2B business to business Business-to-Business
BIC bank identifier code internationaler Bank-Code
BOP balance of payments Zahlungsbilanz
BOT balance of trade Handelsbilanz
BRIC Brazil, Russia, India, China Brasilien, Russland, Indien, China
cc carbon copy, copy circulated, cubic centimeters (Kohle-papier-)Durchschlag, Verteiler, Kubikzentimeter
CEO Chief Executive Officer *(etwa:)* (Haupt-)Geschäfts-führer / in, Firmenchef / in, Vorstandsvorsitzende / r
CFO Chief Financial Officer Finanzleiter / in
CFR cost and freight (Incoterm) Kosten und Fracht
CIF cost, insurance and freight (Incoterm) Kosten, Versicherung und Fracht; frachtfrei versichert
COD cash on delivery Lieferung per Nachnahme
CPT carriage paid to (Incoterm) frachtfrei, Fracht bezahlt
CRM customer relationship management Kundendienst, Kundenbetreuung
CV curriculum vitae Lebenslauf
CWO cash with order Zahlung bei Auftragserteilung
D / A documents against acceptance Dokumente gegen Akzept
D / P documents against payment Dokumente gegen Zahlung
DAP delivery at place (Incoterm) geliefert benannter Ort
DAT delivery at terminal (Incoterm) geliefert Terminal
DDP delivered, duty paid (Incoterm) frei Haus, verzollt geliefert
dept. department Abteilung
e.g. exempli gratia = for example zum Beispiel (z. B.)
encl. enclosed beiliegend, in der Anlage
etc. etcetera und so weiter (usw.)
EU European Union Europäische Union (EU)
EXW ex works (Incoterm) ab Werk
FAO for the attention of zu Händen von
FAQ frequently asked question häufig gestellte Frage
FAS free alongside ship (Incoterm) frei Längsseite Schiff
FCA free carrier (Incoterm) frei Frachtführer
FOB free on board (Incoterm) frei an Bord
GDP gross domestic product Bruttoinlandsprodukt (BIP)
GNP gross national product Bruttosozialprodukt (BSP)
HQ headquarters Hauptsitz, Zentrale
HR human resources Personalabteilung, -wesen
i.e. id est (Latin) = that is das heißt (d. h.)
IBAN International Bank Account Number Internationale Kontonummer
ICC International Chamber of Commerce Internationale Industrie- und Handelskammer (ICC)

IMF International Monetary Fund Internationaler Währungsfond
Inc.; inc incorporated *(AE)* Aktiengesellschaft
ISO International Standards Organisation ISO (Norm)
JIT just-in-time bedarfsorientierte Produktion (gerade rechtzeitig)
L / C letter of credit Akkreditiv
lbs pounds Pfunde *(Gewicht)*
Ltd. limited mit beschränkter Haftung
MD managing director Geschäftsführer / in
MNC multinational company multinationales Unternehmen
mph miles per hour Meilen pro Stunde *(Geschwindigkeit)*
NGO non-governmental organisation Nichtregierungs-organisation
no. number Nummer (Nr.)
OPEC Organisation of the Petroleum Exporting Countries Organisation erdölexportierender Länder (OPEC)
P&L Profit and Loss Gewinn und Verlust
p.a. per annum jährlich, pro Jahr
p.m. / pm post meridian nachmittags / abends (12 Uhr – 24 Uhr)
PIN Personal Identification Number PIN (Erkennungsnummer)
plc; PLC public limited company *(etwa:)* AG
pp paginae = pages Seiten
pp / ppa per procurationem = on behalf of im Auftrag von
PR public relations Öffentlichkeitsarbeit
R&D research and development Forschung und Entwicklung
Re. regarding bezüglich
Re. reply (e-mail) Antwort
Ref. reference Aktenzeichen
ROI return on investment Rentabilität, Kapitalertrag
SME small and medium(-sized) enterprise *(BE)*; small to mid-sized enterprise *(AE)* Mittelstand; kleines und mit-telständisches Unternehmen (KMU)
sq. square Quadrat *(Maß)*, Platz *(Ort)*
SWOT Strengths, Weaknesses, Opportunities, Threats Stärken, Schwächen, Möglichkeiten, Gefahren / Risiken
WTO World Trade Organisation Welthandelsorganisation

283

Countries, nationalities, languages

Land	Bürger	Eigenschaftswort / Sprache (wenn abweichend vom Eigenschaftswort oder bei mehreren Sprachen)
Algeria	an Algerian	Algerian / Arabic, French
Argentina	an Argentinian	Argentinian / Spanish
Australia	an Australian	Australian / English
Austria	an Austrian	Austrian / German
Belgium	a Belgian	Belgian / Dutch (Flemish), French, German
Bolivia	a Bolivian	Bolivian / Spanish, Quéchua
Brazil	a Brazilian	Brazilian / Portuguese
Bulgaria	a Bulgarian	Bulgarian / Bulgarian, Turkish
Canada	a Canadian	Canadian / English, French
Chile	a Chilean	Chilean / Spanish
China	a Chinese	Chinese
Colombia	a Colombian	Colombian / Spanish
Costa Rica	a Costa Rican	Costa Rican / Spanish
Croatia	a Croatian	Croatian
Cuba	a Cuban	Cuban / Spanish
Cyprus	a Cypriot	Cypriot / Greek, Turkish, English
Czech Republic	a Czech	Czech
Denmark	a Dane	Danish
Dominican Republic	a Dominican	Dominican / Spanish
Ecuador	an Ecuadorian	Ecuadorian / Spanish, Quéchua
Egypt	an Egyptian	Egyptian / Arabic, English
El Salvador	an El Salvadoran	El Salvadoran / Spanish
England	an Englishman an Englishwoman the English	English
Estonia	an Estonian	Estonian / Estonian, Russian
Finland	a Finn	Finnish / Finnish, Swedish
France	a Frenchman a Frenchwoman the French	French
Germany	a German	German
Great Britain	a Britishman a Britishwoman the British	British / English
Greece	a Greek	Greek
Hungary	a Hungarian	Hungarian
Iceland	an Icelander	Icelandic
India	an Indian	Indian / Hindi, English, Bengali, and many others

Land	Bürger	Eigenschaftswort / Sprache (wenn abweichend vom Eigenschaftswort oder bei mehreren Sprachen)
Indonesia	an Indonesian	Indonesian / Bahasa Indonesia (official), English, Dutch, Javanese and others
Iran	an Irani	Iranian / Farsi, Turkic, Kurdish
Iraq	an Iraqi	Iraqi / Arabic, Kurdish
Ireland	an Irishman an Irishwoman the Irish	Irish / English, Gaelic
Israel	an Israeli	Israeli / Hebrew, Arabic, English
Italy	an Italian	Italian
Jamaica	a Jamaican	Jamaican / English, Jamaican Creole
Japan	a Japanese	Japanese
Jordan	a Jordanian	Jordanian / Arabic, English
Kenya	a Kenyan	Kenyan / English, Swahili
Korea, North	a (North) Korean	Korean
Korea, South	a (South) Korean	Korean / Korean, English
Kuwait	a Kuwaiti	Kuwaiti / Arabic, English
Latvia	a Latvian	Latvian / Latvian, Russian, Lithuanian
Lebanon	a Lebanese	Lebanese / Arabic, French, English
Libya	a Libyan	Libyan / Arabic, Italian, English
Liechtenstein	a Liechtensteiner	Liechtensteiner / German
Lithuania	a Lithuanian	Lithuanian / Lithuanian, Russian, Polish
Luxembourg	a Luxembourger	Luxembourger / Luxembourgish, French, German
Malaysia	a Malaysian	Malaysian / Malay, English, Chinese dialects
Malta	a Maltese	Maltese / Maltese, English
Mexico	a Mexican	Mexican / Spanish
Morocco	a Moroccan	Moroccan / Arabic, Berber dialects, French
Namibia	a Namibian	Namibian / English, Afrikaans, German
The Netherlands	a Dutchman a Dutchwoman the Dutch	Dutch / Dutch, Frisian
New Zealand	a New Zealander	New Zealand / English, Maori
Nicaragua	a Nicaraguan	Nicaraguan / Spanish, English
Nigeria	a Nigerian	Nigerian / English, Hausa, Yoruba
Norway	a Norwegian	Norwegian / Norwegian, Sami, Finnish
Northern Ireland	a Britishman a Britishwoman the British	British / English
Pakistan	a Pakistani	Pakistani / Urdu, English, Punjabi
Panama	a Panamanian	Panamanian / Spanish, English
Paraguay	a Paraguayan	Paraguayan / Spanish, Guarani
Peru	a Peruvian	Peruvian / Spanish, Quéchua

285

Land	Bürger	Eigenschaftswort / Sprache (wenn abweichend vom Eigenschaftswort oder bei mehreren Sprachen)
The Philippines	a Philippine	Philippine / Filipino (Tagalog), English
Poland	a Pole	Polish
Portugal	a Portuguese	Portuguese
Romania	a Romanian	Romanian / Romanian, Hungarian
Russia	a Russian	Russian
Saudi Arabia	a Saudi	Saudi Arabian / Arabic
Scotland	a Scotsman a Scotswoman the Scots	Scottish / English, Scots Gaelic
Serbia	a Serb	Serbian / Serbian (official), Romanian, Hungarian, Slovak, Croatian
Singapore	a Singaporean	Singaporean / Mandarin, English, Malay
Slovakia	a Slovak	Slovakian / Slovak, Hungarian
Slovenia	a Slovene	Slovenian / Slovenian, Serbo-Croatian
South Africa	a South African	South African / IsiZulu, IsiXhosa, Afrikaans, Sepedi, English
Spain	a Spaniard	Spanish / Castilian Spanish, Catalan, Galician, Basque
Sri Lanka	a Singhalese	Sri Lankan / Singhalese, Tamil, English
Sweden	a Swede	Swedish / Swedish, Sami, Finnish
Switzerland	a Swiss	Swiss / German, French, Italian
Syria	a Syrian	Syrian / Arabic, Kurdish, Armenian, French
Taiwan	a Taiwanese	Taiwanese / Mandarin Chinese, Taiwanese
Tanzania	a Tanzanian	Tanzanian / Swahili, English, Arabic
Thailand	a Thai	Thai / Thai (Siamese), English
Tunisia	a Tunisian	Tunisian / Arabic, French
Turkey	a Turk	Turkish / Turkish, Kurdish
Uganda	a Ugandan	Ugandan / English, Swahili, Arabic
Ukraine	a Ukrainian	Ukrainian / Ukrainian, Russian, Romanian, Polish, Hungarian
United Arab Emirates	a citizen of the UAE	UAE / Arabic (official), Persian, English, Hindi, Urdu
United Kingdom	a Britishman a Britishwoman the British	British / English, Welsh, Scots Gaelic
United States of America	an American	American / English, Spanish
Uruguay	a Uruguayan	Uruguayan / Spanish, Portuñol, Brazilero
Venezuela	a Venezuelan	Venezuelan / Spanish
Vietnam	a Vietnamese	Vietnamese / Vietnamese, English, French, Chinese, Khmer
Wales	a Welshman a Welshwoman the Welsh	Welsh / English, Welsh

Bildquellennachweis

4 shutterstock (vgstudio), New York, NY; **5** BigStockPhoto.com (rafalstachura), Davis, CA; **6** Corbis RF (Royalty-Free), Düsseldorf; **6** Getty Images RF (Digital Vision), München; **6** Getty Images (PhotoDisc), München; **6** Fotosearch Stock Photography, Waukesha, WI; **7** JupiterImages photos.com (Photos.com), Tucson, AZ; **8** plainpicture GmbH & Co. KG (Maria Simon), Hamburg; **8** Alamy Images (Janine Wiedel Photolibrary), Abingdon, Oxon; **8** iStockphoto (RF/Locke), Calgary, Alberta; **10** Photothek.net Gbr (Ute Grabowsky), Radevormwald; **11** Robert Bosch GmbH, Stuttgart; **11** Imageshop (Imageshop), Düsseldorf; **11** Mauritius Images (Gilsdorf), Mittenwald; **14** BigStockPhoto.com (kgtoh), Davis, CA; **17** BigStockPhoto.com (Martin Arnold), Davis, CA; **18** www.bilderbox.com, Thening; **18** Corbis (Eric K. K. Yu), Düsseldorf; **18** Joker (Marcus Gloger), Bonn; **18** JupiterImages photos.com (RF/Photos.com), Tucson, AZ; **19** Klett-Archiv (Meyle + Müller/Harter), Stuttgart; **20** Klett-Archiv (Meyle + Müller/Harter), Stuttgart; **21** iStockphoto (RF/artydanmark), Calgary, Alberta; **25** Kartographie Huber, München; **25** images.de digital photo GmbH (Giribas), Berlin; **25** MEV Verlag GmbH, Augsburg; **25** Jahns, Rainer, Siegsdorf; **27** Klett-Archiv (Meyle + Müller/Harter), Stuttgart; **28** Fotolia LLC (Ralf Beier), New York; **28** StockFood GmbH (Newedel), München; **28** StockFood GmbH (Joff Lee Studios), München; **28** obs (ABCEuroRSCG), Hamburg; **28** Getty Images RF (PhotoDisc), München; **31** BigStockPhoto.com (ErikdeGraaf), Davis, CA; **31** BigStockPhoto.com (Baloncici), Davis, CA; **32** iStockphoto (Mark Stay), Calgary, Alberta; **33** shutterstock (Diego Cervo), New York, NY; **38** Avenue Images GmbH (Corbis RF/Tom Grill), Hamburg; **38** MEV Verlag GmbH, Augsburg; **39** Picture-Alliance (akg), Frankfurt; **39** Picture-Alliance (epa), Frankfurt; **39** Picture-Alliance (Imaginechina), Frankfurt; **39** Klett-Archiv (Meyle + Müller/Harter), Stuttgart; **41** Dreamstime LLC (Maksim Shmeljov), Brentwood, TN; **43** Klett-Archiv (Meyle + Müller/Harter), Stuttgart; **43** Mauritius Images (Pöhlmann), Mittenwald; **43** MEV Verlag GmbH, Augsburg; **43** Avenue Images GmbH (Ingram Publishing), Hamburg; **43** Ingram Publishing, Tattenhall Chester; **44** Fotosearch Stock Photography, Waukesha, WI; **44** Avenue Images GmbH (Image Source), Hamburg; **44** Avenue Images GmbH (Image Source RF), Hamburg; **44** Bananastock, Watlington/Oxon; **44** Imageshop, Düsseldorf; **44** BBC Information and archives, London; **48** BigStockPhoto.com (EnjoyLife), Davis, CA; **48** BigStockPhoto.com (lagardie), Davis, CA; **48** BigStockPhoto.com (remik44992), Davis, CA; **48** BigStockPhoto.com (photobar), Davis, CA; **50** shutterstock (Marcin Balcerzak), New York, NY; **51** Dreamstime LLC (Tonnywu76), Brentwood, TN; **51** shutterstock (Skocko), New York, NY; **53** shutterstock (Monkey Business Images), New York, NY; **53** Thinkstock (Erik Snyder), München; **53** iStockphoto (Dmitry Kutlayev), Calgary, Alberta; **53** Corbis RF (Image Source), Düsseldorf; **54** Klett-Archiv (Meyle + Müller/Harter), Stuttgart; **55** shutterstock (ArtmannWitte), New York, NY; **56** iStockphoto (Jason Stitt), Calgary, Alberta; **56** iStockphoto (RF/Chen), Calgary, Alberta; **56** iStockphoto (RF/Anna Bryukhanova), Calgary, Alberta; **57** iStockphoto (Anna Bryukhanova), Calgary, Alberta; **57** iStockphoto (Jason Stitt), Calgary, Alberta; **57** iStockphoto (RF/Chen), Calgary, Alberta; **63** Thinkstock (Jupiterimages), München; **63** Avenue Images GmbH (Corbis RF/Jack Hollingsworth), Hamburg; **63** PhotoAlto, Paris; **63** Getty Images RF (Eyewire), München; **65** Klett-Archiv (Meyle + Müller/Harter), Stuttgart; **65** Fotosearch Stock Photography (Banana Stock), Waukesha, WI; **65** Avenue Images GmbH (Image Source), Hamburg; **67** Klett-Archiv (Meyle + Müller/Harter), Stuttgart; **70** iStockphoto (RF/peter chen), Calgary, Alberta; **70** Fotosearch Stock Photography (Banana Stock), Waukesha, WI; **74** BigStockPhoto.com (RF), Davis, CA; **74** Dreamstime LLC (Ronfromyork), Brentwood, TN; **74** iStockphoto (RF), Calgary, Alberta; **77** Thinkstock (Comstock), München; **84** Thinkstock (Ryan McVay), München; **85** Klett-Archiv (Meyle + Müller/Harter), Stuttgart; **85** Fotosearch Stock Photography (Banana Stock), Waukesha, WI; **86** iStockphoto (RF/Thompson), Calgary, Alberta; **86** Klett-Archiv (Meyle + Müller/Harter), Stuttgart; **88** Klett-Archiv (Meyle + Müller/Harter), Stuttgart; **91** Klett-Archiv (Meyle + Müller/Harter), Stuttgart; **92** Klett-Archiv (Meyle + Müller/Harter), Stuttgart; **95** BigStockPhoto.com (Norebbo), Davis, CA; **100** Thinkstock (IT Stock), München; **105** LinguaTV GmbH, Berlin; **108** iStockphoto (Jill Fromer), Calgary, Alberta; **108** Mauritius Images (B. Lehner), Mittenwald; **108** Thinkstock (Hemera/Keith Bell), München; **109** iStockphoto (RF/Hudson), Calgary, Alberta; **113** Thinkstock (Hemera), München; **124** shutterstock (vgstudio), New York, NY; **128** Düsseldorfer Messeges. mbH, Düsseldorf; **131** iStockphoto (McDonald), Calgary, Alberta; **132** LinguaTV GmbH, Berlin; **136** Thinkstock (Jupiterimages), München; **140** Corbis (Talaie), Düsseldorf; **145** MEV Verlag GmbH, Augsburg; **146** Thinkstock (Jupiterimages), München; **147** MEV Verlag GmbH, Augsburg; **151** shutterstock (Ralf Beier), New York, NY; **151** iStockphoto (Bogdan Lazar), Calgary, Alberta; **151** Avenue Images GmbH (Corbis RF/Jose Luis Pelaez, Inc./Blend Images), Hamburg; **151** Fotosearch Stock Photography (Corbis RF), Waukesha, WI; **153** BigStockPhoto.com (Yuri Arcurs), Davis, CA; **154** Fotosearch Stock Photography (Banana Stock), Waukesha, WI; **155** BigStockPhoto.com (visual28), Davis, CA; **155** shutterstock (Morgan Lane Photography), New York, NY; **159** BLG Logistics Group AG, Bremen; **163** MEV Verlag GmbH, Augsburg; **163** Fotosearch Stock Photography (Digital Vision), Waukesha, WI; **163** Corel Corporation Deutschland, Unterschleissheim; **164** Thomas Gremmelspacher, Stuttgart; **165** BBC Information and archives, London; **166** shutterstock (Stephen Coburn), New York, NY; **169** Corbis (Saloutos), Düsseldorf; **170** Fotosearch Stock Photography (PhotoDisc), Waukesha, WI; **170** Flughafen Frankfurt-Hahn, Hahn-Flughafen; **171** iStockphoto (bluenemo), Calgary, Alberta; **171** iStockphoto (RF/Prikhodho), Calgary, Alberta; **171** creativ collection Verlag GmbH, Freiburg; **172** iStockphoto (RF/David Meharey), Calgary, Alberta; **172** iStockphoto (RF/Paul Senyszyn), Calgary, Alberta; **172** iStockphoto (RF/Joe Gough), Calgary, Alberta; **172** iStockphoto (RF/Tschakert), Calgary, Alberta; **172** Thinkstock (Hemera Technologies, Getty Images), München; **172** Klett-Archiv (Ruth Feiertag), Stuttgart; **172** Thinkstock (iStockphoto), München; **174** iStockphoto (Rohde), Calgary, Alberta; **174** Getty Images RF (Annie Reynolds/PhotoLink), München; **175** Klett-Archiv (Meyle + Müller/Harter), Stuttgart; **177** MEV Verlag GmbH, Augsburg; **178** BBC Information and archives, London; **179** BigStockPhoto.com (kgtoh), Davis, CA; **181** BigStockPhoto.com (XavierMarchant), Davis, CA; **182** BigStockPhoto.com (Carabay), Davis, CA; **182** BigStockPhoto.com (728JET), Davis, CA; **182** BigStockPhoto.com (Kent Christopherson), Davis, CA; **182** shutterstock (Rafael Ramirez Lee), New York, NY; **182** BigStockPhoto.com (Kurt De Bruyn), Davis, CA; **183** BigStockPhoto.com (Airship75), Davis, CA; **184** Hapag-Lloyd AG, Hamburg; **188** iStockphoto (RonTech2000), Calgary, Alberta; **190** iStockphoto (RF/Paul Cowan), Calgary, Alberta; **193** iStockphoto (RF/Hudson), Calgary, Alberta; **193** iStockphoto (RF), Calgary, Alberta; **193** MEV Verlag GmbH, Augsburg; **195** iStockphoto (fazon1), Calgary, Alberta; **196** Fotolia LLC (ExQuisine), New York; **196** iStockphoto (RF/Maureen Perez), Calgary, Alberta; **196** iStockphoto (RF/Caspel), Calgary, Alberta; **196** Mauritius Images (Pöhlmann), Mittenwald; **196** creativ collection Verlag GmbH, Freiburg; **200** Thinkstock (Hemera), München; **201** iStockphoto (exi5), Calgary, Alberta; **204** Thinkstock (Polka Dot Images), München; **206** Fotolia LLC (Sulamith), New York; **209** Getty Images RF (Photodisc), München; **209** Corel Corporation Deutschland, Unterschleissheim; **210** Klett-Archiv (Meyle + Müller), Stuttgart; **214** shutterstock (Iurii Konoval), New York, NY; **221** shutterstock (ary718), New York, NY; **223** MEV Verlag GmbH, Augsburg; **224** Alamy Images (Expuesto - Nicolas Randall), Abingdon, Oxon; **224** Avenue Images GmbH (CorbisRF), Hamburg; **226** BBC Information and archives, London; **228** SkySails GmbH & Co. KG, Hamburg; **229** BigStockPhoto.com (rafalstachura), Davis, CA; **230** iStockphoto (David Jones), Calgary, Alberta; **231** BigStockPhoto.com (CHRONIS CHAMALIDIS), Davis, CA; **233** iStockphoto (Zorani), Calgary, Alberta; **234** Mercedes Benz, Niederlassung, Stuttgart; **234** MEV Verlag GmbH, Augsburg; **234** iStockphoto (RF/Maier), Calgary, Alberta; **242** BBC Information and archives, London; **243** Thinkstock (Digital Vision), München; **246** Mauritius Images (Simone Fichtl), Mittenwald; **247** creativ collection Verlag GmbH, Freiburg; **248** creativ collection Verlag GmbH, Freiburg; **249** iStockphoto (Willie B. Thomas), Calgary, Alberta; **250** Thinkstock (Comstock), München; **259** Klett-Archiv, Stuttgart; **COVER** Corbis (Benelux), Düsseldorf; **COVER** iStockphoto (christian Lagereek), Calgary, Alberta; **COVER** Avenue Images GmbH (Fancy), Hamburg

Textquellennachweis

180 Lufthansa Cargo flies in tokens of love for Valentine's Day, http://www.lufthansa-cargo.com; **218** The German DTV Cargo Insurance Conditions 2000 / 2008 comprise the following two types of coverage, Gesamtverband der Deutschen Versicherungswirtschaft e.V. (www.tis-gdv.de); **184** www.translinkshipping.de

Sollte es in einem Einzelfall nicht gelungen sein, den korrekten Rechteinhaber ausfindig zu machen, so werden berechtigte Ansprüche selbstverständlich im Rahmen der üblichen Regelungen abgegolten.